Experimental Theology in America

Von der
Göttlichen
und
Natürlichen Liebe
durch
B
Mad. GUION.

Experimental Theology in America

Madame Guyon, Fénelon, and Their Readers

Patricia A. Ward

BAYLOR UNIVERSITY PRESS

© 2009 by Baylor University Press
Waco, Texas 76798

All Rights Reserved. No part of this publication may be reproduced,
stored in a retrieval system, or transmitted, in any form or by any means,
electronic, mechanical, photocopying, recording or otherwise, without
the prior permission in writing of Baylor University Press.

Cover design by Amy Stirnkorb
Cover background © Emre Yildiz/iStockphoto

Frontispiece: Flyleaf plate of Madame Guyon's *The Different Effects of
Sacred and Profane Love*, translated by Gerhard Tersteegen into German
as *Holy Godly Love and Unholy Natural Love*, reprinted in Lancaster,
Pennsylvania in 1828. The plate is produced with the permission of Rare
Books and Manuscripts, Special Collections Library, Pennsylvania State
University Libraries.

Ward, Patricia A., 1940-
Experimental theology in America : Madame Guyon, Fénelon, and their
readers / Patricia A. Ward.
p. cm.
Includes bibliographical references and index.
ISBN 978-1-60258-197-5 (hardback : alk. paper)
1. Quietism--United States--History. 2. Pietism--United States--History.
3. United States--Church history. 4. Guyon, Jeanne Marie Bouvier de
La Motte, 1648-1717. 5. Fénelon, François de Salignac de La Mothe-,
1651-1715. I. Title.
BV5099.W37 2009
277.3'07--dc22

2009010373

Printed in the United States of America on acid-free paper with a
minimum of 30% pcw recycled content.

For

H. Blair Ward (1907–1987)

and

Timothy L. Smith (1924–1997)

Contents

Preface

In the eighteenth century, western Protestantism was characterized by an overarching consciousness and set of values, a "protestant frame of mind." The increase in literacy and the circulation of ideas through letters, personal contacts, the press, and translations contributed to this frame of mind and to a desire for religious unity that would extend beyond existing confessional boundaries.[1] As part of this evangelical fervor, there was a significant demand for devotional literature, drawn from both English and continental Catholic and Protestant traditions. W. R. Ward has cited the immense popularity of Thomas à Kempis (*The Imitation of Christ*), Miguel Molinos (*The Spiritual Guide*), François de Sales (*Introduction to the Devout Life*), Lewis Bayly (*The Practice of Piety*), and Johann Arndt (*True Christianity*). Two of these figures, Kempis and de Sales, were Catholics; Molinos was a Catholic Quietist who was condemned and imprisoned; Bayly was a Puritan; and Arndt was a Lutheran.

The crossing over of ecclesiastical boundaries between Catholicism and Protestantism in this particular reading list is of significance. For example, Puritanism, the most closely studied religious influence on early America, has been described as a devotional movement that drew in part on Augustine and on mystics like Teresa of Avila. *The Imitation of Christ*, with its emphasis on inner spirituality and the renunciation of self, was of special appeal to those embarked on the way toward holiness. Puritans made use, as well, of the manuals of Ignatius Loyola and de Sales, adapting the techniques of Catholic spirituality, such as meditation and self-examination, to their own purposes.[2] The vitality of these Puritan devotional practices was still apparent in the eighteenth century. To cite just one instance, the educated Bostonian Sarah Prince Gill (1728–1771) was a friend of Esther Edwards Burr and began to keep a spiritual diary in 1743 at the height of the Great Awakening. Her entries reveal the peaks and valleys in her efforts to grow toward godliness and to follow these devotional practices. For example, part of the entry for February 18, 1757, is Sarah's response to the fourth chapter of the Song of Solomon and the phrase[3] "Behold thou art fair; there is no spot in thee," when she feels overcome with her "sinning heart." This could well be interpreted as a form of *lectio divina*. Christ is speaking to her.

> Come by Faith and take a view of the heaven I am now preparing for you; don't allways [sic] pore on the darkness of the present state, but solace yourself with glorious views of the aproaching [sic] state I design for You and will prepare for you; I have begun to purifye you in the work of renovation; then I implanted a vital Principle of Holiness in you and that is reaching after a perfection of Holiness agreeable to its Nature; it will (under my care) thrive and grow and in one happy Moment (*vis* at Death) arrive at perfection. I now behold you with tender pity, groaning under your Burden of sin. These groans are a part of my Work in delivering you. I see all your distress [and] all your secret struggles. I behold my Image in You with delight, and in due time I shall fully deliver you.

Although unmentioned by Ward, the writings of Jeanne de la Mothe Guyon and of François de Fénelon, two French Catholics linked to the Quietist Molinos, also figured prominently among the preferred devotional authors of Protestants, both on the Continent and in North America. However, Ward has also described the Protestant frame of mind from 1670–1789 from a different angle, labeling it "early Evangelicalism." Among the more radical mystics contributing to the intellectual roots of Evangelicalism, he has discussed Molinos and Madame Guyon, attributing the latter's popularity to her status as a religious martyr. Indicating that her writings were not very "distinctive" and added nothing particularly new to Quietist mysticism, Ward has seemed puzzled by her popularity in Germany, Switzerland, Holland, and Scotland.[4]

The overarching narrative of this book is precisely the transmission or voyage from the Continent and England to the new American colonies of Quietism, the seventeenth-century movement within continental Catholicism, in which Molinos, Jeanne Guyon, and Fénelon were major figures. The dominant characters are Madame Guyon, a lay teacher, and her defender Fénelon, a bishop and a tutor to the grandson of Louis XIV. The story continues with the history of the ways in which their character and their experience were interpreted by an American Protestant readership from the eighteenth century to the end of the twentieth century. This readership represents a related but different tradition from Puritanism; it has included German Pietists, Quakers, Methodists, holiness revivalists, and charismatics (but also New England Abolitionists). The narrative of transmission is often complex, for people read Madame Guyon and Fénelon for a variety of reasons. These were two mythic figures; Fénelon was a canonic author because of the popularity of his epic novel *Telemachus*, so their works were part of the common reading experience of the educated. Some readers were influenced by them and by Quietist spirituality; but others found an affinity between their own religious experience and that described by Madame Guyon and Fénelon. Thus, my narrative of transmission and of diffusion is really a story of perceived affinities between author and reader.[5]

A thread of transcendental unity binds the disparate movements of popular Protestant spirituality to continental Catholic mysticism. That thread is the theme of the interior way, a spirituality in which knowing is centered in the heart, versus the intellect. Thus epistemology becomes an issue at certain points in the narrative. Interior spirituality emphasized pure or disinterested love, submission to the will of God, Christian perfection, union with God, quietude, rest, and stillness. The bands of believers, of travelers on the way to purity of heart, were often marginalized as separatist or radical voices over and against the powerful establishment of the institutionalized church, whether Catholic or Reformed. Thus, the narrative calls for listening and hearing voices from the margins of religious and literary history and responding to their calls toward an alternate way of knowing God.

Chapters 2 and 3 treat the controversies during the reign of Louis XIV involving Madame Guyon, Fénelon, and the perceived political threat of Quietism to the religious unity of France. Chapters 4-6, 8, and 9 spell out the transmission and diffusion of the works of Madame Guyon and Fénelon. These narratives of transmission are set against a backdrop of broader religious and cultural history that is not irrelevant today. In some ways, we continue to rework the debates of the seventeenth and eighteenth centuries over intellectual knowledge about God (abstract theology) versus the understanding of God that comes from the faith journey of the believer (spiritual theology).[6]

Although the overall organization of the book is chronological, it proceeds by means of themes and problems so that the reader will be observing a series of arabesques and will be asked to double back on occasion to pick up the development of a previous issue. This is particularly the case in chapter 7 on experimental religion. "Experience" was the

epistemological element that unified those who have practiced a spirituality of the heart over and against the forces of established ecclesiastical
tradition. "Experimental knowledge" had its roots in the Catholic mystic
tradition where it was viewed as reserved for those with a special calling.
For example, in 1663 the Jesuit mystic Jean-Joseph Surin wrote in a preface to a manuscript on *Experimental Knowledge of Things of the Other Life*
(*La Science expérimentale des choses de l'autre vie*) that there were two ways of
knowing mystical or future life, the way of faith and the way of experience.
Experience, that is mystical experience, was for few persons.[7]

In the age of the waning of mysticism and of popular religious movements, however, experimental religious knowledge soon was not reserved
for those with a special religious calling but was deemed available to everyone. Not long after Surin, Madame Guyon would say that all are called
to interior prayer. In the Protestant tradition treated in this book, both
Scripture and the inner experience of the divine presence, manifested as
pure love or holiness or divine union, have been the criteria for spiritual
"truth." The phrase "experimental theology" refers to the scriptural and
experiential criteria for spiritual truth in the living tradition of the interior life of holiness. Historians of American theology and religion have
emphasized the influence of common sense empirical philosophy on the
Protestant American mind-set until the Civil War, but their overarching
paradigms have paid scant attention to the ways in which religion of the
heart, with its emphasis on inner experience, differed from or merged
with this empiricism. In his history of American theology, E. Brooks
Holifield develops at length the theme of the "Baconian style" of evidential Christianity.[8] In chapter 7 I have borrowed Holifield's notion of a
"Baconian style." However, I have broadened it in sketching a history of
"experimental religion" as it relates to the readership of Madame Guyon
and Fénelon. Nineteenth-century adherents to the holiness movement,
particularly Thomas Upham, represented a unique variation of the "Baconian style" as they examined the life and writings of Madame Guyon and
of Fénelon. In the context of the rise of Fundamentalism, George Marsden has suggested the variations on Baconianism as they characterized
later American revivalism, whether Methodist, Pentecostal, or dispensa-
tionalist, that relied on the authority of the Bible or personal experience
or both. In reality, the question of the nature of spiritual knowledge and
spiritual truth as filtered through the Baconian model was already evident
in the seventeenth and eighteenth centuries.[9]

Another strand within the complex narrative of this study lies precisely in the relationship between the epistemology of experimental religion and the hermeneutics of devotional reading. The communities of

Protestant readers who have valued and reread the biographies and works of these Catholic authors have used "shared experience" as their hermeneutical criterion—a basis for finding meaning that has claimed to surpass all cultural and ecclesiastical boundaries. In broaching the issue of readership, I have used several approaches. Publishing history is recounted where appropriate as a key to prove dissemination and to demonstrate the reliance on certain key editions and translations during almost three centuries. Major figures are cited because of the scope of their influence as readers and disseminators of works of Catholic spirituality. Lesser known readers, editors, and abridgers are also viewed as paradigmatic.

The question of gender also recurs throughout the story line. The issues of the Counter Reformation marked seventeenth-century France, a period of exceptional religious fervor (and of worldliness), but as the century wore on, a modern consciousness was dawning even as the sun was setting on the great age of mysticism.[10] For women who wished to form their own identity as they sought to translate their inner fervor into service, questions of entering orders, taking solemn vows, and becoming cloistered became vital. Even as the number of convents multiplied in France, there was a blossoming of communities and then orders of laywomen who taught, served the poor, and nursed the sick. These women did not take final solemn vows, did not wear habits, and circulated within society. Madame Guyon was not a religious, nor did she belong to a lay community, but her "apostolic vocation" cannot be understood apart from the new ways in which women sought to express their religious identity. At the same time, she was caught between new and old ways of thinking about the world.[11] Similarly, in an American context, the feminization of spirituality and the role of women as spiritual leaders became issues linked indelibly to the story of Madame Guyon.

The consciousness behind this volume is literary, but the method is interdisciplinary, blending questions in the history of religion and spirituality with literary and theoretical issues. In addition to the primary research directed toward tracing the translations, editions, and format of the works of Madame Guyon and Fénelon, there is a synthesis of European and American scholarship, as I have attempted to create in broad strokes the religious and more general cultural backdrop from which the Quietists emerged and against which they were read. I should add, however, that the scholarly foundation of this book is framed by insights growing from my own autobiography. In chapter 1, an overview that is also a complement to chapter 7, I have given a personal narrative about the origins of my research, its twists and turns, and its unexpected relationship to this autobiographical story.

During my career as a student and a scholar, I have benefited from the support and friendship of many mentors. I have dedicated this book to them and to two mentors in particular who have revealed a great deal about the ways in which my personal story affected the research and writing of this book. When I was eight years old, my family moved to southern Maine where my father, H. Blair Ward, became pastor of the South Portland Church of the Nazarene, a congregation that emerged at the beginning of the twentieth century from New England holiness and camp meeting movements. In Portland, a younger congregation of the same denomination was pastored by Timothy L. Smith. Blair Ward, a man of immense integrity and commitment to his holiness heritage, had a career as a pastor, district superintendent, and college president. Timothy L. Smith, a preacher at heart, went on to a career as a university professor and historian. He authored the pathbreaking *Revivalism and Social Reform in Mid-Nineteenth Century America*[12] and many years ago encouraged me to carry to fruition a study of Madame Guyon. This book is a gift to my mentors and to the rich tradition of religions of the heart from which my own life story has been woven.

Acknowledgments

The early stages of research for this book were made possible by leaves granted by Wheaton College and by Vanderbilt University. I also benefited from a fellowship to participate in a summer Coolidge Research Colloquium of the Society for Religion and Intellectual Life. My understanding of Madame Guyon and her context was enriched by my participation in the "Rencontres autour de la vie et l'oeuvre de Madame Guyon" held in Thonon-les-Bains, France, in 1996.

Research, usually in special collections, was carried out at twenty-five libraries abroad and in the United States. Space does not permit me to name all of them, but staff members were always helpful. I am obliged, however, to mention the Divinity School Library of the Alexander Heard Library of Vanderbilt University because access to its fine general collection was of central importance to the completion of the book.

Many people gave me encouragement and specific assistance, particularly, the late Frank Paul Bowman of the University of Pennsylvania, Jacques Le Brun, Marie-Florine Bruneau, Lyle Dorset, Marie-Louise Gondal, Charles Edwin Jones (whose detailed knowledge of the American holiness movement was invaluable), Sharon Kim, Kenneth Minkema, Mark Noll, and Joel Porte. Carey Newman, Director of the Baylor University Press, believed in this book and was always encouraging. Josette Amsilli and Joell Smith-Borne assisted in the preparation of the final manuscript. I, of course, am responsible for any errors in the final product.

The American Society of Church History has given permission to reuse some of the material in the article "Madame Guyon and Experiential Theology in America," in *Church History* 67 (1998): 484–98, as have the editors of *Christianity and Literature* for parts of "Fénelon Among the New England Abolitionists," in *Christianity and Literature* 50, no. 1 (2000): 79–93. The Arthur and Elizabeth Schlesinger Library on the History of Women in America of the Radcliffe Institute for Advanced Study, Harvard University, has given permission to print excerpts from the correspondence of Harriet Beecher Stowe in chapter 8. The Special Collections Library of the Pennsylvania State University Libraries gave permission to reproduce the plate that constitutes the frontispiece of this book.

For all of the above I am most grateful.

Unless indicated otherwise, all translations are my own.

Chapter 1

❧

American Popular Piety
and Continental Spirituality
The Ecumenical Contexts of Nineteenth-Century Holiness Camp Meetings

The origin and evolution of a book often involve unexpected discoveries
that lead to a complex problem. Such is the case with this study.[1] Years
ago I observed that the writings of two seventeenth-century French Catholics, Jeanne-Marie Bouvier de la Mothe (or, Motte) Guyon, better known
as Madame Guyon, and François de Salignac de la Mothe-Fénelon, the
archbishop of Cambrai, have been read continuously in American Protestant circles since the eighteenth century. In their time, Jeanne Guyon and
Fénelon played leading roles in a public dispute over the nature of Quietism as they espoused it. Fénelon would risk his career to defend Madame
Guyon and would engage in a debate with his one-time mentor Bossuet,
the leading intellectual at the court of Louis XIV and archbishop of Meaux.
Bossuet viewed Quietism as a form of "new mysticism." Louis saw the Quietists as threats to the religious unity of France at the very moment that the
monarch was also suppressing the Huguenots and the Jansenists. Louis XIV
and Bossuet inevitably would get the upper hand. Madame Guyon would
spend years in the Bastille and Fénelon would be exiled from the court to
his bishopric, humbly accepting the pope's condemnation of certain of his
views. Madame Guyon and Fénelon would quickly be seen as religious and
political martyrs; they were household names in certain Protestant circles.
Now, although the two are no longer household names, their works are still
read by Americans. Why? I wondered.

My curiosity peaked with the discovery of an emblem book. This book
of engraved scenes, accompanied by mottos, poems, and commentaries,

1

was in the special collections of the Pennsylvania State University Library. The emblem book in question, a German translation of spiritual poetry by Madame Guyon, had been published in Lancaster, Pennsylvania, in 1828 by Johann Baer, who distributed primarily to the Mennonite market. This particular edition has often been thought to be Madame Guyon's *L'Âme amante de son Dieu* (*The Soul in Love with Its God*). The original collection of poems by that title, written after Madame Guyon's release from prison, had been published in Amsterdam as part of her collected works in 1717, to accompany well-known engravings by Hermann Hugo and Otho Vaenius. In 1751, Gerhard Tersteegen, a German Pietist, published a translation of another emblem book of Madame Guyon's poetry, but with different pictures and mottos from the 1717 work in French. He entitled his work *Holy Godly Love and Unholy Natural Love* (*Die heilige Liebe Gottes und die unheilige Naturliebe*). Tersteegen's emblem book, reproduced in Pennsylvania in the nineteenth century with a crude reproduction of the original engravings, was indeed a translation of poetry by Madame Guyon, but it was not *The Soul in Love with Its God*. Rather, Tersteegen had translated emblems and poems that had been published in 1722 under the title *The Different Effects of Sacred and Profane Love* (*Les éfets diferens de l'Amour sacré & profane*).[2]

American readers also discovered Madame Guyon and Fénelon in English translations quite early in the eighteenth century. For example, in Philadelphia in 1738, Andrew Bradford published *The Archbishop of Cambray's Dissertation on Pure Love, with an account of the life and writings of the lady, for whose sake the archbishop was banish'd from Court.* The Lady in question was, of course, Madame Guyon. Christopher Sauer Sr. (also spelled Saur or Sower) published a reprint of this work in 1750, in Germantown (now part of Philadelphia). These early printers gave me a clue as to the religious roots of the American readers of my French authors. Andrew Bradford was the son of William, who had apprenticed as a printer with a Quaker in England and had accompanied William Penn to America.[3] Later, William left the Quakers and joined the Church of England. Sauer was the son of Johann Christoph Sauer, a Reformed pastor in Germany; Christopher was a radical Pietist who was closely associated in Germantown with the Brethren, also called Dunkers or German Baptists. (Whether Sauer actually joined the Brethren is unclear, but his son and successor as a printer-publisher did indeed join the Brethren.) Because the German emblem book was published in Lancaster county, where not only Mennonites lived but where the Ephrata Cloister of radical mystics had recently closed, it became clear to me that this early readership of Madame Guyon and Fénelon was centered among noncreedal popular religious movements of the eighteenth century that were outside established state churches.

Then, as time went on and I searched for editions of my authors, I began to encounter a twentieth-century underground readership. People interested in spirituality seemed to hear about Madame Guyon and Fénelon through word-of-mouth. A student at Wheaton College in Illinois came to my home for a painting job and, to my astonishment, brought along a volume of the autobiography of Madame Guyon to read during his lunch break. "Why are you reading Madame Guyon?" "I heard it was good," was the reply. Near Columbus, Ohio, a Lutheran of mystic tendencies who was part of a group of bicycle riders explained to me during a breakfast break that she had been told, "Oh, you're a Madame Guyon." In Nashville, Tennessee, a member of a small group at a United Methodist Church asked me, "Have you read Fénelon's *Christian Perfection?* It's really good."[4] At a conference on Madame Guyon that I attended in Thonon-les-Bains, France, a French reader asked the audience of scholars and amateurs why Madame Guyon was so little-read in France when she was widely appreciated in charismatic circles in the United States.[5]

As a scholar, I was intrigued by this diverse set of readers who yet all seemed to be part of a broad community of evangelical faith experience. Unexpectedly, however, the nature of my research took a personal turn. After the death of my father, an ordained elder in the Church of the Nazarene, among his papers that I was sorting I found a little article entitled, "She Paid the Price!" The article recounted the life of Madame Guyon, with quotations from her autobiography, and portrayed her as a "Sufferer for Holiness Truth." Madame Guyon's spiritual experience was cast in the language of the experiential theology of the American holiness movement: she had experienced two instantaneous works of grace, justification and sanctification. Referring to the years of trials that followed Madame Guyon's "new birth experience," the author commented, "In God's good time, however, this 'wilderness' state came to an end and Madame Guyon entered into the 'Canaan' of Perfect Love and the Rest of Faith. The Spirit worked as instantaneously in her deliverance as in the case of her new birth."[6]

During my growing-up years, I had never heard of Madame Guyon, but obviously my father had. Yet, through the circumstances of family history, I was a grandchild of the very American holiness movement that read her works. Unexpectedly, the sensibility of that particular tradition of spirituality came to play an ever more important role in my research as I explored the implications of the reading of Madame Guyon and Fénelon in America.

The families of both my parents were Methodists. In West Virginia, the Wards and Hugheses welcomed circuit riders into their homes and helped to found Methodist churches. My maternal grandmother, whom I never knew, lived from 1865 to 1927. Raised on a farm in Ohio, she married at the age of fifteen, later experienced a conversion, and became a member of the Methodist church in East Liverpool, Ohio, a prosperous pottery manufacturing town at the time. There are few pictures of Cora Anis Maple, but in one of them she is standing in a full-length dress, is holding a well-worn Bible, and is surrounded by a small group of earnest-looking persons. Only one letter exists. My mother was then a student at Eastern Nazarene College, and the letter was to tell her of the death of the husband of one of her much older sisters. "Don't come home till the end of the semester," wrote my grandmother, "but hold on to Jesus, for you could easily cool off in a Holiness school without him. [. . .] Lovingly, your Mama."

Grandmother and one of her older daughters each owned a cottage at Hollow Rock Camp Meeting, "America's Oldest Continuing Holiness Camp Meeting," according to the sign at the entrance, as I recall it. When I visited Hollow Rock, I found a little village of old, white, wooden cottages, tightly clustered in rows around the centrally located tabernacle. Grandma's and Aunt Lizzie's cottages, with a water pump between them, were still there—located at the back corner of the tabernacle. In going to Hollow Rock I was stepping back in time to the era of the National Camp-Meeting Association for the Promotion of Holiness. In 1867, the first holiness camp meeting had been held at Vineland, New Jersey. Great Methodist camp meetings already existed at places such as Wesleyan Grove on Martha's Vineyard; the new wave of camp meetings after the Civil War was the result of attempts to promote the experience of sanctification within Methodism, but it reached across denominations. As the camp meeting became institutionalized, the rustic encampment villages often evolved into cities in the woods or by the seashore, such as Wesleyan Grove or Ocean Grove, New Jersey, models of varying styles of late Victorian cottage architecture. The encampments had represented Bunyan's Beulah Land, an Elysium of spiritual renewal and respite in an increasingly urban society.[7] The image of "Hollow Rock" recalled biblical imagery, particularly that of Exodus 33:22, when, after the incident of the golden calf, Moses asked God for a revelation and grace for the people of Israel. God promised to place Moses in the cleft of a rock; he could not see God face-to-face, but he would see the evidence of the divine glory. Moses would then return to Mount Sinai for a new copy of the Ten Commandments. The desire to glimpse the glory of God was a major motivation for the camp meeting experience. During my visit to Hollow Rock, I felt I was returning to a lost world. Other great camp meetings had disappeared or become more and more like resorts; the camp meeting of my grandmother's time was now almost an artifact of a once vibrant movement. Hollow Rock may be an artifact from the past, but camp meetings are still held for ten days each summer with about four hundred people in attendance. One hundred cottages exist on this little twenty-five acre site, which has been owned by the interdenominational Hollow Rock Holiness Camp Meeting Association since 1875. The members of this association are devoted to keeping the camp meeting tradition alive. The tract of land was purchased by the Methodist conference in 1815 for its annual meeting, and camp meetings began to be held there in 1838. The eventual creation of an independent, interdenominational association to purchase the land and govern the camp meeting coincided with the phenomenon of the rise of regional holiness associations around the country. What is unusual is that this little holiness hamlet perseveres as a living artifact.[8]

As a teenager, my mother established a reputation in western New York and Pennsylvania and in eastern Ohio as a gifted camp meeting pianist. Both she and my father as teenagers became members of the Church of the Nazarene shortly after the controversies over fundamentalism and liberalism touched American Protestanism early in the twentieth century. My grandmother remained a Methodist, but the National Camp-Meeting Association for the Promotion of Holiness did not succeed in reinstating the seeking after Christian perfection in the post-Civil War period. Rather, the doctrine and experience of holiness became divisive within Methodism. As holiness camp meetings flourished, regional, interdenominational or independent holiness associations flourished. These would eventually lead to the founding of new denominations, such as the Church of the Nazarene, still in its early days during the youth of my parents. In my own childhood, I attended camp meetings in Ohio, Massachusetts, Maine (where my father helped in the rehabilitation of an old camp meeting ground with rickety Victorian structures), and Ontario, where he had coordinated the union of a Canadian holiness association (the Gospel Workers) with the Church of the Nazarene. In most cases, such camp meetings would now be conference centers.

As I recall, there used to be book tables at these camp meetings where one could buy short, readable, paperback books concerning the Christian life, the church, and missions. (The National Camp-Meeting Association had quickly established its own publishing arm in Philadelphia as the National Publishing Association for the Promotion of Holiness.[9] Diffusing material to a broad reading public through magazines and books characterized the movement.) My memories of devotional reading were another clue in my search to understand why and how Americans read my two French authors. In addition to the impact of the publication of their works within early immigrant circles of Quakers and Pietists, a second wave of readers born of the holiness revivals and camp meetings of the nineteenth century participated in a uniquely American form of piety that drew upon continental European spirituality, sometimes without knowing it.

The religious history of my parents and their families mirrored a major phase in the narrative of the transmission of the works of Madame Guyon and Fénelon to an American reading public. Despite the ambiguous relationship between American Methodism and the post-Civil War holiness revivals, much of holiness theology and piety was rooted in the Wesleyan tradition. John Wesley's systematic attention to spirituality, or "practical divinity," led him to publish in his fifty-volume *A Christian Library* (printed by Jonathan Pounder in Philadelphia between 1819 and 1827) not only abstracts and selections of the great works of English spirituality, but also those of the Continent—Pascal, Antoinette Bourignon, Fénelon, Brother Lawrence, Pierre Poiret, Madame Guyon, and Miguel de Molinos. Some of these texts were borrowed from a devotional work edited by John Heylin, *Devotional Tracts Concerning the Presence of God*.[10] Wesley, then, took what was useful for his readers from the continental Catholic or Protestant literature of spirituality, particularly devotional and autobiographical works dealing with disinterested or perfect love. This approach to reading was to influence many of his American followers, especially those who became part of the holiness movement.

Nevertheless, Wesley had mixed feelings about Madame Guyon. (Fénelon was a thinker of a different order.) It is known that early on, Wesley read her treatise on prayer, as well as *The Torrents*. Much later, in 1770, he defended her, saying that, despite her errors, she was not an "enthusiast." She possessed an exceptional intelligence and piety. She was no more a lunatic than a heretic. But after the publication of a Quaker translation of Madame Guyon's autobiography in 1772, Wesley became concerned about the risk of excess among its Methodist readers, especially at Bristol. In 1776, he published an abstract of the autobiography, saying that he had never read an autobiography with "so wonderful a mixture" of both the "excellent and of the unscriptural." In his preface he states:

> As to Madam Guion herself, I believe she was not only a good woman but good in an eminent degree; deeply devoted to God, and often favoured with uncommon communications of his Spirit. But I know, from her own words, she was far from infallible; yea, that she was actually deceived in many instances: the more frequently because she imagined herself to be infallible, incapable of being deceived. She had naturally a most fertile imagination, together with vast impetuosity of spirit.[11]

Yet Wesley recommended his authorized life to those readers inter-ested in going on to "perfection." In his *Christian Library*, however, he published only the "devotional tracts" cited above, including two letters on the love of God addressed by Fénelon to the Duke of Bourgogne, as well as Fénelon's "Pious Reflexions" and a text by Madame Guyon, "A Mother's Advice to Her Daughter."[12]

The attitude of Thomas Upham (1799–1872) toward Madame Guyon was less tempered than that of Wesley, and Upham became the key inter-preter of Madame Guyon for American readers who would be touched by nineteenth-century revivals and camp meetings. A professor at Bowdoin College who was interested in the psychology of the will and was also a peace activist, Upham was a Congregationalist minister who experienced sanctification partially due to the tutelage of Phoebe Palmer, a Methodist lay leader and evangelist who spoke at camp meetings in North America and in England. Upham already knew of Madame Guyon and of the doc-trine of Quietism with which she was connected before his experience of sanctification. However, he had become deeply interested in Continental spirituality and had studied Pierre Poiret, the editor of Guyon and her intermediary to German Pietists. Upham published a series of treatises on spirituality in the 1840s that related the interior or sanctified life to Continental mysticism.[13] Upham's interpretive categories, I decided, were evident in the little article "She Paid the Price!" among my father's papers. Upham's two-volume *Life and Religious Opinions and Experience of Madame de la Mothe Guyon*, which also treated Fénelon, went through numerous editions and reprintings in the United States and England.

Upham placed Madame Guyon (and, by extension, Fénelon) within a tradition of inner piety from the Middle Ages to the seventeenth century. Upham also equated this tradition with spiritual reform and renewal; the major figures included Jan Van Ruysbroeck, Johannes Tauler, Benoît de Canfield, Saint John of the Cross, and Miguel de Molinos. For Upham, Madame Guyon was a living example of pure love. This meant that the theology of perfect or disinterested love could best be understood only by those who had experienced it and in whom others could observe its fruit. In the context of the holiness movement he commented that "the doctrine of Sanctification as well as of Justification, will in due time have its philosophi-cal and practical, as well as its exegetical exposition. And all will be tested, and *must* be tested, so far as we can perceive, by LIVING EXAMPLES."[14]

Thus, in this spiritual tradition where experience became the test of the knowledge and presence of God in individual lives, testimonies and biographies were tremendously important as a form of living theology, validating the reality of a deeper or higher life in Christ. I recall that even in my childhood in the Church of the Nazarene, testimony meetings still took place. Spiritual autobiographies and biographies, as well as devotional tracts, played a parallel role to oral testimonies, creating a reading public who craved guidance for their own inner spirituality as well as confirmation of their own religious experience.

By the 1880s and 1890s, leaders of popular Protestant movements were seriously engaged in educating believers by making available collections, abridgments, and abstracts of the works of the spiritual "giants" of Continental spirituality. (This was the phenomenon I observed as a child at camp meeting "book tables" where easy-to-read, short, paperback books were sold at low prices.) For example, G. W. McCalla published a series of books on the "Interior Life" in Philadelphia in the 1880s and 1890s. He had been the editor of *Words of Faith*, a periodical of the National Holiness Association, a successor to the original camp meeting association. The authors McCalla printed ranged from Tauler and John of the Cross, to Mother Angélique Arnaud and Juan Falconi de Bustamente, to Fénelon, Madame Guyon, and Upham. Upham was represented in McCalla's series by *Inward Divine Guidance*, the third part of *The Life of Faith*, often reprinted with a preface by Hannah Whitall Smith, the evangelist from Quaker roots who was also connected with the Keswick movement.

This "democratization" of the spirituality of holiness (both Continental and American) in its U.S. context is perhaps best illustrated by an anonymous article of 1903 that I discovered in a paper called *Living Water*, published in Nashville, Tennessee. The paper had originally been called the *Tennessee Methodist*, first edited by B. F. Haynes and then E. M. Bounds, both well-known figures in the popular spiritual awakenings of the later nineteenth century. The paper became *Zion's Outlet*, edited by J. O. McClurkan, a Cumberland Presbyterian. *Zion's Outlet* was the mouthpiece of the Pentecostal Alliance, a holiness group that crossed denominational boundaries, held camp meetings, and met in the Tulip Street Methodist Church in Nashville. The Alliance started a school that would become Trevecca Nazarene University. McClurkan had ties with dispensationalists and particularly with A. B. Simpson, founder of the Christian and Missionary Alliance.[15] Eventually, in 1915, the McClurkan group united with the Church of the Nazarene.

In 1903, *Zion's Outlet* merged with *Living Water*, an Atlanta publication of the Christian and Missionary Alliance. An article from that same year, entitled "Points in Holiness Theology," succinctly summarizes much of the complex tradition behind the reading of Fénelon and Madame Guyon in America. "Holiness theology" is grounded, above all, in the "Baconian" theology of the nineteenth-century holiness movement, a compromise between the proofs of inner experience and Scripture. The first point in holiness theology "is its note of certitude concerning matters of experience. [. . .] We know because of testing over centuries every promise." Holiness theology is "a growth that reaches across centuries," and it is rooted in the lives of people. "It is a system that grows out of the undesigned, yet united, studies of the holiest men and women this world has even seen." This theology "knows no authority [. . .] except the word of God, as understood by plain people who are filled and guided by the Holy Spirit, who is the author of the book. Finally, holiness theology is "non-sectarian."

> Bernard of Clairvaux, Thomas à Kempis, Madam Guyon, Fénelon, etc., are not to be ostracized from Wesley, Fletcher, Watson, and Asbury, because they are governed by the times in which they lived and the churches to which they belonged in many of their views and utterances.[16]

This little article is really quite remarkable. The tradition of holiness or deep inner spirituality spans the centuries, is broad and ecumenical, includes women as well as men, is rooted in a practical exegesis of Scripture, is expressed in the biographies and autobiographies of the saints of the church, and is available to plain people, the common folk. Above all, this is a practical spirituality, grounded in unshakable experimental knowledge.

Equally remarkable was the educational mission the Alliance and its paper had in mind. The paper abounded with articles summarizing the lives and thought of great figures of the church; often these articles became short books that were advertised to readers. McClurkan himself published a collection of the lives of famous Christians under the title *Chosen Vessels*. These were individuals who represented the doctrine of sanctification by their lives, according to McClurkan, and they included George Whitefield, Frances Willard, Robert Moffatt, Madame Guyon, and Charles G. Finney, among others.[17]

The challenge for me in understanding this American spirituality of the common person was to discover how its historical rootedness in continental Catholic mysticism and popular Protestant Pietism was subsumed into both a theology of experience and an unbounded hermeneutics that were to transcend temporal and cultural contexts.

The complicated issue of Quietism within the Christian tradition illustrates this conundrum. As part of my research, I wrote to a publishing house that has printed a series of abridgments and modern versions of the works of Madame Guyon. I asked why this publisher had chosen to print books by a Quietist author. This is the reply I received.

It isn't that we are interested in Quietist authors per se. In fact, I have no idea which of our authors would be considered Quietist. What we are interested in publishing is Christian literature that is Christ-centered and can help the reader develop a deeper relationship with his Lord. That is what we would call the "deeper Christian life." We publish the finest works we can find on that subject and our editors have found that much of it dates back several hundred years. There is a real hunger for this kind of spiritual depth among our customers.[18]

Despite such disclaimers, the language of American popular piety is permeated by expressions with roots in Puritan and continental Catholic spirituality. Such is the case with Quietism. Madame Guyon and Fénelon have been labeled as Quietists in the history of religion. The language of "rest," or stillness, so prevalent in Quaker, Methodist, and holiness hymns and writing, represents the often-unrecognized impact of Quietist spirituality on the vocabulary of American religious experience. A. B. Simpson (1843–1919) of the Christian and Missionary Alliance, for example, spoke of seeking and hearing only the still, small voice of God within the self.

The best thing about this stillness is that it gives God a chance to work. "He that is entered into his rest, he also hath ceased from his own works, as God did from his"; and when we cease from our works, God works in us; and when we cease from our thoughts, God's thoughts come into us; when we get still from our restless activity, God worketh in us both to will and do of His good pleasure, and we have but to work it out.[19]

On the other hand, Thomas Upham expressed the same sense of quietude, but in more abstract language.

The doctrine of religious quietude conveys the notion of a state of intellect so free from all unnecessary worldly intruders, that God can take up his abode there as the one great idea, which shall either exclusively occupy the mind, or shall so far occupy it as to bring all other thoughts and reflections into entire harmony with itself. [. . .] A state of religious or spiritual quietude is, in other words, a state of rest in God.[20]

Such language takes on profound reverberations once one reads it in the context of the historical context of the Quietist controversies that brought together Madame Guyon and Fénelon, two unlikely companions in the religious conflicts of the later reign of Louis XIV.

Chapter 2

The Reputation of Madame Guyon
Personalities, Politics, and Religious Controversy under Louis XIV

Readers and Madame Guyon the Person

John Wesley published his abridged version of the autobiography of Madame Guyon because he was concerned about the response of early English Methodists to her life, that is, to the power of her account of her spiritual experience. Although he emphasized in his preface that Madame Guyon was an eminently good woman favored with "uncommon communications" of God's spirit, he expressed concern about the autobiography as a whole.

> [The book] contains abundance of excellent things, uncommonly excellent: such as may greatly tend to the spiritual advantage of the children of God. And at the same time it contains several things, which are utterly false and unscriptural: nay such as are dangerously false; such as have a natural tendency to hinder the progress of the children of God; to prevent their growth in grace, yea, to turn them out of the plain, scriptural way, into that of imagination and delusion.[1]

True to eighteenth-century common sense and to his belief in the importance of Scripture, Wesley went on to say that Madame Guyon's errors were on less important matters, but that they were errors common to mystics. She erred when she relied on her confessors and her "inner light" and not on Scripture. "And yet with all this dross, how much pure gold is mixt! So did God wink at involuntary ignorance! What a depth of religion did she enjoy! Of the mind that was in Christ Jesus!"[2]

Although the vocabulary of "imagination," "delusion," and "ignorance" seems to smack of a denigration of female spirituality, Wesley's
comments are quite measured compared with those of Bossuet, Voltaire, and Diderot who ridiculed Madame Guyon, thus consigning her
to obscurity in France as a delusional female mystic. Jacques Bénigne
Bossuet, archbishop of Meaux (1627–1704), became the great opponent
of Madame Guyon in the Quietist controversy at the end of the seventeenth century, engaging in an exchange of polemicals with Fénelon, her
defender. Bossuet's *Account of Quietism* (*Relation sur le quiétisme*) was published in 1698 near the end of the public conflict when Madame Guyon
was already imprisoned in the Bastille. Having debated in writing with
Fénelon regarding the nature of mysticism and how Madame Guyon represented an unacceptable brand of "new" mysticism, Bossuet resorted in
this text to satire in order to undermine the reputations of both Madame
Guyon and Fénelon, especially in court circles.

Bossuet also made insinuations concerning the propriety of Madame
Guyon's relationships, both with her earlier spiritual director Père LaCombe
and with Fénelon. He suggested she was a self-appointed prophetess, deluded
in her sense of apostolic vocation, a fanatic. He poked fun at the occasional
physical manifestations of Madame Guyon's mystic states.

> In the autobiography of this lady, I read that God bestowed upon her such
> an abundance of grace that she literally was bursting and that her corset
> had to be unlaced. She did not forget to mention that a duchess had once
> performed this office. In such a state, she often was placed upon her bed;
> one would just remain seated near her in order to receive her overflowing
> grace, and this was the only means for giving her relief.[3]

By the time of the death of Madame Guyon, a negative and ironic
perspective toward Quietism was already entrenched in France. Montesquieu's satiric *Persian Letters* (*Lettres Persanes*) appeared in 1721. In letter 134,
Rica, one of the Persian visitors, reports on a visit to a library. This visit
gives Montesquieu the opportunity to satirize the proliferation of books
of Scriptural interpretation; interpretation is a battlefield of skirmishes
and attacks among sects and nations. The librarian goes on to explain
to Rica that books on asceticism, devotion, theology, and morality, all
incomprehensible, are on the shelves next to the commentaries. And then
a section devoted to mystical books follows. These are for devout people
of a tender heart, says the librarian. When Rica interrupts and asks for an
explanation of mysticism, his guide replies that devotion warms tender-
hearted people, exciting the brain that then gives birth to delirious states
of ecstasy and ravishment. "Often the delirium of devotion is perfected,

that is, it degenerates into quietism; you know that a quietist is nothing but an individual who is mad, devout, and a libertine."[4] With his subtle language, Montesquieu has ironically mocked the Quietists' claims of perfect love and of the annihilation of the self. Quietists are libertines in the sense that their claims of passive submission to the divine will can make all sorts of behavior excusable because they are no longer worried about the voluntary disciplines of the Christian life.

When Voltaire, the great voice of reason and critic of organized religion, came to write his history of the age of Louis XIV (*Siècle de Louis XIV,* 1752), the negative tradition inaugurated by Bossuet and Montesquieu was refined further. Voltaire's scenario centered on the debate between Bossuet and Fénelon, two gifted princes and rivals of the church. Voltaire relegated Madame Guyon to a secondary role as a misguided hysteric. "It was strange that [Fénelon] was seduced by a woman of revelations, prophecies, and gibberish, who suffocated from interior grace, to the point of having to be unlaced."[5]

In response to eighteenth-century discussions of the physiology, education and social role of women, Diderot wrote an essay "On Women," published in 1774, in which he emphasized the physiological basis of female hysterics. According to him, young women who are prone to hysterics become excessively devout as they age. "The woman dominated by 'hysterism' experiences something of the internal and celestial. [. . .] The Guyon has eloquent lines in her book *The Torrents* for which there are no models. Saint Teresa said of demons: 'How unhappy they are! They do not love at all!' Quietism is the hypocrisy of perverse men and the true religion of tender-hearted women." Here, Diderot situates the Quietist movement in the eighteenth-century cult of sensibility. Then, referring to spiritual direction, he says that Fénelon's character was exceptional among directors who were for the most part perverse and that women could depend on him to bring them closer to God.[6]

This negative view of Madame Guyon continued into the twentieth century, especially among Catholic commentators, because of Rome's condemnation of what it deemed to be the theological excesses of Miguel de Molinos (of which more will be said). All "Quietists" became categorized as adherents to "Molinism." In his history of Catholic spirituality, Pierre Pourat characterized Madame Guyon as "a rather unhealthy and eccentric mystic" with "hysterical tendencies." Her public discourses and teaching were solidly pious; her natural gifts of personality and speech gained her followers. Her esoteric teaching for her inner circle, however, was quite different. And her ability to write with facility, as well as to speak persuasively, "struck her as an invitation from Heaven to spread her ideas."[7] In her general study of mysticism, Anglo-Catholic Evelyn Underhill commented that Madame Guyon was "an example of the unfortunate results of an alliance of mystical tendencies with a feeble surface intelligence. Had she possessed the robust common sense so often found in the great contemplatives, her temperamental inclination to passivity would have been checked, and she would hardly have made use of the exaggerated expressions which brought about the official condemnation of her works."[8] Similarly, in his work on "enthusiasts," Ronald Knox linked Madame Guyon the person and the writer.

> What genuine mystical experiences [Madame Guyon] may have had we shall never know; it was all hopelessly overlaid by the workings of an exuberant, yet strictly logical, imagination. Madame Guyon had ceased to exist; that which spoke and acted in her was God. [. . .] There is a smugness about her autobiography which forbids me to credit the legend of her sanctity; yet she was no ordinary woman, even if she imagined the stranger features of it—what friends she made, and what enemies![9]

Only with the rise of feminism later in the twentieth century and with the ensuing interest in rediscovering the women who had been lost to mainstream history did critics begin to read Madame Guyon in a more balanced light. This rereading began in France with studies by the writer Françoise Mallet-Joris and the theologian Marie-Louise Gondal.[10] Gondal and other women critics have also confronted the profound psychological implications of Jeanne Guyon's childhood, physical distress, periods of depression or spiritual dryness, dreams, and relationships.[11] Although these issues link her to the vast post-Freudian literature about women mystics, they have been a key reason for the dismissive way in which she has been treated by historians.

Questions about Jeanne Guyon's mental and emotional makeup have played a different kind of role, however, in how Americans have responded to her, for they have usually read her works and interpreted her life with minimal reference to her cultural context. If we look at one example from the early twenty-first century, we can see other challenges posed by American readings of this devotional icon. In 2001, *Weavings*, a journal of spirituality published by the Upper Room, published an article describing the spiritual insights that Jan Johnson, the author, had received as she interacted with the life and writings of Madame Guyon.[12] Johnson had recently authored a modern abridgment and paraphrase of Madame Guyon's autobiography and first became acquainted with Madame Guyon's work when she read *Experiencing the Depths of Jesus Christ*, an American version of *A Short and Easy Method of Prayer* (*Moyen court et très facile de faire oraison*, 1685). It is relevant to the understanding of the readership of this material to note that the editor of *Experiencing the Depths of Jesus Christ* claimed that when he discovered Madame Guyon's book, "it was in the form of a very clumsy, mimeographed edition. Whoever prepared that simple edition had added a preface [. . .]: 'That this little book has fallen into your hands is an indication that God desires to do a special work in your heart.'"[13]

Jan Johnson herself was moved by Madame Guyon's desire "to enjoy uninterrupted fellowship with God, a practice [Johnson had] been working at for years." However, after completing her task of paraphrasing the life of Madame Guyon, Johnson "drew back" from Madame Guyon's suffering. "I had dismissed her as a religious crackpot who acquiesced when she should have put her hands on her hips and demanded justice. [. . .] I would never have been so passive." Johnson valued Madame Guyon's use of specific passages of Scripture to sense the presence of God and Guyon's form of holy waiting or "beholding the Lord." Johnson wondered if such practices really brought results, so, anxious to "reclaim [her] hero," she reread the treatise on prayer and discovered also the emphasis on abandonment. In this American version of Madame Guyon's beliefs, one should abandon one's own existence to God since "everything that has happened to you is from God and is exactly what you need." Johnson then decided as an experiment to act out the model of Madame Guyon's advice as a form of spiritual discipline that led in time to the transformation of her own cynicism into spiritual renewal.[14]

Johnson's initial responses to Madame Guyon—admiration for some of her teaching, unease that she might be a fanatic, and rejection of her passivity—are of particular relevance. In one sense, they are not unlike those of John Wesley or of others who have viewed Jeanne Guyon as an isolated figure apart from the religious and political context of which she was so much a part.

The versions of Madame Guyon's writings known to Johnson present an image of Madame Guyon that is the reflection of a brand of modern American evangelical spirituality. The lens of this spirituality has led to both a reading of Madame Guyon that sometimes transforms her into a charismatic and, subsequently, to the dissemination of abridgments of her writings that reinforce this spirituality. Is it possible for modern readers to approach devotional literature in a different way—to read simultaneously with a sensitivity to cultural differences, but with an experientially based hermeneutic that transcends cultural boundaries? This is one of the challenges posed by the history of the transmission and reception of the works of Madame Guyon and Fénelon in America. To get at this challenge, it is important to understand how she was formed by her seventeenth-century context.

The Religious Climate under Louis XIV

Louis XIV came to the throne in 1643 at the age of five. His minority lasted until 1651 and he died in 1715. Jeanne-Marie Bouvier de la Mothe (later, Guyon) was born in 1648 and died in 1717. François de Salignac de la Mothe-Fénelon was born in 1651 and died in 1715. The lives of these two cannot be understood apart from the political and religious complexities of the reign of Louis XIV. Indeed, the early foreign reputation of Madame Guyon and Fénelon was as martyrs to Louis' political and religious policies.

From 1648 to 1653, a revolt of the Parliament of Paris and then of many of the nobles, called "La Fronde," so weakened the monarchy that at one point Louis and his mother, Anne d'Autriche, had to flee Paris. After the death in 1661 of Cardinal Mazarin, the chief minister who had been allied with Anne, Louis took over the direct control of the government, serving as his own chief minister, relying heavily on members of the bourgeoisie such as Jean-Baptiste Colbert. With the experience of the Fronde at the back of his mind, Louis was to institute an absolute and highly centralized government, epitomized by his palace at Versailles. Life at Versailles in the 1660s and 1670s was one of splendor and extravagance and also one that controlled the nobility. Aristocrats who wished to remain in the king's favor had to be present at the court. After the death of Louis' first wife and his secret marriage in 1683 to Françoise d'Aubigné, the Marquise of Maintenon, the tone of the court became noticeably more severe. Raised by a Protestant aunt, Madame de Maintenon had returned to Catholicism; she exercised considerable influence over the king in religious matters and represented the power of a social segment of zealots called *dévots*.

It was to Louis XIV's advantage to ally his monarchy with Catholicism. This was still the age of the Counter Reformation. Engaged in conflicts with the pope about the degree of power of the French throne over church affairs, Louis also followed a policy of internal religious intolerance. During the Renaissance and Reformation, France had been torn apart by religious wars; an uneasy truce had been reached when Henri IV, a Protestant who had converted to Catholicism, issued the Edict of Nantes in 1598, giving a degree of freedom to the Calvinists or Huguenots, as they were called, to worship, to live in secured enclaves, and to enjoy protection within the courts. Under Louis XIII, Catholic-Protestant struggles continued, and Louis XIV followed a policy of forced conversions to Catholicism. In 1685, he revoked the previous edict, depriving Protestants of their freedom of worship and forbidding their emigration. Nevertheless, a major exodus occurred, with significant repercussions, including war.

Nor was Louis tolerant of new movements within Catholicism. For example, Jansenism, the Catholic movement heavily influenced by Augustinian notions of grace and sin, and centered at Port Royal, was viewed with suspicion by Louis who came to openly oppose it, razing the convent of Port Royal in 1711 and lobbying with the pope for the bull that would condemn some of its tenets in 1713. Louis' opposition to the Jansenists was also conditioned by the power of the Jesuits, their archenemies; two of the king's confessors, in fact, were Jesuits.

Against such a backdrop of court intrigue and power politics, linking religion and absolutism, it is not surprising that Madame Guyon and Fénelon would run afoul of the régime. Their paths would cross that of Madame de Maintenon, eventually bringing to a head the religious and personal conflicts embedded in the French cultural context.

The intellectual and religious climate was, however, even more complex than the politics of Louis XIV. The seventeenth century represents what has been called "the twilight of mysticism."[15] Forms of mysticism continued to be practiced and great mystics such as John of the Cross and Teresa of Avila were read and valued. Marie of the Incarnation, the Ursuline who would travel to Quebec, was a mystic of the highest order. As the century wore on, interest in various forms of mental prayer was great so that as Quietism (the "new" mysticism) spread, there were groups and societies meeting in Spain, Italy, and France.[16] Spiritual directors exercised great influence and were one way in which specific traditions of devotional practice and spirituality were disseminated and passed on. Sermons, pulpit oratory, and funeral ceremonies were powerful public rites, particularly in Paris.

Religious orders flourished and multiplied. At the same time, orders of laywomen, such as the Visitandines (Order of the Visitation), permitted women to circulate within society to minister to the poor and needy. Francois de Sales' vision for this particular order, founded first in Annecy in Savoy and then in Lyon, was that there would be no *clausura* and that a life of service would be linked to perfection of the inner spiritual life. But by 1616, he was forced to impose monastic vows in the Augustinian tradition and *clausura* was instituted. Nevertheless, orders such as Vincent de Paul's Daughters of Charity, founded later, were able to succeed at first by avoiding religious institutionalization and remaining as lay communities serving the needy in the broader world.[17]

New ways of thinking were already at work in France. In the aftermath of the Counter Reformation, Ignatian forms of spiritual practice, emphasizing meditative versus contemplative spirituality, had become increasingly important. Descartes had published his *Discourse on Method*

(*Discours sur la méthode*) in 1637. Rational analysis was an entirely different approach to truth than the experiential knowledge of apophatic or non-verbal mysticism. During the lifetimes of Madame Guyon and Fénelon, Baconian science was to be superseded by the theories of Leibniz and Newton. In such a context, mystics, whatever their stripe, were caught between old and new ways of thinking, knowing, and writing in a climate that was highly politically charged. Michel Certeau has demonstrated how the desire for a radical Christianity in the midst of loss and absence was a "fable" inscribed in the details of the mystical texts of the period, and those of Jeanne Guyon were no exception.[18]

The Drama of the Life of Jeanne Guyon

Jeanne-Marie Bouvier de la Mothe (Motte) was born in Montargis, south of Paris and east of Orléans, to a pious aristocratic family.[19] This was the second marriage for both Jeanne's parents and, during her childhood, she would suffer from a lack of maternal love that in retrospect, with the insights of psychology and psychoanalysis, can be seen as a contributing factor to her inclination toward religion. As a natural outcome of her family milieu in which her brother, half-brothers, and sisters were members of religious orders, Jeanne was to come in contact with the major crosscurrents of spirituality and religious practice in seventeenth-century France. Dominique de la Mothe, a half-brother, became a Barnabite and through him she was to come in contact later with Père LaCombe, the spiritual director who would suffer immensely from accusations that he was a Quietist. At the age of two and a half, Jeanne was sent off to spend her childhood in a variety of pensions; she suffered from fragile health and from her mother's disinterest, factors that were to play a role in her spiritual experience.

From 1655 to approximately 1658, she was under the care of a paternal half-sister in an Ursuline pension where she made rapid progress in her intellectual and spiritual education. The Ursulines were the great teaching order of the time, specializing in the education of young girls and their catechesis. Originally not monastic, the Ursulines became an order, and the prestigious house in Paris had close ties to the court. The social and institutional pressures on the Ursulines to move from less formal communities to cloistered convents meant that their mission also shifted to include the education of the aristocracy.[20] Jeanne later commented that at this early age she thought only of giving herself to God and that she often experienced the conflict between her good intentions and bad habits, even doing penances sometimes. After her first communion in 1659, she returned home where she lived a sheltered and boring life, still without much maternal attention, and her spiritual tendencies gradually waned. At one point, her father sent her to a Dominican convent for several months where, when she was ill and not particularly well cared for, she found a Bible in her sickroom. Jeanne wrote in her autobiography that she loved reading. (In fact, she had a passion for reading novels and would give them up around the time of her marriage in 1664.) In her sickroom at the convent, she latched on to the Bible that she found and read it from morning until evening. She had a very good memory and retained what she read. Biblical echoes, allusions, and quotations would characterize her writing style, and one can discern the origins of the imprint of the biblical text on her consciousness in this experience.[21]

In 1661, the family received a visit from a nephew of her father who was about to leave as a missionary to the Far East. Under his influence, Jeanne read spiritual works, notably François de Sales' *Introduction to the Devout Life* (*Introduction à la vie dévote*, 1609), as well as a biography of Jeanne de Chantal by Henri de Maupas, published in 1644. The influence of the lives and ideas of these two figures on the young Jeanne was profound. De Sales (1567–1622) was from Savoy and achieved recognition as a spiritual director, preacher, and writer and as the bishop of Geneva. Early in his career he spent four years on a mission to convert the Calvinist Protestants of the Chablais region. The *Introduction to the Devout Life* was a powerful and popular manual written for the laity because de Sales felt that it was not necessary to lead a cloistered, separate life in order to advance in inner spirituality. A second, equally popular work, *Treatise on the Love of God* (*Traité de l'amour de Dieu*), appeared in 1616. The themes of the teaching of François de Sales would prove appealing to adherents of Quietism who, however, pushed them beyond the limits that Catholicism could tolerate. The spirituality of de Sales was optimistic, emphasizing the grace of God, when coupled with meditation and confession, in the efforts of the individual to purge sinful affections and renounce the attachment to sin. The disciplines or exercises of piety included mental prayer, morning and evening prayers, examination of the conscience, devotional reading, spiritual recollection, confession, and communion. For the laity de Sales recommended a simplified method of mental prayer that included "preparation, considerations, affections and resolutions, and the spiritual bouquet." The last was to recall during the day an element from the meditation from that particular morning. De Sales emphasized as well the active exercise of virtue, and his mysticism was a state in which divine love occupied the mind, bringing the individual will in conformity through obedience with the divine will. The soul progressed toward perfection through prayer that encouraged disinterested love.[22]

Jeanne de Chantal (1572–1641) had been widowed at an early age and had returned home with her four children where she practiced austere piety. She then was forced to live with her father-in-law when he threatened to disinherit her children. In 1604, during a visit from her father, she met François de Sales and then asked him to become her spiritual director. Formed under his principles, she vowed not to remarry and to obey him. Her desire to enter a religious order was delayed. In 1607 de Sales conveyed to her his plan to found the new order of the Visitation (based on the example of Mary's visit to her cousin Elizabeth) referred to earlier. In 1610, Jeanne de Chantal and two others received the rule for this order and a convent was formed. They took their first vows two years later, and in 1618, after *clausura* was established, the pope officially approved the order. Jeanne de Chantal's concern was the spiritual perfection of herself and others in the order, and in this aim she was an example of Salesian spirituality. There were eighty "Visitadine" houses established by the time she died.

Naturally, the young Jeanne Bouvier de la Mothe wanted to enter the Order of the Visitation, for there was a convent in Montargis. Her parents refused, in part because, as a beautiful young aristocrat, she was very eligible for marriage. Nevertheless, the themes of the lives of de Sales and Chantal were to enter into her consciousness, and she was to imitate them later in her initial sense of vocation to Savoy. Further, Jeanne was exposed very early on to spiritual values and practices that were to become her own: to disinterested love, to a spirituality of the laity, and to the importance of mental prayer.

Sent to Paris for a stay of several months in 1663, Jeanne was attracted by sophisticated worldly society; frivolous "worldliness" for a time exercised a powerful pull on her deep spiritual tendencies. In early 1664, her parents arranged her marriage to a well-off bourgeois from Montargis, Jacques Guyon, who was twenty-two years older than she. Jeanne was a bride of fifteen; she came to view the twelve unhappy years of this marriage as a prolonged trial. The young Jeanne shared the Guyon residence with her mother-in-law, who mistreated her. Her husband, a difficult man who also suffered from gout, was unable to respond to his young wife's emotional needs. Of five children, three survived. Both of her parents died. Jeanne Guyon herself suffered from ill health, including disfiguring smallpox.

These difficult circumstances coincided with Madame Guyon's discovery of a mystical interior life that would lead eventually to a vocation, but not to the life of a religious. Contacts with a range of persons contributed to her spiritual development. In the summer of 1667, her father hosted the mother and daughter of Nicolas Fouquet, the disgraced and imprisoned superintendent of finances of Louis XIV. The daughter, Madame de Béthune, the Duchess of Charost, was a person of piety and mystical leanings. Jeanne Guyon formed an unshakable friendship with her. Additional contacts reinforced the influence toward mysticism she had received from the duchess.

In a well-known passage of her autobiography, Madame Guyon describes the first of three critical events in her spiritual life. (Louis Cognet has suggested that Madame Guyon's account was influenced by her later reading of a similar event in the life of Madame Adorna, known as Catharine of Genoa.)[23] Distressed by the lack of progress in her effort to please God and by her inability to meditate and to imagine as part of her prayer life (probably in the manner counseled by François de Sales), on the advice of her father Jeanne went to see a Franciscan who was visiting Montargis. He responded to her distress by telling her that she was looking outside herself for that which was within. "Develop the habit of looking for God in your heart and you will find him there." The next day, on July 22, 1668, Jeanne experienced what she called a deep wound, "as delicious as it was loving, from which I would never desire to be cured." Her happiness, in the midst of the distress of her life, lay within. "O Lord, you were in my heart and you were asking only a simple return within to cause me to feel your presence."[24] For Jeanne Guyon the interior life was a return home, a return to her origins and to the reintegration of the self. She was given the gift of nonconceptual prayer, was enveloped in disinterested love, and had a sense of being moved in all things by God. The following description, written years later, is notable for its attempt to explain the psychology of the will and for its use of natural imagery—both reflections of her reading of mystical literature after this experience.

> My prayer was, from then on, empty of all forms, types, and images; none of my prayer took place in my head; but it was a prayer of delight and possession in the will, where the taste for God was so grand, so pure, and so simple that it attracted and absorbed the two other capacities of the soul [memory and understanding] into a deep contemplation (*recueillement*) without act or discourse. [. . .] It was a prayer of faith which excluded all distinctions, for I had no sight of Jesus Christ nor of divine attributes: everything was absorbed into a delicious faith, where all distinctions were lost in order to give way to the love of loving with more amplitude, without motives or reasons to love. This sovereign power, the will, swallowed up the two other [faculties], depriving them of every distinct object in order to better unite them in her. [. . .] It is

not that they remain passive and unknown in their operations, but it is that the light of faith, like light in general, similar to the Sun, absorbs all distinct lights and puts them in obscurity from our perspective, because the excess of its light surpasses them all.[25]

Madame Guyon gave herself over to this experience of interior prayer, renouncing amusements such as dancing and practicing extreme forms of corporal mortification. Her piety brought about even greater opposition from her mother-in-law and husband. For spiritual guidance Madame Guyon consulted Geneviève Granger, prioress of a convent in Montargis. Later, her spiritual director became Jacques Bertot, a friend of Mère Granger. Bertot was greatly respected in Paris and had been a disciple of Jean de Bernières, a lay Norman mystic and spiritual director whose works would be condemned in 1689 and 1690. Bernières taught that Christian perfection was in abnegation (humility and the love of humiliations).[26] The spiritual guidance of Granger and Bertot illustrates the complex strands of affinities and communication that connected Jeanne Guyon with the spiritual *courants* of her time. In addition, a general pattern began to emerge in her life in which periods of loss and suffering would be followed by intense periods of mystical exaltation.

In July of 1672, she lost both her father and first daughter, to whom she was very attached. After a period of fasting and mortification, on the advice of Mère Granger she celebrated her spiritual marriage to the infant Jesus. The dowry of this mystical union was "crosses, scorn, confusion, opposition, and ignominy." From then on, she considered Jesus as her divine husband. "These words were first placed in my mind, that he would be 'a bridegroom of blood' [Exod 4:25]. Since then he has taken me so strongly as his own, that he has perfectly consecrated my body and my mind unto himself by the cross." These are the words of a writer looking back on the pattern of suffering in her life as an intimate part of her marriage to Jesus. Yet, she goes beyond this imagery to say that, although she often experienced consolation, there were extended periods when she was overwhelmed and abandoned, when her food was "a desolation without consolation."[27] Such dark nights of the soul place her directly in the *via negativa* of mystics like Saint John of the Cross.

In 1676, Jacques Guyon died, and the young widow astutely handled the affairs of the estate, separated herself from her mother-in-law, and lived quietly. Her spiritual life was marked by passive purification and aridity. In 1679, circumstances brought her into contact again with Père La Combe, whom she had met earlier in Montargis. La Combe was a Barnabite known to Jeanne's half-brother, and was also superior of the house of that order in Savoy. (He came into contact with Quietism in

Savoy and Italy.) Madame Guyon felt a deep spiritual affinity with La Combe, and the two exchanged letters. A new phase of Jeanne's spiritual life began, one in which a sense of vocation emerged, and La Combe was pulled along into this increasingly high drama.

In July of 1680, again on the feast day of Mary Magdalene, the third crucial experience of Jeanne Guyon's spiritual journey took place. She had asked La Combe to pray for her deliverance from her desolate spiritual state. In the autobiography she speaks of this day as characterized by a "union of unity" with God, marked not by the cross, but by plenitude, joy, and freedom.

> A single day of this happiness would be the payment with interest for several years of suffering. Although this happiness was only then just dawning, it was not limited to what I describe. Every capacity for good was given back to me enlarged, so free and so exempt from embarrassment that it seemed to become natural.[28]

This emphasis on spontaneity and naturalness is a recurring theme, but the language here also suggests a purification of motive and desire in moving toward the perfection of disinterested love.

> I felt a kind of beatitude increase each day in me. I was completely delivered from all suffering and from all the inclinations I believed I had toward sin. It seemed to me that I did all sorts of good without ownership or benefit and if a recompense was present, it was first dissipated. [. . .] I was astonished at the clearness of my mind and the purity of my heart.[29]

The effect of this union on the daily life of Madame Guyon illustrates a psychology or theology in which the individual's will is subsumed into the divine will. This psychology of the will is at the root of the Quietism that she espoused—an annihilation of the self (will) as it is enveloped by the divine, leading to a passive repose before God, a confidence that one's actions are in accord with God's will, and an acceptance of suffering and of opposition.

> I no longer found the will to submit; it was though it had disappeared, or rather, as though it had passed on into another will. It seems that this powerful and strong will did whatever it pleased. I no longer found that soul which [the divine will] had previously led with extreme love by a shepherd's staff. It seemed only that [my] soul had ceded its place to that will, had passed into that will in order to do only the same thing with it.[30]

The natural imagery used to illustrate this psychology of the will is that of the sea. A drop of water cast into the sea keeps taking on more and more of the qualities of that sea; such is the effect on the individual who experiences union with the divine will.

In line with her admiration of François de Sales, Madame Guyon began to feel that she had a vocation to carry out in Geneva. She met the bishop, Jean d'Arenthon d'Alex, his successor. Madame Guyon's wealth made her an attractive candidate for a lay vocation. D'Arenthon's project was the establishment of a house for "new Catholics" in Gex in Savoy. (These Catholics were Protestant converts.) Jeanne Guyon worked secretly on her plans, consulting Bertot, her spiritual director, LaCombe, and Claude Martin, the son of Marie of the Incarnation, the great mystic and missionary to Quebec. Jeanne left Montargis with her daughter in early July of 1682, going first to Paris where she made arrangements for the management of the assets of her two sons and for her own and her daughter's income. Then she continued to Gex, arriving on July 22.

Sisters from the Order of the Propagation of the Faith were responsibile for the foundation in Gex, and relations with them quickly deteriorated. Jeanne began to feel that she had made a colossal mistake. The bishop asked La Combe to come from nearby Thonon to encourage her. Bertot, her spiritual director in Paris, had died. She felt an immediate spiritual communication with La Combe and he become her next director.

> As soon as I saw the father, I was surprised to feel an interior grace that I can call communication and that I had never had with anyone. It seemed that an influence of grace came from him to me via the most intimate part of the soul and then returned from me to him so that he experienced the same effect; but this was a grace so pure, so clean, so unattached from any feeling that it was like a flowing and ebbing. From there it went on to be lost in the divine and invisible One. There was nothing human or natural, but all was pure spirit, and this union, all pure and holy, which has always remained, becoming more and more one, has never stopped or engaged the soul, always leaving it in perfect freedom. [. . .] The grace that I experienced, that caused this interior influence from him to me and from me to him, dissipated all my troubles and put me in a state of very deep repose.[31]

Retrospectively, Madame Guyon goes out of her way to emphasize that no sexual or emotional bond existed in such special cases of silent communication, but the psychological effect of La Combe's presence is clear. The word "repose" connotes deep peace and detachment. Without resorting to modern psychoanalytic categories, one can immediately discern a refined pattern in Madame Guyon's special revelatory experiences. Circumstances that posed dire threats to the integrity of the self were followed eventually by the reestablishment of an equilibrium through special acts of grace; the integration of the self occurred through a return home (what might be a place of maternal or paternal love) or through a liberating act of communication, whether silent as recounted here, or verbal, an outpouring of speech.

Madame Guyon placed her daughter in an Ursuline pension in Thonon and carried on in Gex; experiencing serious illness, she gave La Combe credit for her recovery, which seemed miraculous. During the difficult winter of 1681–1682, her family, including Dominique de la Mothe, tried to have her return to Montargis. She resisted and ended by turning over the guardianship of her sons to her mother-in-law and by renouncing all her personal assets except for a substantial pension. Other difficulties continued in Gex, including tensions with the Jansenist head of the community. (Opposition by Jansenists was to become a recurring pattern.) Jeanne moved to Thonon in February of 1682, living with her daughter at the Ursuline establishment, giving contributions to the foundation at Gex, but resisting the efforts of the bishop to force her to resume her work there. (La Combe was initially absent on a mission in Italy.) Madame Guyon's half-sister, Jeanne de Sainte-Marie, who was an Ursuline, spent one year in Thonon, taking charge of the education of the young daughter, Jeanne-Marie, who was six years old. The visiting religious did not, however, share her half-sister's gift for inner prayer and mystical union. La Combe himself was not initially inclined toward mysticism but came to share Madame Guyon's experience.

During the two years she spent in Thonon, the bishop of Geneva continued to try to force her to return to Gex and then, according to the autobiography, "persecuted" Jeanne. Ultimately, she had to face the failure of her original vocation to serve new Catholics. She was gravely ill again during the winter of 1682–1683. During much of her stay, she was with the Ursuline nuns, but in the summer of 1683, she withdrew to an uncomfortable house because her situation had become dangerous. She felt demons were at work to oppose her. This period was marked by a severe psychological crisis, but it was also a turning point. Marie-Louise Gondal had delineated a series of births that came out of this darkness: the birth of a woman with a sense of her own identity, the birth of a new kind of spiritual discourse, and the birth of a new form of mysticism, one that crossed from the enclosed world of religious orders to the external, public scene.[32]

Several events delineated the turning points of this rebirth. In the summer of 1683, Jeanne completed a retreat under La Combe in which she experienced a liberation from some of her distress, evidenced in a pouring forth of language that ensued. Shortly after the retreat, through a form of automatic writing in which she herself was not always conscious of what she had written, she produced her first work, *The Torrents* (*Les Torrents*). (The text was subsequently revised slightly and was circulated in manuscript form during her lifetime.)

The metaphor of the title suggests the gathered force of the currents of water as the soul, itself a torrent, is on its interior journey into a state of complete abandonment (a descent into nothingness) and then union with God. The imagery conveys, of course, Madame Guyon's own experience. The soul turns inward through prayer and, in the various stages of contemplation, is drawn into annihilation as its will becomes one with that of God. What is fascinating in this context is that Madame Guyon speaks of the very act of writing *The Torrents* as an illustration of this abandonment.

> When such a soul [i.e., Madame Guyon] writes, she is astonished that she writes things that she didn't think she knew, although she cannot doubt that she possessed them while writing them down. It is not the same with [other souls]: their reason precedes their expression because they are like a person seeing from a distance things which he does not possess. He describes what he has seen, known heard, etc. But this soul [abandoned to the will of God] is like a person who contains a treasure that it sees only after its manifestation. [. . .] God is in this soul, or rather, this soul no longer is: and it no longer acts, but God acts and the soul is the instrument.[33]

Madame Guyon's discourse is spontaneous; its force lies in the fact that is the transcription of a voice. The style seems oral, an address to a common reader. (Despite the use of the third person in this particular passage, a Guyon text is often dialogic; there is an "I" who shifts constantly into direct addresses to God, as though to reinforce the identity of the self.) This particular passage is highly imagistic, and throughout the Guyon corpus there is an interplay of imagery from the Bible, from mystic and devotional literature, and even from her early reading of novels. Despite Madame Guyon's sense that the act of writing seemed directed by a force beyond her control, she had been gaining experience in writing because Père La Combe, as her spiritual director, asked her to record her experiences during spiritual retreats in notebooks.[34]

It was often in dreams that revelations came to her, and such was the case at Thonon. A dream became the means of salvaging her failed initial vocation. During her prolonged illness, on the night of February 2–3, 1683, in a dream she foresaw a persecution against the form of prayer she practiced, but a vindication as well, because this persecution would lead to the establishment of this very form of spirituality. Addressing God, she recalls the dream; the imagery of the womb reinforces her new apostolic mission of spiritual motherhood.

> [. . .] You showed me to myself in the form [. . .] of that woman of the Apocalypse who had the Moon beneath her feet, surrounded by the Sun, twelve stars on her head, and, pregnant, was crying in the pain of childbirth. You made me understand that this Moon [. . .] indicated that my soul was above the vicissitude and inconstancy of events, that I was surrounded and penetrated by you [. . .], that I was pregnant with a fruit that was the spirit that you wanted me to communicate to my children, either by what I said or by my writings, that the Demon was that frightening dragon who would try to devour the fruit [. . .].[35]

This new lay vocation of spiritual motherhood, resulting from Jeanne's spiritual marriage with Jesus, was thus a kind of compensation for the forsaking of her own sons. Madame Guyon began to engage in a ministry of proselytizing, seeking to teach the inner spirituality and form of prayer she had discovered. The bishop of Geneva saw it as a divisive move within the religious communities under his jurisdiction and basically brought her connection to the house in Gex to an end.

When Père La Combe was sent on a mission to Vercelli in Piedmont, Madame Guyon took advantage of the opportunity to go to Turin, where a friend, the Marquise of Pruney, had invited her to come. La Combe and Madame Guyon left Thonon in October of 1683. Her life as a wanderer had begun. La Combe accompanied her to Turin and then continued on his mission. In the meantime, Madame Guyon's mother-in-law had died and a cousin of her late husband took over the guardianship of her two sons. The oldest boy went to Turin to beg her to come home, but she refused. She began her teaching ministry in Turin and again faced opposition, which she blamed on both the bishop of Geneva and her Barnabite half-brother. Madame Guyon's friend began to tire of her presence, and Jeanne thought of leaving Turin in the spring of 1684.

Père La Combe did not want her to come to Vercelli, so he went to Turin to tell Madame Guyon that she should go to Paris. Because she was afraid to travel by herself, La Combe accompanied her to as far as Grenoble where she was again welcomed by a friend. The stay was prolonged. Madame Guyon had enormous success, receiving visitors all day long, and her influence spread among a variety of religious orders. Her apostolic vocation seemed confirmed. At the urging of a counselor at the local *parlement*, or court, Madame Guyon published her *Short and Easy Method of*

Prayer (*Moyen court et très facile de faire oraison*), which would be reprinted in 1686 in Lyon and in Paris. This popular book was by no means the first of its kind to be published during the seventeenth century. It explained a method to practice the "prayer of the heart," but it was remarkable because of the immediacy of the prose with its repetitions, its images, and its affirmation that acquired contemplation of silence and abandonment is available to everyone, especially the unlearned.

> All those who want to pray can. It is the key to perfection and to sov-
> ereign happiness, the efficient means to undo all vices and acquire all
> the virtues. There is only one thing to do to be perfect—to walk into the
> presence of God. God himself has told us this: "*Walk in my presence and
> be perfect*" (Gen 17:1). Prayer alone can give you this presence and give
> it to you continually.[36]

The bishop of Grenoble, who had Jansenist leanings, became concerned about Madame Guyon's influence. As in Turin, a campaign of
rumor and innuendo occurred about her relationship with La Combe.
(No grounds for these insinuations were ever found.) Despite the increasing opposition, or perhaps as a result of it, Madame Guyon's automatic
writing resumed. Between July and December of 1684 she wrote a mystical commentary on the Bible that came to twenty volumes when it was
printed after her death. (Only the commentary on the Song of Solomon
was published during her lifetime, in Lyon in 1688.)

Leaving her daughter in a pension run by the Ursulines, Madame
Guyon set off in March of 1685 without a fixed destination for the next
phase of her vocation. She was briefly in Marseille, a center of Quietism,
where she met the mystic François Malaval. (He was the author of *An Easy
Practice to Elevate the Soul to Contemplation* [*Pratique facile pour élever l'âme à
la contemplation*], and the Italian translation was condemned by Rome in
1688. At the height of Madame Guyon's later involvement in the Quietist
affair, her little treatise would be belittled for being little more than a version of Malaval.)[37] She tried to return to Turin and then went to Vercelli,
where she was protected by the bishop. Because the climate did not suit
her, she then decided to try to go to Geneva, but the bishop refused to
give permission for the move. In Vercelli, false accusations were raised
against her, so in March of 1686 she set out on a circuitous route for Paris.
In Grenoble, the bishop advised her to break off her contacts with La
Combe and to stop teaching and stay there. By then Madame Guyon was
intent on going to Paris, where she arrived in July of 1686.

A laywoman with a sense of vocation, an aristocrat with financial
resources, a mother who had abandoned her sons and her home, a mystic

with an exuberant personality and charismatic presence—these various roles set Jeanne Guyon on a path that easily caused her to be a threat to the religious establishment. As one follows her life in the next few years, one can ponder again the charges that Madame Guyon was mad, ignorant, deluded, and emotionally unstable, that her erotic and emotional needs were displaced into the religious realm and that her revelatory dreams were expressions, not of the will of God, but of her own deep-seated wishes and complexes. However, such an overriding sense of mission and of inner power appears in the next part of her life that one can hardly dismiss her mystical faith as self-delusion. In this sense she was no exception but shared the same sense of apostolic mission with the many women within lay orders and communities who were serving and teaching in society.

In addition, she was no fool. Her education would have been typical of an aristocrat of her time—reading in Latin and French, catechism, writing, the graces of conversation, good manners, and piety, the management of a household. She took advantage of her son's tutor to study Latin, and she was widely versed in both the Latin and French Bible and in the literature of the church fathers. She astutely managed her finances so that she was never poverty stricken. She adroitly judged the personalities of her disciples. As a laywoman, an itinerant at that, she continuously led a risky life, despite her aristocratic connections. She must have known the danger of confronting the political and religious establishment head-on in Paris. One is forced to admire the courage of this woman whose way of thinking was out of sync with the rise of modern rationalism and whose style of communication was so different from our own.

Paris and the Initial Charges of Quietism

Madame Guyon rented a house in the city, brought her daughter to live with her, and once again began to create a circle of influence. She was more prudent than she had been elsewhere, but she did not abandon the spiritual directorship of Père La Combe, so some rumors continued to follow them. She quickly established contacts with her old friend, the Duchess of Béthune who by now considered Jeanne Guyon to be a mystic of advanced standing. She also became part of the circle of the dukes of Beauvillier and of Chevreuse and their wives. The latter, daughters of Colbert, were among the most highly placed of the court *dévots*.

The root of Jeanne Guyon's first encounter with the church establishment in Paris had less to do with her mystical vocation than with the sizeable dowry her daughter would bring to a future marriage. François de Harlay de Champvallon, the archbishop of Paris, wanted to arrange a marriage between Jeanne-Marie Guyon and his grandnephew, who had a questionable reputation. Père la Mothe, the Barnabite, supported the idea. His sister refused. (In 1689, she would have her daughter marry the Duke of Vaux, the youngest brother of the Duchess of Béthune.) To bring pressure on Madame Guyon to consent to the marriage proposed by the archbishop, charges that Madame Guyon was a Quietist were spread informally. In October of 1687, the charges became very serious.

There was a growing climate in Paris against the passive form of mysticism practiced by the Quietists. The popularity of the *Spiritual Guide* by the Spaniard Molinos made him into its leading seventèenth-century proponent. This Spanish mystic had gone to Rome in 1664, where he belonged to a Quietist group. He was arrested in July of 1686, just before Madame Guyon's arrival in Paris. In 1687, Molinos accepted his guilt, retracted his teaching, and was condemned to life in prison, where he died in 1696. The reasons for his condemnation lay less with his *Guide* than with his teaching expanding upon it and his spiritual direction. Rome accused Molinos of teaching that the annihilation of the self involved the soul's faculties, that God's activity replaced the individual's volitional activity, leading to perfection and an incapacity to sin. The inert or passive soul did not have to engage in the active resistance to temptation. The Quietists in general cited mystics such as John of the Cross, Teresa of Avila, and de Sales, but their emphasis was on a state of continuous contemplation leading to perfection, disinterested love (including indifference to the state of one's soul after death), and a state of passive quietude as the will of the individual was absorbed into the divine will. Traditional practices of piety and charity risked being superseded by the state of contemplative prayer, and in this the Quietists ran afoul of Ignatian spirituality.[38]

Père La Combe had been in Rome, so he could be easily accused of links with Molinos. After a sermon La Combe preached in September of 1687, the archbishop obtained an arrest order (a "lettre de cachet") against him and he was arrested in October. Imprisoned in various places, without a normal trial, he was never freed. Jeanne Guyon remained in contact with him, but as La Combe became increasingly unbalanced, he was gradually consumed by a sense of guilt; that guilt, expressed in some of his letters, was later cited when attempts were made to undermine Madame Guyon's character.

An arrest order was also obtained against Madame Guyon, who became gravely ill. In January of 1688 she was placed in imposed seclusion in the Visitation convent in Paris, where she spent seven-and-a-half months while her treatise on prayer and unpublished writings were investigated. Her daughter was placed in a pension. (During this imprisonment,

Jeanne finished writing the first part of her autobiography, of which there are several drafts.) In July, she was brought before a group that included her brother and the tutor of her sons and was pressured to agree to the marriage. Once again she refused.

The details of her release from the Visitandines are interesting, for they reveal the degree to which Jeanne Guyon was a part of the aristocratic lay world of the "devout." According to her autobiography, she was befriended by Madame de Miramion, who had heard of her situation and came to visit the convent to find out the truth because of the negative rumors circulating. Hearing nothing but positive reports from the superior and others at the convent, Madame de Miramion resolved to help Madame Guyon out of "pure charity." Now, Madame de Miramion was a well-known lay *devote*. After the death of her husband in 1645, she had sponsored an orphanage for girls, a shelter workshop, a refuge for delinquent girls, and a retreat house, among other projects. Wanting to be part of a lay order, she became the founding patron of the Daughters of Saint Geneviève in 1670. This was a unique parish-based secular order that ran workshops, schools, and the mothering functions of parish life. Madame de Miramion would die in 1696, during the latter stages of the Quietist controversy, but the lay order endured as a secular entity until it was dispersed during the Revolution.[39] The fact that she took an interest in Madame Guyon's plight was typical of the calling she followed. She and others interceded on her behalf with Madame de Maintenon, who disliked Archbishop Harlay. No error had been found in Madame Guyon's writings; she was freed in September of 1688, but the archbishop forced her to sign a document disavowing any errors in her works. Madame Guyon was taken in by Madame de Miramion.

Madame Guyon and Fénelon

Living quietly, Madame Guyon returned to her circle of aristocratic sympathizers. In October, at a château belonging to the Duchess of Béthune, she met Fénelon, a close friend of the dukes of Chevreuse and Beauvillier. Madame Guyon sensed immediately that she might have a rich spiritual friendship with Fénelon, but he was a person of extreme reserve and little feeling. Their personalities were opposites, and Fénelon would repeat subsequently that Madame Guyon the person was of little interest to him. The meeting, however, coincided with an increasing sense of spiritual dryness or emptiness on his part. Madame Guyon would become Fénelon's spiritual counselor; he would become her defender. Louis Cognet has aptly commented that "Fénelon sought in her the experience of God much more than an intellectual system: with respect to the latter, he himself constructed his own synthesis relatively independently [. . .]. But the horizons of the soul and heart that she opened to him completely renewed his inner world and caused him to discover the mystic domain."[40]

A rich exchange of letters between the two figures exists, particularly for the years 1688 to 1690. Madame Guyon's view of the interior life as a return to one's origins can be seen as giving her a maternal role with Fénelon by which she calls him back to the faith and dependence of a child. She also emphasizes the necessity of abandonment of the self. Hers is an anti-intellectual call in that the way to God and the way of union with God are not reached through meditation or reason but through non-discursive contemplation. The following passages from an undated letter to Fénelon reveal some of these themes.

> I have to warn you and I pray God with all my heart that his word of truth may have its effect on your soul. Its effect will be temporary and of a substance that will impress on you the necessity of abandonment [renunciation] and will cause you to walk without the consolation some-times of knowing where this spirit of truth resides. It is like a lamp that is lit in order to get you started on the way and then is removed at the same time.
>
> The truth for you will always be in my mouth and in my heart and at the tip of my pen. Seek as much as you want, you will find elsewhere enough truth from reason, but you will only find substantive truth [to be] that truth which is never in agreement with reason, [. . .] truth that finds an echo in the substance of your soul and is in accord with it. The more your reason fights truth the more it will [turn out to be] only that substantive truth that can agree with the substance of your soul and put there peace, pure love, and the supreme will of God.
>
> One can trick your reason, but not that intimate part of the soul where that substantial truth of God dwells. [. . .]
>
> I will say to you that the light without light will never be more for you than in abandonment and in loss. If you depart from this path, you will lose it. [. . .] The light of truth [. . .] and the precipices where it will lead you will often frighten your reason [. . .].[41]

This abandonment of reason and of reflective self-awareness accom-panies the theme that the interior way is open to those with the faith of a child. Madame Guyon and Fénelon exchanged many poems, often set to popular tunes. A single example written by her is a sufficient illustration of this emphasis within her counsel. The interior way is one of spontaneous naturalness, a way in which adult self-consciousness does not intervene.

Those in Whom Childhood Is Real
[Ceux en qui l'enfance est réelle]

You have a taste for childhood / And fear the reality.
This is to be a child in appearance / Without truth. /
Those in whom Childhood is real / Do not know how to see or savour
it. /
It is so natural to them / That they can not surmount it.
You cannot counterfeit / Or hide it: when God wants to/
He will reveal its mystery. / The person who hears him is happy.

The desire for littleness / Is contained in this state. /
It intimidates wisdom / And causes it to lose its brilliance.
O Wisdom that I revere, / You alone know its nothingness: /
The state of utter poverty / Is stripped less naked than that of a child.
It contains all weakness, / powerlessness, inability; /
But it is the very suppleness: / In which God does his will.

A few stanzas by Fénelon, who held the title of doctor, had precipi-
tated this call to childhood.

I have the taste for Childhood: / Weakness and obedience
Of me have made a little child, / Content with my toy rattle.
[. . .]
Doctors, let me live / Far from you, far from myself.
Leave me alone, for I want to follow / the blind law of Childhood. /
What good to my brain / Are Aristotle and Plato?
Must your serious reason / Argue like a beetle?
Once I thought myself / Wise like Cato
But under my small Master [Jesus] / I have instead of a doctor become
a simple boy.[42]

When Fénelon met Madame Guyon in the fall of 1688, he had
recently made the acquaintance of Madame de Maintenon via the dukes
of Chevreuse and Beauvillier. The entry of Louis XIV's wife into the little
group of aristocratic *dévots* signaled a turning point in the ecclesiastical
career of Fénelon.

François de Salignac de la Mothe-Fénelon was from an aristocratic
family in Périgord with little money. His uncle François was bishop of
Sarlat, and the family picked the nephew for an ecclesiastical career. After
tutoring and studies at a Jesuit college, he was sent to Paris for further education under the protection of another uncle, Antoine, the Marquis of
Fénelon, who was well known in devout circles and had counted Vincent

de Paul among his friends. A brilliant student, the younger Fénelon eventually was trained at the seminary of Saint-Sulpice, where his piety was highly intellectual and his venerated mentor was Louis Tronson.

After serving as a priest in the parish of Saint-Sulpice, in 1678 Fénelon became superior of the community of New Catholics in Paris. Although Harlay, the archbishop of Paris, named François to the position, his uncle Antoine would have been influential in the nomination. Fénelon's early experience thus paralleled Madame Guyon's original mission to Gex, for the Paris community had been founded for young female converts from Protestantism who needed protection. Fénelon was successful as the intellectual and spiritual director of this foundation. After the revocation of the Edict of Nantes, he was drawn further into the religious controversies of the time when Protestants were being forced to convert. Fénelon was in charge of missionaries sent on two occasions between 1685 and 1687 to Aunis and Saintonge in the west of France. Conversions occurred for pragmatic reasons, and often under duress. Fénelon was severe in his judgment of the Calvinists, but he condemned the use of force in these missions. The participation of both Madame Guyon and Fénelon in the effort to convert Protestants is particularly interesting in the light of their subsequent reputations for tolerance.

In addition to his acquaintance with the dukes of Chevreuse and Beauvillier, the two sons-in-law of Colbert, Fénelon's friendship with Bossuet was of fundamental importance in the events that were to envelop Jeanne Guyon. The older Bossuet was already a major intellectual and theological figure, noted particularly for his sermons. He had close ties to the court, having become tutor to Louis XIV's son in 1670, and had entered the French Academy in 1671. Bossuet became archbishop of Meaux in 1681. He supported the king's policies against the Huguenots and wrote a justification of absolute monarchy that was published after his death.

Fénelon became Bossuet's most brilliant protégé. He was invited to Bossuet's residences, helped in some of his duties, preached in his presence, and undertook writing assignments for him. During this period Fénelon's first published work, *Treatise on the Education of Girls* (*Traité de l'éducation des filles*, 1687), was completed for the Beauvillier family; it was to play a part in his later reputation as a gifted pedagogue.

As a member of the devout circle that included the Beauvilliers, the Chevreuses, Fénelon, Jeanne Guyon, and a few other high aristocrats, Madame de Maintenon immediately implicated this group in the intricate web of religion and court politics merely by her presence among friends. She was quite taken with both Fénelon and Madame Guyon, whose freedom she was responsible for. In 1686, just prior to her contacts with the two, Madame de Maintenon had founded a convent school for girls from poor aristocratic families at Saint-Cyr, not far from Paris. Early in 1689 she introduced Fénelon as a spiritual director at the school, and some of his spiritual writings date from that period, showing his particular emphasis on disinterested or pure love. Madame Guyon also visited the school for short stays of two or three days. Fénelon's fortunes at the court continued to rise, for in August of that same year, he was named tutor to the Duke of Bourgogne, the grandson of the king, and he would do a remarkable job in molding the unruly youth into a promising future king. Fénelon's *Dialogues of the Dead* (*Dialogues des morts*), another influential pedagogical work, resulted from his lessons with the young duke and included the use of fables and short narratives in order to teach moral lessons.

In that same August of 1689, Madame Guyon's young daughter was married to the Count of Vaux, and the mother lived with the young couple in the country for two years. Jeanne Guyon's circle of immediate influence was limited to a few aristocrats and the Saint-Cyr school. Her writings, particularly her *Short and Easy Method of Prayer*, were circulating among the young women at Saint-Cyr. This concerned Fénelon, who thought the readers were not mature enough for this spirituality. Madame Guyon's influence was particularly strong among the novices, partly because of one of her cousins who was a nun at the school. Toward the middle of 1691, Madame de Maintenon decided to take action when Guyonian spirituality began to take over the novices, some of whom were not following agreed-upon expectations of conduct. The ladies of Saint-Cyr were required to take solemn vows. Madame de la Maisonfort, the cousin of Madame Guyon, led the resistance to the suppression of the influence of the latter's teachings. The bishop of Chartres, who was responsible for the convent and school, was brought into the picture. In March of 1693, Madame de Maintenon asked Madame Guyon not to return to the school and began to distance Fénelon from the establishment. (The removal of Fénelon from the scene would be complete when he was named to the bishopric of Cambrai in 1695.) The bishop of Chartres made an official visit to the school in July of 1693, removing all the books and manuscripts of Madame Guyon from the premises.

These events became public knowledge, probably as a result of court intrigue, and Jeanne Guyon soon found her orthodoxy in question. She was in a potentially dangerous position, so her faithful aristocratic friends began to look around for ecclesiastical help. They sought someone who would examine her writings and declare them acceptable to the church. Unfortunately for the Guyonian group, they eventually turned to Bossuet, Fénelon's mentor, who was the leading ecclesiastical intellectual at the court and who was not a specialist in mystic spirituality. Madame Guyon handed over to Bossuet her published works and manuscripts, including her autobiography that she considered confidential; Bossuet would use the autobiography in his demeaning comments about her in his *Account of Quietism*. But late in the summer of 1693, his initial decision concerning the orthodoxy of the writings was positive.

In the meantime, Madame de Maintenon herself thought she would take advantage of Bossuet to stabilize her establishment at Saint-Cyr. She invited Bossuet there and asked him to examine Madame Guyon's writings, intimating that she expected a negative decision. The friends of Jeanne looked around for more help, including Louis Tronson, Fénelon's old teacher. Later in the fall, Bossuet began to stake out a negative position with regard to Madame Guyon's form of apophatic, passive mysticism. According to Jacques Le Brun, Bossuet could accept the possibility of mystical union, but he could not accept the possibility that communication with the divine could occur apart from discourse. Furthermore, Bossuet could give only "ontological" status to the possibility of mystic union, refusing to concede that such experience could be analyzed systematically. Bossuet, as quoted by Le Brun, said that God approaches us "without rules."[43]

Bossuet would go on to label Madame Guyon as an example of "new mysticism." On one level, his approach to her can be viewed as an example of the miscommunication that can occur between old and new ways of seeing the world, with Bossuet himself viewing the world in a "modern" way. His analytical style was at odds with Jeanne Guyon's description of an experience for which she and Fénelon would both seek supportive examples in the writings of the church fathers and preceding mystics. This bifurcation in ways of thinking is a key to understanding later responses to Madame Guyon and her writings, for hers was a theology of experience that could be incorporated easily into a variety of religious traditions, only to be dismissed by some systematic theologians.

After interviews with Madame Guyon, Bossuet issued a long letter in March of 1694, condemning both passive union and pure or disinterested love. Madame Guyon retreated to the countryside and cut off correspondence with her close supporters. Rumors circulated. To put an end to them, Madame Guyon wrote to Madame de Maintenon in June, asking for a public review of both her faith and her behavior. With the consent of the king, Madame de Maintenon agreed to such an examination. The examiners were to be Bossuet, Tronson, and Louis-Antoine de Noailles, a protégé of Madame de Maintenon and the future archbishop of Paris. Madame de Maintenon maneuvered adeptly to isolate Fénelon in this process, implicating him in the affair, turning over to the examiners her secret notebooks in which she had taken down Fénelon's spiritual precepts. The Issy inquiry or council took place from July 1694 to March 1695. The examiners looked at the writings of Madame Guyon in the context of all Quietist teaching. When thirty-four articles of faith, heavily influenced by Bossuet, were published, Madame Guyon would sign them, and Fénelon would also add his signature.

What did Madame Guyon say about her writings? In her autobiography she makes clear her intent as well as her complete fidelity to the church.

> I wrote simply my thoughts: I submit them with sincerity. It is said that they can have a good and a bad meaning. I know that I wrote them with the good sense in mind and that I am even ignorant of the bad. [. . .] If I am condemned, I cannot be taken from the bosom of the Church my Mother, because I condemn everything that she could condemn in my writings. I can in no way admit to having had thoughts I never had, nor to having committed crimes with which I am unacquainted; that would be to lie to the Holy Spirit. Just as I am ready to die for the faith and decision of the Church, I am ready to die to maintain that I have in no way thought what it is wished that I may have thought while writing and that I have in no way committed the crimes that have been imputed to me.[44]

In the space of two months during the summer of 1694, Madame Guyon had prepared a defense in manuscript form, *Justifications*, which she sent to the examiners in the fall. This text was organized by headings, followed by examples from her own writings, from those of authoritative figures in church history, from commentaries, and from the Bible. The first sections dealt with mystical theology, including pure love, prayer, abnegation, the different states of the mystical life, and the operations of God in the interior life; these were followed by a section on "the solidity of the experiences and devotion of Madame Guyon." The final part of the work was a list of forty-seven different terms, again followed by authoritative citations. In her preface Madame Guyon declared quite simply that the essential parts of Christian morality and of mystic theology were "to love God with all our heart, pray without ceasing, and carry our cross daily." "The Gospel presents Charity as the consummation of the Law and continuous Prayer and the abnegation of the self as the two ways to attain it."[45] The reading of the *Justifications* seems to have irritated Bossuet, making him more rigid and unable to enter into Madame Guyon's mindset. From the start she took the position that intellectual judgments were inappropriate for writings that proceeded from the heart.[46]

At the same time, Fénelon took up the defense of Madame Guyon, and of himself, sending to the Issy examiners several essays. He staked out a position that would be his own in this controversy, maintaining that disinterested or pure love was one and the same with the state of passivity and was identifiable with the teachings of François de Sales on holy indifference. (A point of contention was the notion that extreme passivity was characterized by a love for God so pure that one was indifferent to the state of one's soul after death.) Another essay by Fénelon analyzed the thought of Clement of Alexandria as a precedent. Bossuet disagreed, writing a piece, "Tradition of the New Mystics." The disagreement between Bossuet and his protégé would become sharper and sharper, particularly as Fénelon remained faithful in defending Madame Guyon.

While the discussions at Issy were going on, Harlay, the archbishop of Paris and Madame Guyon's old nemesis, entered the picture independently. In October of 1694 he issued a condemnation of her two published works, the method of prayer and the commentary on the Song of Songs (or Solomon). This was a very hard blow for Madame Guyon, but once again, in the face of adversity, she received the gift of a special mystical experience, an alliance with the archangel of pure love, Saint Michael. She created an order or brotherhood of pure love called "the children of the Infant Jesus," and the members were divided into little Christs and little Michaels, "Christofflets" and "Michelins," to whom she referred in her letters. It was not until December of 1694 that Madame Guyon was able to meet her examiners, and she favorably impressed Tronson.

Madame de Maintenon kept the pressure on Bossuet, however, and in January of 1695, Madame Guyon was forced to go to the convent of the Visitandines in Meaux where she was confined until July. She won over the superior, who lobbied for the improvement of the living conditions of Madame Guyon, but even the signing of the articles in March and their dissemination did not remove the pressure. Bossuet now tried to get Jeanne to sign a document admitting heresy regarding faith in the incarnate Christ. She refused but did agree to sign a general act of submission. Bossuet again pressured her, and Madame Guyon prepared a document with a notary protesting in advance any signature that might be extorted from her. Stormy conversations seemed to have occurred, and Bossuet decided he had reached an impasse.

In July, after serving communion to Madame Guyon, he again had her sign an act of submission but also gave to her a concise document attesting to her orthodoxy. Astute as she was, Madame Guyon quickly sent the documents off to Paris for safekeeping. Bossuet returned and could not get them back. On July 9, Madame Guyon left for Paris while

Bossuet led Madame de Maintenon to believe that Madame Guyon had left without permission. She refused to return to Meaux and basically lived in hiding in Paris or nearby for the next months. Bossuet's animosity toward Madame Guyon was an extension of his growing public quarrel with Fénelon.

In December of 1695, Madame Guyon was arrested, her papers and books were seized, and she was interned at Vincennes with two servants. During the next four months she was questioned numerous times by civil authorities whose goal seems to have been to compromise Fénelon. Noailles had become bishop of Paris by April. He intervened, asked Madame Guyon to sign an act of submission, and then transferred her to a convent at Vaugirard where her living conditions were easier and where she would stay until 1698. She carried on an active correspondence and followed the ongoing public debates between Fénelon and Bossuet.

By now Jeanne Guyon was of no importance in the doctrinal disputes and struggles between the two bishops, but Bossuet tried to gain ground on Fénelon by bringing Père La Combe into the picture. It was clear that the latter's mental state had been impaired as a result of his imprisonment. Papers in which La Combe seemed to incriminate himself were seized. He was transferred from a prison in Lourdes to the castle at Vincennes.

Madame Guyon was confronted in April of 1698 with a letter from La Combe in which he asked her to admit that there was error in her teachings and that sin had occurred between them. Madame Guyon said that this was either a forgery or that La Combe was mad and asked to see him. That did not happen. On June 4 of 1698, Jeanne Guyon was led off to the Bastille; she was permitted to have some furniture, and a maid chosen by the archbishop was assigned to her. Her personal servants were put in prison in Vincennes. Jeanne Guyon stayed in the Bastille until March 24, 1703. By then Bossuet had died. Her son intervened and obtained her release. She was carried out on a litter.

Such is the stuff of which legend is made. Jeanne Guyon did not permit any writing about her imprisonment to be published as part of her autobiography when her works were edited. But a recently published manuscript describing her experience includes a chilling description of the psychological duress she experienced. A nearby prisoner committed suicide and she wrote:

> Such things happen often in these places and I am not surprised. There are only the love of God, abandonment to his will, conformity to the suffering Jesus Christ, joined to innocence, that allow you to live in peace in such a place; otherwise the hard things that you experience without consolation throw you into despair. In this place they let you

know only what can distress you, not what can cause you pleasure. You see only terrible faces that treat you with the latest indignities. You are without defense when you are accused. Outside they circulate whatever they want to be heard. In other prisons, you have counsel if you are accused.

[. . .] But here you have no one. You have only a judge. [. . .] They try to persuade you that you are guilty; they make you believe there are many things against you. And poor individuals who do not know what confidence in God and abandonment to his will are, and who further-more feel guilty, despair.[47]

The Dénouement of the Quietist Drama and Early Intermediaries to Protestant Circles

Fénelon's Eclipse

While Jeanne Guyon was confined first at Vincennes and then in the Bastille, an increasingly public dispute between Bossuet and Fénelon played out to its bitter end. This polemic was in part a feud between an ecclesiastical father who felt betrayed by his ecclesiastical son. In part it was a debate between two approaches to an old mystical tradition. It was also a quarrel fueled by the political and personal agenda of members of the court.

During the Issy examination of Madame Guyon's writings, Fénelon was busy writing manuscripts that he sent to the three church representatives and that also circulated privately to his supporters. Simultaneously, Bossuet was working on an important manuscript, *Instruction on the States of Prayer* (*Instruction sur les états d'oraison*, to be published in 1697). In the summer of 1696, Fénelon had been given the opportunity to read the text on prayer because both Bossuet and Madame de Maintenon hoped he would approve it. Fénelon looked briefly at the manuscript, noting that Madame Guyon was criticized, and returned it via an intermediary without studying it in detail. That same summer, while in Cambrai, he himself worked on a manuscript, *Explanation of the Maxims of the Saints on the Interior Life* (*Explication des maximes des saints sur la vie intérieure*, also published in 1697). When Fénelon returned to Paris in November of 1696, he had completed the book, including illustrative citations. A degree of intrigue, of which Fénelon was not totally aware, surrounded the publication of his work when Bossuet discovered the existence of the manuscript and the permit to publish it. The *Explanation*, without its illustrations, was rushed into print and distributed to the court at the beginning of February; Bossuet was taken off guard. Sure of the support of Madame de Maintenon, he took a decisive step later that month and approached the king while he was at Marly, a royal residence near Paris. Bossuet asked forgiveness for having supported Fénelon for a bishopric when Bossuet already suspected he was a Quietist. The king was moved but did not immediately withdraw his support from Fénelon. Bossuet's own work was published in March.

Fénelon's *Maxims* had created something of a shock among intellectuals because of his support of a moderate form of mysticism. Bossuet's work gained popular acclaim because of his persuasive literary style and ample illustrations. He remained unsympathetic to the idea that the interior life is available to all, emphasizing that mystical grace is unpredictably available to an exceptional few. Without its illustrative texts, Fénelon's book seemed a dry series of definitions and expositions of arguments. Nevertheless, his work was important, for he articulated more fully the position he had already set out for the examiners at Issy.

Fénelon's preface states that his goal is to articulate a tradition that justified mysticism but to explain to "simple, uninstructed, and docile" mystics the tenets of that tradition so that they will not fall prey to illusion.

> All interior ways lead toward pure or disinterested love. This pure love is the highest degree of Christian perfection. It is the end of all the ways known by the saints. [. . .] Whoever goes beyond the limits [of this tradition] has already gone astray. If anyone doubts the truth of the perfection of this love, I offer to show him a universal and evident tradition, without interruption from the apostles to Saint François de Sales.

Fenelon continues that the "indifference" praised by de Sales was nothing more than that of pure love, "always without self-interested will, but always determined and desirous of all that God causes us to desire through his written law and the attraction of his grace." All the tests of the interior life purify love and "even the most passive form of contemplation is nothing but the peaceful and uniform exercise of pure love." Responding to church condemnation of Quietists like Molinos, Fénelon makes clear that very few people experience the habitual state of spiritual marriage or union and that this state is not continuous or uninterrupted.[1]

In the aftermath of the publicity surrounding the two books, Fénelon found himself gradually distanced from the king and cut off from ecclesiastical discussions in Paris about his *Maxims*. He obtained permission to send to the pope a Latin translation of the book for examination in

Rome. Fénelon was ordered to reside in Cambrai, effectively banished from the court, and on August 3, 1697, he left for his bishopric, never again to return to Versailles. (He would be discharged as royal tutor at the beginning of 1699, and members of his family and entourage would gradually be disgraced by the king.)

Once in Cambrai, Fénelon published his *Pastoral Instruction* (*Instruction pastorale*), in which he refined his position, using illustrative material, drawn in part from two other figures from the late seventeenth century whose works had been approved by Bossuet and Noailles, the archbishop of Paris. These figures were Jean-Joseph Surin (1600–1665) and Nicolas Herman, better known as Laurent de la Résurrection, or Brother Lawrence (ca. 1605–1691).[2] The pastoral letter was quite admired among specialists; further documents and exchanges of letters occurred, and the tide of affairs turned in Fénelon's favor by 1698.

In May of 1698, Bossuet abandoned doctrinal issues in favor of a cruel and satiric account of Madame Guyon and her relationship with Fénelon. In the *Account of Quietism*, Fénelon was as ridiculed as was Madame Guyon, for he was called "the husband of this woman." In August, Fénelon wrote his *Response*. He defended the integrity of Madame Guyon and her description of the special graces she had received. Again, he cited a variety of sources, including Brother Lawrence and Surin. At the end of the book, he defended his own *Maxims*, saying that he had written them neither to weaken church doctrine by defending Quietism nor to excuse illusion. He left the future open to the judgment of the pope concerning the content of the book.

By the end of 1698, Madame Guyon fell gravely ill, so ill that people were speaking of her death by January. At the time, Fénelon said in a letter, "I must say, after her death, and during her life, that I learned from her only what strongly edified me."[3] Madame Guyon had not died, but the dénouement to the final act of the Quietist controversy was fast approaching for Fénelon.

In Rome, the church had been slowly organizing itself for the examination of Fénelon's *Maxims*. Although Fénelon was a moderate gallican, that is, supporter of the power of the French monarchy in church affairs, the tide of events was continuing to turn against him. Innocent XII was reluctant to act but was under pressure from Louis XIV. In May of 1698, a commission reported that thirty-eight propositions in the *Maxims* were questionable, but the commission was divided. Finally, in March of 1699 the pope issued a letter condemning twenty-three of the propositions without going into detail and with qualifications. In general, the "errors" involved the implications of Fénelon's theology of pure or disinterested love—that it is a continuous state, that the individual is indifferent to his salvation or damnation, that the active practice of the virtues disappears in this state, and that the highest form of contemplative mysticism centers on the divine, but not on Jesus Christ.[4] Fénelon was in no way declared outside the faith as Molinos had been, and the victory for Bossuet was not totally what he had wanted. In April, Fénelon submitted himself fully to the condemnation by the pope, who thanked him.

However, Fénelon's political situation within France continued to deteriorate. In April of 1699 *Telemachus* (*Télémaque*), his epic novel, was published in an unauthorized version. This long work had been written for the Duke of Bourgogne as a continuation of part of the *Odyssey*. It was a narrative about the education of a future ruler, and Fénelon was again using fiction for pedagogical ends. The fluid style of the book prefigured preromantic aesthetic values of the eighteenth century, although the pre-suppositions of the epic were classical. One incident in particular seemed to readers to be an indictment of the desperate circumstances in France in the waning years of the reign of Louis XIV. In their travels, Telemachus and Mentor, his teacher, visit Salentum, an island kingdom. Under Mentor's guidance, it becomes an ideal state. *Telemachus* would become the most reprinted French novel of the eighteenth century.

The Final Years and New Circles of Influence

In Cambrai, Fénelon gathered a small group of supporters, among them a number of priests who had been disgraced along with him, as well as nephews whose education he supervised. He devoted himself to the affairs of his bishopric and also gave much of his energy to the ongoing efforts to suppress Jansenism. Perhaps the cruelest blow of the exile in Cambrai was the untimely death in 1712 of the Duke of Bourgogne, the dauphin, who had remained loyal to his brilliant mentor with whom he had maintained a discreet contact.

Until the death of Bossuet in 1703, Madame Guyon languished in the Bastille, isolated from her family, her health in peril. Armand-Jacques Guyon, the older son, obtained permission to take his mother from the Bastille, but she was to remain under the supervision of the Bishop of Blois. On March 24 of 1703, Jeanne Guyon was freed and went to live with her son and daughter-in-law in the château of Diziers, near Blois. This was a kind of house arrest; her outside communication was strictly limited. Eventually, Madame Guyon, who did not get along with her daughter-in-law, was granted permission to buy a house in Blois in 1706, where she lived until her death.

This was not the end of the story, however. Fénelon's *Maxims* had been translated into English in 1698 and the *Telemachus* appeared almost simultaneously in London in 1699; three editions were quickly printed. Fénelon's early reputation was as a pedagogue and political martyr. His character was also greatly admired. In 1700, the writer of the preface to the second edition of *Telemachus* stated, "That Virtue, Wisdom, and Ardent Desire to procure the Good of Mankind, which are interwoven with the following Story, show the fitness of the Author for so great a Trust."[5] By 1707, a translation of his essay on the education of young girls contained the following comments about Fénelon's character and hospitality in Cambrai.

> He himself is a Person of noble Extraction, and of great Soul, answerable to the Greatness of his Birth; and as he is of easie Accession, so in his Conversation he is sweet, affable, genteel, frank and generous, without affected State and Stiffness, and perfectly free from Pedantry, and Disguise. I had this Character of him, from a *Protestant Gentleman*, who having Business in the *French Flanders*, out of Respect, more than Curiosity, went to wait upon him. The great Archbishop, though he knew his Character and Religion, tenderly embraced him, and treated him familiarly, as a Brother, and was so Unreserv'd and Open to him, as to tell him, he lived as a Prisoner in his own Palace, having none with whom he could freely communicate his thoughts, about genuine and solid Matters of Divinity.[6]

Within just a few years of the exile to Cambrai the legend of Fénelon's gentleness, tolerance, and saintly hospitality had already been formed and his standing among Protestants had been solidified.

This appeal to Protestants was also due to the practicalities of internal and external politics. For example, England and Spain were allied against France in the final wars of the reign of Louis XIV, and Fénelon gained a reputation for opening his palace to wounded and needy officers and soldiers of the opposing armies during the War of the Spanish Succession from 1701 to 1714. The Duke of Marlborough, commanding general of the British forces, was often in contact with Fénelon. When the congress met to prepare what would be the Treaty of Utrecht, British representatives stopped in Cambrai.

If Cambrai was a place often visited by Protestants and foreigners, so was Blois. In her final years, Madame Guyon's sense of vocation to Protestants finally came to fruition, but not in the form it had taken with the New Catholics in Gex. She became the center of a circle of followers, Catholics from France ("les Cis") and non-French, of whom the majority were Protestants ("les Trans"). For the faithful, Jeanne Guyon was their Mother ("notre Mère"). This maternal role was in keeping with that of members of the lay teaching orders of the seventeenth century who were instructed to act "as true mothers." But, to avoid controversy about issues of authority, a line was drawn between their maternal teaching role and the domain of the teaching of faith where they had no authority.[7] Nevertheless, Jeanne Guyon, while assiduously practicing her Catholic faith in Blois, assumed spiritual authority over her group of followers in a way not seen in the earlier lay orders.

Both Fénelon and Madame Guyon were in touch with a large circle of correspondents. Through his letters Fénelon cemented his reputation as a spiritual director and Madame Guyon served as a lay equivalent. Fénelon's *Letters and Spiritual Works* (*Lettres et opuscules spirituels*) were first published in collected form in 1718, and extracts soon began to be published in English as tracts. For example, "Pious Thoughts Concerning the Knowledge and Love of God" appeared in 1720. Readers quickly associated Fénelon with the doctrine of pure or disinterested love. His well-known pastoral letter that was more eloquent than the *Maxims* appeared in 1715 as *Fenelon's Pastoral Letter Concerning the Love of God*.

Fénelon and Madame Guyon themselves kept in contact through intermediaries such as Fénelon's nephew, the Marquis de Fénelon, but letters between the two were destroyed. The rapid translation of their works, along with their letters and personal networks, permitted Madame Guyon and Fénelon to exert a surprising international influence during the final years of their lives while they were in eclipse in France. For example, Guyonian Quietist circles were soon to be found in Scotland, Switzerland, Holland, and Germany.[8]

Pierre Poiret (1646–1719)

The printed dissemination of Madame Guyon's teachings began in 1704, when Pierre Poiret published an anthology called *Spiritual Works* (*Opuscules spirituels*), with a Cologne imprint, although Amsterdam was the actual place of publication.[9] Subsequent editions occurred in 1712 and 1720. In addition to the *Short and Easy Method* and *The Torrents*, the anthology included a letter by Jean Falconi, a Quietist predecessor of Molinos; a defense of the *Short and Easy Method*; other treatises by Madame Guyon— on purgatory, on the way to union of the soul with God; the *Rules of the Associates of the Childhood of Jesus* (*Règles des associés à l'enfance de Jésus*), the group she formed; *Christian Instruction for Young People*; two works by La Combe; and *The Rules of the Michelins*. The works were of uneven quality, but the availability of the most important texts permitted them to be read in French or in translation in Germany, Holland, Switzerland, and the British Isles, where they were quickly picked up by Guyonian circles of various sorts. The correspondence of Madame Guyon with key individuals from these countries, many of whom had visited her in Blois, assured that her teachings would endure.

Trained in Basel, Hanau, and Heidelberg, Pierre Poiret had been a French Huguenot pastor and a disciple of Descartes and Calvin. His early pastoral career had been spent serving Huguenot refugees in Germany. Two important sets of contacts had caused him to turn in dramatic new directions. In Frankfurt, he visited early schismatic Pietists led by Philipp Jakob Spener and through this group he also discovered the writings of Antoinette Bourignon (1616–1680), whom the French would call an "illuminist," and the English, an "enthusiast." Bourignon was an older contemporary of Jeanne Guyon, one of a number of singular women leaders in popular religious movements of the period. Bourignon was more radical than Jeanne Guyon, however, in her independence from the organized church and her reliance on her visions and revelations. She was an itinerant who gathered around her circles of followers whom she called to a radical, primitive form of the teachings of the Gospels.

Poiret set out to follow Antoinette Bourignon, separating from his wife (who went on to join French Camisard prophets in London) and associating with Bourignon during the last four years of her life, as one of her "spiritual sons." He edited and published Bourignon's writings in Amsterdam from 1678 to 1684. Won over to a religion of the heart, to calls for a return to a true expression of Christianity, and to a vision of the New Jerusalem, Poiret abandoned his earlier intellectual training, and turned to mysticism. W. R. Ward, always rather skeptical about Bourignon and Guyon, has commented about Poiret's Quietism: "The curiosity of this somewhat bleak doctrine in Poiret's case was that it was so often stated in defence [sic] of persecuted women as to achieve a somewhat liberationist effect. Since the veneration of saints had died out in Protestantism, male punditry had reigned unchecked in matters of doctrine; now, in an almost Arnoldian way, the pattern of 'true Christianity' was discovered in harassed females."[10] Nevertheless, Poiret produced influential works of his own. In line with contemporary interest in moral training and pedagogy, his *True Principles of the Christian Training of Children* (*Vrais Principes de l'éducation des enfants*, 1690) went through several editions in French and in English, Dutch, and German. John Wesley published a reworked version of this text. Poiret's most important theological treatise was *The Divine Economy* (*L'Economie divine*, 1687), a summa of his theology of salvation and of revelation.

It is unclear just when Poiret and Madame Guyon began to correspond. The two never met, although Poiret visited Fénelon in Cambrai. Madame

Guyon believed in the silent communication between souls advanced on the interior way. She had felt this union with her spiritual directors and with Fénelon, and she also felt intimately linked to Poiret. (Much could be said of the psychological implications of these spiritual attachments.) To Poiret she wrote on one occasion of "the intimate union" that she had with his soul. "I assure you that no one shares your pain more than I, but one must suffer in this life in order to be conformed to Jesus Christ." On another occasion, a letter to Poiret opens in this way: "I always receive great joy, my dear brother in Our Savior, when I see your letters: God has united your heart to mine in a very special way, it seems to me."[11] Poiret was also a valued supporter, of course, because his editorial work would ensure Jeanne Guyon's legacy. His edition of her works, totaling forty volumes, was printed between 1704 and 1722 and was of supreme importance in disseminating Jeanne Guyon's thinking. Her autobiography would not appear until 1720, but her mystical commentary on the Bible came out between 1713 and 1715, followed by one volume of poetry in 1717, with four additional volumes of poetry that appeared after Poiret's death.

To understand why American readers would later mention Madame Guyon in the same breath with Thomas à Kempis or Saint John of the Cross, it is important to note the wide-ranging editions in French of other devotional or mystical writers published by Poiret, for these would work their ways into translations and anthologies in English. One can mention the anonymous *Theologia Germanica*, *The Imitation of Christ*, a mystical anthology called *Theology of the Heart*, Catharine Adorna's (or Catharine of Genoa's) *Theology of Love*, Brother Lawrence's *The Practice of the Presence of God*, and works by La Combe and Malaval, among others. Poiret's publications complemented the references of Madame Guyon and of Fénelon themselves to a specific tradition of Catholic mystic literature.

If Poiret was the key intermediary in disseminating Guyonian ideas among German Pietists, he also was pivotal in bringing a group of Scottish mystics in contact with Madame Guyon.

The Scottish Mystics and Andrew Michael Ramsay (1686–1743)

Politics and religion had also combined after the rule of Cromwell to create a confused picture in Britain. Tolerance had been legally established by the Toleration Act of 1689. In Scotland, the situation was particularly complicated by the Stuart claim to the throne, as well as longstanding conflicts between Scottish Calvinism and Anglicanism. Early in the eighteenth century, a group of mystics had formed in Aberdeen whose central figure was an Anglican priest named George Garden (1647–1728). These mystics had been influenced by the teachings of Antoinette Bourignon and had formed a community at Rosehearty on the lands of Lord Forbes. The brothers of Forbes and Garden were also in the group. (George Garden published a defense of Antoinette Bourignon in 1699, and James Garden, a professor of theology at Aberdeen, was asked by Poiret in 1708 to edit a collection of mystical writers, *Bibliotheca Mysticorum*.) Members of the group were also Jacobites. George Garden came into contact with Pierre Poiret, who turned him from Bourignon to the spirituality of Madame Guyon, and the group followed. George Garden and other members of this Aberdeen group then formed part of the circle of visitors at Bois, along with others from the Continent. In London, Dr. James Keith served as the intermediary with the Continent for these Scottish mystics, and Pierre Poiret maintained an active correspondence with him.

Andrew Michael Ramsay had been destined by his family to be a Presbyterian clergyman and completed studies in philosophy and theology, with a master of arts in 1707.[12] He abandoned the idea of a vocation as a pastor, however, largely because of his rejection of tenets such as predestination, began a religious quest, and joined the Aberdeen circle of mystics in 1708. The following year he was in London studying mathematics and contacting Philadelphians, as well as exiled Camisards. The former were members of a short-lived sect formed among followers of the mystic Jakob Böhme (1575-1624). Its most famous member was Jane Leade, noted for her visions.[13] The Camisards were called the "French prophets" and were Protestants who had led a 1702 revolt in the southern Cevennes Mountains, which Louis XIV had crushed in 1705. These leaders believed they were inspired and predicted the overthrow of the pope and the establishment of a Protestant France. During this period, Ramsay supported himself by serving as a tutor, as he would later in France. In 1710, he was in Europe, spending several months with Pierre Poiret then proceeding to Cambrai in April of 1710. Fénelon accepted Ramsay into his inner circle. At the end of six months, the bishop succeeded in converting him to Catholicism, supposedly by demonstrating that one could not be a deist without becoming a Christian, and one could not be a Christian without becoming a Catholic. Ramsay's exact responsibilities at Cambrai are not known, but in 1714, he went to Blois where he joined the entourage of Jeanne Guyon, serving as her secretary for two years, handling in particular her correspondence with foreigners.

Ramsay left Madame Guyon before her death to tutor in Paris, where he had contacts with exiled Jacobites, becoming a tutor to the son of James III for a brief time in 1724. He was back in Paris from 1725 to 1728 under the protection of the Duke of Sully, the second husband of Jeanne Guyon's daughter, who had been widowed.

Ramsay had already written a discourse about *Telemachus* and had edited philosophical works by Fénelon. But he achieved a certain degree of renown with the publication in French and in English of the *Life of Fenelon* (*Vie de Fénelon*) in 1723 and a novel, *The Travels of Cyrus* (*Les Voyages de Cyrus*) in 1728. In 1729–1730, he was in England where he was elected to the Royal Society and given an honorary degree at Oxford. The rest of his career was spent in France. He became involved with freemasonry, developing a theory and history that placed its origins with the crusades. He continued to write and to tutor; after his death, the synthesis of his thinking appeared as *The Philosophical Principles of Natural and Revealed Religion*, which was only known among English-speaking readers. Ramsay's vision was of a historical process whereby the fall came slowly as pure love gave way to self-love and of a future in which the love of God would reign and the differences between various religions would be diminished and then erased.

Ramsay contributed less to the legend of Madame Guyon than to that of Fénelon, "canonizing" him, one might say. In his early prefaces and discussion of his master, Ramsay seized on the importance of the doctrine of pure love as central to Fénelon's writing and thought. But the Jeanne Guyon autobiography also contributed widely to the evolving image of the saintly, tolerant Fénelon.

The autobiography had just appeared in 1720. Members of the Aberdeen groups of mystics were loyalists to her, while Ramsay was profoundly attached to Fénelon. In writing his life of his master, Ramsay was responding to the autobiography, protecting and expanding the reputation of Fénelon, and systematizing the central tenets of the latter's thought. Ramsay praises Fénelon's educational methods with the Duke of Bourgogne, noting that study was organized "not by Rules, but according as Curiosity, which they took Pains to excite in him, led him to it." One can see why Fénelon, in addition to Locke, was an influence on Rousseau's educational theories. "They endeavored to inspire [the duke] with the Love of Virtue, not be dry Precepts, nor moral Sentences [. . .], but by a Word, a Look, some touching Reflection well tim'd, they gave him every Moment new Lessons, without his being disgusted with it, or even so much as perceiving it."[14]

According to Ramsay, Fénelon conducted himself with disinterestedness at the court until the Quietist controversy arose. Ramsay recounts the history, taking care to emphasize the "simple," "artless," "lively," and "feeling" style of Madame Guyon's writings about her aspiration for divine love.[15] Her spontaneous, natural outpourings are those of a woman whom Ramsay subtly casts into a secondary role.

When charming Nature speaks she is never anxious about the method-
ological Disposition of Words and Phrases; she paints the great Passions
by a beautiful Disorder, where all flows from the Heart without Study or
Contrivance. So likewise the noble and unconfin'd Soarings of divine
Love are not subjected to a theological Strictness in the use of Terms.[16]

Fénelon knew that Madame Guyon was innocent but that her expression
was "inexact," so he opposed Bossuet, choosing "rather to suffer the Exile
and Disgrace, which from that Moment he foresaw would befall him, than
to do an Action so unworthy of his Heart and of his Character."[17]

According to Ramsay, once Fénelon was settled in his bishopric, he
carried out his duties conscientiously. He preached sermons of "Evangelical simplicity" on the theme of love. He carried out acts of charity, opening
his palace to the poor. His attitude was one of inner peace and submission
to the divine will. Fénelon was Christ-like. "He endeavoured to imitate
our great Model, whose simple and affable Manner of conversing gave
Offence to the *Pharisees* of his Time."[18] During this period of scarcity and
suffering, Fénelon's tolerance and generosity set him apart, as his palace
was open to care for the sick, needy, and wounded. Ramsay also describes
his own interaction with Fénelon, whose arguments persuaded him to
convert to Catholicism. He emphasizes the unifying theme of Fénelon's
thought; the bishop was really interested in establishing an exact and correct interpretation of pure love. Only charity in its proper sense teaches
the poverty of spirit that quiets the imagination and reason.

Reception and Communities of Readers

Ramsay and Poiret were the most well-known early disseminators of the
legend and teachings of Madame Guyon and Fénelon; through these two
disciples the writings would be absorbed into German Pietism and the
Quaker movement, passing quickly to the colonies of North America. The
early readers of the writings of Guyon and Fenelon exhibited a tendency
that was to be repeated again and again; they internalized and assimilated
them into the specific cultural context of each new community of readers.[19]
A community in this context was a group governed by shared faith history,
shared narratives, and shared values that governed its interpretive practices.
The language of its faith experience and of its reading practices was characterized by certain dominant semantic fields. For example, "perfection,"
"abnegation," and "repose" generated a host of interlocking themes and
lexical choices. Communities could overlap. The Aberdeen mystics were
connected as a community to Rosehearty; Poiret had his own communal
setting at Rhynsburg in Holland. Blois and Cambrai served as settings for
the circles of Madame Guyon and Fénelon. Interactions occurred among

all four communities, with ensuing enrichment of each communal narrative. The interpretive principles at work in such groups resulted in a hermeneutics of similitude. Readers had a tendency to look for thematic or experiential markers like their own narratives, discarding or disregarding any dissonances. Thus, Ramsay, who had frequented all four communities, finally opted for a hermeneutic that gave dominance to the Catholic values of Cambrai and of Fénelon, while others seemed to absorb Madame Guyon, and to a lesser extent Fénelon, into a Protestant narrative.

The interpretive strategies of such communities were also governed by their reading and writing practices. Parallel and contiguous to the Quietist and Pietist circles on the Continent was Puritan spiritual practice in England and then in New England. Driven by the energy of their belief that all of life, after conversion, was a preparation for death by means of the practice of holiness, Puritans engaged in communal and personal disciplines that furthered that end. Understanding their personal experience was essential to their growth. For this reason, the narrative of the pilgrimage of which John Bunyan's *Pilgrim's Progress* was the seminal example was coupled with the examination of the self. Autobiographical narratives of conversion, biographies, journals, and testimonies were all part of the practices of the community. Richard Baxter recommended the reading of "the true History of exemplary Lives" as better than cards, games, romances, and chat because such reading in young people might "secretly work them to a liking of Godliness and value of good men."[20]

Were Madame Guyon and Fénelon Really Protestants in Disguise?

Madame Guyon and Fénelon declared themselves to be orthodox, loyal Catholics and submitted to the censure of the church. Although both in their later years showed marked tolerance toward Protestants, Madame Guyon was the more flexible of the two. She did not pressure her followers to convert because Catholics and Protestants participated in a shared faith around the person of Jesus and Scripture. As a bishop of the church, Fénelon was less tolerant than some of the legends surrounding him have implied. He was a severe opponent of Jansenism; he pressured Poiret to convert when he visited him; and, of course, he did succeed in converting Ramsay.

In the *Justifications* and *Maxims*, in particular, both figures situated their beliefs within a long tradition, starting with the Bible and the church fathers.[21] Madame Guyon saw in Scripture a confirmation of the interior way, with Paul as an important model. In *The Torrents* she cites Romans 8:26 ("Who will ever be able to separate me from the love [*charité*] of Jesus Christ?") in discussing the highest state of passive union with the divine.

Referring to St. Paul, she asks,

> O, great Saint! Where was your certainty? It was in the infallibility of God alone. Often the epistles of this apostle, this mystic Doctor, are read and not understood. Nevertheless, all the mystic life, its beginning, its progress, and its end are described by St. Paul, and even the divine life, but it is not understood, but a person to whom intelligence [special insight] is given sees it more clearly than the day. O, if those who have so much difficulty in yielding themselves to God could understand the ineffable happiness of a soul that has arrived [at this state], how many would yield themselves to God [. . .].[22]

Madame Guyon and Fénelon sought precedents in the church for their key themes. For example, Dionysius the Areopagite (Pseudo-Dyonysius) was seen to support the abandonment of the active will, the union of the soul with the divine through love, and habitual indifference. Cassian, Gregory of Nazanzus, and Augustine were proponents of passive prayer. Fénelon's study of Clement of Alexandria depicted his mystic knowledge as superior to that of the Greeks; for Clement, perpetual advanced contemplation was possible. The *Mystical Theology* and *Source of Light and of the Way of Life* by Denis the Carthusian from the fifteenth century were thought to uphold apophatic contemplation.

Northern mystics from France, the Rhine, and Holland contributed to the tradition of mystical perfection and habitual union with the divine. The figures who would influence Spain and then France included Jan Van Ruysbroeck (*The Little Book of Enlightenment* and *The Treatise of Perfection of the Sons of God*) and Johannes Tauler, who combined the themes of the contemplative and the active life. Luther had published the *Theologia Germanica*, an anonymous medieval text from Frankfurt that stressed the unimportance of works in achieving perfection or union with God. The writings of the Flemish mystic Harphius were collected in a well-known *Theologia mystica*.

In Spain, the *Alumbrados*, Illuminists, adhered to a spirituality of abandonment and were attacked by the Inquisition in the sixteenth century. Charges of "illuminism" would often carry over into the debates in France in the seventeenth century. But the two figures, Teresa of Avila and John of the Cross, were particularly influential in France, and they knew northern mysticism by way of translations. For example, Teresa referred to "mystical theology" in chapter ten of her autobiography when she spoke of being suddenly seized with a strong presence of God when she in her mind went to the side of Jesus. "I could in no way doubt that he was in me and that I myself was completely swallowed up in Him. That is not a vision; it is what is called, I think, mystical theology."[23] John of the Cross retained from the northern mystics the idea that contemplation is not attained and is a gift from God, but he also emphasized asceticism and the imitation of Christ in his spirituality. Fénelon's accent on the abnegation of the self showed an indebtedness to St. John of the Cross, to whom Fénelon usually refers as the "bienheureux" or "blessed."

Various writers in France had taken up the themes of perfection, indifference, pure love, infused, apophatic contemplation, or passive union before Madame Guyon and Fénelon. We have seen some of them, such as François de Sales. Without delineating in detail this French tradition, we need only note one of Fénelon's responses to Bossuet. In the reply to the latter's detailed criticisms in the *Account of Quietism*, Fénelon said that he had intentionally cited both ancient and recent mystics to show that "the ancients had not exaggerated less than the mystics of these last centuries." The essence of the thought of these great proponents of infused contemplation shows them to be "enemies of illusion." Fénelon set out a list that suggests his sense of mystic continuity from Clement of Alexandria, through Harphius and Tauler, to Catherine of Genoa and Teresa of Avila, to John of the Cross, François de Sales, Madame Chantal, and Surin.[24]

In addition to their identification with this ongoing tradition of passive mysticism, Fénelon and Madame Guyon were utterly Catholic in their adherence to the practices and traditions of the church, for example, to the necessity of spiritual directorship, of confession, and of forms of asceticism. Madame Guyon, however, was a practitioner of extreme forms of mortification and asceticism at certain points, and the language of disgust for the self expressed in *The Torrents* is replete with so many images of stench and decay that an essential part of her quest for transcendence seems to have been to escape from the body.

> Take a sponge that is full of dirt; wash it as much as you want; you will clean it outside, but you will not make it clean at its very center unless you squeeze the sponge to expel all the filth. Then you will easily clean it. This is just what God does; he squeezes this soul in a painful and distressing way; then he causes the most hidden element to come out.[25]

Part of Fénelon's appeal to later readers was the practical, unsystematic approach to issues of humility and disinterestedness in his surviving letters of spiritual direction. However, Madame Guyon reused in varying triadic, metaphoric, and descriptive combinations the categories or degrees of Catholic mysticism—for example, the purgative, illuminative, and unitive mystic ways or the external, interior, and essential degrees of the souls embarked on the way toward perfection. (The latter are the degrees of conformity to the divine will described by Benoît of Canfield in his *Rule of Perfection.*)

In the *Short and Easy Method*, there are three degrees of interior prayer. Meditation or meditative reading can lead in the first degree to an "experimental taste" of the presence of God in silence and repose. The second degree is the prayer of simplicity in which more extended periods of rest in the presence of God are enjoyed. The third degree is contemplation leading to the consummation of the union of the soul with the divine, with the resulting perfection of intention. In *The Torrents* the souls embarked on the interior journey are first slow-flowing, trickling streams, then majestic, broad rivers, and then fast-flowing torrents bound for the ocean of the divine will in which they will be engulfed.

A final example suffices. In a letter to Fénelon, Madame Guyon describes three categories of faith. "Luminous faith" takes pleasure in the light that comes to it, but the soul is still rooted in the world of the senses. The second level of faith is a distinctly separate way. It is "tasty" (*savoureuse*). It is not entirely pure, but is confident and knows what the divine will is because it is illumined by the taste of the presence of God. The last state is that of "pure faith," which goes beyond the material and sense-bound toward an essential "nudity" or purity. And within pure faith itself there are "degrees" leading to complete abandonment.[26]

One can thus conclude that Madame Guyon and Fénelon did not see themselves as anything other than Catholics situated in a tradition of passive contemplation leading to the experience of disinterested love. What, then, caught the attention of early eighteenth-century Protestants?

The Way of Interiority

Madame Guyon, more so than Fénelon, lent herself to the currents of Counter Reformation spirituality—from the last stages of Catholic mysticism, to independent prophetic communities on the Continent, to German Pietism, to Puritan spirituality of the seventeenth and eighteenth centuries. One historian has called all these movements "the religion of the heart" and has included among them Eastern European Hasidic Judaism of the same period. The context for the rise of such movements was complex but included the wars of religion, such as the Thirty Years War, and new epistemologies that led to the questioning of old authority.[27] We will see the relevance of these epistemological shifts in the American reconstitution of Madame Guyon's personal experience of the interior way.

Madame Guyon herself recognized that there was a tie among the adherents to an intense form of inner piety; this is reflected in her commentary on Matthew 18:20 where Jesus says that if two or three are gathered in his name, he is among them. She says that Christians have been so little united because they have been external Christians without the spirit of the faith.

> But interior persons, wherever they may meet, find themselves united by such a strong and intimate liaison of the heart that they discover that unions of nature and of the closest relatives do not equal it. It is such a pure, simple, and clean union that nothing human is mixed with it. And individuals are united whether far or near.
>
> Now the "interiors" experience this union because they are animated by a single spirit, because they are in a sacred link in the heart and soul of the Church. The result is that, from their first meeting, they are taken with one another in a reciprocal cordiality and confidence as free and complete as if they had known each other for a hundred years. This is an agreeable surprise to them.[28]

Leszek Kolakowski has taken a hard-nosed approach to this type of stance. Contrary to her protestations, he maintains, Jeanne Guyon was as intent as Molinos in making contemplative piety one of the pillars of Christianity, "accomplishing *within the Church* a grand work of correction" (emphasis in original). She was "the type of the prophetess incontestably convinced of her divine mission through which a radical reform of all Christianity must be accomplished." Quietism, he concludes, in one fell swoop proposed to do away with the structure of the received spirituality of the means of grace, the practice of the virtues, and the disciplines of works. Rather, all was reduced to and enveloped in a single, undifferentiated act of faith that was not the result of any effort on the part of the individual. This act, without image, thought, or representation was identical with a sense of the presence of God in the believer's soul. "The structure of quietist religiosity is an absence of structure; in sum, all the formulas by which this devotion is expressed are explications of a single idea [. . .] without the least complexity." In this sense and against the backdrop of the religious conflicts of the times, Quietism was "*a return to the first attempt of the Reformation.*"[29]

This is a strong interpretation, but one that makes sense. Could a reader of the time have picked up this reforming drive in the writings of Jeanne Guyon? I think so, and one can see how this drive was indeed a threat to the political and religious establishment in France, as well as the basis of her appeal to other proponents of a religion of the heart. If we take as an example the *Short and Easy Method of Prayer*, the most well-known text of her life, we note a democratization of spirituality that constitutes a condemnation of the way church leaders have excluded the masses from the interior way. After all, "conversion is nothing but diverting the self away from the creature in order to return to God. Conversion is only half perfect, although it is good and valid for salvation, when it is from sin to grace. To be complete, it must be made from without to within."[30]

"All, yes, all," Madame Guyon cries, are called to the way of interior prayer. The simple are the most suited to this way, and if priests and curates would only try to conquer souls by means of the heart, they would have an infinite number of lasting conversions. She appeals to priests to get the illiterate started on the way by having them repeat aloud the "Our Father" in French, learning its meaning, combining it with acts of adoration, trust, silence, and repose.

Finally, she infuses her little treatise with citations in French from the Bible. In doing so, she effectively substitutes the authority of the biblical text for that of the church. In this sense, her *Short and Easy Method* is a subversive, or Protestant, book. Madame Guyon was not the first writer of a treatise on prayer directed toward the laity. But the intensity of her style and the rhetoric of the handbook can be seen as a provocation in their universal call to prayer, their bypassing of many Ignatian spiritual practices, and their establishment of a biblical basis for the authority of the pronouncements.

All are suited for prayer, and it is an appalling misfortune that almost everyone puts himself in a mindset not to be called to prayer. We are all called to prayer, as we are all called to salvation. Prayer is nothing other than the affection of the heart and love. To love God, to occupy oneself with him, is absolutely necessary. Saint Paul orders us to "*pray without ceasing*" (I Thessalonians 5:17). Our Lord says "*I say to you all: watch and pray*" (Mark 13:33-37). Therefore all are able to pray and all must do it. But I admit that all are not able to meditate and very few are suited to it. It is not this sort of prayer that God asks for or that is desired of you.[31]

Chapter 4

Madame Guyon and the Pietist Mind-Set
The Transmission of Quietism to
German-Speaking Pennsylvania

The rise of various expressions of a religion of the heart gave birth to a Protestant theology of experience that Georges Gusdorf has labeled "European Pietism." Across the Continent and in England, subjective religious experience counterbalanced the ever more powerful Enlightenment doctrines of reason, progress, and optimism that were accompanied by the critical study of the Bible and by skepticism regarding special revelation. In one sense, this pietism was an outgrowth of Catholic mystic literature and seventeenth-century psychology that emphasized the analysis of inner spiritual states and autobiographical narratives of the spiritual life.

Gusdorf notes that this highly personal and individualized religious experience was so important that it relegated to a secondary level the rites and teachings of the institutionalized church. "Released from formulas and institutions, subjectivity [was] opened to access to divinity in its total presence." The mystical tendency of much of this pietistic movement was marked by "a conversion of the soul to the space within; a solitary conscience, in its particular vocation, [was] exposed to the peril of God, pursuing in secret an odyssey that [had] to lead it to the happiness of the elect." Gusdorf illustrates these themes by citing J. S. Karl, a pastor in Halle in the 1740s. Karl speaks in a triumphant tone, announcing the arrival of the age of the Holy Spirit, which the prophets and apostles had predicted. "The light shines; the shadows are dissipating." But this new age is not one of external signs, for it is in the "deepest part of ourselves that we must look for the Kingdom of Jesus, in a life hidden in God in

Christ, in a full and complete negation, an abandonment and sacrifice of our being in God. God demands a free people who serve him out of voluntary obedience and submission."[1]

Most of the major themes of German Pietism are evident in this passage from Karl—the necessity of an inner experience of Christ, the eschatological expectation of a new kingdom, the call for reform to usher in a new age of vitality in the church, the abnegation of the self in total submission to God. The latter idea is, of course, related to the experiential theology of Quietism. Furthermore, German Pietism was shot through with mystical elements.[2] Johann Arndt, whose *True Christianity* became so widely popular, was the forerunner of German Pietism; his book was the standard work of Lutheran spirituality and drew heavily on the mystical tradition. Arndt had edited two fifteenth-century works, *German Theology* (*Theologia Deutsch*) and the *Imitation of Christ*. *True Christianity* synthesized elements of Catholic mysticism, particularly the christological mysticism of Bernard of Clairvaux, Meister Eckart, and Tauler. W. R. Ward has claimed that the first three books of *True Christianity* are variations of the mystical *via purgativa*, *via illuminativa*, and *via unitiva*.[3]

Philipp Jakob Spener (1635–1705), the pastor whom Pierre Poiret visited in Frankfurt, was key to the development of Pietism. His call for reform in the hope of ushering in the kingdom of God were best illustrated in his *Pia Desideria: or Heartfelt Desires for a God-Pleasing Improvement of the True Protestant Church* (1675). Spener placed great authority on Scripture and emphasized individual piety through individual regeneration and sanctification (or *renovation*). His teaching also emphasized the priesthood of believers and the small group (*collegium pietatis*) in the spirituality of the interior life. In part because of his relationship to the established Lutheran church, Spener was very cautious about mystics such as Jakob Böhme and Antoinette Bourignon, but he had many contacts with the leaders of other religious movements, not just Bourignon; these contacts illustrate how extensive the communication was among groups espousing new forms of spirituality. Quakers were making mission trips into Germany and William Penn met with Spener's group of Pietists in 1678.[4] Spener was aware of the Quietist debates surrounding Molinos as early as 1686, but, if anything, Molinos signified for him the hope of ecclesiastical change.

In Geneva, Spener had known Jean de Labadie (1610–1674), and in 1667 he had translated Labadie's treatise on contemplation and meditation, *La Pratique de l'Oraison et méditation chrétienne*.[5] Labadie is a figure worth noting in passing because he was a former Jesuit who studied theology at Bordeaux, where he had had contacts with J.-J. Surin, the mystic. Labadie sensed a mission to return to primitive Christianity and to gather together the redeemed. He first converted to the Huguenot church and served as a pastor and engaged in debates about church reform and the interpretation of Scripture; unsuccessful in his attempts at church reform, Labadie moved on to found communities in Amsterdam and then Denmark. Labadie taught that only the inspired soul could understand the Bible. Labadie's community in Amsterdam included Anna Maria Schurman, who would be connected with the Philadelphians, and he was also in contact with Bourignon. Labadists in Wiewand were visited at one point by William Penn and George Fox to discuss union. Labadists founded an ill-fated colony in Maryland and were also to be found in New Castle County, Pennsylvania, in the fall of 1684. Although Labadie was not really a Quietist, he illustrates how mysticism was to be found everywhere. His movement was short-lived, however, and ended legally in 1737.

Quietism and German Pietism

The hopes for renewal, the individualism of spiritual experience, and the mystic elements that influenced the roots of Pietism were expressed in an interest in Quietism, and this interest was thematized over time. August Hermann Francke (1663-1727) was a supporter of Spener who was appointed at the university at Halle in 1692 and made it a center of Pietism, emphasizing the new birth. An extensive printing program at Halle disseminated Bibles, prayer books, songbooks, and devotional materials to a broad reading public. Francke was interested in mysticism and borrowed its language. Most importantly for this narrative, he translated from an Italian version Molinos' *Spiritual Guide* and published a Latin version just at the height of the controversy in Rome. The guide would be widely read at Halle. Although Francke denied he was a follower of Molinos and was not a mystic, his language of tranquility (*Gelassenheit*) demonstrates how the vocabulary of inner spirituality was layered by an overlapping of devotional traditions.

Gottfried Arnold (1666-1714) would be the link between Halle and the radical Pietists of the next generation. After academic positions, he served as a Lutheran pastor. In addition to the new birth, Arnold emphasized the illumination and renovation of the soul as it moved toward perfection and union with the divine. His critique of the church's repression of dissent through declarations of heresy in his first important volume of history laid the groundwork for later separatist groups. Moreover, his interest in mysticism was evident in his book on mystical theology, *History and Description of Mystical Theology or the Secret Teaching of God as in the Old and New Mystics* (1703), which demonstrated the perceived continuity of tradition between Catholic and Protestant practitioners of the inner life as did Poiret's editions of the same period. Arnold also translated Molinos' *Guide* into German. The first edition in 1699 coincided as well with the appearance of an English translation in London; other editions of the German translation were printed in 1732 and 1743.[6]

Translations of the works of Madame Guyon began to appear in the 1720s in Leipzig. Samuel Benjamin Walter published the autobiography in 1727, followed by translations of her *Christian and Spiritual Letters* and *The Torrents* in 1728 and of the *Short and Easy Method of Prayer* in 1730. But Madame Guyon's influence on German Pietism is best measured by looking at her spiritual commentary on the Bible and its impact on the Berleburg Bible.

The Guyon Commentary on the Bible

The Guyon mystical commentary, *La Sainte Bible*, edited by Pierre Poiret, coincided in an unusual way with the Pietist mind-set. Her approach to Scripture was isolated from contemporary critical discussions of the nature of the biblical text, which Spinoza had set off. Jacques Le Brun has noted that "all of Madame Guyon's work [was] haunted by Scripture, by the Bible, by the act of writing which, divinely demonstrated in the Bible, [was] again accomplished on a daily basis in the act of the mystic and the writer."[7]

In her preface to the biblical commentary, she asks readers to set aside a critical mind-set and its accompanying prejudices and to approach the Bible with indifference and openness. She contrasts the literal meaning of the text, which she insists is the purview of scholars, and the mystical sense. Although she is aware of the tradition of patristic readings of Scripture on several levels and seems to have been influenced by Pseudo-Dyonisius, Madame Guyon's hermeneutic is distinctly her own.[8]

The "mystical" sense of Scripture is the "interior" meaning. Thus, all of the Bible is "an immense allegory" of the interior way.[9] In the move to the spiritual meaning of the text, Christology plays a key role, serving as a "pivot" in the shift away from the literal.[10] A kind of cosmology lies behind this hermeneutic as the individual is a microcosm of the larger universe. God is the source of every being who is characterized by an innate instinct to return to that source and to rediscover a lost unity.[11] The consequence of this approach to the Bible is a circular hermeneutic. "Interior experience guarantees the truth of Scripture in which the interpreter rediscovers it; Scripture guarantees the authenticity of an interior experience that corresponds to it; and the writing of the commentary constitutes for the interpreter [. . .] what in turn becomes an experience of the truth of Scripture."[12]

I would put it this way. Reading the Scripture for Jeanne Guyon became a way of affirming her own experience, and her experience was paradigmatic for all souls who engage in the interior way. Thus, her hermeneutic escapes or sidesteps the horizons or boundaries of understanding postulated by later theorists, such as Hans-Georg Gadamer, who have been concerned with establishing a basis for the meaning of a text and the significance of a text. Culture and time disappear in this form of spiritual reading based on a universally available experience.

These principles are evident in much of the Guyonian commentary on Apocalypse (Revelation), also linked thematically to the Song of Songs (Song of Solomon) and Gospel of John. Everything begins with the Word.

> All is given *by Jesus Christ*, and nothing can be given except by him. [. . .] It is in this new birth that you communicate life and immortality to all those who are happy enough to follow you. [. . .] The Word is *the beginning and the end.* [. . .] He is the principle of all things because everything has been made by him: He also wants to be the principle in us of all our works.[13]

Thus, in chapter 7, the "mark and seal" of the faithful is "the sign of all interior persons, marked by the character of the Spirit of God."[14] The multitudes clothed in white before the throne of the Lamb are "the annihilated souls" who are in a permanent and intimate union" with God. "This is why [the soul] is always *before the throne of God*; it is incessantly before him and with him; it itself is his throne."[15] The woman of chapter 12, verses 1 and 2, who is clothed with the sun, is pregnant and has the moon beneath her feet. She appears elsewhere in the dream Madame Guyon recounts in her autobiography to which I have already referred. Here, the woman is the truth that must be nourished on earth; she is the church, and she is also prayer. The dragon that threatens this woman in verses 3 and 4 is self-love. The war in heaven is between this self-love and pure love. In the end, the character and mark of the servants of God are "God alone in all things," only his glory, and only his interest. No thought of self, of self-interest, or of desire exists. In chapter 18, Babylon is the figure of self-will and of corrupted nature. Finally, the marriage supper of chapter 19 is "the mystical death by which souls are called to the nuptial bed."[16] The new heaven and earth of chapter 21 signify that the soul has passed through all the degrees or mystical states to a final consummation in which all is renewed. The vision of a new Jerusalem is TRUTH, by which and in which God will reign.[17]

The commentary on the Apocalypse concludes with a defense. There are terms and expressions in "mystical theology" that must not be viewed as rigorously as in "scholastic theology." This writer (Madame Guyon) has used no other book but the Bible and has written what came immediately into her mind through faith and in abandon.[18]

If the commentary on the Bible is a confirmation of the interior way, it is also an affirmation of Madame Guyon's own identity and calling. Nowhere is this more evident than in her prophetic, modern commentary on Matthew 20:5-7, when the news of the resurrection of Jesus is revealed to the two Maries, and they are empowered to tell the news. The commentary is also, perhaps, desperate as an act of self-integration by Jeanne Guyon.

> The mission is given to these women to exercise the office of apostles. And toward whom? Toward the apostles themselves. Why? The pillars of the Church will learn from women the resurrection of its Savior who is the fundamental truth of religion? O Lord, is it to keep the apostles humble or to reward with this sublime task the love that these women have for you that you honor them with such a celebrated embassy? At the least it is to reveal your sovereign authority and your absolute will that cannot be embarrassed or limited by any sex or condition in life.
>
> Who will not be surprised that God can use ordinary women to teach the greatest mysteries to learned men? But they must be annihilated in order to be fit for the great things to which God destines them.[19]

The Berleburg Bible

What did German Pietists find in this biblical commentary that resonated with their own theology? Many of the themes were also their own: the centrality of Jesus, of Scripture, of the interior life, of individual conversion, of disinterested love, and of the community of those who have experienced union with God. Madame Guyon's commentary on the Song of Songs was the first of her works to be translated into German. After Pierre Poiret published the entire commentary on the Bible, Casimir, Count of Berleburg, translated it into German, except for the previously published Song of Songs. Madame Guyon's text was then incorporated into the *Berleburg Bible* (*Der Berleburger Bibel*), a commentary published between 1726 and 1742 under the direction of Johann Friedrich Haug.[20] This influential German commentary was a repository of the themes of the Pietists; the commentaters viewed the literal text as an envelope containing the secret, the "spirit" and "life" of the Scripture.

The German commentary gave a literal and then mystical sense for the biblical text, and Madame Guyon's interpretation was incorporated into this second sense. Sometimes, her commentaries were adapted to fit the format of the German text. Sometimes she was used word for word, sometimes in excerpts. The Pietists relied primarily on her commentaries on the Pentateuch, Jeremiah, Ezekiel, Job, the Song of Songs, the Psalms, and Matthew. Nothing is used from the Apocalypse. This is understandable, given the emphasis on eschatology among the Pietists. In addition, references to Catholic dogma and practice were also suppressed in the Protestant commentary. In the end, Madame Guyon's ideas were absorbed and synthesized into dominant German Pietist themes.

Johann Kelpius (1673–1708) and the Arrival of Quietism in America

Among the German Pietist separatists, Johann Kelpius introduced Quietist thought directly into the New World. The son of a pastor, with excellent university training, he was interested in the teachings of Böhme and of the Philadelphians, as well as the Quietists. Kelpius had formed a "Chapter of Perfection" in Germany, and his party of future colonists had gone first to Holland and London before arriving in Philadelphia in June of 1694. The goal was to found a mystic community, and Kelpius thought the native Americans also shared mystic and occult dogmas. The sense of belonging to a country of the soul, to a timeless band, is evident in his journal from the trip to America that begins with a reference to Seneca. This mind-set was not unlike that of Madame Guyon and of many of the other "true believers" of the period.

> I cannot go beyond my country: it is the one of all; no one can be banished outside of this. My country is not forbidden to me, but only a locality. Into whatever land I come, I come into my own: none is exile, but only another country. My country is wherever it is well; for if one is wise he is a traveler; if foolish an exile. The great principle of virtue is [. . .] a mind gradually trained first to barter visible and transitory things, that it may afterward be able to give them up.[21]

Kelpius' vision was of a wilderness society of the elect who would recapture the qualities of the early church and usher in an ecumenical new age. He foresaw a society based on communal property that was quite distinct from the Quaker approach to property. His band of forty set up a hermitage that included a chapter house and surrounding huts on the Wissahickon, outside of Philadelphia, where they achieved a reputation for mystic spirituality. Kelpius himself was viewed as a kind of medieval monk.

Kelpius had a perceptive and acute intelligence and saw himself as participating in a broader movement than his own. In a letter of December 1699 to Steven Mumford, a leader of Brethren in Rhode Island, he implied that "this late Revolution in Europe (not to speak of that in other parts) which in the Roman Church goes under the Name of Quietism, in the Protestant Church under the Name of Pietism, Cheliasm, and Philadelphianism" shared the same miraculous power as that of the early church.[22]

Kelpius' abilities are evident in the tract or pamphlet on prayer that he wrote for German settlers in Pennsylvania. *Eine kurtze und begreiflige Anleitung aum stillen Gebet* was then translated into English as *A Short, Easy, and Comprehensive Method of Prayer* and was published anonymously in 1741, with further editions with Kelpius as the author in 1743 and 1761. The pamphlet may be related to a book on prayer by Francke, but many of its themes are those of Madame Guyon's *Short and Easy Method*. Kelpius' work is a remarkable synthesis of Quietist and Pietist practice and thought. Like the Quietists, he maintains that all are called to "inward prayer," a mystic practice bringing souls into conformity with the will of God.

> [. . .] And as all Christians [. . .] are called to this state of pure love and perfection, and will, by the Power of this Call, have the necessary Grace offered to them, to attain to such a State: so this inward Prayer suits all Persons, even the most simple and ignorant, who are also capable of performing this Order or Manner of Prayer.[23]

Inward prayer has been performed in all ages and is available to the "simple and unlearned." It is just as important as faith, hope, and love.

Kelpius, however, simplifies his introduction to prayer and avoids all mention of the mystic degrees or states that occur in Catholic treatises. Inward prayer can be active or passive. Active prayer can be articulated by words and thoughts, but the active prayer of the heart is much more efficacious.

> One may pray without forming or uttering any words, without consideration or speculation of the mind, without holding rational discourses, or making conclusions, yea, without knowing the least thing in a manner relative to the outward senses. And this prayer is the Prayer of the heart, the unutterable prayer, the most perfect of which is the Fruit of Love, and the less perfect a sensibility of our indigences.[24]

This prayer of the heart can be practiced at all times and in all places because it becomes "an everlasting Inclination of the Heart to God, which Inclination flows from Love."[25] The method of inward prayer involves the representation of the presence of God through faith and the resigned commitment of the soul to the will of God. In one sense, Kelpius also upholds Brother Lawrence's practice of the presence of God but suggests that even when the individual is in a state of continuous inward prayer, there are specific moments for the prayer of the affections ("Have mercy upon me, make me whole") and the prayer of presentation ("If thou wilt, thou canst make me whole"). The latter is really an act of complete submission to the will of God.

Kelpius emphasizes that inward prayer is possible only through the working of the Holy Spirit and he does not mention the annilation of the self so necessary to Quietist union with God. He does, however, indicate that inward prayer much be accompanied by the subduing or mortification of the "flesh" and of inclinations to be busy with the outward world. Since the spirit of prayer can be lost, it is important to set aside time for the prayer of silence. Kelpius' final admonition is, "Resign yourselves to the Lord, and make him your Refuge by Means of Prayer, and forget not to perform it."[26]

After Kelpius' death in 1708, the community did not last long. It was succeeded, however, by the Ephrata community. Kelpius himself did achieve some degree of influence, including a readership among Quakers, despite John Greenleaf Whittier's description of him as "maddest of good men."[27] As late as 1951, Pendle Hill, a Quaker study and retreat center, cooperated in the publication of the 1761 edition of Kelpius' method of prayer.

Johann Conrad Beissel (1698–1768)

In colonial Pennsylvania, Conrad Beissel would be a controversial figure.[28] Before his emigration, he experienced a conversion after he came into contact with Pietists in Heidelberg and eventually was expelled as a result of his beliefs. In Büdingen and Schwarzenau, where freedom of religion was permitted, he came into contact with many of the strands of current religions of the heart. He was influenced by Christian Hochmann von Hohenau of the Dunkers (Baptist Brethren); at Marienborn, he was involved in the community of Inspirationists, the same Camisard-derived prophets whom Ramsay, Fénelon's editor, met in London. Beissel also encountered Philadelphians, so he knew the doctrines of Jakob Böhme.

Charles de Marsay (1688–1755)

Beissel also came into contact with Charles de Marsay, whose spirituality was based on the teachings of Labadie, Bourignon, and Guyon.[29] Marsay is an interesting figure because he was a Huguenot whose family had gone into hiding and then exile after the Revocation of the Edict of Nantes. Marsay was in the service of the Elector of Hanover when he read the works of Antoinette Bourignon. He was won over by her ideas and left the military service, settling in Schwartzenau, where he lived as an ascetic hermit. His wife and two followers of Bourignon accompanied him. (Schwarzenau was close to Berleburg.) Marsay eventually supported himself by working as a watchmaker.

In 1715, while visiting Switzerland, he discovered the writings of Madame Guyon. Later, in his autobiography, he spoke of the effect on him of the poem describing the seventeenth emblem of her *L'Âme amante de son dieu.* (This is *The Soul in Love with Its God,* referred to in chapter 1.) "I felt a very strong emotion in my heart, and God caused me to see my interior state expressed in these rhymes. May God always lead me blindly through faith and abandonment."[30] In these comments, Marsay is referring explicitly to the emblem by Hermannus Hugo showing the female pilgrim soul in a garden labyrinth as she sees in the distance, on a distant peak, Love whom she seeks. Farther on in the labyrinth, she sees a blind man, led by a dog. A few stanzas in a prose translation indicate the themes of Madame Guyon's poem.

> Dear husband, with faith in your help, I walk without fear in this terrible labyrinth, so filled with twists and turns.
>
> I watch in the distance the most daring and perceptive fall into the precipice: without seeing I go on, and all my cleverness lies in abandoning myself to the care of my Lover.
>
> This blind man is a great example of abandonment and faith; when I contemplate him from afar, I feel delighted beyond myself. He follows his little dog and walks with assurance, without stumbling or making a false step. I am guided by your providence and can I not abandon myself? [. . .]
>
> This life is a labyrinth; if we want to walk with certainty, may our faith be blind and without pretense, our love, pure and without disguise.[31]

In his own writings, published at Berleburg in French and German, Marsay combined themes from Böhme, Bourignon, and Guyon but specifically gave counsel on how to engage in interior prayer and reach a mystic state of death to the self. His primary influence was as spiritual advisor to Count Johann Friedrich von Fleischbein (a grandnephew of Goethe) as part of a Guyonian community at the castle of Hainchen. (Fleischbein is a figure to whom I will return). Marsay himself was in touch with Pietists in Pennsylvania and even thought of emigrating at one point.

Beissel and the Ephrata Community in Pennsylvania
Quietist Themes and Mystic Syncretism

Beissel was expelled from the community of Inspirationists in Germany and emigrated to Pennsylvania in 1720 where he was apprenticed as a weaver in Germantown for a year to Peter Becker, a Brethren leader. In the fall of 1721, Beissel left for Mill Creek in Conestoga (Lebanon County), where he and three friends lived as hermits. He apparently had contacts with several religious groups during these early years and may have even visited the Labadist colony in Maryland. He came into contact with a group of Brethren visiting the backcountry, and he and his group were baptized by Peter Becker in 1724. Problems quickly emerged because Beissel and his group preached the keeping of some Jewish observances, such as the Sabbath. In 1728 a schism occurred between most of Beissel's group at Conestoga and the Brethren at Germantown. Even Alexander Mack, the founder of the Brethren in Friesland, who came to Pennsylvania in 1729, was unable to resolve the conflict. In 1732, Beissel founded the Ephrata Cloister, near Lancaster, and it quickly took on the characteristics of a monastic community. Ephrata evolved and changed over the next decades but remained a force until late in the century. Its last publication was in 1793, and its buildings were taken over in 1812.[32]

A detailed history of Ephrata is not pertinent here, but it is sufficient to note that the community was composed both of solitaries who lived at the Cloister and also of householders. The men and women at Ephrata itself wore habits and observed a rigorous life, including a midnight service, of watch for the second coming. The community was known for its extraordinary singing. Christopher Sauer himself printed the first hymnal in 1735, despite the fact that his wife had defected from the Germantown Brethren and had joined Beissel's group. Sabbath worship, the Lord's Supper, the copying of manuscripts, and, finally, an influential printing press were part of the life at Ephrata. The spirituality or theology of Ephrata was syncretic. Beissel was not an original thinker, but the roots of German Pietism, including Quietist strains, were blended with major doses of the theosophy of Jakob Böhme. As time wore on, alchemy and Rosacrutianism also influenced the practices of the members of the Cloister.

Böhme has already appeared as an illuminating presence among the popular religious movements of the late seventeenth and early eighteenth centuries, which we have encountered.[33] Before his death in 1624, Böhme, the cobbler with mystic leanings and an erudition that also included naturalist philosophy, alchemy, and astrology, quickly achieved a following that included the nobility of Silesia. His works began to appear in French and in English by the 1640s, and Böhme's mysticism and rejection of classic Lutheran theology found a favorable response among religionists of the "heart." In 1613, he was forbidden to continue writing by the authorities of Goerlitz, his town. This was because his manuscript, *The Rising Dawn* (*Morgenröte im Aufgang*), begun in 1612, had gained Böhme notoriety and brought him into conflict with the established Lutheran church. He reassumed writing in 1618, and another influential book, *The Way to Christ*

(*Christosophia, oder der Weg zu Christo*), appeared in 1624; his complete works were published after his death. Part of Böhme's appeal was the fact that his works appeared in German, not in Latin.

Conrad Beissel's teachings early in his career were a blend of Pietist teachings, reflecting in part Böhme's influence on separatists in Germany. Central to this theology was the teaching that "our salvation is in the life of Jesus Christ within us."[34] F. Ernst Stoeffler has maintained that Böhme laid the foundation for subsequent criticism of both the established church and its theological formulations by this emphasis on the need for a living faith in a "living God."[35] Thus an existential union with Christ and a wisdom revealed by his Spirit would replace dry intellectual knowledge. Böhme's distinction between the Church of Abel (those experiencing the life of Christ) and the Church of Cain (the established historical church) led the way for the splintering caused by the Pietist movement in Germany and the rise of independent groups such as the Philadelphians and Beissel's monastic community.

There was a Quietist strain in the teachings of Beissel at Ephrata, but it illustrates the fact that as time wore on, Quietist themes were diffused and subsumed into a variety of theological contexts, often losing their original specificity. Thus, in Beissel's *Mystical Poems*, one can find a selection of aphorisms that sound as though they are Quietist, but they could derive from Böhme or from German Pietism itself.

> #3 Leave your thoughts which rejoice in vain pleasure,
> Or you will regret [your actions] in eternity.
>
> #8 Go into the ground of the soul, away from all the world's turmoil;
> There in yourself you will find the quiet heaven of God.
>
> #15 The quiet rest of peace which God's children have
> A man finds in the tents of Salem where soul and spirit refresh themselves.
>
> #24 He who possesses himself in God forgets time and place;
> Is free from sorrow and pain and can rest in any place.
>
> #35 If you wish to live in God you must first die;
> [Your] best appearance and light must first completely die in you.
>
> #36 Destroy self-love; you are a bitter death
> To the heart which has given itself completely to God.
>
> #56 How beautiful does it flourish here in the still soul
> Which out of a desire for heaven betroths itself to nothing here.

Elsewhere, for example in sermons, Beissel contrasts those who follow Christ out of self-interest or self-love and those who have followed God out of pure love. The first of Beissel's maxims, collected by Peter Miller, shows very well the incorporation of Quietist themes into a new meta-phoric context.

> Be still and retire within youself. In all things which you undertake to do, do not be moved by anything except that which brings you out of the quiet chamber of your own essentiality. For from the stillness of Zion proceeds the brightness of God; therefore always be still and attend to what the Lord speaks within you.[36]

Walter C. Klein has noted an "unmistakable strain of quietism" at Ephrata, attributing it to both the influence of Madame Guyon and to the theosophy of Böhme or his followers. Klein takes a somewhat negative view of Ephrata's lack of emphasis on the "active virtues." "Union with God is vouch-safed only to those who have annihilated all that characterizes them as human beings. The end to which the seeker directs his efforts is the extinction of his impure desires."[37] On the other hand, such themes went hand in hand at Ephrata with beliefs such as the revelation of the divine *Urgrund* as Sophia, in whom the true church finds wisdom. As with other movements such as the Philadelphians or Labadists, the followers of Beissel reached a dead end. The demise of Ephrata suggests the way in which many of the most radical expressions of a religion of the heart, into which Quietism found its way, were doomed to fail as times changed and leaders disappeared.

Reading Habits among German-Speaking Immigrants

The history of early printing in Philadelphia, Ephrata, and Lancaster County in general gives some clues as to the reading habits of the early German Pietists from the mid-eighteenth to the early nineteenth centuries. A Lutheran account on early Brethren taste in reading, published in 1813, is worth citing. "These people read all the writings of the mystics—Bernier, Madame Guyon, Tauler, John of the Cross, Bertot, Molinos, Arnold, etc. and even the writings of Jacob Böhme—mornings and evenings for their home worship! and this as regularly as their bibles."[38]

The taste for mystical devotional literature is also illustrated by exam-ples of what was printed.[39] These books are proof of the enduring influ-ence of Ephrata on the reading of mystical literature and, for about a century, of the ongoing reading in German of devotional literature and spiritual treatises of continental Pietism. The readers were not only the various descendants of the Brethren and Moravians, but also of the Ana-baptist Mennonites, who had made use of Pietist sources.

Jakob Böhme continued to be published in the nineteenth century. For example, *Christosophia, oder der Weg zu Christo* was printed by J. Ruth in

Ephrata as late as 1811-1812, but an interesting detail is that the edition includes an introduction of letters, including one by Gerhard Tersteegen, along with a testimony by Gottfried Arnold. An introduction to Böhme and his collected writings appeared in Ephrata in 1822, with a second edition in 1824.

Thomas à Kempis appeared in the translation, *Der Kleine Kempis, oder Kurze Sprüche und Gebätlein*, a collection of short writings and prayers. The Sauer press in Germantown produced four editions between 1750 and 1795.[40] And editions of various German Pietists—Francke, Mack, Bauman, among others—were printed in Lancaster county in the 1820s, along with song and hymn books, and even John Bunyan's *Pilgrim's Progress* (*Der Himlische Wandersmann, Oder Eine Beschriebung vom Menschen des in Himmel kommt*), Lancaster, 1828.

This taste for Pietist literature, for mystical and devotional texts, for poetry and hymns, was the specific context for what would seem to be the inexplicable printing of the emblem book, with poems by Madame Guyon, referred to in chapter 1. The German translation by Gerhard Tersteegen, printed in Lancaster in 1828, was, I discovered, just one of many of his works published in Pennsylvania and was one of many books about the inner life in Christ to appear in Philadelphia and nearby as long as German remained a powerful force among settlers in Pennsylvania. The first Christopher Sauer was an important intermediary in the contacts between Tersteegen and America.

Gerhard Tersteegen (1697-1769) and Madame Guyon

To my mind, Tersteegen's deep and earnest spirituality makes him one of the most appealing figures in the large cast of characters of this narrative.[41] He was born in Moers in the lower region of the Rhine, was baptized, and made his confession of faith in the reformed church. From 1713 to 1717, he served as an apprentice to his uncle in Mühlheim, where he came under Pietist influence and had a conversion experience. It was during this period that Tersteegen became acquainted with Quietist thought. He soon abandoned his own business to earn a living weaving ribbons until 1730, when, supported by friends, he devoted himself full time to his spiritual work. His craft allowed him the time and austere solitude to devote to serious reading and contemplation and to good works among the poor. (Tersteegen would always have a sense of responsibility toward others.)

The road to certainty was long and difficult, but, in 1724, on April 13, Maundy Thursday, Tersteegen had a second mystical experience, not unlike Jeanne Guyon's betrothal to Christ. He wrote a contract, often cited, that reflects the *Brautmystik* of the Cistercian tradition, Dominican mysticism emphasizing love and wisdom (via Suso) as well as devotion to the infant Jesus (as in Renty and Bernières-Louvigny.)

> To my Jesus! I pledge myself to You, my only Saviour and Groom, Christ Jesus, to be completely and eternally Your own. From this evening on I gladly deny all right and power over myself, which Satan may wrongfully have given to me.—From this evening on my heart and my entire love shall eternally and out of due gratitude be devoted to You and sacrificed. Not mine but Your will be done from now on and to all eternity! May Your Spirit seal what has been written in humility.[42]

After this experience, Tersteegen began to write both treatises and poetry, as well as to translate. It was first as a writer that he began to achieve a reputation. A religious awakening occurred in Mühlheim in 1725–1727, and its leader, Wilhelm Hoffman (who would be a mentor), asked Tersteegen to assist in the gatherings of these Pietists. (These gatherings or "conventicles" were forbidden in Mühlheim from 1740 to 1750.) In 1727, Tersteegen founded the Oterrbeck "Pilgerhütte," house of pilgrims, a unique Protestant community of brothers devoted to vows of obedience, celibacy, and poverty. He began to travel widely in Germany, and from 1732 on, he made almost yearly trips to Holland. In 1733, he began to have serious health problems, and these would continue until his death. This ill health was viewed by Tersteegen as a call to follow the crucified Christ even more closely. It also permitted him to become something of a healer, using herbal methods.

Tersteegen was in touch with Pietist groups and movements in both Europe and America through his extensive personal contacts and by his extensive correspondence. From 1750 to 1756, when the Seven Years' War began, he was the inspiration for a spiritual awakening throughout the Rhine region. Always living simply and always administering aid to the poor and ill, Tersteegen was visited continuously by spiritual pilgrims who sought not simply his wisdom but also the benefit of being in the presence of a genuine Christlike spirit.

In his belief in the necessity of a personal conversion and the centrality of Christ and in the Bible as the basis for his theology, Tersteegen was situated precisely in the German Pietist tradition. He drew on the Catholic tradition in his emphasis on the necessity of living a saintly life, on the importance of solitude and prayer, the cross as the sign of God's love, and a mystical union with Christ. Christ is a *Liebesmagnet* (a magnet of love) drawing the soul toward total union. In these ways, Tersteegen synthesized in a remarkable way the great Catholic traditions of the cross and of mystical love with a reformed, Pietist theology and evangelical experience.

Tersteegen's writings included numerous translations and adaptations—for example, of Labadie, Bernières, Kempis, Neandri, and Guyon. His hymns still figure within the life of the church. His spiritual poetry, *A Little Spiritual Flower Garden of the Inner Soul* (*Geistliches Blumen-Gärtlein Inniger Seelen*), was first published in 1729, reprinted later with an appendix, *The Lottery of Devotion* (*Der Frommen Lotterie*), and went through many editions. A compendium of theological works was published in 1750 as *The Way of Truth, in which is God's Blessedness* (*Weg der Wahrheit, die da ist nach der Gottseligkeit*).

The influence of Quietism, particularly that of Madame Guyon, on Tersteegen was profound. Through his mentor, Hoffman, he discovered this tradition, but he was oriented by his reading of Pierre Poiret. The cultivation of the inner life, the necessity of saintliness, the mystic marriage of the soul in union with Christ, and the resulting quietness or stillness are all variations on themes he found in Madame Guyon and others. Thus, Tersteegen, in addition to Poiret, became a contributor to the tradition of writing the biographies of saints, of holy lives, read by Protestants. He published *Selected Biographies of Saintly Souls* (*Auserlesene Lebensbeschreibungen Heiliger*), starting with volume one in 1733. Tersteegen differed from Catholics with whom he felt an affinity in that he emphasized the necessity of conversion as a prelude to the growth toward union in Christ and de-emphasized the acts of mortification of Catholic mysticism; at the same time, he followed them in underlining the importance of suffering as a sign of the love embodied in the cross. The phraseology of the annihilation of the self was displaced by a stress on the single-minded desire for nothing but the will of God. The life in Christ was to be a life lived out in service toward others. Although Tersteegen's interest in growth into a holy life had its roots in a reformed theology of sanctification, his own union with Christ was also experienced as a mystic union.

Tersteegen's tremendously popular poetry spread the themes of the stillness or quietness that results from living in God's will. Two examples will suffice.

God and His Will Bring Stillness

Whoever longs for nothing but God and his dearest will
In all circumstances can best be still;
Come what may, he has what he requires:
Whoever craves something more only multiplies his own pain.

Whoever Wills Only God Is Always Still

[. . .] I have and will only God; I live pleased and still:
Then mine and my Father's Will.[43]

Tersteegen and Madame Guyon's Emblem Books

Tersteegen knew Madame Guyon both in Poiret's French editions and in German translations. One of the most popular of these translations was her spiritual poetry that accompanied two famous sets of emblems from the Counter Reformation in Holland: Vaenius' *Emblems of Divine Love* (*Amoris Divini Emblemata*), published in 1615, and Hermann Hugo's *Godly Desires* (*Pia Desideria*), which appeared in 1624. Emblem books had traditionally conveyed narratives by means of pictures replete with symbols, often in a sequence. These images were often accompanied by mottos; poetry was often added as a gloss on the pictures. Vaenius was important because he transferred the secular love tradition of sixteenth-century emblems to a sacred context. Thus, the Cupid of the prior tradition became the child Jesus, pursuing the human soul, represented as a young girl, Anima. Hugo's emblems depict the soul in pursuit of sainthood.

Madame Guyon probably wrote her spiritual poetry to accompany these popular emblems while she was in Blois, after her release from prison. In 1717, Pierre Poiret published the two sets of poems, along with the emblems, as *L'Âme amante de son Dieu* (*The Soul in Love with Its God*). An anonymous German translation was published in 1719 as *Die Ihren Gott liebende Seele* that remained in print for some time and was popular among Pietists. It has been thought that Tersteegen, who wanted to translate Madame Guyon but was deterred by the fact that so much of her work had already appeared in German, retranslated the 1717 Poiret edition of *The Soul in Love with Its God*. This is a scholarly error of long standing.[44] A detailed comparison of the French and German texts reveals that Tersteegen had done something quite different.

He had discovered another set of emblems, with accompanying poems by Madame Guyon, *The Different Effects of Sacred and Profane Love* (*Les éfets diferens de l'Amour sacré et profane*), which Poiret had published in 1722 in the fourth volume of a collection of her poetry. Tersteegen set out to publish these emblems with his own translation of the poems.[45] In his preface, he indicates that the emblems were published in both Paris and Antwerp in the seventeenth century and that Madame Guyon had worked with a Paris edition. The emblems are a variation of the tradition of Vaenius and Hugo, for they depict Cupid as the representative of profane love and Jesus as the embodiment of divine love. The soul, or Anima, is a young woman. Latin mottos, usually quotations from the Vulgate, accompany the engravings, but Madame Guyon's poems are in French. The wonderful sequence of emblems depicts first the conflict of the soul torn between the two loves until profane love is conquered and divine love is triumphant. In emblem 18, the triumphant Jesus, accompanied by two angels, carries a banner and is followed by the young woman who bears a cross. Subsequent emblems depict the soul's life in Christ as it is purified, whether it is refined by fire so that it is as gold or it is nailed to the cross. Emblem 28, referring to Galatians 2 in which Paul says that he is crucified in Christ, depicts divine love nailing the soul to a cross. Eventually there is a union of love, and the soul is increasingly conformed to the image of Christ. (In emblem 37, the woman is seated at an easel painting an image of divine love.) Finally, there is a consummation of the two beings into one, as divine love and an angelic woman hold a circle in which the Greek iota is in the center.

Tersteegen's German text was published first in 1751 and then in 1787.[46] The title page makes clear that this is a translation of Madame Guyon's poetry, but that the poetry is "illustrated by further observations from her collected biblical writings." Opposite the title page is the engraving that preceded the Poiret four-volume edition of the *Spiritual Poetry*; this depicts a pastoral idyllic scene of the new kingdom in which all the animal kingdom dwells in peace, as prophesied in Isaiah 11:6. The Latin citation, "Puer parvulus minabit eos" ("a little child shall lead them"), is also accompanied by its German translation. In the foreground of the picture is Madame Guyon, with a small child in her arms, and another small child in the foreground is playing with snakes. Poiret added the name of Madame Guyon to the engraving, but Tersteegen has substituted in German, "About Godly and Genuine Love according to Madame Guyon."

Tersteegen has brilliantly translated the poems, but he has added selections from Madame Guyon's biblical commentary as a gloss to these poems; in the few instances where emblems have mottos but no scriptural citations, he has added biblical citations. In one instance where Ambrose is cited, Tersteegen has substituted a biblical verse. At the end of the book he has appended his own description of the "title picture": "the blessed strand of restored innocence, and its universal spreading over the whole earth, in the splendid kingdom of Jesus Christ on Earth," infusing a prophetic tone to the book quite appropriate to a Pietist. Tersteegen then adds a number of passages from Madame Guyon's scriptural commentary, concluding with her reference on Revelation 22:20, "O Jesus, you promised it: 'Yes, I am coming soon!' [. . .] So then, o my King, come and begin your kingdom and do not delay any longer."[47]

In his preface to the volume, Tersteegen notes that he hopes that he has brought out the true meaning of the author through the addition of the selections of her biblical commentaries. He also defends emblems and the godliness of Madame Guyon and her innocence in the Quietist affair. Her writings, according to Tersteegen, emphasize the way to God through the heart, faith, and love. Although a Roman Catholic, she lived with a "pious and God-surrendered" heart.

His choices of passages from the biblical commentaries on both the Old and New Testaments can be seen as an interpretive act, one that emphasizes the centrality of Jesus and of the cross to the vision of divine love in the original emblems. What he does with emblem 18, "The Triumph of Love," illustrates this interpretive act. Madame Guyon's verses read as follows:

> The triumph of Love is found in the cross, / In pain and thorns; / these are what Jesus chose; / these are the divine routes and paths. / Let us follow Jesus and walk in his steps; / let us not lose sight of our standard: / the cross with Jesus has charming appeal; / to carry it one must have a poor and naked soul. / Let us leave vain amusements: / Let us do more, Let us leave ourselves behind: / We will have contentment / In the most extreme pain. / Happy is the person in this lowly dwelling place who follows the banner of pure love![48]

This particular emblem is without a scriptural reference, so Tersteegen has added a reference to the triumph of the crucified Christ over principalities and powers in Colossians 2:15. Then, in the eight pages of selections from the biblical commentary that he has added from the Old and New Testaments, the theme is set forth in his heading: "How Christ triumphed over all enemies for us and in us, and how we shall follow our triumphant Lord on the way of the Cross." The overriding theme from Madame Guyon's commentary is "the more that we are subject to Jesus Christ and he reigns in us, so that we have no other will but his, the more he subdues our enemies. [. . .] He will triumph in you; and you will overcome in him."[49]

By means of such additions from the scriptural commentaries, Tersteegen has set up a hermeneutical framework for the Guyon poetry, one that assures that readers will interpret both the emblems and the poems in a Protestant framework. Madame Guyon has been transformed for non-Catholic readers. The theological framework for the emblems has become the biblical, Christ-centered, and cross-oriented grid of radical German Pietism.

Tersteegen in Pennsylvania

Numerous editions of Tersteegen's works were printed in German in Pennsylvania in the eighteenth and early nineteenth centuries. Notably, very early in Germantown, the first Christopher Sauer produced a number of these texts: *The Godly Lottery or Little Spiritual Treasure Chest* (*Der Frommen Lotterie*, *oder Geistliches Schatzkaestlein*) in 1741, the *Little Spiritual Flower Garden of the Inner Soul* (*Geistliches Blumen-Gärtlein*) in 1747, *Warning Writings Against Carelessness* (*Warnung-Schreiben wider die Leichtsinigkeit*), from the Dutch, in 1748, and *Der kleine Kempis*, mentioned above, which is probably Tersteegen's translation and edition, in 1750. The Sauer press produced additional reprints of most of the above, but other printers also produced editions of Tersteegen in the eighteenth century; there were at least thirteen editions, including a hymn book published at Ephrata in 1792.

It is known that Tersteegen was in correspondence with believers in Pennsylvania, and it is thought that the first Sauer was among these correspondents. Peter Erb has translated and reproduced a letter written by Tersteegen in 1753 from Mulheim, probably to Christopher Sauer the first, in which he thanks his correspondent for three English books that had been sent to him. These probably included an abridgment of Kempis' *The Imitation of Christ* (published by Sauer in 1749), Fénelon's *Dissertation on Pure Love* (1750), and perhaps *Religions of the Ancient Brahmans* (1752).

The letter is interesting because of its discussion of current spirituality, mysticism, and divisions among believers. Apparently the American writer had given an account of the sectarianism in early Pennsylvania, including an account of Ephrata (about which Sauer was particularly negative because of his wife's defection to Beissel's group). Tersteegen responds, "May God eventually bring all that is divided and dispersed together in Christ. This probably will not happen in the future otherwise than through the inward and real way, when one forgets the images and non-essentials in view of the reality, or, at least, when in the happy fusion of the hearts in the spirit (not in the intellects), one gladly yields and bears with another [. . .]."

Tersteegen then goes on to discuss the mystical tendencies of the time: "I myself believe that we do not need so many mystical books, many Germans have educated themselves too early in beautiful and high things without any reality." He says that false mysticism is the result of souls who have not experienced regeneration or have "only been crucified." "God Himself," he says, "must indeed lead one into the reality of the inward life." But Tersteegen continues that he values the judicious use of books about the inner life.

The letter concludes with more discussion of the church. "I too fear that those at Ephrata are too narrow-minded and biased in their forms." Tersteegen has met English-speaking Quakers in Amsterdam among whom he has found some "devout hearts." In Mulheim there is no new sectarianism or division. In a postscript, he adds further specific references to the situation in Germany and then writes this final sentence:

"The writings of the Bishop of Cambray are for the most part all printed in German." This may be a reponse to an inquiry from Sauer about publishing Fénelon in a German translation.[50]

This particular letter illustrates well the international nature of eighteenth-century religious movements emphasizing the inner life, as well as the increasingly cautious tone taken by many leaders regarding the dangers of popular mysticism apart from spiritual maturity. In Pennsylvania, however, interest both in Tersteegen and in mystical spirituality continued into the 1830s, partly as a result of the lingering shadow of Ephrata and the powerful influence of German Pietism among the various communities of Brethren and Anabaptists.

Approximately half a dozen editions of Tersteegen were printed between 1800 and 1820. As noted above, in Lancaster County, between 1820 and 1830, a variety of spiritual books in German appeared, including two editions of the *Little Spiritual Flower Garden of the Inner Soul* along with the *Godly Lottery* in 1822 and 1823. This was the spiritual climate, then, for the publication of the German translation of Madame Guyon that originally attracted my attention, despite the fact that bibliographies had made a misattribution of the original work in French. The reprint of Tersteegen's translation of *Sacred and Profane Love* as *Die heilige Liebe Gottes, und die unheilige Naturliebe* in Lancaster in 1828 was perfectly explicable given both his popularity and the ways in which Quietist thought had permeated German Pietism. Jacob Schweitzer, the publisher, and the printer, Johann Bär or Baer, were connected with several other spiritual publications for the Lancaster market. The emblems are the same in their edition as those in the eighteenth-century continental editions. One later reprint of these emblems appeared in York in 1834, but they are simpler and cruder, not from the original plates. It includes a preface by Tersteegen to the 1751 German edition, but the title is different this time: *Signposts to Eternal Life in Forty-two Contemplations and Edifying Verses* (*Wegweiser zum Ewigen Leben in Zweiundvierzig Betrachtungen und erbaulichen Versen*).[51]

American readership for German translations imbued with the direct or indirect influence of Quietism would die out as succeeding generations became more anglicized. Yet, the hymnody of the tradition, whether in translation or in German, continued to convey to American believers the experiential theology of Molinos and Jeanne Guyon, but the Quietist phraseology, filtered through Pietism, was by then also intertwined with other elements of theological tradition. The following hymn by Tersteegen, translated by John Wesley, demonstrates how a living faith was built from these complex historical strands. "Thou hidden Love" in translation suggests the language of Augustine; yet, the themes of love, submission to the divine will, and repose can all be seen as distant echoes of the Quietist experience.

> Thou hidden Love of God, whose height, / Whose depth, unfathomed, no man knows, / I see from far Thy beauteous light, / And inly sigh for Thy repose; / My heart is pained, nor can it be / At rest till it finds rest in Thee. // Thy secret voice invites me still / The sweetness of Thy yoke to prove. / And fain I would; but though my will / Seems fix'd, yet wide my passions rove; / Yet hindrances strew all the way, / I aim at Thee, yet from Thee stray. // 'Tis mercy all that Thou hast brought / My mind to seek her peace in Thee. / Yet while I seek, but find Thee not, / No peace my wand'ring soul shall see. / Oh, when shall all my wand'rings end, / And all my steps to thee-ward tend! // Is there a thing beneath the sun / That strives with Thee my heart to share? / Ah, tear it thence, and reign alone, / The Lord of evr'y motion there! / Then shall my heart from earth be free, / When it hath found repose in Thee. // Oh, hide this self from me, that I / No more, but Christ in me, may live. / My vile affections crucify, / Nor let one darling lust survive! / In all things nothing may I see, / Nothing desire or seek, but Thee! // O Love, Thy sovereign aid impart, / To save me from low-thoughted care; / Chase this self-will from all my heart, / From all its hidden mazes there; / Make me Thy duteous child, that I / Ceaseless may, "Abba, Father," cry. // Each moment draw from earth away / My heart, that lowly waits Thy call; / Speak to my inmost soul, and say, / "I am thy Love, thy God, thy All!" / To feel Thy power, to hear Thy voice, / To taste Thy love, be all my choice.[52]

Madame Guyon and the Reading Public in Germany
An Ironic Postscript

If Tersteegen's mysticism represented an enduring legacy of Guyonian influence, Karl Philipp Moritz's *Anton Reiser: A Psychological Novel* (1785–1790) served as an ironic postscript on the subject of Quietist circles of the eighteenth century. Moritz was editor of the *Magazine for Experiential Psychology* (*Magazin für Erfahrungsseelenkunde*) and brought to his autobiographical novel a secularized sensibility marked by the writings of Goethe and Rousseau. The novel/biography is narrated in the third person, but the narrator is Anton's mature alter ego who presents the first twenty years of the gifted, but immature, protagonist's life as he himself perceived events at a particular moment. Through the somewhat ironic but unmediated narration, a modern consciousness has subverted and undercut the earnest Pietism of the earlier part of the century.

Anton's distorted view of himself, his loneliness, his inability to relate socially, and his depressive tendencies result from his parents' disastrous marriage, his unhappy childhood, and his exposure to Quietism. His inner life has been nourished in large part by reading, and he eventually leads his life through the lives of the characters in the books he reads or, at a later point, those that he sees on the stage.

A Pietism nourished in the writings of Madame Guyon is at the root of much of Anton's excessive self-consciousness. Through ironic exaggeration, Mortiz makes her a negative force from the beginning of the novel. Anton's father is a follower of a brand of her Quietism as taught and practiced by Herr von Fleischbein, whose band of followers comes to his estate. (This is the historic figure who was a disciple of Charles de Marsay.)[53] Anton's mother is Lutheran, with a respect for both Scripture and reformed theology, so that the conflict between her and her husband over religion is a microcosm of the tension between the established church and separatist groups. "Although Madame Guyon's precept of the total mortification and destruction of all emotions, the gentle and tender ones included, agreed with the hard and insensitive soul of her husband, it was impossible for her ever to come to terms with these ideas, against which her heart rebelled."[54] Herr von Fleischbein, however, finds that her "dry, metaphysical fanaticism" ("die trockne, metaphysische Schwärmerei") suits his temperament, and he enthusiastically sets a reading program for his followers.

> Once a day all these people had to assemble in a great room in the house for a kind of worship service that Herr von Fleischbein himself had arranged and that consisted in their all sitting around a table for half an hour, with eyes closed, their heads on the table, to see whether they might perceive within themselves the voice of God or the "inner Word." Whoever did so made it known to the others.
>
> Herr von Fleischbein also determined the reading of his people, and whoever among the servants or maids had an idle quarter-hour was seen in no other way than sitting in a thoughtful pose with one of Madame Guyon's writings in hand concerning "inner prayer" or the like and reading.[55]

In the Reiser home, the works of Madame Guyon are read aloud (as well as Fénelon's *Telemachus*) and the poetry of Madame Guyon is sung. The young Anton tries earnestly to practice inner prayer. When his father takes him to visit the Fleischbein community (at Pyrmont, in the novel), the young Anton enjoys playing with a wheelbarrow in the orchard of the house where they are staying.

Because he began to regard this as a sin, to justify it he thought up a quite singular whim. He had read much in Guyon's writings and elsewhere about the Little Jesus, of whom it was said He was omnipresent and one could speak with Him everywhere. The "Little" caused him to imagine a boy somewhat smaller than himself, and since he was already on such familiar terms with God Himself, why not all the more with this His Son, whom he trusted not to refuse to play with Him and thus would also not be opposed if he wanted to cart Him about a bit in the wheelbarrow and to give Him pleasure.[56]

Throughout the novel, after Anton has moved on to other forms of enthusiasm, he turns to Madame Guyon's poetry, set to music, to express his melancholy. As Anton matures, he is able to discuss Madame Guyon's mysticism with his father by relating it to his own emerging understanding of metaphysics.

The one truly positive example of the great Pietist tradition in the novel is the aged, learned, and spiritual Herr Tischer whom Anton visits first with his father and later on his own. Eventually, though, in part two of the novel, Anton finds that he cannot recapture his early experiences of piety, and he finds himself accused of being on his way to perdition by another radical Pietist hatmaker for whom he is an apprentice.

Anton learns to live for his obsessive passions—reading, then preaching, and then the theater. He writes poetry, engages in solitary walks, and wanders, living often by chance. He has the opportunity to study at a university and experiences almost delicious moments of despair. His unhappy childhood and his early reading of Madame Guyon have given him no secure inner sense of the self. Devotional literature has led not to peace and union of the self with God, but to preromantic despair and isolation, along with an insatiable *Sehnsucht*. Without religious consolation, the path of subjective solitude is dangerous and ironic. At the end of part four of the novel, when Anton finds a theater troupe that he thinks he can join, he discovers that the manager has sold the costumes and abandoned the actors. The troupe is bankrupt.

Chapter 5

The Praxis of Piety
Quaker and Methodist Mediation of the Works of Fénelon and Madame Guyon

Fénelon and Literature of Instruction in America

Despite Fénelon's ecclesiastical and political eclipse at the end of the seventeeth century, his stature grew so quickly that it is difficult today to comprehend the extent of his popularity. The rapid translation of his works and the idealization of his life contributed to his reputation. Nevertheless, the reading public responded to another strain in his works. Aside from his polemical writings, almost all of Fénelon's work was to instruct, whether his initial reader was the Duke of Bourgogne, his royal pupil, or the recipients of his letters of spiritual guidance. The eighteenth-century reading public was large as a result of the expansion of literacy and the increased dissemination of printed materials. While the novel was emerging as a genre that would please, amuse, and beguile its readers, people still thought they should read to learn, to improve, and to absorb moral lessons. The relative popularity of Fénelon's Quietist works, that is, of his overtly spiritual writings, cannot be isolated from his other instructional works, most notably his *Telemachus* and his treatise on the education of girls.

A version of *Telemachus* had circulated in manuscript form before an unauthorized version was published in Paris in April of 1699. (The edition bearing the name of Fénelon as the author would be published in December in Holland.) As already noted, the novel, really a prose epic, was almost immediately translated into English. By the end of the eighteenth century, there were at least three hundred different editions of the novel in French, and late into the nineteenth century, an edited eighteenth-century English translation was still in print in the United States.[1] *Telemachus* was read in both French and English in colonial America where, although Voltaire was the most popular French author, Fénelon's epic was the most frequently read individual work in French. The 1732 inventory of the library of Richard Hickman of Williamsburg included an edition of *Telemachus* in French. It was cited in the 1744 edition of "A Catalogue of Some of the Most Valuable Authors . . . Proper to Be Read by the Students" at Columbia. One reader exclaimed, "I have entertained myself all day reading *Telemachus*. It is really delightful and very improving." By 1797, a book peddler in Dumfries, Virginia, wrote Matthew Carey, his Philadelphia publisher, "Telemaque Eng & French are *much, much* Wanted . . . it were well to put them for Dumfries as soon as possible."[2]

Interest in France and its culture ebbed and flowed with the political tides of the period, peaking during French support for the American Revolution and receding during the Terror and tensions over trade in the later 1790s. Yet, Philadelphia was a center for French emigrés, and it was there that French editions of *Telemachus* were first published in 1784 and 1791.[3] A new French edition appeared in Boston in 1797, but a more popular edition was bilingual in French and English and was also published in 1797. Numerous reprints in French appeared in Philadelphia between 1806 and 1834. In reality, *Telemachus* was an esteemed cultural commodity by the end of the eighteenth century. Whether Andrew Jackson read the work in French is uncertain, but a copy signed by him of the 1784 edition exists. In 1837, the walls of the grand entrance of Jackson's plantation home, The Hermitage, were papered with scenes from the book.[4]

What accounts for the immense popularity and prestige of Fénelon's book? Although Fénelon himself advocated a responsible and responsive monarchy, the implied criticism of the abuses of absolutism by Louis XIV allowed some readers to see it as revolutionary. A more likely explanation, however, is that the book met the changing tastes of the eighteenth century. On one hand, it was classical, following the epic models of Homer and Virgil. Telemachus and Mentor go through numerous adventures in the ancient Mediterranean world while they look for Ulysses, Telemachus' missing father. Mythological beings and classical allusions dominate the book. The style, however, is a fluid prose that reinforces Fénelon's values of simplicity, nature, and the countryside. Escaping the flattery, artificiality, and corruption of the city is one of the emphases. (One can see these themes pushed to an extreme later in Rousseau.) And, the book is about practical virtue. Readers responded to the pleasure of the adventures and the wisdom of the instruction.

In one sense, Fénelon set the stage for the new kind of reading that would emerge by the time of the publication of Rousseau's wildly popular novel about Julie and St. Preux, *La Nouvelle Héloïse* (1762). Of this novel, Robert Darnton has commented that it "would succeed in proportion to the reader's distance from Parisian high society." But part of the spell of Rousseau was the power of his personality because, although his novel purported to be an exchange of letters, particularly between Julie and St. Preux, "the actual communication took place between the reader and Rousseau himself." Rousseau was viewed by his readers as their "friend" and as a purveyor of truth. "What set Rousseauistic reading apart from its religious antecedents—whether they were Calvinist, Jansenist, or pietistic— was the summons to read the most suspect form of literature, the novel, as if it were the Bible."[5] Although this European paradigm for the reading of Rousseau does not fit American readers exactly, the response of English-speaking readers to Fénelon the author demonstrates the beginnings of this new mode of reading.

Fénelon himself would never have promoted a cult of personality nor a view of authorial authority that would rival a sacred text. In fact, he wrote that the "author must forget himself in his work and must permit me to forget him."[6] Yet, readers of the time did indeed accord a unique authority to him and to his *Telemachus*. A 1795 New York edition of the Hawkesworth translation was preceded by a life of the author in which the link between Fénelon and his work was underscored: "The conduct of the man will illustrate the sublime ethics of the poet, and afford the most impressive lessons of practical virtue."[7] In the epic, the young Telemachus is accompanied by his teacher, Mentor, who is really the goddess Minerva in disguise. Telemachus is on his way back to Ithaca in search of his father, Ulysses. Telemachus proves himself via his adventures and success in battle; when he has been sufficiently instructed by means of these experiences, he discovers his father, and Minerva reveals herself for the last time and then disappears.

This is a novel about paternity, authoritative truth, and instruction. Like Fénelon's actual relationship to the Duke of Bourgogne, the link between Mentor and Telemachus is also paternal. But the particular authority of Mentor is sacred in that he is a revelation of the goddess of wisdom, and the character of this revealed wisdom is androgynous because of the double personality of Mentor-Minerva. Through pagan antiquity, Fénelon is really establishing a Christian framework for the revelation of truth. Thus, eighteenth-century readers would have read *Telemachus* with an eye toward both the Bible and classical mythology, and they would have seen Mentor the fictional character as an authoritative persona of Fénelon himself.[8]

Although pedagogical works such as Fénelon's dialogues and fables were also reprinted and discussed in the eighteenth century, his first published work, the essay on the education of girls, was particularly influential. Published in Paris in 1687 and 1696, with new editions in Amsterdam in 1697, 1702, and 1708, the treatise was often linked to John Locke's essay, "On Education," of 1693. (Fénelon's treatise appeared in an English translation in London in 1699, with several ensuing printings.[9]) However, the essay also appealed to Protestants who were interested in doctrinal education and character formation. Thus, the text would have been read against the backdrop of works such as Poiret's *True Principles of the Christian Education of Children* (*Vrais Principes de l'Education chrétienne des enfants*), published in 1690. This work went through several editions in French and was translated into German, Dutch, and Latin and into English in 1695. (Later, John Wesley published an abridgment of Poiret's book in his *Christian Library*.) Fénelon's essay coincided, as well, with interest in improving the education of women, an interest that caused many people to write on the subject in the eighteenth century. One strand of the influence of Fénelon, and the ripple effect of this interest in the goals and means of education, was to connect him to Rousseau's *Emile*, published in 1762.

Several factors influenced the success of Fénelon's short treatise. He had written the work against this backdrop of an ongoing debate about the nature of education and the role of women. (Indeed, his work appeared at about the same time as Claude Fleury's *Traité du choix et de la méthode des études*, a treatise on the nature of method of study, which Fénelon cites.) However, as time went on, Fénelon's success in transforming the unruly grandson of Louis XIV into a future king became well known, even though his pupil never reached the throne, and the eighteenth-century reader could have confidence in the writer's educational principles. Further, Fénelon set forth his principles for the education of children in such a way that chapters three through eight of the total of thirteen applied to both girls and boys. Above all, Fénelon's goal was "a kind of practical education" that was solid but formed character.[10] Rousseau was particularly drawn to Fénelon's principles: that education should be adapted to the physical development of the child; that learning should take into account the natural temperament of the individual; that learning should occur in an indirect way, giving pleasure, rather than in an abstract manner by rote; and that education should form in the person a preference for the simple, the natural, and the moral, rather than for the artificial, worldly, and ephemeral.

Having supervised the education of young female "converts," Fénelon respected women, but he was no feminist. In his treatise he followed seventeenth-century social mores, assigning them to the domestic sphere or "economy," and he viewed them as weaker physically and inclined to vanity, fashion, excessively "tender" friendships, and imprudent speech. He was really taking on the world of the seventeenth-century salon, the society of the *précieuses*, the aristocratic women who spoke an affected, precious French, promoting learning and conversation that became exaggerated and pretentious over time. He was also taking on "worldly" society, with its superficial devotion to fashion, passion, and relationships outside of marriage. (The contrasting sets of values depicted by Fénelon were similar to those portrayed in Madame de Lafayette's historical novel, *La Princesse de Clèves*, 1678.)

Thus, in Fénelon's view, badly educated girls always have a "wandering imagination," nourished on novels and comedies about profane love, full of "invented adventures" and "generous passions" that have nothing to do with the "true motivations" needed to live in the world. These badly trained girls, who have wit and intelligence, "often develop into *précieuses* and read all the books that can feed their vanity." Because women are of primary importance in the domestic sphere, their education is crucial because their influence touches all of life, including the public domain.[11]

Fénelon's program of study for girls is practical; he is concerned that women be able to manage the affairs of a household, whatever their social class, so that they become not only individuals of mature Christian character but also individuals capable in the practical matters of the private sphere. They should learn to read and write their own language correctly, they should know arithmetic, and they should know the rules of justice (for example, what a contract is). Latin is also useful, but knowing Italian and Spanish could lead them astray into dangerous reading habits. Rather, they should learn from ancient history; with care, they can benefit from works of eloquence and poetry and from exposure to painting and music.[12]

Fénelon's comments on how one teaches reading to young children are particularly interesting because he says that "everything that pleases the imagination facilitates study." One begins with beautiful books with beautiful pictures and then moves on to stories, histories, and fables that the child can recount and in which roles can be played. (Fénelon's own fables and dialogues of the dead, written for his pupil the Duke of Bourgogne, illustrate these principles.) The tutor or governess can use these experiences to arouse curiosity about serious things. This same method can be used for the reading and recounting of biblical stories, and for the introduction of the first principles of religious teaching. The reading of the gospel and of the instructions of Paul is crucial to the understanding of the centrality of Christ and, in girls particularly, to the avoidance of superstition because girls are "naturally credulous."[13]

In the end, Fénelon's model of complete womanhood is the virtu-
ous woman of Proverbs 31, a passage that he quotes to conclude his little
treatise. Fénelon's blending of Christian character, basic education, and
practical domestic administration responded perfectly to the needs of
eighteenth- and nineteenth-century readers.

In America, Fénelon's treatise was particularly popular from the 1790s
through the 1830s, the period also of the peak readership of *Telemachus*.
Interest in education, particularly the formation of Christian character,
was certainly basic to Puritan and Pietist culture in the colonies.[14] Fénelon's
little book reached a broad audience. It appeared in three different printings in 1795 as *Some Advice to Governesses and Teachers. Written by the author
of The Evidence of the Existence of God. Supposed to be translated by Bishop Bar-
clay*.[15] A different translation, *Fenelon's Treatise on the Education of Daughters*,
appeared in Albany, New York in 1806 (printed by Backus & Whiting),
with reprints in Boston (1821 and 1831) and Baltimore (1852). Fénelon's
reputation as a pedagogue continued even as institutions for the education
of young women began to come into being in the United States.

Nevertheless, to American readers, the enduring appeal of both
Fénelon and Madame Guyon lay in their devotional writing and biographical or autobiographical narratives. For an understanding of how English-
speaking readers in the American colonies first became acquainted with
these elements of the stories of the two French Quietists, it is essential
to return to England and to additional contexts of their reception there.
Religious literature at the time was doctrinal or theological, polemical or
"controversial," and "practical"; works in the latter category were directed
toward how to practice the Christian life. Publication was directed toward
a wide audience, usually organized by categories (for example, women,
families, young Christians, and mature Christians). Distribution occurred
by a variety of means, including special organizations such as the Society
for Promoting Christian Knowledge and Wesley's Book Room.[16]

Tracts or pamphlets were one means by which English readers came to
know essential elements of the spirituality of both Fénelon and Madame
Guyon. The earliest edition of Fénelon's spiritual works appeared in
1704 under the title *Réflexions saintes pour tous les jours du mois* (Paris: J.-B.
Delespine), usually translated into English as simply *Pious Reflections*. The
collected spiritual works were published in two volumes in 1718; these
included a "Dissertation on Pure Love," which was written during the
period of Fénelon's dispute with Bossuet.[17] This theme of disinterested
or perfect love proved to be particularly popular among Quakers and
Methodists, although the translated and reprinted texts on pure love
usually included a more easily read letter on the topic to the Duke of

Bourgogne. In addition, Poiret's edition of Madame Guyon's works was being published even as Fénelon's spiritual works were appearing; a collection of her spiritual letters appeared in four volumes in 1717, also giving additional material for translation.[18] (The autobiography would appear in 1720.) John Heylin, curate of Saint Mary's The Strand in London, was closely connected with Aberdeen and continental mystics under the influence of French Quietism. In 1724, he brought out *Devotional Tracts Concerning the Presence of God and Other Religious Subjects*. This collection included Fénelon's letter to the Duke of Bourgogne "On the Love of God" and "Pious Reflections." Also represented were "Letters Concerning and from" Brother Lawrence, "Conversations with B. Lawrence," "A Letter from Mary Henrics [of Amsterdam] to one troubled in mind," and Madame Guyon's "A Mother's Advice to Her Daughter," a short essay of counsel to her daughter, which constituted an easily assimilable summary of Quietist principles.[19] Heylin's translations were but one example of the dissemination of material by and about Fénelon and Madame Guyon. As noted in chapter 3, Ramsay's little biography of Fénelon had just been published in 1723.

The Quakers

Josiah Martin, a Friend, began publishing translations in 1727 with *An Account of Madam Guyon* and continued with various works by Fénelon.[20] An anthology of some of this material by Martin was printed in London by Luke Hinde, and this was quickly reprinted in Philadelphia by Andrew Bradford in 1738 as *The Archbishop of Cambray's Dissertation on Pure Love, with an account of the life and writings of the lady, for whose sake the archbishop was banish'd from Court. And the grievous persecutions she suffer'd in France for her Religion*. (As already noted, Bradford's father, William, had accompanied William Penn to America.) Christopher Sauer reprinted this anthology in 1750.

Howard Mumsford Jones has cited the 1738 edition by Bradford as an example of popular "sub-literary religious literature" in eighteenth-century America that strengthened "the belief that the French papists [were] a wicked lot, and that France [was] to be distrusted."[21] Jones goes on to note that, under the influence of deism and John Locke, Americans gradually became more tolerant of continental Catholicism until the two decades of irreligious attitudes following the War of Independence. Nevertheless, the significance of this particular volume lies less in its antipapal leanings and more in the appeal of Madame Guyon and Fénelon to the dissenting groups of Protestant believers in early America.

George Fox's Quaker movement was born in the seventeenth century along with other religions of the heart, and I have already noted in passing that Quakers were in contact with Continental religious nonconformists. Persecuted because of their dissent during the religious controversies surrounding the overthrow of the monarchy and the rise of Puritanism, Quakers readily sympathized with many of the religious movements on the Continent and viewed the Conventicle Act of 1664, restricting worship, as a call to stand firm but also to disseminate their beliefs and values. When William Penn received the province of Pennsylvania from the Duke of York and landed in 1682, Quakers readily followed him.[22] The affinities between Quakers' beliefs and those of Continental movements lay in their emphasis on inner spirituality, the rejection of the established church, the centrality of Jesus and of the gospel, and pure love. However, the distinctive elements of their movement—the witness of the inner light of the spirit of Christ as a reliable source of truth, tolerance and equality, pacifism and nonviolence, and the Quaker meeting—were a unique blend of elements of all these religions of the heart. They did not, like the Pietists, emphasize "conversion," and women played an important role in the movement generally, whereas key prophetesses or spiritual mothers gathered followers around them in some of the other groups.

Quakers of remarkable spirituality also shared the mystical tendencies of the time. Francis Frost has noted that historians have considered eighteenth-century Quaker mysticism to be essentially Quietist in its reduction of worship to silent waiting for the inspiration of the Spirit in the depths of the heart and in its rejection of intellectual forms of spirituality. However, Frost suggests that Quaker spirituality was not strictly the Quietism of Molinos and Madame Guyon, with their emphasis on a psychological state of absolute abnegation of the self; rather, it was the poverty of spirit of the Beatitudes, evidenced in the practice of an often heroic love of one's neighbor.[23] Quietist, as opposed to rational or ethical, tendencies within Quakerism would turn out to be a source of contention into the early nineteenth century; in the early American colonies, Quietism was a major influence.[24] Quaker readers readily perceived in the life and writings of Fénelon and Madame Guyon elements of their own experience. The public also saw the connection between the Quakers and the Quietists. When the Quietist controversy in France was under discussion in England, the author of an anti-Fénelon tract, giving a translation of Bossuet's history of the controversy, entitled his version *Quakerism A-la-Mode*.[25]

The American reprints by Bradford (1738) and Sauer (1750) of the Fénelon essay on pure love, along with an account of the life of Madame Guyon and other extracts, were really an anthology reflective of Quaker beliefs. The "apologetic preface" is particularly fascinating because the rational-passive debates among the Quakers are evident. The editor defends the inclusion of an extract by Fénelon, "Meditation on the Inward Operation of God's Spirit," against objections from those viewing Scripture or reason as the only standard for truth. The light and voice of God within are reliable sources of truth as well. The editor also suggests a "plan of universal peace and love" that is synonymous with "a society founded upon the love of God & of neighbors." Fénelon has "inculcated" this plan into his *Telemachus*, designed for the instruction of the Duke of Bourgogne.[26] The translator then gives examples of both moral instruction from the prose epic and extracts from Fénelon's letters to the Duke, particularly on disinterested love.

The writer of the preface wished to establish the importance of Madame Guyon's spiritual vocation, showing that it was equally as valid as that of Fénelon. He was banished from court for having defended a woman who "was a great promoter of Piety and Virtue in France, and in her Writings taught and recommended above all Things the knowledge of divine and pure Love."[27] Citations from Madame Guyon's letters emphasize her wise counsel on matters of dress, piety, and the interior life, as opposed to the laxity of many of the spiritual directors of her time. For example,

> Give yourself therefore to God with your whole heart, never more to retake your self. Look upon your self as a person belonging to Him. Love Him above all Things. See that His Will govern all your Actions: Accustom your self to Retire within your self, where God is always present. Strive to preserve this divine Presence. Enter often within your self to speak to God and to hear Him. Set some Times as Mary did at the Feet of Jesus. God loves the Language of the heart abundantly more than that of the Mouth, or the Reasoning of the Mind. Continue in Faith, in Humility, in a Dependence on God, and above all in Charity, and you will run well. I am much concern'd for the good of your Soul.[28]

A striking defense of Madame Guyon's sense of apostolic vocation then ensues, with a series of examples from Scripture. Madame Guyon never usurped authority over a man, but the gospel is available to all women, as in the case of the Samaritan woman whom Jesus encountered at the well. Women can be apostles like Mary Magdalene, the first to announce the resurrection of Jesus. And women have the gift of prophecy. The exegesis of Scripture is drawn from sources such as John Locke, Matthew Henry, and Pasquier Quesnel. Henry (1661–1714) was a nonconformist Presbyterian, noted for his expository commentary on the Old and New Testaments. Quesnel (1634–1719) became the voice of exiled Jansenists in Amsterdam and was the author of *Réflexions*

morales sur le Nouveau Testament. Both interpreted the Bible in a devotional rather than a critical way. (One can compare Madame Guyon's
mystical interpretation of the Bible as another form of devotional commentary.) Quesnel's work was almost as important as Jansenius' study of
Augustine, and sections of it were condemned by the bull "Unigenitus."
Strikingly, then, a feminist argument is developed to justify the life and
teachings of Madame Guyon.

In the anthology itself, Fénelon's somewhat abstract treatise on the
nature of pure love is the first reprinted work. The essence of this love is
the ability of the individual to cease to look at himself as independent and
to view himself as part of the family of humankind, all children of a common Father "who would have us prefer the general Good of his Family to
our own particular Interest." Such love is made possible by the ceaseless
operation of God in the heart.²⁹

Then follows an account, with commentary, of the life of Madame
Guyon, illustrated also with excerpts from her autobiography, the *Short
and Easy Method*, her letters, and her poetry.³⁰ All of these works had been
published in Poiret's French edition not long before. It is important to
note this method of putting together an interpreted "life and works" for
Madame Guyon because Pierre Poiret had used this approach for his work
on Catherine of Genoa (Madame Adorna), and Thomas Upham would
adapt this style in his influential nineteenth-century study of Madame
Guyon. In Martin's narrative, she is presented as the Lady who cherished
the doctrine of pure love. "The *Reader* now sees the main Scope and Tendency of this Lady's Writings; the ardent Desire of her Soul, the Meditation of her Heart, and the *Burthen* of her *Song*. All her Writings, Verse and
Prose, tend only to the Establishing [of] PURE LOVE, and the *Reign* of
Christ in the Heart."³¹

In concluding, the editor draws on the commentary of Quesnel to
emphasize that the Samaritan woman was an apostle, drawing people to
Christ. Madame Guyon herself issued a "remarkable invitation" to Jesus
Christ to the schismatics (probably Catholics) of her time. To the "Samari-
tans" (probably the established church) of his own time the author says,
"Tis to you the interior Spirit addresses itself, that Spirit of Adoration
in Truth, that prayer worthy of God, that interior Worship, that PURE
LOVE, so much despised by our Nation and People."³² The anthology also
includes several letters and two poems ("hymns") by Madame Guyon, "The
Paths of Divine Love by which the Soul is led to the Divine Union," and
"Directions for a Holy Life by the Archbishop of Cambray." The presence
of samples of Madame Guyon's poetry is of interest, for it would play a role

in her popularity in the early nineteenth century, and the most famous of
these poems, her bird-in-a-cage singing with freedom, now in print, represents her role as one of the persecuted nonconformist dissenters.

> Great God for thy Pleasure / I am put into a Cage. /
> Listen to my Notes, For that's all I desire: /
> I love my Confinement / Great God for thy Pleasure. / [. . .]
> I live in Freedom / Though in Confinement: /
> PURE LOVE sets free / Both Heart and Will: /
> In my little Cage / I live in Freedom.[33]

John Woolman and Fénelon

The affinity that Quakers felt with Fénelon's teachings on disinterested
love and abnegation of the self, along with his reputation for tolerance,
was well represented by John Woolman (1720–1772), best known perhaps
for his opposition to slave-holding by Quakers and for his posthumous
journal. Woolman was, however, an adept of the interior way and well
read in the literature of devotion. In 1740 he wrote,

> I kept steady to meetings, spent first-days in the afternoon chiefly in
> reading the scriptures and other good Books, and was early convinced
> in my mind that true Religion consisted in an inward life, where in the
> Heart doth love and Reverence God the Creator, and learn to Exercise
> true Justice and Goodness [. . .]. That as the mind was moved by an
> inward Principle to Love God as an invisible, incomprehensible Being,
> by the same principle it was moved to love him in all his manifestation
> in the Visible world. [. . .]
>
> While I silently ponder on that change which was wrought in me,
> I find no language equal to it, nor any means to convey to another a
> clear idea of it. I looked upon the works of God in this Visible Cre-
> ation, and an awfullness covered me: my heart was tender and often
> contrite, and a universal Love to my fellow Creatures increased in me.
> This will be understood by such who have trodden in the same path.
>
> Some glance of Real beauty is perceivable in their faces, who dwell
> in true meekness. Some tincture of true Harmony in the sound of that
> voice to which Divine Love give utterance, & Some appearance of right
> order in their temper and Conduct, whose passions are fully regulated,
> yet all these do not fully show forth that inward life to such who have
> not felt it; but this white stone and new name is known rightly to such
> only who have it.[34]

Woolman read a range of works from Thomas à Kempis' *The Imitation of Christ*, John Foxe's *Acts and Monuments*, and William Cave's *Primitive Christianity* to the French Quietists and Jesuits' accounts of their travels in India and Africa. Affinities with Fénelon can be seen in the style of his essays, for example, in a comparison of Woolman's "Essay on Pure Wisdom" and Fénelon's "Dissertation on Pure Love."[35] Woolman also would have known the literature of French spirituality through his close association with Anthony Benezet (1713–1784), the Frenchman who converted to Quakerism and whose writings were important in the opposition to slavery.

In a very short time, Quakers in America associated Woolman and Fénelon in their minds. For example, by the early nineteenth century one can find a short extract of Woolman's journal to which is appended Fénelon's "On Faithfulness in Little Things," one of the most popular of his translated pieces of spiritual advice.

> He who learns, by Divine assistance, to make a right application in small matters of a spiritual nature, will not fail to accumulate much treasure as well as he who is attentive in temporal concerns. Great things are only great because many small materials are brought and combined together—he who is careful to lose nothing, will generally increase his wealth.
>
> True love is watchful and attentive without great and painful restraint of spirit. Augustine saith, '*quod minimum est, minimum est, sed in minima fidelem esse magnum est*. Little things are little things, but to be faithful in little things is something great.'"[36]

John Wesley and Quietism

John Wesley's Aldersgate experience, in which he felt his heart "strangely warmed," confirming his conversion, took place in 1738. The roots of his spiritual quest and his ensuing spirituality were complex, but they can be explained in part by his reading and by his exposure to both English and Continental spirituality, particularly German Pietism. Driven by his earnest good works and lack of inner assurance of his salvation, Wesley was drawn to books about the inner life, whether treatises, devotional works, or biographies giving experiential confirmation of Christian "perfection." A few examples will suffice. Among the books he took with him to Georgia (where he arrived in February of 1736) was Thomas à Kempis' the *Imitation of Christ*, which Wesley would later quote in Latin in his correspondence. (He had read Kempis, Jeremy Taylor, and William Law at Oxford.)[37] He also had with him William Law's *Christian Perfection*, August Hermann Francke's *Nicodemus*, and *The Life of Gregory Lopez* (1542–1596), who lived much of his life as a hermit in Mexico, devoted to doing the will of God. Records of this early reading show a preference for personal religious accounts from the early church. During the 1730s Wesley also read Pierre Poiret's theological treatise, *L'Économie divine*, and Saint-Jure's biography of Gaston Jean-Baptiste de Renty (1611–1649), which Poiret had re-edited as *Le Chrétien réel* (1701); this biography also existed in an English translation.[38] (The biography of Renty was highly influential among some German Pietists and would also draw the attention of adherents to the American holiness movement in the nineteenth century.[39]) Renty was an example of someone who practiced the presence of God and also believed that the laity could experience a life of deep spirituality without choosing a religious vocation. In addition, William Law brought to Wesley's attention the writings of Tauler and Molinos and the *Theologia Germanica* (*German Theology*). Thus in the years leading to his conversion, when Wesley was engaged in his personal quest, in addition to the English literature of spirituality, he was aware of Catholic and Pietist writings about religion of the heart, "primitive" Christianity, and the mystic roots of Quietist spirituality.[40]

If Wesley's disposition was inclined toward the search for an inner experience of faith, to be confirmed by a sense of assurance or peace, his encounters with continental Pietists also influenced him during the 1730s. The story has often been recounted of the calm exhibited by the Moravians in the face of a terrifying storm in January of 1736 during Wesley's voyage to Georgia. During his less-than-satisfying experience as a missionary, Wesley was indelibly marked by his encounters with the Moravian Herrnhut brethren under the leadership of August Gottlieb Spangenberg, who would later succeed Count Zinzendorf as the leader of the Moravians,[41] as well as with German Brethren. After his return to England, Wesley kept up his contacts with Moravians; Peter Böhler, who had remarkable ministries in Oxford and London, organizing "bands" of Moravians, played a key role in the events leading to Wesley's conversion. Wesley was particularly affected by the biographical testimonies of believers of their inner assurance of the experience of justification in Christ. After the Aldersgate event, Wesley went to the Continent in the summer of 1738, spending time at the Herrnhut and with other communities of believers.[42]

Wesley, nevertheless, was not uncritical in his reading about devotional practices and the mystical way of abnegation of the self and union with God and in his observations of Moravian belief and practice. In the mid 1730s he rejected the mystical way of union through contemplative prayer and solitude. When Peter Böhler was interacting with him in the period leading up to his conversion, Wesley even broke with his mentor William Law, accusing him of emphasizing works of devotion rather than conversion through faith in Christ and his mediating work.[43] Wesley also came to reject the "stillness" of Moravian groups in England as too passive because of his own emphasis on praxis, as well as faith.[44] At the same time, he was well aware of the vogue in England for Quietist authors and the dangers posed for his Methodist followers of the "enthusiasm" engendered by popular Quietism, particularly among Quakers. These factors account for much of his ambivalence (noted in chapters 1 and 2) about Madame Guyon and, to a milder degree, Fénelon. Thus, in his journal entry for June 5, 1742, Wesley noted that he had finished reading Madame Guyon's *Short method of Prayer* and *Les Torrents Spirituels*. Of the people at Epworth, whom he was visiting, Wesley exclaims,

> Ah, my brethren! I can answer your riddle, now I have ploughed with your heifer. The very words I have so often heard some of you use are not your own, no more than they are God's. They are only retailed from this poor Quietist, and that with the utmost faithfuless. Oh that ye knew how much God is wiser than man! Then would you drop Quietists and Mystics together, and at all hazards keep to the plain, practical, written Word of God.[45]

During the 1770s, Wesley's comments were more complicated. In his journal entry for August 27, 1770, he writes that he has read Lord Lyttelton's *Dialogues of the Dead* (which was a takeoff on Fénelon's book by the same name), calling the book "ingenious," and says he can "subscribe" to most of it. In Lyttelton's third dialogue, Plato says to Fénelon that he is surprised "that a man so superior to all other follies could give in to the reveries of Madam Guyon, a distracted enthusiast" and that it is strange that "the two great lights of France [. . .] engaged in a controversy whether a mad woman was a heretic or a saint." Wesley comments in his journal: "I believe Madam Guyon was in several mistakes, speculative and practical too. Yet I would no more dare to call her, than her friend Archbishop Fénelon 'a distracted enthusiast.' She was undoubtedly a woman of a very uncommon understanding, and of excellent piety. Nor was she any more 'a lunatic' than she was a heretic."[46]

The publication in 1772 of a new translation of Madame Guyon's autobiography apparently had a great influence on the Methodists at Bristol. Although this two-volume work was published anonymously, the translator was James Gough, a Quaker. Wesley commented that the people in Bristol were "hurt" by reading mystic writers who refine "plain Christianity" and "spoil it" even though these writers, particularly Madame Guyon, have an "abundance of excellent sayings." Four years later, after a second edition of the translation appeared in Dublin in 1775, Wesley would publish his abridged version of her autobiography, with the much more cautious preface that was noted in chapter 1.[47] In this way, he could try to control the response of Methodist readers to her life and teachings.

Wesley's reading did indeed have an impact on his doctrine of sanctification or Christian perfection, although his distinct stamp on the tradition of sanctification included his emphasis on grace and on growth that prepares the individual for the experience of sanctification. For Wesley, Christian perfection was a purity of intention, and perfect love was active love of one's neighbor, as opposed to passive indifference. Harold Lindström has described a certain continuity before and after 1738 (the year of the Aldersgate experience) in Wesley's view of Christian perfection, a view that had some indebtedness to "practical mysticism." Sanctification was first described as "an inward obedience of the heart and an outward obedience of word and act." It was also "inward and outward conformity with Christ" and then "love to God and our neighbour, the love of a whole and undivided heart." These emphases paralleled his reading of Kempis, William Law, and Jeremy Taylor.[48] Henry D. Rack has added that the notion that sanctification could be obtained instantaneously was Moravian. For Rack, however, Wesley had too much Enlightenment optimism to adopt the "morbid misery" of Kempis and Taylor. And even if Wesley could not accept Madame Guyon's emphasis on passivity, he could admire the practicality of her "short and easy method." The Wesleyan emphasis on grace saved Christian perfection from being the result of human effort.[49]

A Christian Library

Given Wesley's criticism of mysticism, why would he include anything by Madame Guyon or Fénelon or Molinos in his *Christian Library*, that fifty-volume collection of abstracts and abridgments, published between 1749 and 1755 and reprinted in America from 1819 to 1827?[50] Wesley continued to be attracted to Catholic biographies and writings that described the interior state of holiness or perfect love and that presented instructions on the disciplined life. In the preface to his library, Wesley made clear that his interest was "practical divinity" and that he was presenting a choice of scripturally sound extracts in plain language, edited as he deemed necessary.[51] His interests were pastoral, always applied, and geared toward the spiritual formation of Methodists that they might "go on" to Christian perfection or sanctification. Out of faith, sound doctrine, and the disciplines of growth would come Christians who would make an impact on society. Given the nature of Wesley's own spiritual journey, his various mentors, and his reading, he was ecumenical in taste in putting together his vast anthology, but he felt no qualms about excluding the mystical.

The scope of the volumes was astounding, but it was reflective of Wesley's theological and devotional principles drawn from the history of Christianity: the church fathers, Macarius, John Arndt; accounts of martyrs; biographies; Puritan devotional literature; Anglican authors; and mystics, including John of the Cross, Teresa of Avila, and Pascal, not to mention some Quietists. There were also significant omissions, such as Augustine, medieval material, and Bayly's *Practice of Piety*.[52]

Given Wesley's own bent toward systematic means to form and apply true Christianity, he turned to Heylin's *Devotional Tracts* for material by Fénelon and Madame Guyon. Wesley had bought copies in 1731–1732 and had distributed them and used them in his ministry.[53] The French Quietist material was readable, translated rather freely, and edited by the suppression of elements unsuitable to a Protestant readership. (For example, references to Catholic saints were eliminated.) These were essentially letters of spiritual advice and direction: "Letters to the Duke of Burgundy from M. de Fenelon, Archbishop of Cambray," "Pious Reflections: Translated from the French," and "A Mother's Advice to Her Daughter: Translated from the French." Wesley then added extracts from *The Spiritual Guide* by Molinos to follow the French Quietists.

The first letter by Fénelon is a masterfully constructed piece on "the Love of God." "I believe, my Lord, the true way of loving mankind is, to love them in God, and for his sake." Because people do not know what God's love is, they are bound by fear. Fénelon then notes what this love is not and what it does not entail.

> This love requires nothing of us, but to do for the sake of God, what reason itself should incline us to do. We are not desired to add to the number of the good works which we have already learned to practise. All that is incumbent upon is, to do the same things from a principle of love to God, that honest men of a regular life do from principles of honour, and regard to themself. Nothing is to be laid aside but what is wrong. [. . .] Let us do the same honourable and virtuous things as formerly; but let us do them for his sake who made us, and to whom we owe all.[54]

This love does not require the "austerities" of a religious vocation, nor does it add to one's burdens or crosses. It does not upset the natural order of society and the created world. What is this love, then? It is "to love God in" our friends; not to seek perfection in others because that is in God alone; to love God's "workmanship," all of his created world; and it is to love God above all else. Fénelon's sensibility comes through in his description of the nature of this godly love. "This love [. . .] is real, cordial, faithful, constant, and active; and I prefer it in my last and sincerest choices to every other love. It has also its tenderness and transports. [. . .] Nothing is so cold, dry, hard, and reserved as a heart that loves itself in all things. Nothing is so tender, open, lively, sweet, and loving, as a heart possessed and animated with divine love." Aside from the exclusion of a citation from St. Michael, the translation is true to the original.[55]

Wesley added a second letter to the duke that gives the appearance of being a reply to the initial letter. The translation is again accurate; biblical quotations, all in Latin in the original and without exact identification, have of course all been rendered in English.[56] This letter is systematic in its advice; therein lies its interest for Methodism. Fénelon exhorts his protégé to love God in all things, and learn "to seek him in your heart with the simplicity of a child," one of the themes of Madame Guyon's original advice to Fénelon himself. Then the letter goes on to encourage the duke to pray in a systematic fashion, including a little prayer in the morning. Echoing themes in Brother Lawrence, Fénelon urges the "recollection of the presence of God" as a "renewal of prayer" thoughout the day. Morning prayer "more with the heart than with understanding; more in the way of simple affection than reasoning" will nourish one throughout the day. Regular reading encourages "familiarity with God" and participation in the sacraments "when you have occasion and inclination" is also important. "Dread sin," but be quick to return to "the Father of Mercies," and, above all, be humble. At the time of the writing of the letter, Fénelon is separated from the duke and reveals the depth of his affection: "I would give a thousand lives as a drop of water, to see you such as God would have you."[57]

The original version of *Pious Reflections* contained thirty-one brief meditations on passages of Scripture, one for each day of the month. Wesley included sixteen of these.[58] His extracts emphasize the qualities of the Christian (patience, faithfulness, humility, obedience to the will of God, inner peace, love, prayer, and growth through suffering and affliction). One of Fénelon's themes that are picked up again and again by both Quaker and Methodist readers is that of the wise use of time. In reflection 13 in the *Library*, the use of time is seen as a preparation for eternity. "God, most liberal and bounteous of all other things, teaches us by the frugal dispensation of his providence, how careful we ought to be to make use of time, because he never gives two moments together, nor grants us a second, till he has withdrawn the first, keeping the third in his own hand, so that we are in a perfect uncertainty whether we shall have it or not." . . . "We cannot every moment do great matters for him, but we may always do what is proper for our condition."[59]

Madame Guyon's "A Mother's Advice to Her Daughter" contains five of the six sections of the original: "Some Direction for Devotion," "Of the Divine Presence," "How to Pass the Day Religiously," "Concerning Mortification," and "Some Rules for Conversation." The last, omitted section, is a sample meditation on the words of Christ in Matthew 11:19, emphasizing humility and repose. As in the material from Fénelon, the emphasis on a method for the devotional life, the wise use of time, and simplicity in lifestyle would have appealed to Wesley. Again, the translation is generally true to the original, but there is some compression that eliminates the vividness of the French text. For example, early in the letter, Madame Guyon adopts a subtly feminist stance when she distinguishes between Christian and pagan devotion. Citing Romans 8:17, she feminizes the theological concept in the text and also inserts a Catholic notion of baptism: "Vous êtes donc Chrétienne, ma fille, c'est à dire, *enfant de Dieu*, & par conséquent, *cohéritière de Jésus-Christ*, apellée à jouïr de Dieu, à être son temple, & c'est pour cela que vous avez été consacrée au Batême [sic]." The feminized "cohéritier" of the French, suggesting theological equality before God by gender, cannot be conveyed in English, and the reference to baptism has been removed: "My child, 'you are the temple of God,' if so be that 'God dwell in you by faith.' His will is, that he may reign in you; and how can he reign there, if he does not dwell there?" The translation eliminates the issue of gender and does not convey how Madame Guyon develops the image of the temple, noting that her daughter is composed of an "interior" and an "exterior," both of which must be regulated, but that God dwells in us as his temple if we do his will.[60]

There are some significant comments about the reading process in this essay of instruction, and these are related to what Madame Guyon says in her *Short and Easy Method*. The Bible is the preeminent text to be read daily to "edify and nourish" the soul and to instruct in one's duty or conduct. The more interesting comments concern spiritual reading, both because of the mention of other devotional texts and because of the method suggested which seems to be an extension of *lectio divina*.

> Never pass the morning without reading some spiritual book, such as *Thomas à Kempis, John Arndt*, or the like. Read slowly, that you may profit by it; and when you come from devotion, be careful not to dissipate your thoughts, but preserve what you have received thereby, as a precious liquor, which you fear will be evaporated. The fire kindles in prayer, but it soon goes out, if it be not kept up the rest of the day. The fuel you must feed it with, is frequent recollection, and acts of love, thanksgiving, and oblation of yourself to God; and, as it were, sinking inwards, to find him there, who is the centre of your soul.[61]

The Protestant translation has omitted François de Sales of the original, replacing him with the Lutheran Arndt. Significantly, Madame Guyon's understanding of spiritual reading is in the tradition of de Sales, whom she so admired. The psychology of the experience is primary. The nourishment of the soul incites a form of inner prayer leading to an awareness of God's presence that is to be carefully nourished and guarded throughout the day.

Quietist emphasis on the inner sense of the divine presence (already seen in the extracts from Fénelon) is repeated in the section of this tract on how to spend the day "religiously."

> Keep always an inward solitude, without which the outward is unprofitable. By an inward solitude, I mean, that you should shut out the thoughts of the world and yourself, that your mind may be vacant to God, but you should not disturb yourself for things that come into your mind against your will.
>
> All that we desire with passion and eagerness, is not of God. God dwells in peace.[62]

The extracts from Molinos' much-abridged *Spiritual Guide* further develop the themes of the preceding material from both Fénelon and Madame Guyon: "Thou oughtest always then to keep thine heart in peace, that thou mayest keep pure that temple of God; and with a right and pure intention, thou art to work, pray, obey, and suffer, without being in the least moved, whatever it pleases the Lord to send unto thee."[63] Prayer is the best defense as the soul is beset by crosses and temptations. The practice of the presence of God ("internal recollection") also appears here: "Thou oughtest to be accustomed to recollect thyself in his presence, with an affectionate attention, as one that is given up to God, and united unto him, with reverence, humility, and submission."[64] Few persons can achieve the annihilation of the self, but the spiritual person is marked by inner self-denial, humility, resignation, and peace. The soul that reaches true inner solitude is spacious, ready to be filled by the spirit of God. Because holiness results from self-denial, it is more frequently found among the simple. The fruits of the presence of the Spirit ("the perfections of spiritual beauty") are evident "in the throne of quiet."[65]

Wesley, then, has minimized mystical contemplative prayer and the complete annihilation of the self in mystical union with the divine will from the Quietist tradition. Through carefully choosing examples of the counsel from this tradition, he has incorporated it into Methodist spirituality and practice. Although the roots of the language of "rest" and "repose" are ultimately in Augustine, the hymnody of the Wesleys perpetuates the experiential teaching that the assurance of justification by faith and that submission to the divine will are characterized by inner peace or quiet.

> Thou hidden Source of calm repose, / Thou all sufficient Love divine, / My help and Refuge from my foes, / Secure I am, if Thou art mine; / And lo! from sin and grief and shame / I hide me, Jesus, in Thy name. // Thy mighty name salvation is, / And keeps my happy soul above; / Comfort it brings, and pow'r, and peace, / And joy, and everlasting love / To me, with Thy great name are giv'n / Pardon, and holiness, and heav'n. // Jesus, my All in All Thou art: / My Rest in toil, my ease in pain, / The med'cine of my broken heart, / In war my peace, in loss my gain, / My smile beneath the tyrant's frown, / In shame my glory and my crown! // In want my plentiful supply, / In weakness my almighty pow'r, / In bonds my perfect liberty, / My light in Satan's darkest hour, / In grief my joy unspeakable, / My life in death, my heav'n in hell![66]

James Gough and Thomas Digby Brooke

James Gough (1712-1780) played an unheralded role in the reading of the autobiography of Madame Guyon, especially in America, because he was the anonymous translator of the first more or less complete version in English that appeared in Bristol in 1772. Gough was a schoolmaster who became a Quaker leader, but he was also a poet (who largely abandoned that calling after his experience of divine love) and author, for example, of a lexicon and a grammar book. In his posthumously published memoirs, he describes a classic spiritual crisis in which his soul became married to Jesus. Having grown up in northern England and having chosen the dress of the Friends, Gough had just moved to Bristol at the age of twenty-one, but he found himself much like a "speckled bird" in a "strange land" where there were few others who dressed as he.

> [. . .] in this my solitary situation it pleased divine Goodness to take notice of me, and to favour me afresh with a merciful and reaching visitation of his love to my soul, and more clearly to reveal his Son in me, whereby I was given plainly to see that my safety here, and happiness hereafter, depended upon my yielding faithful obedience to his requirings by his light in my heart, and that his requirings would be only what tended to my real good, and last welfare.
>
> This was a day of my soul's espousal to Christ Jesus. I was overcome with his love, and with admiration of his condescending goodness to such an unworthy creature; it being the day of the Lord's power, I was ready and willing to do any things that I saw I should or ought to do.[67]

In 1738, Gough moved to Cork and soon after became a minister, travel-ing in England and Wales, including the yearly meetings in Wales, Bris-tol, and London. Once back in Ireland, he settled in Mountmelick and then Dublin.

Wesley's reaction to the first printing in Bristol of Gough's transla-tion of Madame Guyon may have been more complicated than simply the issue of enthusiasm. According to Gough, the Methodists were beginning to become established in Ireland, particularly in Mountmelick. John Cur-tis, who had briefly been a Methodist in Bristol but had become a Friend, made a "religious visit" to Ireland. Later, John Wesley himself made an appearance in Mountmelick, and Gough went to hear him preach in the marketplace. However, Wesley began with an attack on John Curtis: "I understand one John Curtis from Bristol hath of late been travelling in these parts, and endeavoring to lay waste that good work, which it hath pleased God to carry on by our hands, giving out that he was formerly a Methodist and acquainted with me." Gough went to confront Wesley later in the day, quoting Scripture that Wesley should not judge and indi-cating that Curtis was "influenced with the universal love of God and that he has endeavoured to propagate the same in others."[68] The least one can conclude from Gough's account of this interesting episode is that the appearance of his translation of Madame Guyon coincided with Quaker-Methodist tensions, that he himself had confronted Wesley about the issue, and that more than theological concerns lay behind Wesley's concerns about Methodists who read Madame Guyon in Bristol.

We know that Gough was the anonymous translator of *The Life of Lady Guion, Written by herself in French, now abridged, and translated into English* because two other works by the translator are advertised at the end of the second volume, most notably his *Select Lives of Foreigners, Eminent in Piety,* listed as in press. (This work would be reprinted in the United States.) Gough's interest in the power of biography and autobiography, evident in his *Lives,* is also apparent in the preface to the Guyon translation. "The reader will view, in the course of this translation, the progress of a holy pilgrim, not fictitious but real; a life of no common sort; from its birth upwarded attended with remarkable events, assaulted with troubles and inured to oppositions; a soul filled with the love of God."[69] The power of biography is also apparent in the appendices to part one: the lives of Teresa of Avila and François de Sales and a comparison of the lives of the two women.[70] The appendix to volume two includes the lives of Molinos and Fénelon, the latter based on the biography written by Fénelon's grand-nephew, along with extracts of "Directions for a Holy Life" as previously translated by Josiah Martin.[71] Part of Gough's inspiration for his approach to editing Madame Guyon by surrounding her text with the lives of other eminently pious people is Pierre Poiret himself. The original French editor is cited, including his remarks on the life of Madame Guyon in his preface.[72] Gough also defends Madame Guyon as a Catholic, noting that Thomas à Kempis is read by "christians [sic] of all denominations." "And what is the reason thereof," he asks, "but that his lines are found to be lively and experimental, edifying, and suiting the inward concern of every true christian?"[73]

Gough was a free translator and he had no qualms about suppressing elements that would not suit his Protestant readers in the text. He also inserted historical and theological explanations where he deemed fit, for example, giving the reader a summary of the events surrounding the examinations at Issy and the aftermath. Because this translation became identified with the entire tradition of American nineteenth-century publication and commentary, the kinds of changes Gough made become significant in Protestant preemption of this Catholic. The key "conversion" experience in which Jeanne Guyon discovered the interior life and contemplative prayer is described at length in the original.

> It was a prayer of faith which excluded all distinctions, for I had no sight of Jesus Christ nor of divine attributes: everything was absorbed into a delicious faith, where all distinctions were lost in order to give way to the love of loving with more amplitude, without motives or reasons to love.[74]

In the Bristol translation, this becomes the following:

> It was a prayer of rejoicing and of possession; wherein the taste of God was so great, so pure, unblended and uninterrupted, that it drew and absorbed the powers of the soul into a profound recollection, without act or discourse. For I had now no sight but of Jesus Christ alone.[75]

Similarly, the details of Madame Guyon's marriage contract with Jesus on the feast day of Mary Magdalene in 1672 are omitted, and the event is alluded to within the narration, followed by a note by the translator about the marriage contract. Referring to the "crosses" that preceded this experience, the translation mentions the even more severe crosses that followed: "And tho' I have had abundance of them hitherto, yet they were only the shadows of those which I have been since obligated to pass through, pursuant to a marriage contract, which I had newly entered into with our Lord Jesus Christ."[76]

The Bristol edition is thus an edited translation and an anthology, more complete but similar to the earlier text that was reprinted in 1738 and 1750 in Philadelphia. However, the appendices are much more voluminous and also give access to more of Madame Guyon's writings. Volume two includes a selection of poems inserted before the last chapter of the autobiography, "An Abstract of Lady Guion's Short and Easy Method of Prayer," an "Extract from the Spiritual Torrents," and "On Christian Perfection" (the title given to a letter for Father La Combe). The extract of the treatise on prayer is again freely translated; the order of the original chapters is retained, but the final chapters of the original are omitted.

The history of the publication of this particular anonymous translation is complicated because a new edition, again anonymous, was published in Dublin in 1775, this time with a different title and a new translation of the treatise on prayer by Thomas Digby Brooke. The work is in one volume, minus the appendices of the earlier edition, but it does include the translations of Madame Guyon's poems.[77] The preface seems also to be by Brooke.

> Biography, in all its various kinds, is the most captivating species of reading to the human mind—do but adapt the subject to the reader, and its entertainment becomes delightful, and its influence irresistible.
>
> —The secret cause of this lies deep in the heart of man.—every one has some subject that he admires—some aim that he stretches after. —The life of the man who possesses in any degree his revered idol, becomes to him as a precious mine, —wherein his treasure lies hid—and he searches therein with diligence, to discover by what method it was attained, and by what power secured, that he also may become partaker of his happiness, and possessor of this favourite object.[78]

Digby Brooke's translation of Madame Guyon's *Short and Easy Method* is livelier in style than the Gough text, and Brooke has simplified the original work so that it can be read as a handbook of devotion without a Catholic context; all twenty-four chapters are included. "We should, indeed, surrender our whole being unto CHRIST JESUS; and cease to live any longer in ourselves, that he himself may become our life; 'that being dead, our life may be hid with CHRIST IN GOD' (Col. iii.3)."[79]

It is likely that Thomas Digby Brooke was the younger brother of Henry Brooke (1766–1783), an Irish writer with Methodist connections. His novel, *The Fool of Quality; or, The History of Henry Earl of Moreland* (1766), on the education and character of a younger son as opposed to his libertine older brother, was edited by John Wesley for Methodist readers and had an eighteenth-century American reprinting. Moreover, the values of the novel are those of the tradition of the interior life: humility, love, and submission to the divine will.[80]

The translation of Madame Guyon's treatise on prayer by Henry's younger brother had considerable influence. It was published separately in both London and Bristol in 1775. (Perhaps the Bristol publication was yet one more reason for John Wesley's abstracted life of the lady, published in 1776). The Bristol printing was entitled *The Worship of God in Spirit and in Truth: or, A Short and Easy Method of Prayer, Suited to every capacity* and would quickly reappear in Philadelphia.[81] When the Bristol and Dublin editions of Madame Guyon's autobiography were reprinted in America, Thomas Digby Brooke would eventually be thought to be the translator of the entire edited autobiography of Madame Guyon, but that is a story that awaits telling.

Chapter 6

Persons of Eminent Piety and Writers of Spiritual Wisdom
Fénelon, Madame Guyon, and Their American Readership, 1800–1840

The writer of *Telemachus* was held in such esteem that, as his spiritual writings became known, they also joined the corpus of common reading material in early America. The great Jonathan Edwards (1703–1758) listed among his early reading not only *Telemachus* but also Fénelon's "Pious Thoughts" and the *Spiritual Works*.[1] In the late seventeenth and early eighteenth centuries the Quietist debates on the Continent over the nature of passive spirituality, the annihilation of the self, and disinterested love were very well known. It is difficult to determine what editions of the Quietists the Puritans of New England read, but the Quietist controversies were one factor in the background of public discussions of the theological issues raised by the problem of a proper love of God and a healthy love of self. The problem took the specific form of the question of whether one should be willing to be damned for the glory of God. Samuel Willard, the pastor of Old South Church in Boston, discussed the issue of happiness (self-love) as part of a monthly series of lectures on the *Westminster Catechism* between 1687 and 1707. (These were published posthumously in 1726 as *A Complete Body of Divinity*.) Willard's position was an argument from the natural order, namely, that the nature of humanity was a part of creation and could not be denied. Later, Edwards would also oppose the espousal of a theology of disinterested love or universal benevolence as espoused by his disciple Samuel Hopkins.[2] (Hopkins, as presented by Edwards A. Park, would attract considerable interest among the perfectionists of the nineteenth century.) If one assumes that Edwards reflected on

107

the issues of the nature of the divine order, the glory of God, self-love, and disinterested love, he would have found much to attract him in Fénelon's writings, which show an Augustinian bent and a clear discussion of these themes. It would have been the conclusion of Fénelon's arguments with which Edwards would have disagreed. Fénelon could write:

> O my God, O love, love thyself in me! In this way thou will be loved as thou art lovable. I only want to live to be consumed before thee, as a lamp burns ceaselessly before thine altars. I do not exist for myself at all. It is only thou who existest for thine own self. Nothing for me, all for thee. This is not too much. I am jealous for thee against my own self. Better perish than allow the love which should be given to thee, ever to return to me. Love on, O love! Love in thy weak creature! Love thy supreme beauty! O beauty, O infinite goodness, O infinite love: burn, consume, transport, annihilate my heart, make it a perfect holocaust![3]

Edwards was an early example of readers who saw Fénelon as a canonic author for both his didactic novel and his works of spiritual direction. As the popular revivals of the early nineteenth century succeeded the deism and irreligion of the revolutionary period, and as the printing and circulation of books increased, Fénelon's writings of spiritual direction became increasingly popular. Although Madame Guyon did not share Fénelon's eminence, she too, was read as an author in her own right. Quaker interest in the two of them remained constant and even increased.

In his study of French culture in early America, Howard Mumsford Jones noted the waves of revivals among New England Congregationalists that spread westward between 1799 and 1842, as well as the westward and southern movement of revivals and camp meetings via Presbyterian, Baptist, and Methodist outreach. However, he concluded that there was a renewed interest in Fénelon in the 1820s and that it was related to historically complicated American attitudes toward French Catholicism and French politics. The continuing prestige of *Telemachus* had made Fénelon into something of a progressive, and thus any evidence of "modernity" in a Catholic bishop such as the archbishop of Cambrai was viewed favorably by Americans.[4]

Actually, the reading of Fénelon as a canonic author and of Madame Guyon as a figure of persecution and forbearance in suffering was quite continuous throughout the early decades of the nineteenth century. Issues of American anti-Catholicism, central to Howard Mumsford Jones' analysis of attitudes toward French culture, became increasingly irrelevant as the two Quietists entered the broader spectrum of American culture. For an understanding of the nature of their stature and their readership, some knowledge of their publishing history is essential, given that eighteenth-century English translations played a crucial and continuous role in creating the myths and images surrounding these figures. In addition, the prefaces and formats of these editions provide important clues to the use to which the texts were put.

Early Publications of Fénelon's Writings of Spiritual Direction

Proof of the reading public's taste for Fénelon as a spiritual author lies in the publishing history of his *Pious Reflections*, which appeared in over a dozen editions between 1803 and 1818; some of these editions were in a miniature or small format and continued to appear as late as the 1850s.[5] The format indicated that these reflections were for devotional use. A miniature or tract format was also allotted to the single text "On Faithfulness in Little Things," which appeared in several versions starting in 1801 in New York when Isaac Collins printed a ten-page edition also in a small format.

Extracts of Fénelon's spiritual writings began to appear, along with versions of his life. These extracts were not always the same; there were variations in the choice of texts. The preface to the first of these collections (1802) indicated that the translation was based on the 1718 edition of the *Oeuvres spirituelles*. About half of Fénelon's prayers or meditations for the major days of the liturgical calendar were included, along with "Meditations on the Apostle's words" (Phil 2:13 and Acts 17:28), "Directions for a Holy Life, and the Attaining of Christian Perfection" and "A Letter on the Truth of Religion." Evidence of Catholic observances was absent, and other selections in the volume were already known in some form. Fénelon's life and character were almost always cited as a justification for reading his spiritual writings, and this was the case even in the brief preface to the 1802 work. "The Character of the Archbishop of Cambray is so well known and established, that 'tis needless to say any thing of him in order to enhance the value of the following Meditations and Soliloquies, or to excite the reader to a perusal of them."[6]

Philadelphia, 1804

Remarkably, four publications of Quietist works, two by Fénelon and two by Madame Guyon, appeared in a single year, and they tell us a great deal about the appeal of these individuals as persons of eminent piety and as authors of spiritual wisdom. The publisher Kimber, Conrad, and Company brought out an eight-page tract of Fénelon's "Faithfulness in Little Things."[7] More significantly, the same publisher produced an important anthology of Fénelon material, put together by the Quaker John Kendall. In his preface, Kendall relied on previous biographies of Fénelon that emphasized his exemplary character. In fact, parts of the preface were only slight variations of passages from James Gough, who in turn echoed Ramsay and Josiah Martin. (Gough would be relied upon repeatedly throughout the entire nineteenth century.) Those who sent Fénelon into exile in Cambrai chose to disregard his character and reputation. "His good understanding, and the purity of his life, were no longer considered: his friend [Madame Guyon] was to pass for a whimsical enthusiastical woman; and himself for the promoter of a senseless and profane sect." During the years in the bishopric, Fénelon "walked with God, like Enoch," displaying immense inner tranquility while carrying out his external acts of charity. "Christianity alone," writes Kendall, "can raise to that peace of the Holy Spirit, and inward tranquility, which excludes, not only unprofitable actions, but even useless thoughts. This internal quietude he endeavoured to attain, while he was outwardly employed in performing the duties of humanity, religion, and his vocation."[8]

The extracts themselves in the Kendall anthology constituted approximately thirty items drawn from the spiritual works, approximately half of them from the collection often entitled *Instructions and Advice on Various Points of Morality and Christian Perfection*, followed by meditations (reflections). The excerpts were often familiar, for example "On Fidelity in small Matters," "On Crosses," and "On the Employment of Our Time." But the titles given to others reflected the Quaker tradition: "On the true Light," "On the Presence of God," and "On Conformity to the Will of God." These spiritual extracts were followed by a large selection of letters. This anthology, like the one published in 1802, shows how a tradition was formed in which Fénelon's life and character informed the selections chosen for a particular anthology.

The third volume published by Kimber, Conrad, and Company was not by Fénelon; it was the first American edition of a collection of thirty-seven poems by Madame Guyon, as translated by William Cowper, that had been published in England in 1801. Cowper (1731–1800), whose depressive mental illness had caused him to retire to the country, had come under the influence of evangelical Methodism in Olney. (John Newton, the curate of the Olney parish, although a Calvinist, had been influenced in particular by George Whitefield. Newton made much use of hymns in his work, and he and Cowper collaborated while the latter was able.) Despite his morbid fear of damnation, Cowper was known in these circles for his contributions to *Olney Hymns* (1779), of which "God moves in a mysterious way" was one of the best known.[9] In 1782, William Bull, an evangelical minister with whom Cowper had become acquainted, gave volumes two, three, and four of the *Poésies et cantiques spirituels* (1722) to the English poet. Bull asked Cowper to translate a selection of the poems with an English readership specifically in mind. Cowper completed thirty-seven translations over a two-year period, choosing texts he liked and thought could be set to English verse. For a variety of reasons, Bull did not publish the collection until after Cowper's death.[10]

Kimber, Conrad, and Company brought out the first American edition, but the volume was quickly reprinted in 1806 and 1808, with other printings to follow. Cowper was popular, and these translations marked a shift in the taste of American readers.[11] The English poet succeeded in transforming Madame Guyon's Quietist themes and improvisational style to a polished verse that communicated her experience as religious sensibility or religious feeling, often in a natural setting. This late eighteenth-century sensibility coincided with the slow emergence of romantic taste among American readers. Furthermore, the publication of Cowper's translations came during the rising tide of popular religion in the early nineteenth century, particularly with the explosive growth of American Methodism.[12]

Madame Guyon's Poetry in Translation

William Bull, an enthusiastic admirer of Madame Guyon, may have been prompted to ask Cowper to translate some of her verse because a few examples of her poetry had been included by James Gough in his abridged and annotated version of her life in both the Bristol and Dublin editions. Gough himself was dissatisfied with the examples of her poetry that had already appeared in print, calling them "inadequate." "Her poetic vein was free, flowing, with warm devotion and gratitude."[13] Just before the last chapter of the autobiography, Gough inserted eleven translations, ranging from short stanzaic songs to a long address of Christ to his spouse and the ensuing reply, illustrating divine union. Gough chose three poems related to Madame Guyon's imprisonment to begin his extracts, and the first, the well-known piece built around the metaphor of a caged bird, was a distinct improvement upon the translation in the 1735 London anthology that was reprinted in Philadelphia in 1738. The following stanzas avoid the language of pure love in the two stanzas cited in chapter 5.

> Great God here at ease,
> Thee singly to please.
> I sing all the length of the day;
> / Shut up in a cage,
> Yes shelter'd from rage:
> Oh listen and smile on the lay!
> [. . .]

> O pleasure divine,
> All excellence thine;
> And thee will I love and adore:
> The more piercing my pain
> The more freedom I gain,
> And of every choice blessing the[e] more.[14]

The translator relies heavily on riming couplets, but the rhythm of his lines is often awkward. The diction reflects the generalized aesthetic of eighteenth-century classicism. Of the effect of divine love, Gough's translation reads as follows,

> To thee then adhering, wherever they go,
> With how virtuous ardor thy votaries glow.
> Tho' rocks in the road, or tho' desarts [sic] are found,
> Harmonious appears the creation around.
> All nature looks chearful, if foul or if fair,
> New fragrance diffusing throughout the mild air.
> The joy that's *within* issues forth in their views,
> And paradise, gracing all objects, renews.[15]

Other excerpts read like hymns. (Many of the Guyon poems were meant to be sung to popular tunes indicated in the manuscript.) "O love ever true, / Ever ancient and new / How thy favours unbounded amaze! / How grace from on high, / Like an angel of joy, / All around me thy glory displays!"[16] Finally, the very formal address of Christ, the divine bridegroom, to his spouse is entitled "M. Guion's Experience of Divine Communion, A Poem."

> O Thou dear object of my first delight,
> True to my laws, and beauteous in my sight,
> Obsequious, chase, effervent with the dart
> Of pure affection in they constant heart!
> My BRIDE elected! All THY SELF resign:
> For ever faithful to thy bridegroom shine [. . .].[17]

William Cowper's translations are of quite another order, elegant and versatile in versification, transforming Madame Guyon's quite varied form and style into English equivalents. Cowper has attempted to create a poetic equivalent, not an exact translation. It is not surprising that the volume of the Cowper translations was popular, for he expresses the Quietist themes in the language of evangelical Methodism and of preromantic naturalism.

There were 890 poems in the four volumes published in French in 1722; volumes one through three were organized in headings concerning instructions for souls seeking the interior life, the states of the interior life, and the emotions and transports of souls lost in God and called to help others. Volume four was a miscellany, including a poetic version of the Song of Songs, and poems written in alexandrines.[18]

There was no particular principle guiding Cowper's choice of poems to translate other than his own taste and sense that the particular piece could become English verse. The majority of these poems are on divine love, submission to the will of God, and bearing one's crosses. In his free poetic versions, Cowper eliminates the intimate, erotic language often used to address Christ in the original, and he introduces the diction of English evangelicalism, toning down the intensity of Quietist themes.[19] For example, the theme of indifference becomes that of acquiescence in "Veiller à Dieu de coeur pendant la nuit" ("Watching unto God in the Night Season").

> L'amour qui m'instruit au silence,
> M'enseigne aussi de ne désirer rien;
> Et m'apprend que l'indifférence
> Non le choix, est le plus grand bien.

> Love this gentle admonition
> Whispers soft within my breast;
> "Choice befits not they condition,
> Acquiescence suits thee best."

Similarly, the repose within nothingness of "Sacrifice dans les vicissitudes du divin Amour" disappears in "The Vicissitudes experienced in the Christian Life."

> Si vous me demandez ce que je crois de moi,
> Je n'en connois aucune chose:
> Jadis je vivois par la foi;
> C'est dans le rien que je repose.

> My claim to life, though sought with earnest care,
> No light within me or without me shows;
> Once I had faith, but now in self-despair
> Find my chief cordial and my best repose.[20]

Madame Guyon's mysticism in which the continual presence of God transcends all the categories of time and space becomes in Cowper a sense of concrete belonging.

> Tout est mon pays, ma retraite;
> Il n'est pour moi ni temps ni lieu;

L'âme est contente et satisfaite,
Tous les lieux lui deviennent Dieu.

To me remains not place nor time;
My country is in every clime;
I can be calm and free from care
On any shore, since God is there.[21]

The experiential theology of the forgiveness of sin and of divine love, with echos of Methodist hymnody, is evident in stanzas such as these from "Pure Love, On a Principle of Gratitude."

All are indebted much to thee,
But I far more than all,
From many a deadly snare set free,
And rais'd from many a Fall.
Overwhelm me from above
Daily with thy boundless Love.

What bonds of Gratitude I feel
No language can declare,
Beneath th'oppressive weight I reel,
'Tis more than I can bear;
When shall I that blessing prove,
To return thee Love for Love? [. . .]

Oh blessedness all bliss above,
When thy pure fires prevail,
Love only teaches what is Love,
All other lessons fail,
We learn its name but not its pow'rs,
Experience only makes it ours.[22]

Nature, a source of refuge and consolation, figures in several of the Cowper translations that are fine examples of eighteenth-century taste, even the taste for the wild and the sublime. In "Scenes Favorable to Meditation," the speaker, isolated from humankind, addresses the wild countryside, pondering the paradoxes of the soul that is dead to herself but nourished in the love of her divine spouse.

Wilds horrid and dark with o'ershadowing trees,
Rocks that ivy and briars infold,
Scenes Nature with dread and astonishment sees,
But I with a pleasure untold.

Though awfully silent and shaggy and rude,
I am charm'd with the peace ye afford,
Your shades are a temple where none will intrude,
The abode of my Lover and Lord. [. . .]

Here let me though fixt in a desert, be free,
A Little One whom they despise
Though lost to the world, if in union with thee,
Shall be holy and happy and wise.[23]

One of the most successful of Cowper's versions is a narrative built on the figures of the winged figure of love and his bride who learns to trust him entirely. This sort of erotic context is often found in Madame Guyon's emblem poetry, as it was in the entire mystic tradition, but it is often more playful in her poems.

'Twas my purpose on a day,
To embark and sail away;
As I climb'd the vessel's side,
Love was sporting in the tide,
Come he said—ascend—make haste,
Launch into the boundless waste.

Many Mariners were there,
Having each his sep'rate care,
They that row'd us, held their eyes
Fixt upon the starry skies,
Others steer'd, or turn'd the sails
To receive the shifting gales.

The voyager accepts the invitation to leap into the sea, only to find herself without courage, overwhelmed by the ocean, and abandoned by Love. But the beloved resigns herself to whatever the will of her king and lord is; this acceptance is the key to the resolution of the absence of the divine presence.

This was just what Love intended,
He was now no more offended,
Soon as I became a child,
Love return'd to me and smiled:
Never strife shall more betide
Twixt the Bridegroom and his Bride.[24]

Autobiographies and Exemplary Lives—"Good Men and Women of Every Denomination under the Sun"

The three publications brought out by Kimber, Conrad, and Company were not the only books that contributed to the popularity of Fénelon and Madame Guyon among nineteenth-century Quakers and Methodists. (German Pietists were no doubt also reading these books in English.) Joseph Crukshank, a Philadelphia printing establishment with Quaker roots, also published an edition of the 1775 Dublin edition of the Gough edition of the life of Madame Guyon, along with the Brooke translation of the *Short and Easy Method*. Not to be outdone, the New Bedford publisher Abraham Shearman then printed the 1772 Bristol edition of the Guyon autobiography, with some abridgments, in 1805.[25]

Nor was American interest in the life of Madame Guyon limited to her story alone. As already noted in chapter 5, James Gough had included a number of short biographies as appendices to his 1772 Bristol edition of the Guyon autobiography. He extended his interest in the exemplary lives of Christians on the interior way in an anonymously edited anthology, *Select Lives of Foreigners, Eminent in Piety* (Bristol, ca. 1772), and then reprinted in a second edition. Benjamin and Thomas Kite reprinted this anthology with a few changes in a third edition in Philadelphia in 1807.[26] The Kites changed the order of the biographies, placing the life of Fénelon first, followed by "Directions for a Holy Life, and the Attaining Christian Perfection." They then followed the order of the previous edition, presenting the life of Molinos and the "Progress of Quietism," the lives of Peter Poiret and Antonia Bourignon, followed by "Her Sentiments, on the Essentials of the Christian Religion," the lives of de Renty and de Sales, including some of the latter's "maxims of piety," and the life of Gregory Lopez.

Some of this material was included in the 1772 edition of the Guyon autobiography and reflects Gough's use of Pierre Poiret as a source; there was an overlapping of interest with that of John Wesley, both in his personal spiritual development and in some of the extracts he included in his *Christian Library*. The preface to the *Select Lives* included an ecumenical defense of the value of reading biographies of the truly pious, no matter what their Christian tradition. The ecumenical flavor, then, of this tradition of holiness and pure love was entrenched early on in American popular religion of the nineteenth century. "I love to read the lives of good men and women, who were truly such, of every denomination under the sun," writes the "translator." Although these individuals may sometimes be mistaken in "externals," "they all aim at one great point, viz. to honour God, to live in his fear, to have the heart made clean and kept so, their words few and savoury, ministering grace to the hearers, and [. . .] to be, good examples to others in conversation, in charity, in spirit, in faith, in purity. 1 Tim. iv. 12."[27]

This biography of Fénelon in the American edition of *Select Lives* was different from that included in the 1772 Guyon autobiography. In that version, Gough relied both on Ramsay and on the abbé Fénelon's *Vie de Fénelon*, a longer, drier account. Here, the account drew on Ramsay again, but also the excerpts published by Josiah Martin and the anthology that followed (*A Dissertation on Pure Love by the Archbishop of Cambray* [. . .]), published in London in 1735, which Gough apparently knew in a 1739 Dublin edition.[28] (This was the anthology reprinted earlier in Pennsylvania by Bradford and by Sauer.) The account of Fénelon's life in *Select Lives* was lively and included commentary about *Telemachus* and its importance, an abridged version of the letter of Fénelon to the Duke of Bourgogne on disinterested love ("the true way of loving"), and other short abstracts of letters and meditations. Like Ramsay, the editor emphasized Fénelon's exemplary life as a bishop while in exile, his acts of charity during a time of war and suffering, and his inner detachment and spirit of quietude. The editor also stressed that Fénelon was faithful to his friendship with the Lady Guyon until the end of his life. Fénelon died without money and without debts, and an editorial note compares Fénelon and the Marquis de Renty as examples of those "who found religion not to be a mere speculative notion, but a practical duty, not to consist in preaching and praying only, but in doing good to *all*."[29] As noted, this account of Fénelon's life was followed by "Directions for a Holy Life, and the Attaining of Christian Perfection" ("Instructions et avis sur divers points de la morale et de la perfection chrétienne"). This was the Josiah Martin translation of just the seventh chapter of this collection, with each point highlighted numerically.

Proof of American interest in the French Quietists lies in the editions that followed, for example, *A Short and Easy Method of Prayer* with a life of the author (Baltimore: B. W. Sower, 1812). And a series of printings of the 1775 edition of the autobiography began to appear by 1820; these editions would bring together the strands of the tradition I have been tracing because they combined the Gough version of the life (with the appended biographies of people like Fénelon and Molinos), a selection of the poems by Cowper, and the Digby Brooke translation of the treatise on prayer. The preface was that of the 1775 edition. The first of these editions appeared as *The Life and Religious Experience of the Celebrated Lady Guion* (New York: Hoyt and Bolmore, 1820) and included seventeen of the Cowper translations.[30] Quaker interest in Quietism would prove to be continuous. A devotional anthology entitled *A Guide to True Peace*, containing excerpts from Fénelon's *Maxims of the Saints*, Madame Guyon's *Short and Easy Method of Prayer*, and Molinos' *Spiritual Guide*, was first published in 1813 and continued to be in print through the twentieth century.[31]

Unitarian and Abolitionist Readers

By the 1820s, our French Quietists had found a new foothold among noncreedal American Protestants. Fénelon had been read in eighteenth-century New England; despite the fact that he and Madame Guyon represented a theological tradition quite different from the dominant Calvinist models, their emphasis on inner piety certainly paralleled elements of Puritan spirituality. In nineteenth-century New England, the two figures would be read anew by Unitarians and Abolitionists and cast into a different mold.

In Boston, Fénelon came to stand for tolerance and love. These elements were present in the mythic tradition surrounding him from Ramsay on, but the tradition suppressed certain elements of his ecclesiastical career. To recap, he had been responsible early on for promoting the conversion of Hugenots and was the noted director of a school for "new Catholic" girls. During his exile in Cambrai, he forcefully opposed the Jansenists and was supportive of their suppression. However, his doctrine of pure love, his temperament, and his acts of charity to the poor and to the soldiers on both the French and English sides during the war raging around Cambrai won the day in the hagiography that came to surround his life. The preface to an 1814 edition of *Pious Reflections*, published in Boston, emphasized Fénelon's ability to relate to people of all social classes and to transcend the boundaries of religious intolerance. Fénelon seems to have been transformed from a gifted pedagogue into a Christ figure incarnating democratic values.

> The qualities which rendered Fenelon an object of esteem and admiration, and which will endear his name to every future age, consisted in a temper always mild and serene; a polite yet simple address; an animated conversation, a mild cheerfulness tempering the dignity of his station; a religious zeal highly tinctured with enthusiasm, yet unaccompanied with the bitterness of fanaticism; and a wonderful perspecuity of expression in explaining the most abstruse and difficult subjects. He possessed also the power of reducing himself to a level with persons of all capacities, and never appeared anxious to display the superiority of his own understanding. His exalted talents and profound learning, instead of filling him with pride and supercilliousness, rendered him more humble and unassuming.[32]

Against the background of such portraits of Fénelon, in 1829 Eliza Follen published an anonymous anthology, *Selections from the Writings of Fenelon with a Memoir of His Life*. This anthology would go through six editions until 1859. The initial edition coincided with the publication in France of the first complete edition of the Duc de Saint-Simon's *Mémoires* in 1829 and 1830 (reprinted in 1835, 1840, and 1841). Saint-Simon treated the episodes of the Quietist controversy with irony and detachment, noting Fénelon's ecclesiastical ambitions. However, his account of Fénelon in Cambrai was sympathetic, painting him as a saint.[33] Eliza Follen's connections were with literary, Unitarian, and early abolitionist circles in Boston.

A Cabot, Follen was active in the Sunday school at the Federal Street Church where she participated in a group that regularly discussed religious issues with William Ellery Channing. Her writing career centered on children's literature and Sunday school material.[34] Eliza's husband Charles was a German social activist who was a political refugee in Boston and who had anglicized his name. After Eliza introduced Charles to Channing, the two became close friends. Eliza and Charles married in 1828, and Charles became a professor of German at Harvard in 1830. He also established his credentials as an abolitionist in his "Lectures on Moral Philosophy," also in 1830, when he denounced slavery. William Lloyd Garrison and John Greenleaf Whittier influenced Cabot to join the New England Anti-Slavery Society in 1834. Follen's first speech to the convention of this society, "Address to the People of the United States," was the immediate cause of the decision by Harvard College not to renew his contract the next year. He then became a lecturer, Unitarian minister, and more zealous abolitionist. Follen also became something of a martyr after his death in 1840 on the steamer Lexington that caught fire in Long Island Sound. Garrison, in fact, named a son after Charles Follen.

The milieu of the Follens ranged from active abolitionists such as Garrison to intellectual abolitionists such as William Ellery Channing and Henry Wadsworth Longfellow. Longfellow, although younger, certainly knew Follen as a result of his Harvard connection and in 1842 published his *Poems on Slavery* that was dedicated to Channing, a friend of his father. In a letter to William Plumer Jr., an active abolitionist, Longfellow said that he hoped Plumer would not be offended by his poems "as the spirit in which they are written is that of kindness—not denunication;—at all events not violence."[35]

Henry Sedgwick, whose wife had introduced Eliza to Charles Follen, wrote the preface to the first edition of the *Selections from the Writings of Fenelon*. Sedgwick cast Fénelon in an exemplary role as a figure of

nonviolence in what was to be a dominant issue as the abolitionist movement evolved. Fénelon belonged to the "whole of mankind," as a church-
man without creed who was pious "in the highest sense" of the word. "He
loved men, not because they were of the same race as himself, but because
they were susceptible of virtue and happiness."[36]

Eliza Follen's "Memoir of Fenelon" continued many of the themes
of preceding portraits but made use of additional sources, such as Saint-
Simon. She gives a rather full account of Fénelon's career and the range of
his writings. The account of the Quietist controversy is rather brief, with
little emphasis on Madame Guyon, but considerable attention is given to
the years in Cambrai and Fénelon's charitable actions that crossed the
boundaries of social class and, in war, national identity: "All distinctions
of religion and sect, all feelings of hatred and jealousy that divided the
nations, seemed to disappear in the presence of Fenelon." "The spirit of
Christian love" was "immortalized" in Fénelon.[37]

Most remarkable are Follen's comments about the relationship
between the reader and Fénelon the writer. She emphasizes the deep
relationship between the reader and Fénelon the man and the moral
effect of that spiritual contact. These comments mark the emergence
of a hermeneutics of the reading process that was not based on a tradition derived from *lectio divina*, but one that accorded tremendous power
to the transforming spirit of Fénelon. Follen notes that the "feeling of
quiet and of tranquillity" of these writings is also excited in the reader
and then continues,

> It is a friend, who approaches you and pours his soul into yours. You
> feel that you are holding an intimate communion with a gifted mind.
> He moderates, and suspends, at least for a while, your worldly cares and
> your sorrows; you enter for a time into that spirit of self-sacrifice and
> self-oblivion which seems to be the key-note of all his writings. Your
> whole heart seems to expand with the [C]hristian love that inspired
> him. We are ready to forgive human nature so many men who make us
> hate it, on account of Fenelon, who makes us love it.[38]

The nuances of the comments by both Sedgwick and Follen suggest
a subtle transformation in the portrait of Fénelon emerging in New England. Fénelon was an exemplary figure, but his Quietist roots and his
place within the ongoing popular tradition of religions of the heart were
minimized or ignored; his exemplary power represented those qualities
of Christianity that were universal religious traits to be imitated. In addition, Eliza Follen represented the first significant American woman to
interpret the French Quietist tradition, marking the emergence of women

as powerful readers within this theological and devotional current that lay outside the boundaries of the well-established, creedal church.

Eliza Follen's table of contents of her own translated extracts is also revealing. Her selections reinforce the portait of the universal religious figure. The first selection is taken from "On the Existence of God" (*Démonstration de l'existence de Dieu*), which was well known in the eighteenth century.[39] A nineteenth-century American edition had appeared in 1811.[40] This treatise was situated in a complex intellectual tradition involving Descartes, Spinoza, and Malebranche; Fénelon had already written a refutation of the system of Malebranche, and his apologetic for the existence of God was an original contribution, drawing on Augustine and Descartes in particular. Radically simplifying Fénelon's arguments, one can note his argument for God from nature, but emphasizing the aesthetic quality of the design and marvel of the natural world. Secondly, building a psychology based on mind-body dualism, Fénelon suggested that the conception of the infinite in the human mind can be none other than the idea of God. Follen's inclusion of extracts from this treatise at the beginning of her anthology set Fénelon in a broad intellectual context, certainly acceptable to Unitarian emphases on a non-Trinitarian view of God, the cultivation of Christian virtue, and an inner experience of truth.[41]

Other extracts in the Follan anthology were drawn from various sections of Fénelon's spiritual writings as they were collected in the *Manual of Piety* (*Manuel de Piété*), including, for example, "On the Knowledge and Love of God," "On Piety," "On Prayer," "Upon Fidelity in Little Things," and all of the "Pious Reflections," here called "Reflections for Every Day of the Month," but abridged. The scope of Fénelon's writings was also illustrated by the inclusion of extracts from "On the Education of Girls" and from the "Letters." The latter were not samples of Fénelon's missives of spiritual direction, but rather a series of occasional letters that were really apologetic in nature on such topics as the psychology of the self, belief, the necessity of worship, and the superiority of Christian worship to Jewish worship, the immortality of the soul, and free will. Interestingly, an American edition of excerpts had appeared as a catechism in 1810; this was a rare early example of Catholic use of Fénelon's spiritual or doctrinal writings.[42]

The overall impression of Follen's reinterpretation of Fénelon's Quietism is that she changed it into an active, outward-looking morality. The reflection for day thirty includes this representative passage: "To love God is to make his will ours; it is to obey faithfully his laws; it is to abhor sin. To love God is to love all that Jesus Christ loved,—poverty, humiliation, suffering; it is to hate what he hated, the vanities of the world, our own passions."[43]

William Ellery Channing reviewed the first edition of Follen's *Selec-tions* in the *Christian Examiner* in 1829. The review was reprinted separately in Boston that same year and then in London in 1830. Channing sets the character and writings of Fénelon against the "paralyzing influence" of Christian theology that has inhibited free inquiry and action. Progress in religion is to be defined as the "supreme law of the soul." Even though Fénelon was a Catholic, he is admirable because he was "essentially free." "Fenelon saw far into the human heart, and especially into the lurkings of self-love."[44] In the context of a Unitarian worldview and preceding Puritan debates about self-love, Channing's comments about Fénelon are mea-sured; in particular his view of self-love was too "dark." Fénelon's notion of self-abnegation implies a conflict between the will of God and that of the individual when this is impossible; in fact, complete denial of the self would also be impossible. Channing praises Fénelon's view of God "as the pitying and purifying friend of the soul." And although Fénelon might seem to some to be an "enthusiast," his idea that "love to mankind, directed aright, is the germ and element of love to the Divinity."[45]

The fourth edition of Eliza Follen's anthology was published in 1841, just after the death of her husband. Channing wrote some "Introductory Remarks" for this edition in which he took up some of his earlier themes about Fénelon but placed them in a general context. Fénelon "belongs to no sect" but represents the "universal spirit of Christianity." It is the qual-ity of Fénelon's character that matters, for his writings were not marked by "logical accuracy of thought and expression." Rather, "they came from his heart. They were transcripts of his own experience."[46] The portrait of Fénelon drawn by Channing is marked by qualities traditionally assigned to women:

> . . . his light, though so mild and tender, was still so clear, and pure, and penetrating, that he left on all around him one and the same impres-sion; and the voice of his generation has come down to us uncontra-dicted, undivided, in attestation of his rare sanctity and goodness. This great soul breathed itself out with child-like simplicity in his writings. In reading these, we commune not with his intellect alone, but with his whole spirit, not with an author, but with Fenelon, as he spoke and lived in his common walks, and among the men of his own age.[47]

The growth of a female readership interested in the biographies and beliefs of people like Fénelon and Madame Guyon is also illustrated by the figure of Lydia Maria Child (1802–1880), a Unitarian equivalent to Harriet Beecher Stowe. (Stowe, who admired Fénelon but not Madame Guyon, will appear in chapter 8.) Child's husband was a member of the group that founded the American Anti-Slavery Society in 1832, and Lydia went on to edit the *National Anti-Slavery Standard.* Originally a Congregationalist, Child wrote popular romances such as *Philothea,* as well as Sunday school material. She epitomizes many of the New England women writers for mass culture in the nineteenth century, whom Ann Douglas has portrayed as succeeding the established Congregationalist clergy in influence.[48]

Lydia desperately needed to write to earn money and, in the late 1820s and early 1830s, became an expert on domestic "economy," publishing *The Frugal Housewife* (1829), a volume with many editions, and *The Mother's Book* (1831). She then conceived of a series, The Ladies' Family Library, to promote the education of her female readers through biography and literature. In 1831–1832, Child produced the biographies of Madame de Staël and Madame Roland (two figures of political resistance) and then of Lady Russell and Madame Guyon (two exemplary women of suffering and piety).[49] The Guyon material was based primarily on the autobiography and gave few details of the religious dispute over Quietism. Child set up a contrast between Fénelon and Madame Guyon and portrayed the cleric as her disciple. Madame Guyon represented ideal Christian womanhood.

> Having a dislike to everything like an affectation of singularity, he was at first disposed to avoid her; but the modesty of her demeanor, and the extreme simplicity and gentleness of her manners, soon prepossessed him in her favor. Although she was more unreserved and incautious than the Abbé Fenelon, she strongly resembled him in her disinterestedness, her love of God, her conscientious courage, and her total abandonment to the guidance of Divine Providence: it is not strange, therefore, that he became one of her disciples, as well as a zealous friend and admirer.[50]

Later, Child would produce a comparative study of religions, indicating that the Christian religion represented historical progress within world religions. E. Brooks Holifield sees Child as among the figures promoting a "more pietist, devotional side of Unitarianism," in her case, a "religion of the heart" so pronounced that she rejected theology. Child defined religion as "'sentiments of reverence toward God, and of justice and benevolence toward our fellow men.'"[51]

One can claim no lasting influence of Quietist thought on Lydia Maria Child, but her journalistic biography of Madame Guyon was a sign of the French woman's enduring place in the popular imagination, and other such biographies would continue to occur. Soon, readers caught up in the perfectionist revivalism that would ensue in the 1840s would claim Madame Guyon as a familiar figure. In 1841, Thomas C. Upham, of whom more will be said, would refer readers of the new *Guide to Christian Perfection* to the Lydia Child biography and say that Madame Guyon was "distinguished alike for her talents and her piety" and that "her religious history has attracted considerable attention."[52]

Emerson and the Alcotts

Although Austin Warren has said that Emerson was largely responsible for the "vogue" of Fénelon among the Transcendentalists, Fénelon was such a cultural icon in New England by the 1830s that most educated readers encountered the author of *Telemachus* during their early years.[53] When he was thirteen, Emerson tried to read *Telemachus* in French.[54] Rather than assigning to Emerson the role of popularizing Fénelon, we can probably conclude that Emerson illustrates the fact that many American readers of the writings of Fénelon and of Madame Guyon were not necessarily influenced by them in a lasting way. Some indeed were, but others read them as cultural artifacts or figures to admire; still others recognized affinities between their religious experience or beliefs and those of Fénelon and Madame Guyon.

Throughout his career, Emerson expressed admiration for Fénelon and cited him from time to time as a representative religious thinker. He certainly knew Follen's and Channing's commentaries on Fénelon, but Robert D. Richardson has called Emerson's early sense of dependency and self-abnegation his "Fénelon mood" that he had to learn to throw off before proceeding to his later calls for self-reliance and to his sense that the self provides the path to the divine.[55] Emerson's references to Fénelon in the key period of about 1830 to 1836 illustrate this admiration. Like Channing, Emerson had resisted the label of "Unitarian," but Channing had been a theological mentor and Emerson was a pastor in that mold until he resigned his Second Church pastorate in 1832. Emerson was gradually emphasizing the intuitive inner moral sense that leads one to act ethically, that Jesus' teachings were authoritative to the degree that they "confirmed" this moral sense.[56] Influenced by Swedenborg's view that there were universal analogies or correspondences between the natural and spiritual worlds and by Coleridge's theory of the faculties of the mind, Emerson moved toward a view that nature was a source of ethical truth, recognized by the mind, a sign of the God within us. Although the evolution of Emerson's thought was complex during the years leading to the publication in 1836 of *Nature*, his lecture on Martin Luther in 1835 illustrates how Fénelon played a role in his thinking as a representative figure, in this context, one who combined Scripture and nature in his religious views.

There never has been since Luther a great man of the first class who believed as he did, unless Cromwell be deemed a sort of continuation of him. All others, if religious men as Milton, Newton, Leibnitz, Bacon, Montesquieu, Fenelon, Pascal, Locke, Cuvier, Goethe have joined Nature to Revelation to form their religion or like Spinoza, Rousseau, Laplace have worshipped like the Indian, Nature alone. Luther's religion is exclusively and literally from the Scriptures.[57]

Emerson's diaries of the 1830s reveal how he was working out his early thinking and include allusions to both Fénelon and Madame Guyon. In January of 1830, he wrote,

That man will always speak with authority who speaks his own convictions—not the knowledge of his ear or eye—[i.e.] supersitions got in conversations, or errors or truths remembered from his reading—but that which true or false he hath perceived with his own inward eye—which therefore is true to him—true even as he tells it, & absolutely true in some element through distorted & discoloured by some disease in the soul.

During this period, Emerson was thinking about a range of issues in the comparative history of philosophy as well as mentioning anecdotes from the life of Fénelon. After citing a quotation attributed to Fénelon that he was more a man than a Frenchman or a Fénelon, Emerson wrote that the "greatness of human desires is surely one element of the greatness of man. The love of the marvelous, all the fantastic theories of mystics, the deification of the faculties &c &c are in that view good."[58]

In 1833, Emerson was exploring the issues of the moral law and virtue with respect to organized religion and he situated these questions in the context of his intellectual and spiritual heroes: "I believe that the error of religionists lies in this, that they do not know the extent or the harmony or the depth of their moral nature, that they are clinging to little, positive, verbal, formal versions of the moral and & very imperfect versions too [. . .]." Calvinism and Unitarianism and any religious faith in the hands of an incapable teacher are insufficient versions of the moral law. But a "true Teacher" makes the "sublimity & depth of the Original"—that is, Moral Truth—shine forth. Because of this moral core of truth ("this One bottom"), "the eminent men of each church, Socrates, A Kempis, Fenelon, Butler, Penn, Swedenborg, Channing think & say the same thing." Then Emerson discusses the principles of "the moral law of human nature," all of which "may be penetrated unto" within the individual.

A man contains all that is needful to his government within himself. He is made a law unto himself. All real good or evil that can befal [sic] him must be from himself. He only can do himself any good or any harm. Nothing can be given to him or taken from him but always there is a compensation. There is a correspondence between the human soul & everything that exists in the world [. . .]. The highest revelation is that God is in every man.[59]

Madame Guyon also figured among the enthusiasts of a religion of the heart, who gave a clue to Emerson as to the essence of a religious experience. When he was preparing his first public lectures on the biographies of great men in January of 1835, including the lecture on Luther quoted above, Emerson included Madame Guyon in a list that demonstrates his awareness of the nature of popular religious fervor.

[. . .] Bitter cold days, yet I read of that inward fervor which ran as fire from heart to heart through England in George Fox's time. How precisely parallel are the biographies of religious enthusiasts. Swedenborg, Guyon, Fox, Luther & perhaps Bohmen [sic]. Each owes all to the discovery that God must be sought within, not without. That is the discovery of Jesus. Each perceives the worthlessness of all instruction, & the infinity of wisdom that issues from meditation. Each perceives the nullity of all conditions but one, innocence; & the absolute submission which attends it. All become simple, plain in word & act. Swedenborg & the Quakers have much to say of a new Name that shall be given in heaven.[60]

One can extrapolate from these early references in Emerson the conclusion that in the climate of Transcendentalist thinking, Quietists, Pietists, and Quakers, as well as Platonists, Swedenborgians, and others, were all part of a single, broad group of those seeking contact with the divine by means of both an escape from the boundaries of creed and a powerful inner experience of truth. When Bronson Alcott, the gifted educator and friend of Emerson, visited England in 1842 and conceived the idea of founding Fruitlands, an agrarian society founded upon Transcendentalist and communal principles, he and Charles Love brought back a library featuring mystical books. In April of 1843, *The Dial*, the official organ of the Transcendentalists, printed a catalogue of the books. The list included Kempis, de Sales, Molinos, Guyon, Fénelon, Bourignon, Poiret, Hugo, Franck, Ramsay, Law, and Swedenborg, to name a few authors. Under the catalogue entries for Guyon, there seems to have been a reprint of the 1775 edition of her life, misattributed to Digby Brooke, French editions of her letters, spiritual works, and autobiography, "selections in German" that appear to be the Teersteegen edition of emblems with biblical commentary, *The Holy Love of God*, and a volume called *Polemics* (London, 1841). Under Fénelon, the anthology we have encountered under the title *The Archbishop of Cambray's Dissertation on Pure Love* [. . .] seems to have been listed, along with an account of Madame Guyon and her *Justifications*, as well as Fénelon's *Maxims of the Saints*, *Dialogues of the Dead*, and *Lives and Maxims of Ancient Philosophers*. In the library these books were equally as important as those by Jakob Böhme, only to be exceeded by the number of books by William Law (who also became a proponent of Böhme in England). Among the books listed under Law were *Way to Divine Knowledge*, *Spirit of Prayer*, *Spirit of Love*, *Christian Perfection*, and *A Serious Call*.[61]

The library at Fruitlands was a physical testimony to the presence in America of the popular religious and mystical movements of the seventeenth and eighteenth centuries on the Continent and in England. Fruitlands, of course, did not last long as an agricultural community, completing its brief life in 1844-1845. But figures like Fénelon and Madame Guyon by then had a sure place in the popular imagination. In what she called her "sentimental" phase of early adolescence, Louisa May Alcott recalled the day she "got religion" in a nature experience.

> I remember running over the hills just at dawn one summer morning, & pausing to rest in the silent woods, saw, through an arch of trees, the sun rise over river, hill, and wide green meadows as I never saw it before.
>
> Something born of the lovely hour, a happy mood, and the unfolding aspirations of a child's soul seemed to bring me very near to God; and in the hush of that morning hour I always felt that I "got religion," as the phrase goes. A new and vital sense of His presence, tender and sustaining as a father's arms, came to me then, never to change through forty years of life's vicissitudes, but to grow stronger for the sharp disciplines of poverty and pain, sorrow and success.[62]

In 1852 Louisa recorded in her diary a resolution to improve her reading by choosing good books and reducing the number of novels. She included a list of authors and titles she liked: Carlyle, Goethe, Plutarch, Madame Guyon, Milton, Schiller, and Madame de Staël, among others.[63] Madame Guyon's place in this ranking says a great deal about her popular status in New England; even today visitors to the Emerson house in Concord will find among the books a small, leather-bound volume, marked "Madame Guion" on the spine.

Chapter 7

From Experimental Religion to Experimental Holiness
Contexts of Thomas Upham's Reinterpretation of Madame Guyon, 1840–1860

In the late 1830s, two new periodicals appeared that represented the unique blend of pietism, revivalism, and Christian perfectionism that gave birth to the holiness movements of nineteenth-century America.[1] The *Oberlin Evangelist* began publication in 1837; this was the vehicle for the theology of a second conversion leading to Christian perfection as preached by the evangelist Charles Grandison Finney, who had become a professor of theology at Oberlin College in 1835. *The Guide to Christian Perfection* (later, *Guide to Holiness*) was inaugurated in 1839 by Timothy Merritt (1775–1845), a Methodist minister of the New England Conference who had served in Boston and in Lowell, Massachusetts, had done other editorial work, and had also been an officer of the Methodist anti-slavery society when it had convened in Lowell.[2] The Oberlin paper was the voice of the new Calvinist wing of revivalism and perfectionism; the *Guide* was the purveyor of Wesleyan holiness, emphasizing revivals and a notion that sanctification was a state of Christian perfection attainable in this life.

The uniqueness of Timothy Merritt's new publication was its emphasis on "experimental and practical piety." Although the magazine featured excerpts from Wesley, John Fletcher, and notable proponents of Christian perfection, it also regularly published reports on "religious experience"— biographical and autobiographical accounts, letters, and articles on the experience of sanctification. An 1854 article, written in a popular style on "Experimental Holiness," epitomizes this applied theology. The author contrasts "argumentative sermons" with the power of testimonies in reaching people: "Learned theories could never move a sceptic's heart, or kindle in human breasts that deep sense of conscious guilt, and that panting for salvation which the living, experimental testimony of the child of God produces." The author does not wish "to under value argument, reasoning, or entreaty." No, it should be "interwoven" with experimental testimony that is the "cementing element" in reaching sinners and in "making holiness the savor of 'life unto life' to very many imperfect believers." When it began, the *Guide* had a monthly circulation of 3,000, by the beginning of the Civil War, a circulation of 15,300 in the United States and abroad, and by 1870, a circulation of 37,000, showing something of the appeal of holiness revivalism.[3] The *Guide* is of particular interest in establishing the ongoing legacy of the figures of Madame Guyon and Fénelon. Thomas Cogswell Upham, their key interpreter to the holiness movement, began to publish in the *Guide* in 1840 after he himself had come to claim the experience of sanctification.

Until this point in our narrative, I have relied on the language of the religions of the heart—of piety and of Pietism—to describe the tradition and broad community of believers in which the readership of the Quietists was placed. But the language of experimental theology, because Upham placed the Quietists in the camp of experimental holiness, is at this point more useful in understanding why adherents of Wesleyan perfectionism in America could claim Madame Guyon and Fénelon as one of their own. Some examples of the language of experimental religion and of the experimental knowledge of God are important in understanding where the "holiness people" fit in the history of Christian piety and the epistemological issues related to it.

"The Inward and Experimental Knowledge of God in the Soul"

When the first English translation of Madame Guyon's *A Short and Easy Method of Prayer* appeared in 1704, a preface for the English reader was affixed that set forth an explanation of the importance of "internal prayer." The author of the preface defended the type of prayer practiced and promoted by Madame Guyon in terms of its theology and its effect. In fact, the "effect" or experiential result of such prayer was synonymous with its "doctrine."

> For want of the right Understanding of *Internal Prayer*, Men have generally conceived very preposterous Notions of it, and of the *Doctrine* which chiefly recommends it; tho' in Effect this last is nothing else but the Inward and Experimental Knowledge of God in the Soul, the Practical Doctrine of Mortification and the New Birth, the real Participation of the Divine Nature, and an entire Conformity to the Spirit

and Life of *Jesus Christ*: in a Word, it is the Doctrine of pure and disinterested Love, raising the Soul to the living Contemplation of God,
and a vital Union with him, so far as is attainable in this moral State;
which is the very End and Design, the Substance and Accomplishment
of the Christian Religion.[4]

The doctrinal basis of interior prayer is solid, the writer maintains; God is
"pure Spirit," invisible in nature, so that it is "just and reasonable" that a
man [sic] should search within "his Interiour" to come into possession of
good and spiritual things. As a result of the fall, the impediments must be
removed that make it impossible for individuals to let God abide in them.

> The inmost Centre of our hearts was design'd to be the place of his
> Abode, the Temple of his Holiness, and the Habitation of his Peace;
> Now the peculiar End and Tendency of this Doctrine is, to point to this
> Centre, to introduce all into the inward Temple, and to teach us how to
> worship in the Holy Place; [. . .] that our Hearts being enflamed with
> the Divine Fire of *Love*, our whole Being may be purified, enlightened
> and transform'd into the Living Image of *Jesus Christ*.[5]

The key to this interior life that transforms the soul is "the entire Surrender of the whole Being to God" and continual attention of the heart
to the divine presence. The growth and progress of the soul occur as the
spirit of Jesus becomes "the Principle of its Life, the Spring of its Motions
and Actions."[6] Because the prayer that characterizes the interior way is
one of the heart, not the head, and is the "internal Exercise of Love,"
all persons of all classes can perform it at all times.[7] If those who have
pastoral responsibilities trained people in "internal prayer," it would put
an end to religious controversy by leading to the discernment of truth,
apart from the practice and doctrine of a particular party. "'Tis true, this
Author is *Romanist*, but 'tis as true, that she is a Persecuted one; persecuted, I say, for *Truth and Righteousness sake*."[8]

This preface summarizes an essential component of the tradition of
the interior way as it passed from the Continent and England to America;
its doctrine, while derived from Scripture, was confirmed by experience.
The language of the "experimental" or experiential was commonplace. In
the preface to his 1772 edition of the autobiography of Madame Guyon,
James Gough, the anonymous editor/translator, defended her as a Catholic by referring to Thomas à Kempis, the author of the *Imitation of Christ*.
"What book of divinity, after the bible [sic], is now more in use among
Christians of all denominations, than that of *Thomas à Kempis*, who was a
strict member of the church of Rome? And what is the reason thereof, but

that his lines are found to be lively and experimental, edifying, and suiting the inward concern of every true christian?"[9] One other example from
Gough's collection of biographies of individuals "eminent in piety" illustrates how much value was placed on narratives of spiritual experience.
Commenting on a spiritual account by Poiret, the anonymous translater
notes, "I love to meet with such experimental relations [accounts] of the
Lord's mercies, in any language, as this of Peter Poiret, handed down to
us in the Latin."[10]

Experimental Knowledge and Religious Experience

In Latin, *experimentia* denoted "the process of trying, "trial," or "testing"
and then evolved to mean "knowledge gained by experience." These
meanings carried over into early English and French, coming to mean also
"practical demonstration" or knowledge gained by the observation of facts
or events. "Experience" also applied to the conscious awareness of being
affected by events. The mystic tradition made use of the word *experimentia*
to describe the inner operations of God within the soul with the ensuing
understanding of divine love and goodness.[11] But the meaning of "experience" and of "experimental" knowledge became much more complicated
in the sixteenth and seventeenth centuries with the advent of Baconian
science, the psychology of the self arising from spiritual self-awareness as
well as from Cartesianism, followed by the influence of John Locke's *Essay
on Human Understanding* in the eighteenth century. In both French and
English, the words "experience" and "experimental" became prevalent in
religious contexts. The *Oxford English Dictionary* cites the phrase "experimental divinity" in the context of spiritual knowledge as early as 1614. In
a letter to Madame de Chantal in 1607, François de Sales analyzed the
psychology of worry and then commented, "I feel myself consoled by this
experimental knowledge which God gives me of myself."[12] References to
"experimental knowledge" (*la science expérimentale*) can be found throughout the literature of seventeenth-century French spirituality.

Marie de l'Incarnation (Marie Guyart), one of the great mystics of the
period and a founder of the Ursuline convent in Quebec, made frequent
references to the realm of the experiential, using the verb *expérimenter* or the
adjective *expérimental*. In her autobiographical account of 1633, she speaks
of "experiencing" the diversity of God's grace in the variety of her interior
life. In citing the Song of Songs and her divine marriage with the Beloved,
she notes the insufficiency of language: "These sorts of favors must be felt
and experienced, not named and written down." Marie's autobiographical
account of 1654 continues the use of experimental language to describe the
highest forms of mystical union and apostolic vocation; at the same time,

she notes the insufficiency of the language of the senses to describe what is essentially totally spiritual: "The soul experiences (*expérimente*) continuously the gracious movement which in spiritual marriage has taken possession of her and burns and consumes her with such a gracious and sweet fire that it is not possible to describe it." One can only sing a "continual epithalamium" in response; "books and studiousness cannot teach this language which is entirely celestial and divine."[13]

The seventeenth century in France saw the rise of both a theology based on the evidence of historical documents (the Bible, the church fathers, and ecclesiastical history) and a mystical theology based on the documents of experience (biography and autobiography). In this second tradition, certain accounts, such as those of Theresa of Avila, attained quasi-canonical status. This recourse to experience was new and highly individualized and was a response to charges of illusion. Yet, it was self-referential. The thrust of this tradition was to emphasize a psychology of the will, and it was not until the end of the century, as mystical fervor faded and Cartesian rationalism began to dominate discourse, that "experience" began to be equated with religious feeling.[14]

When Madame Guyon came under scrutiny for her Quietist beliefs late in the century, she exchanged letters in the fall of 1693 with Bossuet after she had been interviewed by him. The issue discussed in these letters was the validity of her experience of "silent communication." For Bossuet, the issue was ontological; the experience of special acts of God's grace could not be subject to a method or to scientific verification. (In this sense, Bossuet was "modern," although he labeled Quietism a new or modern form of mysticism.) Madame Guyon, on the other hand, claimed experience as a validation in and of itself.[15] In observing these two conflicting mind-sets, one finds it difficult to determine to what extent the appeals to theological and scriptural tradition were also articulated against cultural commonplaces derived from Baconian science of experimental truth or from Cartesian reason. Madame Guyon wrote to Bossuet that the question of "silent interior communication" was easy to settle because of "the large number of persons of merit and of honesty who had experienced it."[16] She contrasts the active and contemplative ways of Martha and Mary, as well: "This truth is not that of simple speculation like many others; it is from experience. How I wish for you, Monsignor, this happy experience, that renders bitterness sweet, that changes grief into felicity, that makes the miserable happy, that teaches that the only solid pleasure lies in the loss of everything that men of little enlightenment call by that name."[17]

Bossuet, on the other hand, wrote to someone else during the same period that the "new spirituals" were creating jargon and speaking too much about passivity. He went on to say that these "spirituals" were creating "many rules from experience or *raisonnement*, but neither our experience, no more than that of persons whom we know, makes the ways of God, nor do our reasonings make his law." Bossuet then goes on to reject the state of permanent union on logical terms: "If one had complete and absolute permanence, one would have eternity."[18]

When her formal examination at Issy occurred, Madame Guyon gave a clear statement of the epistemological status of experiential knowledge in the *Justifications* by placing the criterion of experience within established church tradition. Section 19 was entitled "Experience. Intelligence [Knowledge or Understanding]" and constituted her response to those who questioned whether the inner way of silent contemplation could lead to the knowledge of God: "Let them have the experience themselves and they will see that what we have told them of it is little in comparison to what it is. In these things, the intelligence understands only as much as experience has attained." She then cites Thomas Aquinas' well-known commentary on Psalm 34:8 ("O taste and see that the Lord is good") as the spiritual injunction to "taste" or "experience" the divine presence. The mystical literature was replete with the language of these senses to describe the experimental knowledge of the presence of God. Madame Guyon, for example, had spoken of the "experimental taste of the presence of God" as setting the stage for a more advanced form of interior prayer in the *Short and Easy Method*.[19] As the argument proceeds in the *Justifications*, it becomes apparent that spiritual understanding and psychological certainty are the results of the inner prayer of silence leading to union with God, but only those who share the experience understand this: "Two effects are assigned to experience, one is a certainty of understanding; the other is an assurance of affection."[20]

The emphasis on conversion and then on Christian growth in German Pietism as it responded to the intellectualism of Lutheranism paralleled these themes in Madame Guyon. Although faith was always seen as a gift of God, the assurance of conversion and then its transforming effects were special emphases among the Pietists and their forerunners. *True Christianity* (1605–1610) by Johann Arndt, the precursor of German Pietism as it is commonly understood, had the widest circulation of any book within Protestantism apart from the Bible and became a classic of Christian devotional literature. In fact, an edition printed in Philadelphia in 1751 was the first book in German to be printed in America.[21] Arndt's influence, however, was not limited to readers within the Lutheran, Pietist, and Puritan traditions; John Wesley included extracts from *True Christianity* in volumes one and two of his *Christian Library*, and even

The Guide to Christian Perfection included a few extracts from Arndt with the comment that "the work is very favorable to the doctrine of present sanctification."[22]

In his preface, Arndt defines true Christianity as "the Demonstration of a true, lively, and practical Faith, manifesting and exerting its Life and Energy by unfeigned Godliness, and suitable Fruits of Righteousness." He calls his treatise a "piece of Practical Christianity" and sets this lively faith in opposition of the "notional and speculative Science" of divinity. This Christianity is "a living Experience and practical Exercise of the Soul." At various places in his treatise, he repeats the imagery of the senses, drawn from the language of Psalm 34. For example, in commenting on the nature of faith as defined in Hebrews 11, Arndt notes that the phrase "substance of things hoped for" suggests "undoubted, solid, and firm Trust" and "a certain manifest and notable Conviction, Sensation, and Experience of such Things as are invisible."

> And so great and powerful indeed is the Consolation of a true living Faith in our Hearts, as it cannot but convince, by arguing most firmly and most solidly from Experience and from a great Taste of the sovereign Good in the Soul, from the Quietude of Heart, and from Peace in God: Whereby that Preservation remains most certain, and that Hope of Salvation unshaken, which a Christian Man doubt not even to seal with his very Life.[23]

"Two Sorts of Knowledge"—The Puritan Tradition and Jonathan Edwards

If Arndt's *True Christianity* continued to be widely read in the eighteenth century, so was the Bishop of Bangor Lewis Bayly's *The Practise of Piety* (1605), a key to Puritan spirituality, a parallel movement to the various manifestations of religion of the heart to which Quietism was tied. Puritan spirituality also emphasized conversion and the practical effects of salvation. However, its Calvinist-Augustinian accent on human sinfulness, coupled with the theology of election, set it apart from many of these other movements of renewal. In their pilgrimage toward the Celestial city, self-examination played a prominent role among the disciplines practiced by Puritans. This introspection led to the preeminence of journals, autobiographies, and biographies; in this sense, experience was as important as in other heartfelt religious movements. However, reason tempered Puritan spirituality so that it was much more compatible with Ignatian practice (which Madame Guyon, for example, rejected) than some of the forms of inner revelation cultivated by other groups.[24]

John Bunyan (1628–1688) recounted his own "experience" (often as tortured self-examination) in his autobiography *Grace Abounding*. Interestingly, in chapter 2, he noted that in the extreme poverty of his early marriage, his wife still owned two books that her father had left her when he died: *The Plain Man's Pathway to Heaven* and (Bayly's) *The Practice of Piety*.

In Bunyan's *Pilgrim's Progress*, the fifth stage of the journey brings Christian and Faithful face to face with Talkative, a character who loves to speak about spiritual topics but who is without true faith. As the two pilgrims converse with Talkative, Christian, who has previously known Talkative, tries to get his companion to understand the nature of Talkative's discourse. "Heavenly knowledge" is a gift of grace, and religion has no place in Talkative's heart. "His house is as empty of religion as the white of an egg is of savor," writes Bunyan. "There is there neither prayer, nor sign of repentance for sin; yea, the brute, in his kind, serves God far better than he." Talkative's life just does not bear out what he says: "The soul of religion is the practical part." Christian then encourages Faithful to confront Talkative with the truth. Faithful explains the difference between two types of knowledge—"knowledge that resteth in the bare speculation of things, and knowledge that is accompanied with the grace of faith and love, which puts a man doing even the will of God from the heart."[25] A "work of grace" reveals itself to the individual through the conviction of sin or "by an experimental confession of his faith in Christ" and "a life answerable to that confession: to wit, a life of holiness—heart holiness, family holiness [. . .] and by conversation holiness in the world."[26] Talkative is embarrassed by such questions of "experience" and "conscience" and departs, accusing Faithful of being a "peevish or melancholy man."[27]

Later in the journey, after the martyr's death of Faithful, Hopeful succeeds him as Christian's companion, and Hopeful readily recounts the story of the beginning of his own journey "to look after the good of [his] soul" and his conversion after Faithful had explained the way. Hopeful had repeatedly prayed for forgiveness until "the Father showed [him] his Son." "I did not see him with my bodily eyes," he says, "but with the eyes of my understanding, Eph. 1:18, 19; and thus it was."[28]

These issues of spiritual knowledge and experimental religion were to be addressed in America by Jonathan Edwards, who distinguished between speculative theological knowledge, the result of the understanding, and practical theological knowledge and "the sense of the heart," the result of the understanding and the will.[29] In one sense, Edwards fleshes out the Puritan emphases of the much-read *The Practice of Piety* by Lewis Bayly, for whom knowing and glorifying God were the essence of godliness. Bayly's work went through sixty editions in the seventeenth century and, like Bunyan and the metaphor of the pilgrimage, played an important role in New England Puritan devotional practice.[30] Bayly prefaced his guide to piety with a schematic representation showing that the knowledge of God consists in understanding the nature of the trinity and its attributes. Knowledge is also of the self, its corruption and its "renovation." But this knowledge also leads to a life glorifying God in private and in public, including extraordinary means such as fasting and feasting, then in death, through dying in and for the Lord.[31]

Edwards, on the other hand, broached the issue of spiritual knowledge out of a broad intellectual background; for example, he not only had read Fénelon but also Locke's *Essay on Human Understanding* at Yale. Edwards was interested in Newtonian science, as well as in the Cambridge Platonists, not to mention Calvinist theology as opposed to Arminianism. Like Arndt and many others, Edwards distinguished between speculative theology and practical theology, "the sense of the heart."[32] The phraseology "sense of the heart" came not only from Edwards' intellectual interests but also from his own inner experience after his conversion around 1721. In his "Personal Narrative" he wrote of his first sense of "that sort of inward, sweet delight in God and divine things that I have lived much in since" when he read 1 Timothy 1:17: "There came into my soul, and was as it were diffused through it, a sense of the glory of the Divine Being; a new sense, quite different from any thing I ever experienced before."[33]

In the 1720s, before the first Great Awakening, Edwards wrote two texts that he delivered as sermons in which he analyzed systematically the nature of spiritual understanding and praxis in the context of an exposition of Scripture. "A Spiritual Understanding of Divine Things Denied to the Unregenerate" was a sermon based on 1 Corinthians 2:14. Like Bunyan's fictional characters Christian and Faithful, Edwards discusses two kinds of knowledge: "Natural men may obtain a large notional knowledge and understanding of the doctrine of divinity. They may be very well [versed] in theology, and may have read abundance of books which treat of divinity with much learning and great strength of reason." Natural men may be able to discuss and argue religious issues and be very orthodox in their "notional knowledge," but they do not have spiritual understanding.

> This spiritual knowledge of divine things consists in a certain clear apprehension and a lively infixed sensibleness of them that the godly have, which wicked men are destitute of. Men may have a great deal of notional knowledge about things, and yet not have a lively and sensible idea of them. [. . .] The eyes of believers are opened, they do as it were see divine things. There is a certain intenseness and sensibleness in their apprehension of [them], a certain seeing and feeling.

Edwards combines the experiential or sensory quality of knowing with his idealism. Knowledge of a thing is in proportion not only to the "extensiveness of our notions" and the "number of circumstances known" but also "chiefly in the intensiveness of the idea." Spiritual illumination is like tasting or smelling, and Edwards cites the Song of Songs. This "spiritual light" consists of three aspects: first, "'tis a sight of the truth and reality of spiritual things"; second, it is "the knowledge of the excellency of divine things"; third, "it is the experimental knowledge of the saving operations of God's Spirit."[34] Spiritual knowledge complements natural understanding, but it is transformative because it changes the heart, purifies one's life, results in joy, and induces humility.

In the context of the hermeneutics of the spiritual reading of Scripture and of devotional literature, Edwards' comments are of particular interest. Spiritual knowledge affects the reading process because transformed readers, as opposed to intellectually knowledgeable readers, recognize within the text their own experience.

> The godly, having this experimental knowledge, it wonderfully enlightens to the understanding the gospel and the spiritual and true meaning of Scripture, because he finds the same things in his own heart that he reads of. He knows how it is, because he feels it himself. And this makes that he reads, the Scripture and other spiritual books, with much more delight than otherwise he would do. This makes him delight much more in those discourses, books and sermons that are most spiritual, which others have the least relish of.[35]

Although spiritual knowledge is unavailable to the unregenerate heart, those who have experienced regeneration should seek it, for it is available to them. In this sense, Edwards is true to his Calvinist roots, for he includes "doctrinal knowledge" as something to strive after, a form of knowledge many adherents to "religion of the heart" would not have been encouraged to seek. Believers are to practice—that is, act—on the level of their knowledge of God, and to seek more knowledge through Scripture, meditation, hearing the word, and prayer. These are the means to "improvement," according to Edwards, but are what Pietists might have called "sanctification."

A later sermon, "Profitable Hearers of the Word" (dating from 1728 to 1729), was based on the parable of the sower in Matthew 13 and developed the themes of the earlier text. Edwards emphasizes the nature of the understanding as the faculty of spiritual knowledge and its fruitfulness. This understanding is two-fold, involving "a sensible apprehension" of what is revealed in Scripture and the "judgment" that Scripture is true.

In this approach, Edwards is post-Lockean, and in this particular text he expands the hermeneutic of experience suggested in the earlier sermon. In contrast to the unregenerate, the godly "apprehend" the glory of God, the nature of Christ, the means of salvation, and the nature of duty as revealed in Scripture. Further, "they have the experimental knowledge of the nature of that holiness which is recommended and required by the Word." A person who has not experienced holiness of heart through the influence of God's spirit is like a blind person who cannot conceive of colors. In other words, experience leads to the understanding and application of doctrine: "The godly have experience, and therefore know what it is: they know what the several graces of the Spirit are, they know what faith is, they know what divine love is, they know what repentance is and what spiritual joy is. And therefore when they read or hear of these things, they understand the Word."[36] Although "natural man" may become aware of his blindness and sinfulness through observing God's glory and revelation, only the godly can be fruitful or apply the word of God because they understand it. That fruitfulness is dependent upon obedience and conformity to the life of Christ, evident in internal and external evidence of God's grace.

Experimental Religion and "Baconian Style"

Although there is more to Edwards' argument than the preceding summary suggests, his emphasis on spiritual experience as the root to the understanding of God's Word constitutes an important boundary for an experimental theology.[37] Edwards' mature thought could be explored in this respect, but these two early sermons demonstrate how "the experimental" had become part of the mind-set of the post-Lockean world. Sarah Pierpont Edwards' ecstatic spiritual experience in 1742 during the Great Awakening added depth to Edwards' testing of the legitimacy of unusual spiritual experience versus mere enthusiasm. Her narrative described a period when her husband was absent from the home and another minister was visiting, during which she carried out her normal household responsibilities while going through an intense religious experience. The experience was marked by physical symptoms, but seems to have been a state of continuous union with God. Sarah Edwards experienced a complete "resignation" of her will to God, an acceptance of her willingness to die or live as God willed, and a sublime love of God and fellow human beings, marked by an acceptance and a refusal to judge them.

> [. . .] I felt a love to all mankind, wholly peculiar in its strength and sweetness, far beyond all that I had ever felt before. The power of that

love seemed to be inexpressible. I thought, if I were surrounded by enemies, who were venting their malice and cruelty upon me, in torment-
ing me, it would still be impossible that I should cherish any feelings
towards them but those of love, and pity and ardent desires for their
happiness. At the same time I thought, if I were cast off by my nearest
and dearest friends, and if the feelings and conduct of my husband were
to be changed from tenderness and affection, to extreme hatred and
cruelty, and that every day, I could so rest in God, that it would not
touch my heart, or diminish my happiness. I could still go on with alac-
rity in the performance of every act of duty, and my happiness remain
undiminished and entire.[38]

Edwards had asked his wife to write down the narrative and then, without
naming her, summarized it in *Some Thoughts Concerning the Present Revival of
Religion*. From this instance and others he observed, in good Baconian fashion
and with the support of Scripture, he drew conclusions about their validity.

The great affections and high transports that others have lately been
under, are in general of the same kind with those in the instance that
has been given, though not to so high a degree, and many of them, not
so pure and unmixed, and so well regulated. I have had opportunity to
observe many instances here and elsewhere; and though there are some
instances of great affections in which there has been a great mixture of
nature with grace, and in some a sad degenerating of religious affections; yet there is that uniformity observable, that 'tis easy to be seen
that in general 'tis the same spirit from whence the work in all parts of
the land has originated.[39]

Edwards' *Treatise Concerning Religious Affections* (1746) underscored
the importance of experience in spiritual understanding and the inclinations of the will or heart, but he cautioned that the claim of experience
alone was not a sign of the regenerate heart; it had to be accompanied by
the signs of consistent outward piety.

[. . .] If we see a man, who in the course of his life, seems to follow and
imitate Christ, and greatly to exert and deny himself for the honor of
Christ and to promote his kingdom and interest in the world; reason
teaches that this is an evidence of love to Christ, more to be depended
on, than if a man only says he has love to Christ, and tells of the inward
experiences he has had of love to him, what strong love he felt, and how
his heart was drawn out in love at such and such a time, when it may
be there appears but little imitation of Christ in his behavior, and he
seems backward to do any great matter for him, or to put himself out of

the way for the promoting of his kingdom, but seems to be apt to excuse himself, whenever he is called to deny himself for Christ.

Edwards continues with other examples of claims to experience that are at odds with the evidence of the individual's actual life. In the tradition of Bunyan's description of "Talkative," Edward concludes that "words are cheap" when based on "passing affections." "Christian practice is a costly laborious thing," he says. "The self-denial that is required of Christians, and the narrowness of the way that leads to life, don't consist in words, but in practice. Hypocrites may much more easily be brought to talk like saints, than to act like saints."[40] The assumptions behind Edwards' method of argumentation here are interesting; he is using Baconian inductive reasoning, reaching conclusions by "experimentally" positing examples of discrepancies between claims of spiritual experience and actual Christian practice.

Although I have emphasized the vocabulary of mysticism and of post-Lockean thinking in parts of the preceding discussion, this example of argumentation raises the question of the degree to which Baconian "experimental philosophy" colored the discourse about "experimental religion" from the seventeenth through the nineteenth centuries. Baconian science was connected with the moderns (versus the ancients), progress, and reform, as well as the method of inductive reasoning based on the experimental data of sense experience.[41] Nevertheless, the tradition of experimental religion that I have been tracing, with its emphasis on inner experience and spiritual knowledge, is distinct from the external sense data of Baconianism, but the proofs of inner experience were seen as certain. John Newton, the hymnist and curate of Olney, used a striking image to describe this inner certainty in a letter of 1756: "My own experiences are as good as mathematical demonstrations to me."[42]

Nineteenth-century American usage of the adjective "experimental" would reflect a fusion of these two traditions: that of the certain knowledge of inner experience and that of reasonable truth gained through evidence. But the tradition of spiritual, experimental knowledge and understanding, of which Madame Guyon and Fenelon are major examples, represents a distinct, continuous strain within American religious thinking that has not been fully described by historians of theology and religion; the latter have emphasized the reformulation of Baconian thought by Scottish common-sense philosophers such as Thomas Reid, who then influenced American theology in a relatively continuous way from the early Republic to the period of Fundamentalism in the early twentieth century. Mark Noll has noted three types of "intellectual commonplaces" in this tradition: intuitive ethical common sense, the reliability of direct sense impressions in epistemological matters, and the reliability of inductive reasoning in arriving at truth based on experience. The Bible was viewed as an acceptable source of moral truths about the created world. As the nineteenth century wore on, theologians looked for rational evidence of Christian revelation.[43]

Crisis Experiences

The First Great Awakening, beginning in the 1730s, followed slightly later by the Methodist movement in England, would raise the issue of "experience" in the context of emotion and enthusiasm. John Wesley opted for a balanced approach of Scripture, tradition, common sense, and experience to avoid extremism, and it has been argued that Locke, via Peter Browne, had a significant influence on his thinking. One can maintain as well that the Puritan and Pietist traditions went hand in hand with Lockean experience (and even with Wesley's reading of Edwards' *Religious Affections*, which was extracted in *A Christian Library*). The inner assurance of the experience of conversion was experiential, with evidence of change within the individual, but the biographies of other believers confirmed the validity of that experience. Wesley regularly included autobiographical or biographical articles in the *Arminian Magazine*, in addition to the extracts on spirituality and spiritual lives in his *Christan Library*.[44]

In nineteenth-century America, the issue of religious experience and its relation to theology took on significance in the wake of the Second Great Awakening and the ensuing tradition of camp meetings, dating from about 1800, and then the ongoing revivals emphasizing holiness that occurred during the 1830s and continued until and after the Civil War.[45] The camp meeting movement of the early part of the century played a crucial role in the reformulation of experimental knowledge as a crisis experience, a dramatic turning point. In popular Christianity, the crisis experience initially was that of conversion, confession, and repentance, often accompanied by great emotionalism, in the context of camp meetings or revivals. David Watson has commented on the emotional nature of these camp meeting conversions.

> The atmosphere of the camp meeting was to set the tone for the revivalism of the nineteenth century. It retained the directness of the challenge to the sinner, and the necessity of an inruption of divine grace upon the human will; but the focus was on the experience of this inruption, rather than the change it wrought per se. The new birth was now something to be measured by the intensity and impact of its manifestation in the convert. Leaping, shouting and convulsive jerking were normative, and Methodist leaders, such as Francis Asbury, Peter Cartwright and William McKendree, who endorsed camp meetings to the point where

they became identified as a Methodist institution, found themselves on the crest of a wave of emotional expression which was highly evocative of scenes of Wesley's early outdoor preaching, and which sometimes were difficult to control.[46]

By the late 1820s experimental religion had come to be identified in the American popular imagination both with emotionalism and with a theology of experience, centering on conversion.[47] As early as 1825 Charles G. Finney was having a significant impact in the Northeast through his use of revival techniques. The American Unitarian Association published a tract in 1827 attacking what it viewed as the perversion of the term "experimental religion," and the tract is clearly a response to early revivalism. "Many talk and write about experimental religion, as if it were a mysterious, unintelligible process or possession, the badge to be worn by those few only, who are the special favorites of heaven."

> What they understand by experimental religion seems to be a certain tangible object, which is to be seized or acquired altogether, or else nothing is gained; it is the result of a peculiar call of God, comes from influences entirely supernatural, and is in fact a sort of miraculous power, which enables them, and them only, to step at once out of darkness into light, to leave what is termed the world, and join what is termed the company of the saints. Hence they sometimes speak of getting religion and losing religion, as they would speak of getting or losing property, as if it were an outward possession, and not a temper of mind and heart; [. . .] as if it were a kind of charter for heaven, put into their hands they know not how nor whence, and insuring to them by one stirring process the benefits of salvation.[48]

The writer of the tract sets out to redefine experimental religion, contrasting the "experimental" and the "theoretical." It is "that thorough vital religion, which is planted in the heart, and sanctifies the thoughts, the purposes and the life" in opposition to the speculative and boastful.[49] Experimental religion is also based on a "sense of *personal interest* in the subject" in which the rational truths of Christianity are appropriated by the individual: "Does the voice of nature and of revelation teach us that there is a God, an Infinite Spirit, who rules all worlds? Then let each one say—this God is *my* Father, *my* Creator, *my* Governor, and will be *my* Judge."[50] Finally, the ultimate test of "acquaintance with the spirit of Christianity" is that it becomes "a governing *principle of life and conduct.*"

> We are free to confess, that the only experimental religion, which we deem valuable, is that which consists in being good and doing good on

> Christian principles and with Christian motives,—and not that, which
> consists only or mainly in certain floating feelings and mysterious trans-
> actions between God and the soul.[51]

The writer goes on to attack the necessity of a crisis experience; genuine
experimental religion "is not acquired or finished by one effort or by one
process."

> It does not come at a particular moment, like the sudden arrival of a
> stranger, who merely takes up his abode with us, without feeling any
> interest in our every day business and pursuits; it is rather an unreserved
> and familiar friend, whose intimacy grows every day more close in our
> every day business and pursuits.[52]

The means for acquiring experimental religion are not ecstatic but
involve the study of Scripture and the reading of books and prayer, following the example of teachers, and moral improvement; everyone's experience of religion is different and cannot be cast into a single pattern.
Experimental religion is situated in the heart and makes a difference in
one's life. Although this particular tract is an attack on expressions of religious enthusiasm, particularly the equation of religion with conversion,
the writer has adopted the language of piety and morality of the tradition
of religion of the heart while rejecting a theology of regeneration or transformation through the Holy Spirit.

Christian Perfection and the Holiness Movement

Experimental religion as a theology of crisis experience included not
only conversion but also sanctification by the 1830s and 1840s when, as
noted earlier, holiness (or sanctification or Christian perfection) became
a theme of personal renewal and revival. The yearning for this spiritual
state coincided with broader cultural aspirations for premillennial reform
and utopian dreams. "Sanctification" was not a new theological term; it
existed in several traditions to designate the process of spiritual growth by
which the individual believer, in both character and action, was increasingly in conformity with the model of Christ. John Wesley had emphasized the necessity of "going on to perfection," of which the proofs were
pure love and pure intent (for example, in his *Plain Account of Christian
Perfection*). These evidences were the result of the work of the Holy Spirit,
the obedience of the individual Christian and his or her participation
in the disciplines of the spiritual life. Wesley himself experienced sanctification as a process, but for many of his followers this was a distinct
crisis experience, subsequent to justification, and Wesley accepted this

possibility. Up through the Civil War, American Methodism, influenced by John Fletcher and Adam Clarke, claimed Christian perfection as normative, a crisis experience witnessed to by the Holy Spirit subsequent to justification, characterized by a cleansing of the "bent" toward sinning and complete obedience to the divine will. In his *Letters to Young Ministers of the Gospel*, Nathan Bangs recommended theologians such as Clarke who believed in perfectionism, and by 1825, Timothy Merritt (who would found *The Guide to Christian Perfection*) had published *The Christian's Manual: A Treatise on Christian Perfection*, in which he maintained that "entire" sanctification was both progressive and instantaneous.[53]

One strand of this search for Christian perfection was represented by Oberlin revivalism and reformism under Charles Grandison Finney and Asa Mahan. As noted, Finney, although a lawyer and untrained as a theologian, went to Oberlin as a professor of theology. Viewing himself as a populist who preached biblical truth, Finney was seen in his own time as a follower of Edwards, but his theology evolved and represented a blend of New England Calvinism, both Old School and New. Unlike the Calvinist emphasis on election and the thoroughness of the fall, Finney's theology stressed the voluntary nature of sin and the freedom of the will. He was Baconian in his belief in reason and the rational evidence for Christianity.[54] Finney's conviction that Christian perfection was attainable in this life also marked him as a son of his time and not of Edwards. This brand of perfectionism marked a blend of social millennialism and revivalism, but with an emphasis on perfectionism as conformity of the individual will to God's will in complete obedience. Finney had already begun to lean toward perfectionism before going to Oberlin, but once there he found himself in the middle of the holiness revival movement. Mahan, president of the college, was more influenced by Wesleyan or Methodist perfectionism in its American form than was Finney. The language of holiness at Oberlin was initially in the tradition of John Fletcher—that of a second blessing (or crisis experience), marked by a cleansing of the bent toward sinning.

A holiness revival broke out at Oberlin in 1836 after a student raised the question of whether sanctification was attainable in this life. Finney defined sanctification as a Christian's sense of "unbroken peace, and not come into condemnation, or have the feeling of condemnation or a consciousness of sin." The question and its aftermath were a "practical question," according to Finney.

> We had no theories on the subject, no philosophy to maintain, but simply took it up as a bible question. In this form it existed amongst us as an *experimental* truth, which we did not attempt to reduce to a theological

formula; nor did we attempt to explain its philosophy until years afterwards. But the discussion and settling of this question here was a great
blessing to us, and to a great number of our students [. . .].[55]

Finney has given his pragmatic, biblical, and Baconian slant to the "experimental knowledge" of holiness as an attainable state in this life, setting
this experiential knowledge over and against theological or speculative
formulations.

Phoebe Palmer (1807–1874) was an influential proponent of Christian perfection or sanctification as a second crisis experience subsequent
to conversion. A Methodist layperson and wife of a physician in New
York City, Palmer is an interesting example of the feminization of American religion in the mid-nineteenth century. A proponent of the role of
women as spiritual teachers, Palmer did not herself espouse the ordina-
tion of women, but she articulated a theology of equality in the spiritual
kingdom and the important role of women in promoting revivalism and
the cause of "holiness." She was a camp meeting and revival speaker in
both North America and England before and after the Civil War. Her
holiness ministry evolved in New York when she and her sister Sarah
Lankford began in 1835 to host a Tuesday Meeting for the Promotion
of Holiness in the Palmer home. These meetings were ecumenical and
were only for women until 1839 when Phebe Upham, the wife of Thomas
Upham, a professor at Bowdoin College, asked permission to bring her
husband. Upham would become the influential interpreter of Madame
Guyon and Fénelon to the holiness movement.[56]

Phoebe Palmer dated her entry into the experience of sanctification
to the year 1837; her theology of holiness had several distinct emphases.
Christian perfection is indeed attainable in this life; it entails a complete
surrender of the will to God—"laying all on the altar"—and the state of
holiness is maintained through complete obedience to God. The altar
metaphor was based on Abraham's willingness to sacrifice his son Isaac;
literally, the altar or mourners' bench played an important role in the
camp meetings of the period. Once the act of complete consecration is
accomplished in faith, the believer is entirely sanctified. Initially, a feeling of assurance, the kind of inner witness so important to Pietists and
to Wesley, was stressed to a lesser degree than the importance for the
believer to witness or testify to his or her act of surrender. Palmer was
influenced in her theology by John Fletcher and by the autobiography
of the eighteenth-century Methodist Hester Ann Rogers. In time, Palmer
also emphasized that sanctification is marked by a second blessing of the
Holy Spirit; this theme characterized her later camp meeting work and
was in part a response to criticism that her "altar theology" emphasized

too strongly the volitional act of the believer. For example, Nathan Bangs, the respected Methodist who frequented Palmer's Tuesday meetings, said at an 1857 meeting, "We must be sanctified, and have an evidence of [it] before we have any scriptural authority to believe it."[57]

Palmer's theology of holiness was also marked by "experimental" language. Her feminized account of the pilgrimage toward sanctification appeared first as articles and then in book format. (Parts of the book appeared in *The Guide to Holiness*.) *The Way of Holiness, with Notes by the Way; being A Narrative of Religious Experience resulting from a determination to be a Bible Christian* was published in 1843 and went through many printings. The second edition included prefatory commendations by Asa Mahan (a Congregationalist) from the *Oberlin Evangelist* and by L. L. Hamline (a Methodist) from the *Ladies' Repository*. Palmer had read Bunyan and makes an occasional direct reference to him, as in speaking of his Beulah. (Beulah land would become a theme in the gospel music of the holiness tradition.) The narrative, moreover, is filled with indirect references to the narrative framework of *Pilgrim's Progress*. Palmer also identifies herself overtly with the tradition of the Wesleys and of Fletcher, although her book was viewed at the time as crossing denominational lines.[58]

The initial sections of the account are written in a third-person female voice and define the way of holiness, addressing two issues, "Is There Not a Shorter Way?" and "There is but One Way?" Certainly, the theme of finding a shorter way to Christian perfection rather than a long, gradual process of growth situates the account in the context of American pragmatism or practicality, but one thinks as well of the literature of democratized spirituality such as Madame Guyon's *Short and Easy Method*, which makes interior prayer and even union with God available to all. The way to holiness is one of consecration, obedience, and faith. Once the act of consecration is complete, the state of sanctification is complete because faith indicates that God has accepted this act through this grace. The Holy Spirit bears witness to this second act of grace, but sanctification is contingent in that it depends upon continual obedience. The initial act of consecration and its acceptance by God is a kind of covenant that Phoebe Palmer describes in terms of its experiential effect.

> [. . .] A hallowed sense of consecration took possession of her soul; a divine conviction that the covenant was recognized in heaven, accompanied with the assurance that the seal, proclaiming her wholly the Lord's was set; while a consciousness, deep and abiding, that she had been but a co-worker with God in this matter, added still greater confirmation to her conceptions of the extent and permanency of those heaven-inspired exercises, by which a mighty work had been wrought in and for her soul,

which she felt assured would tell on her eternal destiny, even after myriads of ages had been spent in the eternal world.[59]

The language of experience is even clearer in Palmer's description of the witness of the Spirit to the truth of biblical promises.

> She felt in experimental verity that it was not in vain she had believed; her very experience seemed lost and swallowed up in God; she plunged, as it were, into an immeasurable ocean of love, light, and power, and realized that she was encompassed with the "favor of the Almighty as with a shield; and felt assured, while she continued thus, to rest her entire being on the faithfulness of God, she might confidently stand rejoicing in hope," and exultingly sing with the poet—
> "My steadfast soul from falling free,
> Shall now no longer rove,
> But Christ be all in all to me,
> And *all my soul be LOVE.*"[60]

The verse cited by Palmer is stanza 11 of a well-known hymn by Charles Wesley, "My God! I know, I feel thee mine."[61]

In addition to Palmer's emphasis on the contractual nature of entire consecration (God's grace and individual volition), two additional themes of her ministry are apparent in *The Way of Holiness.* One is the value of giving testimony and of hearing testimony as practical means to reinforce experimental truth as opposed to abstract thought.

> That which is learned by *experience* is much more deeply written upon the heart than what is learned by mere precept. By this painful process, the lessons of grace remain written in *living* characters upon the mind, and we are better able to tell to travelers coming after us, just how and where we met with this and the other difficulty, how we overcame, and the peculiar lessons learned by passing through *this* and *that* trial, and thus be not only advantaged in our experience, but helpful to our fellow-pilgrims.[62]

A second theme is Palmer's continuous reference to the Bible as the ultimate criterion for truth regardless of one's emotional state.

> I have been called, in the first place [. . .] to take the WORD OF THE LORD, to examine myself by its tests, and just so far as I have found its promises suited to my condition, just so far I have rested, most confidently, upon its truth. And having previously made the resolution that, if possessed of these tests, I would venture, whether my *feelings*

warranted the conclusion or not, [. . .] I have invariably found that, just so soon as I have made the venture, the foundation upon which I rested was as *firm as the pillars of eternity!*[63]

Palmer, then, held to a Baconian compromise something like that of Finney. Experimental truth was validated by Scripture and Scripture, in turn, validated experimental truth.

It is on the issue of Scripture that Palmer parted company with the Catholic mystical tradition we have been tracing. In a letter of 1851 to Thomas and Phebe Upham, she addressed this issue.

Surely, the excellency of a religious experience, is only to be tested by its conformity to the Word of God. It is, therefore, that I have long felt, a reservation, in receiving the experience of ancient Catholic writers. I do not wonder that some of our friends, who so evidently have been conforming their experiences to the modes given in these writings, instead of conforming them to the Bible, have missed the mark. One of the friends who have thus been spoiled, through vain philosophy, says, he does not know why we may not in our experience go beyond where the Saviour did when on earth. He also thinks that Paul was in a lower state of experience than some around us, who arrive at this high estate. Now, do you wonder that my heart is indeed sorrowful in view of these matters? Where will they end?[64]

Despite this rejection of the mystical tradition within Catholicism, Phoebe Palmer took over the language of the tradition of the interior way that had come down to her via Wesley and many others, but she sentimentalized it and gradually adapted it to the context of the second blessing of camp meeting enthusiasm. This language is particularly evident in her journal entries, some of which constitute the later sections of *The Way of Holiness.*

All the ardent desires of my soul are sweetly centered on God. I feel that I have not one desire apart from that which may promote his glory. He is my all in all. I enjoy a silent heaven of love. The beauty of holiness more and more captivates my enraptured soul.

    Spirit of holiness, continue to breathe upon me thy purifying, soul-transforming influences![65]

The themes of assurance, rest, quietude, and even of union also figure in this discourse of the experience of holiness and of Phoebe Palmer's own calling, but they are always framed by intertextual references to Scripture.

In reference to my future course, I wish to lie passive in the hands of the Lord, as an instrument to perform his pleasure in all things. My will is lost in the will of God. I would not—dare not choose for myself, though the choice were given. God is my all in all. I walk by faith, and am enabled to endure as *seeing* the Invisible, and my enjoyment consists in a calm, quiet resting on the promises of the gospel, assured that it is my Father's good pleasure to give me the kingdom.[66]

Writing that she feels a "blessed realization" that she "dwells in God," Palmer emphasizes the state of assurance of those who have entered the city of Zion on this side of death, a rest that surpasses language. This language of rest and assurance, although rooted in the hymns of Charles Wesley, reverberates with echoes of the entire tradition of the interior way; it was diffused, thematized, and sentimentalized in the music of nineteenth-century American piety. An example of this thematization is the well-known gospel song "Blessed Assurance," written and composed in 1873. Phoebe Palmer Knapp, the daughter of Phoebe Palmer, was the organist and choir director of the John Street Methodist Church in New York City, where the experience of the deeper Christian life was preached. She wrote the tune and took it to Fanny J. Crosby, the blind composer and poet who also knew the Palmers.[67] Crosby immediately wrote the words of the song, of which stanzas two and three are variations on many of the Quietist themes as they were expressed in an American context.

Perfect submission, perfect delight, / visions of rapture now burst on my sight; /
Angels descending bring from above / echoes of mercy, whispers of love. / [...]
Perfect submission, all is at rest; / I in my Savior am happy and blest, /
Watching and waiting, looking above, / filled with his goodness, lost in his love.[68]

Thomas Cogswell Upham (1799–1872)

A Congregationalist clergyman and son of a representative to Congress, Upham was Professor of Mental and Moral Philosophy at Bowdoin College in Maine from 1824 to 1867. He had studied at Dartmouth and at Andover Theological Seminary where he taught briefly; Upham also served a church in Rochester, New York, in 1823–1824 before going to Bowdoin.[69] Interest in sanctification was already evident in Maine, and Upham's wife Phebe came to the experience before her husband. She brought her husband to one of Palmer's Tuesday meetings and in 1839–1840, partially because of Palmer's tutelage, Thomas Upham experienced sanctification. It not only transformed his inner life, but also redirected the nature of his writing so that he would be responsible for the appropriation of Madame Guyon and of Fénelon by the nineteenth-century holiness movement.

Palmer always viewed herself as something of a spiritual mentor to the Uphams. She described how she interceded in prayer on Upham's behalf so that he would experience sanctification and saw that he, as a professor and a Congregationalist, could have a significant sphere of influence: "I saw that the Redeemer's kingdom needed an advocate in the denomination of Christians to which he belonged, in defence of this doctrine. Standing, as he did, with an important college, it was greatly desirable, that he should be a witness of its attainment." "While pleading for Professor Upham, I promised the Lord, if he would impart the blessing, I would, through grace, make it an especial subject of praise [. . .] and that, if the entire devotion of my life to his service were in any way possible, it should, as a ceaseless thank-offering, be rendered."[70] Yet, as Upham's influence within the holiness movement grew through his writings, Palmer not only expressed reservations about his interest in Catholic mysticism and divine union as a state subsequent to sanctification, but she also worried that theological and spiritual writings like his would supersede the Bible as the central text of believers. In describing the principles of the Tuesday meeting so that they could be replicated, she said that "Not Wesley, not Fletcher, not Finney, not Mahan, not Upham, but the Bible, the holy BIBLE, is the first and last, and in the midst always. The BIBLE is the standard, the groundwork, the platform, the creed. Here we stand on common ground, and nothing but the spirit of this blessed book will finally eradicate and extirpate a sectarian spirit."[71] Palmer's vision of the holiness movement embraced all denominations, but the doctrinal basis was a practical application of Scripture.

True to her pragmatic experimental theology, Palmer disseminated biographical testimonies to the experience of sanctification, and her respect for Upham was such that she included Upham's account (with the note that he was a congregationist) in the 1868 volume *Pioneer Experiences*. Upham recounts that he "experienced religion" in a revival at Dartmouth in 1815 but that he led the "common Christian life of sinning and repenting," in part because of the prevailing doctrine that sanctification is not complete until death. His own account of his experience of sanctification is more nuanced than that by Palmer. In 1839, he began "to examine the subject of holiness *as a matter of personal realization*" and concluded that God required him to be holy. In July, by an act of "simple volition" he "consecrated" himself to God "in body and spirit."[72] This "calm and unchangeable resolution of mind" was followed by two specific results: freedom from a sense of condemnation and an increased love of the Bible and sense that the Bible was to be his guide. Upham "found holiness everywhere" in Scripture and felt that he "began to love it."[73] In December, he frequented meetings of "pious" Methodists in New York, and through their instruction he learned that his act of consecration had put him in a position to exercise faith, a *"sanctifying instrumentality."* On Friday morning, December 27, Upham discovered that he, through faith, had undergone "a great moral revolution" of "abiding peace and consolation." Upon his return to Maine in mid-January, he began his own house meetings to promote "personal godliness," but he found that he still battled with self-love. In early February, after a struggle with his selfishness, which he deemed incompatible with "perfect love," he was able to claim the experience of sanctification. In mid-February, there were "some remarkable operations on [his] mind" which language could not fully detail. Upham implies he had a mystical experience by referring to Paul's description of his own special state as "'whether in the body or out of the body, I cannot tell.'"[74]

> So conscious have I been that inordinate self-love has been the great cause of the separation between my soul and God, that the very idea of self as distinct from God is almost painful to me. When self is destroyed, the divine union, which sanctified hearts only know, takes place. If I know any thing, I know most certainly that the true resting place of my soul is and must be in the infinite mind; that it is not and cannot be any where else. [. . .] Accordingly it is my earnest and constant prayer, that my will may be wholly and for ever lost in the will of God, and that I may never know self any more, except as the instrument of divine glory.[75]

Upham and the Quietist Tradition

The language of Upham's discussion of sanctification in the end is not that of Palmer. His testimony is replete with echoes of Catholic Quietism and of his own work in the psychology of the mind: the painfulness of the notion of self as distinct from God, the resting place of the soul in the infinite mind, divine union, and the individual will lost in the divine will. Although he uses the language of personal godliness, Christ as his own Savior, for instance, his description of the state of sanctification is generically mystic and Quietist. How did Upham move from the crisis experience of sanctification, as espoused by Palmer and other "pious Methodists," to the contextualization of this American experiential theology within the Catholic apophatic mystical tradition?

Upham was a serious academic who is recognized today as the author of the first American textbook in psychology, but this book was really a synthesis of the fields of epistemology and psychology from Locke, through French sensationalists and Scottish empiricists to Jonathan Edwards and Kant. *Elements of Intellectual Philosophy* was published in 1827 and went through fifty-seven editions. Upham maintained that the human mind was indivisible but characterized by "intricate and multiplied varieties of action" of the sensibilities, intellect, and will.[76] The importance of this book within American culture should not be underestimated. E. Brooks Holifield has indicated that "mental science" quickly influenced the direction of nineteenth-century American theology, placing Upham among those influencing the Baconian style of "evidential" Christianity. But if we see this work as a precursor to Upham's efforts to promote a deeper spirituality akin to that of continental Catholic mystics, we can agree with Darius Salter that his importance lay in developing a holiness theology of psychological restoration.[77]

Upham was serious in his pursuit of both a theory of the mind or self and of a satisfying experimental theology of personal holiness. In the 1830s, before his experience of sanctification, this pursuit seems to have absorbed him. In 1834, he published *A Philosophical and Practical Treatise on the Will*, of which the intellectual background ranged from Hobbes, Cudworth, and Baxter to Locke, Reid, and Edwards. He defined the will as "the mental power or susceptibility by which we put forth volitions."[78] After outlining the laws governing the will and the motives that drive volitions, Upham speaks of the potential conflict between personal and moral motives, "the fountain of sweet and of bitter waters, the basis of an internal hostility renewable every day and every hour."[79] This conflict seems to echo Upham's description of his own experience as a Christian before sanctification—a life of inner conflict, of sinning and repenting. On the other hand, the potential exists for the will to be free; that freedom is not an abstraction but can only be realized through the consciousness of consistent acts of volition. The basis of this freedom lies in "mental harmony," and the best example is the person and actions of Jesus, he says: "When each power performs its functions without any unavoidable perplexity existing in itself or infringement from some other source, we are then conscious of liberty in the highest sense of the term."[80] The power of the will is also linked to consistency of character, and this is particularly important in the "religious character." Upham's articulation of the principle of "mental harmony" as the basis for consistent action and character is a wonderful example of the wedding of his intellectual concerns with his own spiritual journey. He was ready to embrace sanctification as espoused by both the American holiness movement and Catholic Quietism.

Upham had been publishing poetry since 1819, and the 1836 edition of *American Cottage Life* shows that he was acquainted with the work of Madame Guyon. This poetry reflected popular Romantic taste. Upham idealized the "religious feeling" of the American farmer whose "consistency of life" had been honed by the reading of the Bible and by prayer. The forms included ballads, songs, hymns, and sonnets, often on religious themes. Madame Guyon's oft-translated poem about the caged bird that is free figured in the collection, along with other poems on Quietist themes such as the freedom that comes from doing the will of God, calm, and rest. The final lines of Upham's translation of the Guyon poem "A Little Bird I Am" go this way: "And in Thy mighty will to find / The joy, the freedom of the mind." Upham's own "The True Rest" also illustrates the parallel between his philosophy of the mind and Quietism.

'Tis not in vain the mind,
    By many a tempest driven,
Shall seek a resting-place to find,
    A calm like that of heaven.
The weak one and dismayed,
    Scarce knowing where to flee,
How happy, when he finds the aid,
    That comes alone from Thee.

In Thee, O god, is REST;—
    Rest from the world's desires,
From pride that agitates the breast,
    From passion's angry fires.

In Thee is rest from fear,
    That brings its strange alarm,
And sorrow, with its rising tear,
    Thou past the power to calm.[81]

The emerging Quietist themes of Upham's theory of the will and subsequently his poetry were echoed by his political ideas as a peace activist. In 1836 he published *The Manual of Peace* in which he maintained that Christians should view the agenda of a "pacific reformation" as equal to the temperance movement. He called for an end to capital punishment and the slave trade, among other evils, and advocated both international law and a congress of nations.[82]

Once Upham could claim as his own the experience of sanctification, the thrust of his writings turned to the interior life. In the 1840s he articulated an experimental theology that was really a psychology of the *state* of sanctification and then of divine union. He began to contribute articles to *The Guide to Christian Perfection* in July of 1840, and a series on the "Principles of the Interior Life" quickly ensued that became the book by that title, published in 1843, the year that Phoebe Palmer's largely auto-biographical *The Way of Holiness* appeared.[83] Upham's goal was to establish a ground for the assurance of sanctification in describing the relationship between faith and love. The third part of the book, "On Inward Divine Guidance," was afterward frequently published separately with a preface by Hannah Whithall Smith. One example was G. W. McCalla's 1887 printing. In her preface, she says that "no one need fear delusion or fanaticism who follows the teachings of this book, and neither can such fail to be led into a more intimate communion with [God]."[84] As indicated in chapter 1, Upham's description of divine guidance is grounded in Scripture, but also in his adaptation of Quietist spirituality. He makes very clear that guidance is by the Holy Ghost (a theological position not articulated by many of the mystics in whom he is interested). The possibility of divine guidance requires a state of receptiveness and cooperation with God and the person guided by the Holy Spirit acts in harmony with Scripture. Self-will is annihilated and God is "the great center" of the individual's being. Upham recommends the "state of inward recollection" as essential to the interior life.

> When it becomes the fixed habit of the soul, it not only restores God to the inward possession, and establishes him upon the throne of the intellect and heart, but, differing from that condition in which he comes in broken and fragmentary visits, it sustains him there essentially, without interruption, in what may be termed a continuance or perpetuity of presence. In a word, it is the devoutly and practically realized presence of God in the soul moment by moment. This is the state of mind which we cannot hesitate in saying all Christians ought to be in. It is hardly necessary to say that it is a scriptural state of mind.[85]

Basically, Upham is taking the principles of interior prayer, set forth by Quietists like Madame Guyon, and setting them forth as spiritual principles with a basis in both Scripture and the psychology of the self. Such a state of recollection requires a nondiscursive and nonpurposeful focus on the present that brings knowledge of divine will through the "still small voice" heard in the soul. It results in a state of rest or quietness to the soul and entails the complete submission of the will to that of God: "A person in this state of mind, being at rest in the will of God, and never out of that divine will, is operative precisely as God would have him so; moving as God moves, stopping where God stops. He is at rest, but never idle."[86]

In his treatise on the will, Upham held out the possibility that the conflicts within the divided self could indeed be overcome so that all the faculties—intellect, will, and sensibilities—could be in powerful harmony, as in the example of Jesus. Here, he cites Madame Guyon in her later life as just such a person who speaks of a simple inner state without "variations," one of annihilation of the self. Upham says that Madame Guyon's state is one of "perfect balance and harmony of the different parts of the mind. There may be deep feeling [. . .] but it is so perfectly controlled by a sense of union with the will of God, that the result is complete simplicity and rest of soul."[87] Upham also quotes Molinos to show that the state of inner annihilation involves no action of desiring, willing, or understanding apart from the will of God: "We seek ourselves every time we get out of our Nothing; and, therefore never get to quiet and perfect contemplation. Creep in, as far as ever thou canst, into the truth of thy Nothing."[88] Finally, Upham steps beyond the standard theology of sanctification to defend the "unitive state" or union with the divine as a special level of experience within the interior life that has been experienced by both Catholics and Protestants, entailing higher levels of consciousness.

The Move to Biography

With his book on the interior life, followed in 1845 by another on the life of faith, Upham the educator had produced clearly written primers that translated the tradition of a spirituality of inner holiness for an American reading public caught up in the perfectionist yearnings of the midcentury. But Upham was practical. His writings in no way encouraged the excesses of enthusiasm because his goal was to educate and teach the interior way to his readers. It was an easy transition for him to make the move to biography to illustrate the experimental theology he was espousing. He began with the life of Catharine Adorna, published in 1845. Catharine was a fifteenth-century aristocrat who was married to a worldly nobleman; she discovered the inner way of holiness, characterized by pure love, even in the midst of her duties as wife and mother. Upham is very clear in his introduction about the aim of this interpretive biography—to illustrate "the doctrine of holiness."

> It has been a matter of no small interest to me, to find individuals, living in different ages of the world, under different social systems, and in Christian denominations variant from each other in many particulars, who have illustrated in a happy manner the great outlines of the doctrine of holiness. Such instances tend to confirm the truth of the doctrine; they show the mighty power of the operations of the Holy Ghost on individual minds, and establish with new motives the great lesson

of Christian charity. If the doctrine of present sanctification is true, as I have no doubt that it is when rightly understood, those, who are the subjects of it, will always possess essentially the same image, though sometimes slightly modified by the circumstances under which they lived [. . .].[89]

In part, this biography was a response to the theological debate as to whether sanctification could be achieved during one's lifetime. Upham alludes to this debate in these comments and speaks to it at various points in the book, likening the discussion of sanctification to the debate over Quietism between Bossuet and Fénelon.[90] Thus, theological truth for him lies in the evidence—not only in Scripture, but in lived experience. In this stance, he is in line with the entire tradition of religion of the heart, but he gives expression to the particular slant of the Baconian style that we have seen in Finney and Palmer. Of pure love, as "a matter of inward consciousness," he comments that it "can be understood only by personal experience. He only, who has it, can fully understand what it is."[91] And here we see the logical impasse posed again and again within the tradition of the interior way; those without the special experience cannot understand it, and yet the experience itself is its own point of reference and its own proof.

In recounting Catharine's inner journey, Upham interprets the meaning of the turning points by referring to the sequence of his own experimental theology. At the age of 25, torn between the worldliness of her personal life and her spiritual yearning that she had been denying, she experienced a moment of illumination while confessing her inner state to a priest. Upham calls this moment "redemptive" as he quotes her as saying that she received knowledge in that moment that language could not express. Upham interpets this initial illumination as an act of consecration in which she "laid upon the divine altar both her inward and her outward powers."[92] The illumination was followed by the repression of the senses, prayer and fasting, and service to the sick so that Catharine became truly pious. Her consecration was accompanied by a true act of faith with the accompanying manifestations of inner quietude and pure love. In this way, she experienced sanctification. Initially, she withdrew from the world and led a secluded life to devote herself to attaining the knowledge of God through praying six hours a day. Eventually, after an extended period of temptation, she arrived at a state in which "all unsanctified desire ceased" and entered into divine union.[93]

Upham is not particularly successful as a biographer in this work because he uses few narrative details from Catharine's life and only selective quotations from her writings, employing this source material primarily as a springboard to expound his ideas of sanctification, its evidence, and divine union. He emphasizes Catharine's themes of pure love and the intellect as a means to a knowing of God that surpasses reason. "Defects of moral judgment arise from those selfish influences, which it is the effect of pure love to clear away," he says. "Let the heart be pure; in other words, let the mind, in its estimate of things, look at them in the light of God alone, and its decision, in relation to moral subjects, at least, can hardly fail to be correct. And if the sanctified mind sees clearly, it also feels deeply. It does not more clearly see the wrong, than it hates the performance of it."[94] Through Catharine, Upham seems to be responding to criticism of the doctrine of sanctification. He clarifies again the nature of rest and quietude, certainty and assurance, living in the moment and in recollection, surrender to the divine will and inner crucifixion, and the relationship between divine and human agency. Phoebe Palmer would express uneasiness about Upham's view of divine union, and here we can see why. Upham sees it as a state that is different from and subsequent to sanctification: "Union, in the experimental sense of the term, is not merely holiness, but is the holiness of the creature united with the holiness of God; [. . .] it is a state of mind which is characterized, perhaps more than in any other way, by the absence of [. . .] unsanctified desire, or desire which may be supposed to exist in the creature, separate from the will of God."[95]

In developing this exposition of his theology and psychology of holiness, Upham cites the tradition of writers, often labeled as mystics, who wrote out of "personal knowledge," setting the "religion of the heart" in opposition to "the theology of the head." These writers included John of the Cross, Suso, Canfield, Ruysbroeck, Tauler, Kempis, Harphius, and the author of the *Theologia Germanica*.[96] He mentions Antoinette Bourignon and Madame Guyon in relation to a life of prayer and faith, and he sees Catharine as embodying the doctrines of assurance, as articulated by Edwards, and of perfection of love, as taught by Fénelon and Wesley. These references show how Upham synthesized theological traditions, including Pierre Poiret's unique blend of mysticism and piety. Poiret's biography, with illustrations from Catharine's writings, was a major source used by Upham. He adopted Poiret's method of the interpretive reordering of Madame Adorna's writings into a theology of pure love, pushing this approach even farther in his next project on Madame Guyon and Fénelon.[97]

The Life and Religious Experience and Opinions of Madame de La Mothe Guyon: Together with some account of the personal history and religious opinions of Fenelon, Archbishop of Cambray, in two volumes, was copyrighted in 1846 and went through thirty-seven editions, not counting translations, abridgments, and borrowings. Why was this work so successful? In part, the success was because of the mythic tradition already surrounding the two figures. In part, it was due to Upham's reputation. This time Upham's use of the form of the interpretive biography was more polished and included extensive use of the writings of Madame Guyon and Fénelon. The success of the work also reflected the quest for holiness that permeated pre- and post-Civil War America. In the book Upham plays an active part as narrator and interpreter, recounting the events of Madame Guyon's life up to her departure from Grenoble for Paris in 1686 in volume 1. In volume 2, he recounts her life until the release from the Bastille in 1702, while also introducing Fénelon, his relationship to Madame Guyon, and the doctrinal controversies with Bossuet. In both volumes, Upham summarizes and quotes from the major works of each protagonist, but he paraphrases and rephrases their thoughts and ideas.

Upham is clear about his method. He has tried to convey the "sentiment" rather than the "precise mode of expression" of Madame Guyon's writings and he has also given an "*interpreted* translation" of the "spirit" of the original, rather than the literal meaning. Sometimes he has used "the judicious translation which Mr. Brooke has made of a portion of her Life, and of the work entitled 'A Short Method of Prayer.'" Upham notes that this translation of the Guyon autobiography was published anonymously along with the treatise on prayer translated by Brooke, but he thinks that Brooke was responsible for the translation and edition of Guyon's life.[98] Upham actually was relying on a reprinting of the Gough translation that had been published anonymously in one volume with the Brooke version of the method of prayer in Dublin in 1775. He also had read in French Poiret's editions of Madame Guyon's works as well as the works of Fénelon and Bossuet and major biographies, including Ramsay's account of Fénelon and Guyon.

In both volumes, Upham makes ample use of Madame Guyon's poetry, again freely contextualizing the stanzas in question to illustrate her spiritual state, her feelings (for example, upon incarceration), or her beliefs or doctrine. In addition to occasional stanzas that are cited in the text, twenty-two poems or sequences of stanzas are reproduced, usually at the end of a chapter. Sometimes the sources of the translations are identified as coming from editions—the anonymous life (Gough), poems edited by "Churchill," or Cowper's translation; some are by Upham or by Cowper, but without attribution.

One example will suffice to describe Upham's use of poetry to illustrate the spiritual and psychological state of Madame Guyon. In the summer of 1681, she embarked on her trip to Savoy, where she felt her vocation lay. She had been in Paris and then, probably in July, accompanied by her young daughter, she embarked on the Seine River at the start of her spiritual adventure. Upham comments that both the autobiography and poetry reflect her state of mind. "No person but a Christian of confirmed and thorough piety could have written [the stanzas]. Poetry is the *heart expressed.* [. . .] The poetry of Madame Guyon, whatever defects may be thought to attach to it in some respects, has the merit of expressing precisely what she *was,* and what she *felt.*" Upham then quotes, without identifying the source this time, Cowper's translation "The Soul That Loves God Finds Him Everywhere," but under the title "God Everywhere to the Soul That Loves Him." The lines "To me remains nor place nor time; / My country is in every clime; / I can be calm and free from care / On any shore, since God is there" (a stanza that Upham italicizes) are represented as a transcription of Madame Guyon's spiritual and psychological state as she leaves Paris. The reader enters into her mind and heart through the poetry.[99]

Like Madame Adorna, Madame Guyon becomes an example of experimental theology in Upham's hands. The interpretive biographies and selective translations by Poiret and Gough seem to have given him license to appropriate Guyon's experience into a Protestant format. After all, Gough had defended Madame Guyon as a Catholic by presenting her discovery of interior or contemplative prayer as a "conversion" experience, and Poiret had spelled out for Protestants the entire tradition of pure love and apophatic mysticism with which they could identify. Upham goes as far as calling Madame Guyon and Fénelon Protestants; thus nineteenth-century American readers were entirely comfortable with these two seventeenth-century Catholics whose religious experience was apparently so like their own.

Later commentators felt differently. Thomas Taylor Allen, a member of the British civil service in Bengal, translated the entire autobiography at the end of the century and called the Upham version of the life "defective and misleading." For Allen, Guyon embodied the universal spirit of the Savior, and her autobiography was intuitive, a "spontaneous overflow from the heart." Upham had bound "her catholic spirit" in "the grave clothes of so-called Evangelical dogma."[100] In the twentieth century, Ronald Knox claimed that the "trick" of Upham's approach was "to substitute, at every turn, the jargon of Evangelical piety for the Quietist jargon in which Madame Guyon wrote. [. . .] The only shred of excuse that can be devised for this habit of laying Protestant eggs in the nest of Quietism is Madame Guyon's use [. . .] of the word 'faith.'"[101]

Upham's narration and interpretation of Madame Guyon's formative journey on the interior way places her within an experimental theology of crisis experiences. In chapter 2, it was noted that three events marked her early spiritual life: the directive to look within and the discovery, on July 22, 1668, the feast day of Mary Magdalene, of the divine presence in her heart—a wound "as delicious as it was loving"; her mystical marriage to the infant Jesus in July of 1672; and her experience of divine union, "a union of unity" again on the same feast day in 1680. Upham plays the role of the interpreter for the American reader. The events leading up to the first of these events were a sign of the providential leading of God, and her conversion was "marked and decisive."

> It is hardly necessary to say, that the change which persons experience in their transition from the life of nature to the life of God in the soul, are very different, in their commencement, in different persons, being much more marked in some cases than in others. In the case of Madame Guyon, although slowly progressive in its preparatory steps, it seems to have been very decisive and marked at the time of its actually taking place. It was obviously a great crisis in her moral and religious being,— one in which the pride and obstinacy of the natural heart were broken down, and in which, for the first time, she became truly willing to receive Christ alone as her hope of salvation.[102]

The descriptions of the marriage with Jesus of 1672 are suppressed, no doubt because the experience was so embedded within Catholic practice, but Upham does reproduce the text of the contract itself. He chooses to see the written contract as the sign of a consecration of the will to God that had been made in 1670. "Her consecration, made in the spirit of entire self-renouncement," he says, "was a consecration to God's will, and not *to her own*; to be what God would have her to be, and not what her fallen nature would have her to be. Two years after this time, she placed her signature to a written act of Covenant or act of Consecration [. . .] but the act itself, she made previously, made it *now*, and made it *irrevocable*."[103] Given Upham's view that consecration precedes the experience of sanctification, we can anticipate then his interpretation of the Magdalene experience of July 1680. It is the day of her deliverance from "seven years of privation" and "the triumph of sanctifying grace." Madame Guyon had described the joy and plenitude of this experience, marked by the union of her will and the divine, and the experience of love: "Whether we call this state of experience pure love or perfect love, whether we denominate it sanctification or assurance of faith, is perhaps not very essential. Certain it is, that it seemed to her [. . .] that she loved her heavenly Father, in accordance with what the Saviour requires of us, her whole power of loving."[104]

To illustrate this state of sanctification, Upham appropriates passages from the latter part of the *Torrents*, "translating not merely her words, which, taken as they stand, would convey but very imperfect and perhaps false ideas to an English reader, but what I suppose her to *mean* by them." For example, Upham's Guyon says "I willed nothing; meaning in the statement that I had no will of my own. As a sanctified heart is always in harmony with the divine providences, I had no will but the divine will [. . .]. How could such a soul have other than a deep peace [. . .]!"[105] In Upham's hands, the story of the crosses and sufferings that Madame Guyon endures is both one of persecution for teaching sanctification and of inner quietude and love in and through her trials. Her initial vocation to go to Gex in Savoy to help in the effort to convert and educate new Catholics (former Protestants) becomes a mission of charity in which she simply speaks of sanctification and elicits the opposition of the bishop who had initially recruited her.

> Thus at the foot of the Alps, when she thought her great business was to make ointments, and cut linen, and bind up wounds, and tend the sick, and teach poor children the alphabet and the catechism, (important vocations to those whom Providence calls to them,) she uttered a word from her burdened heart, in her *simplicity*, without knowing or thinking how widely it would affect the interests of humanity, or through how many distant ages it would be re-echoed. And that word was, Sanctification by Faith.
>
> Both the thing and the manner of the thing struck those who heard her with astonishment. Sanctification itself was repugnant; and sanctification by *faith* inexplicable.[106]

The tone is thus set for much that follows. The story of Madame Guyon's itinerant life of lay teaching—her moves from Gex to Thonon, to Turin, to Grenoble, and to Marseille, and finally her return to Paris in 1786—is cast in a thematic construct of persecution because of her teaching of the doctrine of sanctification.

Upham describes succinctly Madame Guyon's writings of this period, the *Torrents*, the commentary on Scripture, and the treatise on prayer. He notes the "ease and vivacity" with which she wrote, the extent of her correspondence, and the range of her influence: "All classes of persons, no matter how high or how low" benefited from these letters if she thought the recipients could profit from them.[107] But if we look at what Upham does with the influential *Short and Easy Method*, we find that Madame Guyon's vivid, spontaneous, and oral style—called by the translator Thomas Taylor Allen the "spontaneous overflow of the heart"—is obliterated by Upham's paraphrased "analysis." He justifies his method on grounds of gender.

> [. . .] We have not undertaken to follow precisely the language of the original, but have given what we supposed to be the idea or thought, with some slight variations of the original arrangement, such as seemed

to improve the logical and religious relation of the parts. The Method
of Prayer is a work remarkable, in that age of the world, as coming from
a *woman*, and still more remarkable, when considered in contrast with
the prevalent views and practices of the church of which the author was
a member, which tended, as it seemed to her, to substitute the form for
the substance, the ceremonial for the spirit. Its doctrines are essentially
Protestant: making Faith [. . .] the foundation of the religious life, and
even carrying the power of faith in the renovation of our inward nature
beyond what is commonly found in Protestant writers.[108]

If we deconstruct this passage, we find that Upham himself has engaged
in an act of substitution, destroying the spirit and the form of the original
text (which he himself claims as gendered). He appropriates the text on
prayer into nineteen propositions, beginning with "Remarks in explanation of the use of the term Prayer" and ending with "Appeal to religious
pastors and teachers."[109] And Madame Guyon's transformation into a
Protestant is now complete.

Upham's stance toward Madame Guyon throughout his work becomes
contradictory. She epitomizes the potential and power of the sanctified life
when all the faculties are brought into harmony through subjection to the
divine will, thus infusing the individual with pure, selfless love. Yet, as a
woman she is the victim of her time and culture, and thus Upham, the male
interpreter, must step into the gap and rework her thoughts and expressions
for his readers. Early in volume one, he says that her "literary" education,
although comparable to that of other women of her time, was in some
ways "defective." "Her style of writing is eloquent and impressive in a high
degree," he says, "but a critical eye will discover its deficiencies."

> In translating her statements, therefore, it is oftentimes necessary to
> analyze her thoughts and re-arrange them in their logical order, in
> order to present them to the mind of the reader in the same position,
> and with the same import they possessed in her own mind. It is to be
> noticed, also, that the theological and experimental terms which she
> uses, sometimes have a specific meaning, not unknown perhaps in some
> of the mystic writers, but which can certainly be ascertained only by an
> intimate knowledge of her own experience, character, and writings.[110]

These issues of gendered ways of knowing, speaking, writing—and of serving God—are significant in the second volume.

The narrative of this volume follows Madame Guyon's life from her
return to Paris in 1686 until her death. In addition to the autobiography
and poetry, Upham makes extensive use of the letters and summarizes

the *Justifications*. In addition to thematizing Madame Guyon's quietude and courage during her various periods of imprisonment, he emphasizes the debate over doctrine and contrasts Madame Guyon's influence on Fénelon with Bossuet's reaction against her. Upham even creates a dialogue between Bossuet and Madame Guyon in which he represents their different theological positions with regard to religion of the heart. As in the case of the *Short and Easy Method*, Upham summarizes and domesticates Fénelon's *Maxims of the Saints*, paraphrasing the various sections for his Protestant readers.

And these readers were of two sorts—those who were resisting the experimental truth of sanctification in this life and those who were women of sensibility. Upham addresses the first group at various points in underscoring that the Catholics who were on the inner way, to whom Madame Guyon ministered, believed in justification by faith *complemented* by the experience of sanctification.[111] Although Madame Guyon spoke of her calling as an "apostolic vocation," Upham underscores her instrumentality—her role as an instrument of God—for his women readers. In so doing, he sets up a gendered contrast between female sensibility and male intellect. In a letter to her brother, who was a Carthusian, the translation emphasizes that individual instrumentality depends on the state of annihilation of the self.

> And if you ask why it is, that the Lord has seen fit to bless me in my labors, it is because he has first, by taking away my own will, made me a *nothing*. The instrumentality which recognizes God as the sole source of its own strength, and regards itself only as an instrument, is the instrumentality which God blesses. It is thus that he has seen fit to make use of a poor, weak woman, as an instrument in his own mighty hands, in bringing multitudes of different ages and conditions, priests as well as others, to a knowledge of himself. His own good Spirit, in the results which have been wrought in them, has put the seal to that which he has enabled me to say.[112]

This instrumentality is extended to Madame Guyon's role as a spiritual mentor to Fénelon. Upham says that the "truth, purity, and love" that characterizes Fénelon's works are due to Madame Guyon: "If the writings of Fenelon, taken in all their relations and all their results, have exerted an influence probably not inferior to those of any other man, it ought not be concealed nor to be disguised, that it was a woman's mind, operating upon the mind of their author, from which no small portion of the light which pervades and embellishes them first proceeded." Upham then continues to discuss the nature of "woman's influence" in forming men from childhood to mature greatness. Madame Guyon understood "relations and effects"; although the soul of every person has the same value, she grasped the extent of Fénelon's influence in society. "When she considered the relations in which he stood and the influence which he was capable of exerting and that his mind was to be brought into contact with the minds of princes and kings," Upham says, "she felt more deeply than can be expressed, how necessary it was that he should be delivered from the power of inferior motives, and that he should act and live only in the Lord."[113]

It has been noted that the portrait of Fénelon in some ways feminized him, emphasizing his Christlike traits in terms of the traits of male-female stereotypes. If Madame Guyon's influence helped to enhance Fénelon's remarkable traits, her rejection by Bossuet, as recounted by Upham, underscores the contrast between the two men. The difficult confrontations between Guyon and Bossuet are accentuated in the Upham account, beginning with their encounter in January of 1694. Bossuet was a great intellectual with an "acute and discriminating mind." "Accustomed to the supremacy of his intellectual power, he was apt to be dictatorial and rough in his greatness," and he "was but little conciliated and softened by the presence and the finer sensibilities of woman."[114] When Bossuet and Fénelon confront each other publicly in their written defenses of their positions against and for pure love, Upham sets up a dramatic contrast, on the basis of these gendered roles.

> Bossuet and Fenelon [. . .] embodied more of public thought and of public attachment than any other two men in France. And, singularly as it may seem, the object of controversy between them was a poor captive woman, who was at this very time shut up in the fortress of Vincennes, and who was employed in making religious songs, which she sung in concert with her pious maid-servant. Bossuet looked upon her as a heretic. Fenelon was regarded, not without some reason, as her avowed defender.[115]

Banished to his bishopric in Cambrai, Fénelon would become an example of piety and pure love, by which he was a "friend to all mankind." Imprisoned in the Bastille and then finally released, Madame Guyon would be an example of "the *sanctifying* results of religion, in distinction from its mere justifying power." In the context of the debate about the possibility of entire sanctification in this life, Upham ends his book on an experimental note, as well as a millennialist hope, as he envisions the spread of the experience of holiness.

The doctrine of Sanctification as well as of Justification, will in due time have its philosophical and practical, as well as its exegetical exposition. And all will be tested, and *must* be tested, so far as we can perceive, by LIVING EXAMPLES. As the light of holiness arises upon the world, and as the names of those whose lives have been practical illustrations of a pure and perfected love, become more and more dear to the church, it can hardly be overlooked or forgotten. Forgetful of herself, she had no purpose, no desire, of being remembered. But he who forgets himself in the purity and strength of his love for another, necessarily writes his memorial in the heart and in the acts of the being beloved.[116]

How do we evaluate Upham's restatement of the tradition of experimental religion that enveloped the figures of Madame Guyon and, to a lesser extent, Fénelon? Ann Taves has quite correctly noted that both Phoebe Palmer and Thomas Upham downplayed the witness of the Spirit and emphasized the "consciousness of giving one's all," thus removing "sensible assurance" (i.e., enthusiasm) from the doctrine of assurance. Upham was able to unite Wesleyan holiness with the Edwardsian tradition of disinterest benevolence. Both Palmer and Upham made the experience of holiness acceptable to the middle class.[117] However, Palmer, Thomas, and Phebe Upham illustrate that the search for perfection was connected with other contexts of the life of the middle class in the Northeast. The fact that the holiness movement was felt not only within Methodism but also across denominations—for example, among New England Congregationalists—is a fact not treated by Ann Douglas in *The Feminization of American Culture*. Phoebe Palmer, although a New Yorker and a Methodist, played a role in the sentimentalization of the language of sanctification, and, as we shall see in chapter 9, so did both the Uphams.

The Guide to Christian Perfection/Holiness published on occasion short extracts from Madame Guyon, Fénelon, Molinos, Catharine Adorna, François de Sales, Gregory of Lopez, and Francis of Assisi during the 1840s and 1850s. These extracts began with a Cowper translation of Madame Guyon in 1842. Many of these extracts were justified because of John Wesley's interest in Continental spirituality and, of course, because of Upham's writings. Melvin Dieter has noted that Upham established the experiential kinship felt between the American holiness tradition and Catholic mysticism.[118] The *Guide* itself viewed Upham's *Life and Religious Opinions* of Madame Guyon as an attempt to recapture the true piety of the early church. The *Guide* indicated that Upham's earlier writings had presented a detailed plan for attaining Christian character, but now his biography of Madame Guyon had presented a model of that character.

We cannot but think that this book is destined to exert a very favorable influence on the church, in raising the tone of piety to the true standard. Indeed, its effects are already beginning to be felt on many hearts. While many of the memoirs which have been given to the world, present a very defective religion, and consequently, while they do some good, also do some hurt, excluding the great doctrine of present and practical holiness, here is a book, breathing the spirit, the courage, the faith of the apostles and primitive Christians.

Through Pierre Poiret and John Wesley, Upham had discovered the living tradition of experimental theology. He gave it some unique twists, but his appropriation of that tradition into the language of the holiness movement and of a second crisis experience of sanctification allowed American readers to claim *their* experience to be the same as that of Catholic mystics and others. The Pietist phenomenon of reading beyond interpretive cultural horizons would be repeated. A popular culture of devotional literature, with an ensuing hermeneutic of proof through shared experience, would carry on into the twentieth century. And even during the rise of Fundamentalism, when boundaries and lines were to be drawn, an ecumenical current centered on experimental religion would be ever present in America.

Chapter 8

❦

The Turn to Devotional Literature
Readers of Fénelon, from Boardman, Stowe, and Bushnell to Twentieth-Century Evangelicals

The Persistence of Experimental Theology

As Phoebe Palmer had prayed, Thomas Upham's influence was not limited to the holiness movement that grew out of Methodism.[1] Upham's works on the interior life and on the Catholic forerunners of "holiness" coincided with a much broader movement in North America, England, and then the Continent. The desire for a deeper Christian life and even, in some instances, a belief in the necessity of a subsequent crisis experience was evident beyond Methodist circles before and after the Civil War. Revivals and camp meetings gave impetus to a broad search for holiness or deep inner piety that crossed denominations and social classes and touched both urban and rural America. Notable, for example, was the wave of revivals that began in the East in 1857 and spread westward, characterized by small prayer and testimony meetings that were somewhat akin to the original Tuesday meetings in New York City. Such small groups created core communities of believers (and readers) that were all part of larger, loosely knit communities sharing the same inner experience of the deeper life.

A look at three representative figures from Presbyterian and Congregationalist backgrounds during the period of the 1840s to 1860s indicates some of the ways experimental theology affected American religious experience, sending it in diverging directions.

169

W. E. Boardman (1810–1886) and the Keswick Movement

Originally a Presbyterian grocer in Illinois, William E. Boardman experienced a "second conversion" in part through a book that was given to him
by a Methodist circuit rider and that contained testimonies of Charles G.
Finney and Asa Mahan. Boardman and his wife left for Lane Theological Seminary in Cincinnati, and he went on to become an officer of the
American Sunday School Union in Philadelphia in the 1850s. Boardman
also attended the Tuesday meetings of Phoebe Palmer in New York City
and was, of course, influenced by the Oberlin brand of holiness preached
by Finney and Mahan.[2]

As the prewar religious fervor continued, Boardman published *The
Higher Christian Life* in 1859, a book that would sell almost 200,000 copies
in the United States and England. (*The Guide to Holiness* also published a
brief excerpt that year.)[3] The purpose of Boardman's title as a description
of mature Christian experience was to avoid as much as possible the con-
notations and disputes around the word "sanctification." "A wider sphere
for the experimental truth set forth and a clearer delineation are the
things sought," he wrote, "and hackneyed terms, or pre-appointed terms,
or terms against which prejudice is arrayed, would not answer." In fact,
Edwards' phrase "second conversion" could suffice to describe this life
of fullness in God.[4] "Experimental religion" as presented by Boardman
embraces salvation, the ensuing struggle to live a holy life, followed by a
"later, deeper work" in which the believer places full trust in Jesus as the
way, the truth, and the life. This "practical, experimental apprehension of
Christ is instantaneous in every case."[5] In this act of faith, subsequent to
conversion, the soul is placed in the hands of Christ "as the clay in the
hands of the potter" and the soul can then be a "mirror to the Master."[6]
But this is not a life described as sinless Christian perfection; it is a life of
complete trust in Christ and obedience to him.

Boardman knew the works of Upham, and in *The Higher Christian
Life* he refers in passing to *Principles of the Interior Life*.[7] It is also evident
that Boardman was acquainted with the tradition of buttressing experience through biographical accounts, because in his book the higher
Christian life is described in both scriptural and biographical contexts.
Both theological and personal accounts of this higher life have crossed
denominational traditions; "classes of witnesses" are to be found in the
Lutheran, Wesleyan, and Oberlin traditions. These figures have ranged
from Luther to Edwards, from Mrs. Edwards to Hester Ann Rogers,
from Mahan and Finney to a number of unidentified types ("an eminent lady," "a merchant," for example). (The significance of the references to Sarah Edwards and Hester Ann Rogers will become increasingly

apparent in this chapter and the next.) Boardman illustrates how, in the nineteenth century, the assumptions of experimental theology continued to be stated explicitly, but the biographical proofs were drawn from a larger pool of believers.

Boardman became famous because of his book, and after the Civil War he was an evangelist at camp meetings in the East. He then went to England, where his own book and the works of Phoebe Palmer, Finney, and Upham were already known as part of holiness revivals. During Dwight L. Moody's revival campaign in London in 1873, Boardman joined forces with Hannah Whitall Smith and her husband R. Pearsall Smith in promoting "the cause of holiness."[8] (Boardman would reside permanently in London from 1875 on.) A broad group of Christians became part of promoting a second crisis experience so that the holiness movement in the British Isles included the Anglican and Calvinist traditions; the emphasis of American Wesleyan holiness adherents on sanctification as complete surrender, an eradication from the bent to sinning, and an infilling of the Holy Spirit gave way to different theological themes. These emphases included the necessity of a second crisis experience, but the infilling of the Holy Spirit was now an empowering for service, and faith healing and premillennialism also were stressed. In 1875, the Anglican vicar of Keswick arranged for an open-air convention to take place, and within a short period of time the Keswick movement was born from yearly meetings in southern England. These conventions spread to the United States.[9] The "Keswick movement" over time proved to be a useful descriptor for the broad grouping of non-Wesleyan proponents of a deeper life of love and obedience characterized by a key experience following conversion. And in the twentieth century when Evangelicalism succeeded the narrower, separatist tendencies of Fundamentalism, the theological values of the Keswick movement continued in America and England.[10]

Among the readers out of the Keswick tradition who would read devotional literature, Madame Guyon and Fénelon continued to be valued. I have already noted that Ruth Bell Graham, the daughter of Presbyterian missionaries, a Wheaton College graduate, and the wife of the evangelist Billy Graham, wrote the preface to a reprint of extracts of the Thomas Taylor Allen translation of *The Autobiography of Madame Guyon*.[11] Similarly, Elisabeth Elliot, another Wheaton College graduate, former missionary among the Auca Indians, and evangelical author, wrote the preface to a reprint of Fénelon's letters of spiritual direction called *Spiritual Letters to Women*. Elliot stressed Fénelon's message of submission as an act of inner obedience to God and the timeliness of his theme of the abandonment of self-love for an age of narcissistic self-indulgence and self-seeking.[12]

Harriet Beecher Stowe (1811–1874)

At the beginning of Uncle Tom's Cabin (1852), Mr. Shelby and Haley are bargaining over the details of the sale of the slave Tom to settle a debt. Shelby argues that the value of Tom alone is enough to settle the deal because he has an uncommon character. "Tom is a good, steady, sensible, pious fellow. He got religion at a camp-meeting, four years ago; and I believe he really did get it." Haley responds that he considers religion valuable in a slave, and Shelby continues, "Well, Tom's got the real article, if ever a fellow had."[13] Throughout the novel real piety is the test of truth and faith. Tom becomes a Christ figure, exhibiting humility, disinterested love, quietude, and good works.

Joan Hedrick has succinctly summarized the complex issues surrounding Uncle Tom's Cabin that have embroiled the novel and the character of Tom in the politics of race. Stowe drew her study of the character of slaves at least in part from her experiences with her own household servants. She made use of slave narratives of escape and of journalistic accounts of the effects of the Fugitive Slave Law. Stowe's innovation was to center the traditional bondage plot on not a female character, but a male character who, as a perfect Christian, becomes a martyr who permits the escape of the woman. There was also some of Calvin Stowe's interest in continental Pietism embedded in the religious milieu of the novel. On the other hand, Hedrick notes the difficulty that twentieth-century critics have had in accepting the religious values in Uncle Tom's Cabin; for example, Hortense Spillers has emphasized the "theological terror" drawn from Calvinism and the "thematics of sacrifice" in the work.[14]

Given the racism embedded in the stereotypes of Uncle Tom's Cabin, the importance of Tom as the embodiment of authentic piety should not be overlooked. Stowe seems to have intended him to be a radical example of revolutionary Christianity, a figure in the tradition of Fénelon. She thought that when Negroes were freed, they would be a "magnificent revelation of human life [. . .] in their lowly docility of heart, their aptitude to repose on a superior mind and rest on a higher power, their childlike simplicity of affection, and facility of forgiveness."[15] Again, Stowe was not alone in this approach to Tom's character and to the character of Negroes in general as spiritual examples. In 1850, readers had just encountered Sojourner Truth's Narrative of her slave experiences, her spiritual awakening, and her ensuing journey as a speaker in the religious awakenings of the 1840s and the growing abolitionist movement. Phebe Upham also published an account of the life and death of Phebe Ann Jacobs, a former slave and domestic servant in the home of the presidents of Dartmouth

College and Bowdoin College, that appeared in *The Guide to Holiness* in July 1850 and that was also published separately as a tract.

Phebe Jacobs had died the previous February in Brunswick, where she had lived alone after the death of the wife of the college president. Phebe washed and ironed clothes for the college students and was known for her Christian character: "Phebe lived not for earth, but for heaven. While she was diligent and faithful in all the departments of household labor, she was at the same time fervent in spirit, serving the Lord. All her work seemed to be sanctified by prayer and praise, and done *cheerfully, heartily*, as unto the Lord." Phebe, "one of Abraham's children of *faith*," was noted for her prayer life and her humility: "Phebe's humility drew all hearts toward her. This was the mark by which she was every where known. She did not herself seem to be conscious of it, but she was always seeking to be concealed; to pass unnoticed." And before her death Phebe, too, had "come into a new and fuller realization than ever before of Jesus, as a *present* and *all-sufficient* Saviour." In her words, "'she had never let her Saviour go.' 'she had held him by the hand.'" "'He had come into her heart, and *continued to abide* with her.'"[16] No claim can be made for mutual influence between Upham and Stowe, but Phebe was among those welcoming Harriet to Brunswick in the late spring of 1850.

Behind *Uncle Tom's Cabin* lay a complex set of values, an intertext, not only drawn from the context sketched by Joan Hedrick but also drawn from Stowe's exposure in the 1840s to Eliza Follen's version of Fénelon against the backdrop of New England culture and abolitionism, to the values of Oberlin revivalism, and to Thomas Upham's theology of the interior life.

In the early 1840s Stowe began to exhibit a strong interest in the Edwardsian notion of a "second conversion" and the Oberlin holiness revival. Joan D. Hedrick has suggested that Harriet's interest in perfectionism was related to the crisis triggered by the suicide of her brother George in 1843; during this period, Harriet was swept along by millennialism and perfectionism that evoked repression and conflict within women. Hedrick goes on to say that in the 1850s the imitation of Christ would replace this perfectionism: Stowe's "understanding of the life of Christ validated the common and the everyday, both in her personal life and in her literary realism."[17] This spiritual journey, however, had a broader context, growing out of New School Calvinism, the Oberlin revivalist theology, and the figure of Fénelon.

Stowe began to publish articles in the *New-York Evangelist* (a New School paper) in 1835 and continued to be a contributor until the early 1850s. Her article "De Rance and Fenelon—A Contrast" appeared in July of 1842. The impetus for the article may have been the 1841 edition of Mrs. Follen's anthology of Fénelon's writings and the memoirs of Saint-Simon, published in several editions in French between 1829 and 1841. Charles Butler had also published biographies of Fénelon, Bossuet, and de Rancé as part of a six-volume set of "Lives" that appeared in several editions from 1810 on. In 1657 the abbé de Rancé had withdrawn from worldly circles after the death of his lover the Duchesse de Montbazon, according to legend. In 1662, he entered the La Trappe abbey, transforming it by means of a rule of great austerity. Bossuet had drawn de Rancé into the Quietist controversy, and the abbot, from what Saint-Simon called his "desert," condemned Fénelon's writings, without knowing that Bossuet would make his opinion public.

For Stowe, the reign of Louis XIV produced numerous instances of "truth stranger than fiction" in the contrasting values of worldly licentiousness and "excess of religious devotion." "But the developments of the religious sentiment in this very corrupt and licentious time, are fully as wonderful as any other."[18] Stowe narrates the legend of de Rancé's entry into La Trappe and gives a long description of the desolate setting of the abbey, calling the discipline "rigid and death-like." "Every person who entered the Tomb of La Trappe, was supposed to die to his former self, and to the memory of all of his former life," she writes. De Rancé eventually goes into a decline from the exhaustion of this austere regimen, but, says Stowe, when we move to Fénelon it "is like emerging from a dark, damp cavern, into pure air and sunshine."

Stowe describes Fénelon's dignity, his manners, and the way he was able to place himself on the level of his pupil, the Duke of Bourgogne. She attributes the transformation in the latter's character under Fénelon's guidance less to pedagogy than to "the power of the gospel, simply and truthfully exhibited in the life of a consistent Christian." Fénelon's "purity and enlarged benevolence of [. . .] heart carried him beyond the narrow and intolerant spirit of the church." Once in Cambrai, he demonstrated "tenderness, sympathy, and care" to the poor, friendless, and wounded soldiers whom he received in his palace.

According to Stowe, Fénelon defended Madame Guyon out of both pity and an inclination toward Quietist disinterestedness, but the lady herself was an "enthusiast" whose doctrines "if involving somewhat of metaphysical absurdity" were "harmless." Stowe emphasizes the self-annihilation and passivity of the Quietists and quaintly stresses their freedom—"from all hope, fear, or desire of any sort." God was to be loved without regard to any personal happiness, and "the love of happiness itself must be eradicated from our mind to give place to one of absolute submission to the divine will."

If Stowe rejected Madame Guyon and the extremes of Quietism, she adopted Fénelon the person as a model of the traits of Christlikeness, tolerance, and disinterested benevolence. She seems to have connected Fénelon in her mind with Samuel Hopkins, the disciple of Edwards who was the Congregationalist pastor in Newport from 1770 to 1803 and who opposed the slave trade. In the context of New England theological debates about the nature of self-love, Hopkins' teaching that the mark of the true Christian is a form of "divine benevolence" that enables the individual to be willing to be damned for the glory of God had engendered considerable debate and controversy. Stowe would make Hopkins' opposition to the slave trade a test of true Christianity in the novel *The Minister's Wooing* (1859). His character would also become a mouthpiece for a theology of spiritual equality for men and women in the "economy of grace" in this book.[19] Similarly, the portrayal of Mary Scudder, the model of female spirituality in the novel, drew on the account of Sarah Pierpont Edwards by Samuel Hopkins, who had stayed with the Edwards family while he was studying theology. Sarah had been a spiritual mentor to Hopkins, and he subsequently called her "eminent for her piety and experimental religion."[20]

Edwards A. Park, who had given an influential address on "The Theology of the Intellect and That of the Feelings" in 1850 was a Hopkins disciple and faculty colleague of Calvin Stowe at Andover Theological Seminary. He published an edition of the works of Hopkins in 1852, in which was included a long memoir of his life and discussion of his works. This edition drew considerable attention, and Harret Beecher Stowe had read it.[21] In the wake of the continuing discussion of the issue of self-love by people like Channing (who was favorable to Hopkins) and of the interest in the Quietists fostered by Upham, Park introduced a telling analogy in the defense of Hopkins' spirituality.

> There is a striking resemblance between the feelings of Dr. Hopkins and the feelings of Fenelon, Madame Guion, and many other mystics, with regard to the endurance of *pain* for the divine glory. It is unnatural for any man to rise into these heights of sentiment and of reasoning, unless he have an ideality far above that of the masses. Hopkins, with all his logic, had a comprehensive though not an active imagination, and he took into his range the loftiest suppositions conceivable.[22]

The connections between the spiritual experience of Sarah Edwards and the mysticism of Madame Guyon and between the theology of Hopkins and of Fénelon continued to be made in the nineteenth-century imagination. Perfectionists were drawn to the theology of universal benevolence because of their doctrine of perfect love; they were also drawn to Hopkins because of his opposition to slavery and their own interest in social reform. One can conclude that Hopkins, like Fénelon, reflected Harriet Beecher Stowe's spiritual state as she participated in the fervor of New School Calvinism and also searched for a deeper Christian life.[23]

Harriet's letters to her husband during the 1840s expressed a yearning for just such an experience, although she distanced herself from a theology of perfection in this life. In a letter of August of 1844, she puts herself in the camp of experimental religion of the Oberlin type in discussing a second more perfect state of Christian life. She writes to Calvin that "there is a great & real change which Christ is now working in the hearts of his church, a step which bears the same relation to ordinary experience as conversion did to past life. [. . .] There is a longing—a sighing for some more perfect state to be attained in this world [,] & to this sentiment this longing is to be ascribed the success of the Oberlin paper & doctrine."[24] By the next year, there is evidence that Harriet had read Upham's book on the interior life and that she had gained a deeper spiritual experience. In two articles for the *New-York Evangelist* in the spring of 1845, the first of which was entitled "The Interior or Hidden Life," she commented on the significance of Upham's book and staked out her own theological position.[25]

Stowe assures her readers that the book is not related to fanaticism but that it treats "a high form of Christian experience" that has crossed time, circumstances, and denominations and that has been described in various ways. "German, Swede or American, Moravian, Lutheran, Methodist, or Presbyterian experience" includes similar "phenomena," she says. Various names have been applied to it: "'assurance of faith, assurance of hope, baptism of the Spirit, perfect love, perfect trust, entire consecration,'" and, "erroneously," says Stowe, "*Christian perfection, or entire sanctification.*" Stowe describes the current widespread search thoughout the American "Christian community," including "all parts of the West" for this experience. In some cases, the experience has been radical and revolutionary; in others, gradual. Although she disagrees with parts of Upham's book—its disclaimer of the philosophy of Oberlin, its seeming arrival "at mere quietism"—she sees it as timely because millennial action has to be linked to inner experience: "The whole state of the times seems to call for an effort to bring back the Christian mind to a deeper internal scrutiny and life. For these fifty years there has been [. . .] a universal tendency to *outwardness* in religion. The whole great system of benevolent organization, the whole formation of the outward tactics necessary for efficient millennial action, has fallen into these times, and been eliminated with surprising rapidity." The experience described by Upham may appear to be impossible to attain, but the history of the church suggests otherwise.

The title of Stowe's second article—"The Interior Life: Or Primitive Christian Experience"—is an interesting variation on the first piece.[26] By lively dialogue, she explores the question of what would happen if someone attained a high level of Christian experience and whether such an experience is possible. Again, she dismisses the possibility of sinless perfection in this life, but she makes the case for "the apostolic and primitive Christian experience" of the New Testament. In both articles, Stowe also relates the state of this primitive Christianity to Bunyan's land of Beulah; she uses the criteria of Scripture and experience to prove her point.

> But suppose the absolute sinless rest of the blessed is not to be attained here, does it follow that there is nothing that is? Though heaven itself does not lie on this side of the river of death, is there not a land of Beulah that does? And have not multitudes who once were scarce able to keep awake on the Enchanted ground, found themselves renewed as with youthful vigor, when they entered this balmy region? But after all, there is nothing on this point like experience. Let every Christian open his New Testament, and follow with us this question—What *have* mortal men and women like us felt and attained, by the power of the gospel of Christ?

This state that is "like a new conversion" is indeed attainable. Stowe concludes that there are five characteristics of this experience that indicate that it has been attained: "the mind is so bent and absorbed by the love of Christ, that all inducements to worldliness lose their power"; the Christian no longer acts from "constitutional impulse" but "steadily and constantly from the impulse of Christ"; like Paul, the individual is borne along by the power of Christ; the Spirit bears witness to the individual that he or she is a child of God; and "the high devotional language of the Bible becomes the spontaneous and habitual language of the soul."

Harriet herself experienced a "second conversion," according to her sister Catharine Beecher, who wrote to Phoebe Palmer in the fall of 1845 when she was seeking Mrs. Palmer's support for her project of sending women teachers to the frontier. Catharine said that she herself had read *The Way of Holiness* and that her sister had also recently embarked on this way by the "Bible method."[27] It is evident, nevertheless, that Harriet's deeper Christian experience was akin to the teachings of Edwards and Finney. Like those whom we have already encountered, her standards of validation were a modified Baconian proof of Scripture, inner experience, and consistent Christian behavior.

Despite her admiration for Fénelon, Stowe was no Quietist even though she came to admire the Uphams and counted Phebe Upham among her friends. When Harriet preceded Calvin in the move to Maine so that Calvin could join (briefly) the faculty at Bowdoin College, Harriet wrote of the Uphams that "this family is delightful, there is such a perfect sweetness & quietude in all its movements. Not a harsh word or hasty expression is ever heard. It is a beautiful pattern of a Christian family, a beautiful exemplification of religion."[28] Fénelon embodied in Harriet's religious imagination an approach to faith that was intuitional, experiential, charitable, and sentimental as opposed to the intellectual, theological, and rational approach of much of Calvinism. In a letter to her husband in 1853, during her antislavery tour of Europe, she contrasts two traditions within French religious culture by means of the figures of Fénelon and Calvin, but she sentimentalizes Fénelon. "The very sweetest & softest as well as the most austere & rigid type of piety has been given by the French mind—Witness Fenelon & John Calvin. Fenelon standing as the type of the mystic & Calvin as the rationalistic style of religion. Fenelon with his heart so sweet so childlike so simple & tender was essentially French in his nature & essence."[29]

Harriet Beecher Stowe would become an Episcopalian, and her mature Christian faith would be characterized by a tolerant Christ-centered theology as articulated in *Footsteps of the Master* (1877):

> It is this divine wideness of spirit, this tolerance of love, that is the most characteristic element in the stages that mark the higher Christian life. Such spirits as Fénelon, Francis de Sales, Woolman, and the apostle Eliot seem to have risen to the calm regions of clear-sighted love. Hence the maxim of Fénelon[:] "Only perfection can tolerate the imperfect."[30]

Horace Bushnell (1802–1876) and the Turn to Devotional Literature

For Stowe, one of the marks of a deeper experience of Christ was that "the high devotional language of the Bible becomes the spontaneous and habitual language of the soul." This unusual emphasis on the linguistic expression of the deep inner piety resulting from the experience of a "second conversion" provides a link to her contemporary Horace Bushnell. A Congregational minister in Hartford throughout his entire career, Bushnell, like Stowe, moved beyond traditional New England Calvinism. Holifield has aptly remarked that Bushnell represented an alternative to "evidential Christianity," substituting "Christian consciousness" or "religious experience" for rational evidentialism. But, says Holifield, Bushnell's so-called incipient liberalism was underpinned by "an intense supernaturalism."[31] Ann Douglas has underscored Bushnell's liberalism, equating the "Bushnellian Christ, meeting men on mortal terrain, shaping himself to human needs, offering himself as a model not as a governor" with the feminization of American culture that went hand in hand with the disappearance of Old School Calvinism: "Newly sensitized and femininized in image, defined as a lover of all the world's 'little ones,' the liberal Jesus too [was] adept in discovering and tapping the unconscious; he too [was] adept at the small gains which can pass unnoticed."[32]

After the publication of *Discourses on Christian Nurture* (1847), in which his lifelong interest in the formation of Christian character was already evident, Bushnell was engaged in intensive academic study of Coleridge's *Aids to Reflection* and German thinkers like Friedrich Schlegel. However, he also read Upham's *Interior Life* and his account of Madame Guyon, as well as the writings of Fénelon. According to his wife's account, Bushnell later said, "'I believed from reading, especially the New Testament, and from other testimony, that there is a higher, fuller life that can be lived, and set myself to attain it. I swung, for a time towards quietism, but soon passed out into a broader, more positive state."[33] In February of 1848, Bushnell told his wife that he had discovered "'the gospel,'" and it was not through study, but through a personal experience—a revelation—that he came into a relationship with God in Christ. Out of this "experimental knowledge and perception," Bushnell was able to cast the Christian life into "rational forms," but the key was his revelatory spiritual crisis.[34] As late as 1871, Bushnell spoke to his wife about this crisis experience.

> "I seemed to pass a boundary. I had never been very legal in my Christian life, but now I passed from these partial seeings, glimpses and doubts, into a clearer knowledge of God and into his inspirations, which I have never wholly lost. The change was into faith,—a sense of the freeness of God and the ease of approach to him."[35]

Out of this reading of Coleridge and German Romantic philosophers, and of French Quietists and Upham's interpretation of them, came a synthesis that was given a distinct cast by Bushnell's seemingly mystical experience of the friendship of Christ as the embodiment of the spirit of God. It is too facile to see Bushnell as a harbinger of liberalism even as he rejected "scientific theology" (a phrase in his controversial *God in Christ* [1849]). On the one hand, Bushnell grasped the limits of abstract theological language and understood the power and necessity of symbolic and metaphoric language to talk about God. This he derived from his reading of Coleridge and the German idealists. At the same time, he understood from his exposure to apophatic mysticism the limits of language in conveying the mystical experience of the divine. Like others in the tradition of religion of the heart, Bushnell distinguished between knowledge about God and knowledge of God. His understanding of the linguistic basis of this epistemology was distinctive; knowledge of God was immediate and unmediated by language. Bushnell, however, articulated the necessity of knowing Christ personally and in his Christology paralleled the emphases of Stowe and Boardman, but with a much more sophisticated theoretical framework. A liberal? Yes, but with a distinctive foundation in experimental religion.

In 1848, Bushnell was invited to give addresses at Yale, Harvard, and Andover; he published these discourses, along with a preliminary piece on language, as *God in Christ*. He was responding to several issues: Unitarian and Calvinist debates about the nature of Christ as well as New Calvinist revivalism. He was charged with heterodoxy but was supported by Congregationalists in Connecticut. Yet, his views were both "modern" and pietistic. He also gave careful attention as to how one should read abstract discourse, Scripture, and devotional literature. In discussing the limits of representational language and the signifying role of words, he suggests that "language will be ever trying to mend its own deficiencies, by multiplying its forms of representation."[36] Bushnell thus undercuts straightforward texts built around a dominant signifying field, calling for the patient reading of complicated texts with a range of symbols and sometimes apparently antagonistic ideas in order to come to a "complete view" of the author's meaning.[37]

He then extends this "comprehensive manner" of reading to Scripture in which the "repugnances" are allowed to stand as the mind gravitates outward to "that whole of truth in which they coalesce." This whole, however, "will be such a whole as requires a whole universe of rite, symbol, incarnation, historic breathings, and poetic forms, to give it expression,— in a word, just what it now has."[38] Formulations of doctrine have to be held "in a certain letter of accommodation" because of the limits of "the letter"—that is, the limits of abstract language as representational. On the other hand, the Scriptures will be read more frequently if this view of language (growing out of the Romanticism of Coleridge and German thinkers) is taken into account, but they will be read differently: "not as a magazine of proposition and mere dialectic entities, but as inspirations and poetic forms of life; requiring, also, divine inbreathings and exaltations in us, that we may ascend into their meaning." Indeed, Bushnell admits, there is a "mystic element" in all of this.[39] And what of the reading of great devotional literature from different periods and different "forms of worship and opinion"? These texts should be read "for instruction, not for criticism. Here [disciples] will see the Life struggling out through other forms of dogma, and while these other forms are meeting, and, perhaps, neutralizing their own, the image of Christ will shine out more clear and simple than they ever saw it before."⁴⁰

Bushnell's reformulation of the nature of Christ and of the atonement was an effort to modify the legalistic notions inherent in the notion of redemption. Thus, Christ, the Logos or word of God, the perfect character, dissolved the law of social evil and opened the way to eternity and to Christian liberty. Bushnell's language echoes some of the themes of the Quietist authors he had read: "It is going clear of self to live in the objective. It is the passing out of self-love into the love of God; or, what is the same, into a state of faith and devotion, the fundamental distinction of which is that man is moving outward, away from his own centre towards God, to rest on God, and live in God."⁴¹ The simplicity of faith is the "yielding up of the soul" to the altar of Christ, a propitiation of our sin. Piety becomes for Bushnell something quite other than dogma. Bushnell's faith is one of "a living, ingenuous, patient, pure sensibility—a heart [. . .] quickened by the Spirit of God" that leads to "acting as in rest."⁴² Intellect provides a check so that the individual is not acting just from "fancy," but the immediate knowledge of Christ is what matters; dogma has had "mournful effects on piety."⁴³

> It appears evident to me that we embrace a very great and truly unchristian error, in holding the relative estimate we do of the head and the heart. When we speak of talent, ministerial talent for example, how generally is it estimated by the head. How extensively is our judgment of Christian character itself suspended on the question of mere opinions and theoretic beliefs. We seem also to imagine, which is worse than all, that the head is to take care of the heart, the opinions to regulate the faith—that we are first to fill the head or natural understanding with articles and dogmas, and then that the head is to shape the experience of the life, and even to be a law to the working of the Spirit. [. . .] True Christianity holds a very different opinion. It teaches that out of the heart are the issues of life; that God hath given us light in the face of his Son, by shining into our heart; that heresies themselves belong to the natural understanding; and that only the pure in heart can behold the face of God.⁴⁴

Bushnell rejected the periodic heightened spirituality of revivals in favor of an ongoing state of Christ-centered piety that would supersede legalistic dogma, and like others of his time, he yearned for a new age, in this case, a new age of Christian spirituality that would break down the walls of dogma.⁴⁵ As a result, he recommended that "disciples" read and study "the best and most deeply devotional Christian writers in different ages, and under forms of worship and opinion most remote from their own. [. . .] They will see [the image of Christ] as he lives in all his followers, and loving them with a new spirit of catholicity, will worship him with a new sense of oneness with him and his redeemed." Bushnell specifies a number of figures—Fox, Gurnell, Tersteegen, Thomas à Kempis, and "the great archbishop of Cambray." Fénelon's character is singled out—"that most luminous and loveliest of teachers, that most beautiful, most Christlike, and, to human judgment, purest of all living characters since the days of the apostles."[46] In fact, Bushnell recommends that Christian ministers and theological students in New England should read "the mystic and quietistic writers" to counteract the effects of dry dogma.

Both Stowe and Bushnell sought and experienced a deeper Christian life; both moved beyond Quietism, but out of their admiration of Fénelon came a more pliable, tolerant Christology that led each of them beyond nineteenth-century revivalism or New School Calvinism. Whether from the impact of Romanticism or of the heightened spirituality of the time, both identified with a piety that was heart centered and grounded in the literature of devotion.[47] Bushnell was unusual in that his understanding of contemporary philosophical theology enabled him to articulate the epistemological issues at the heart of the tradition of experimental religion. In the sermon "The Immediate Knowledge of God," he refined the distinction between "knowing God and knowing about God" by setting out the epistemological basis of faith.

> But true faith itself discovers another and more absolute knowledge, a knowledge of God himself: immediate, personal knowledge, coming out of no report, or statement, or any thing called truth, as being taught in language. It is knowing God within, even as we know ourselves. The other is only a knowing about God, as from a distance.[48]

Philosophers may say that God is unknowable; Christians may say that we can know propositions about God. Self-centered, sinful humans cut themselves off from "God's internal actuating presence." Being born of God "is the entering of God again into his place." There are two kinds of knowledge: "one is what you know mediately about yourself, through language, and one that which you have immediately as being conscious of yourself." The knowledge of God fits into this second category: "as every soul thus enlightened will testify, that he is now conscious, not of himself only, but of a certain *otherness* moving in him."[49] The immediate knowledge of God does not exclude the necessity of external revelation—Scripture is given to us to show us how to find God. Nor does knowing

Christ as a friend exclude the use of one's intelligence, but the natural understanding of matters about God is of a lower order. "You must rise, you must go up into trust and *know* God–God *himself*–by the inward discovery of his infinite spirit and person."[50]

Devotional Literature and What We Can Learn from Reprints

Upham's study of the life and religious opinions of Madame Guyon and of Fénelon was a weighty, two-volume work. It spawned a number of editions, sometimes in a small format, directed toward the readers of devotional literature. The genres of this literature included letters of spiritual direction; abstracts of previously published guides to prayer; reprints of autobiographies, biographies, and scriptural commentaries; and collections of poetry. Publishers brought out editions not only of Madame Guyon and of Fénelon but also, to a lesser extent, of other mystics mentioned by Upham such as John of the Cross. Often these books were preceded by prefaces indicating how one should read the particular devotional work. In retrospect, this legacy of prefaces and reprints was particularly important because a hermeneutics for the reading of devotional literature emerged over time.

There were spurts in the publication of these devotional works in the 1850s before the Civil War and then in the latter quarter of the nineteenth century. These flurries of publication also paralleled movements within American Protestantism, particularly, the phases of revivalism, the rise of Pentecostalism, and the creation of denominations growing out of nineteenth-century revivalism. A religious publishing industry resulted in which editions and abstracts, drawn from previous books and often recast into "modern" language, brought to devout readers texts that were increasingly distant from the original. In a sense this was a more extreme version of what was done in the eighteenth century. This phenomenon continued into the twentieth and twenty-first centuries, with a new flurry of editions after World War II that paralleled the new Evangelicalism and various manifestations of charismatic Christian faith.

A useful initial example illustrating the tendencies in the evolution of publication of devotional literature surrounding the Quietists is James W. Metcalf's 1853 volume, *Spiritual Progress, or Instructions in the Divine Life of the Soul.* Metcalf translated and edited Fénelon's *Christian Counsel* and *Spiritual Letters* as well as Madame Guyon's *A Short and Easy Method of Prayer* in the Digby Brooke version but corrected against the French version of her works (*Opuscules*), plus extracts entitled *Concise View of the Way to God, And of the State of Union,* followed by *Spiritual Maxims* attributed to Père La Combe. Metcalf was quite scholarly in giving his French sources, but his aim was very practical. In his preface he states "this little work is intended to be simply devotional" so that sectarian or controversial material has been omitted. The reader should approach these texts with an openness to the guidance of the Holy Spirit, and Metcalf implicitly accords a particular revelatory power to devotional literature that is akin to the reading of the Bible. He says that readers who have had the inner experience described within will rejoice and be thankful. Those who have not should not be distrustful: "Reading thus, in absolute dependence, not upon man's wisdom or teaching, but upon the utterances of the blessed Spirit within, you shall infallibly be guided into all Truth. Such is the promise of Him who cannot lie. And may his blessing rest upon you."

In 1893, Metcalf's anthology was reprinted in its entirety by a publishing house associated with the National Holiness Association; a subtitle had been added: "For such as are desirous to count all things but loss that they may win Christ." Charles Blanchard (1848–1925), the president of the nondenominational Wheaton College, read and annotated this 1893 edition. Blanchard, much influenced by figures like George Mueller of the English Keswick Convention, exemplifies how the readership of Catholic Quietist devotional literature spread from the holiness movement through Keswick figures into fundamentalist circles more closely connected with Calvinist theology. Much later, the Metcalf anthology in its 1893 form as *Christian Counsel* would reappear on the Internet.[51]

John Greenleaf Whittier (1807–1892), the Quaker poet and Abolitionist, was well known as a Quietist. On his seventieth birthday, Henry Wadsworth Longfellow dedicated a poem to him in which the silences of speech, desire, and thought of Molinos were equated to Whittier's silence unless moved by spiritual "voices and melodies."[52] In 1862, during the Civil War, Whittier published the preface to the American edition of *The Patience of Hope*, a collection of devotional poetry by the Scottish writer Dora Greenwell. For Whittier there has been a continuing series within Christianity of great individuals or "devout souls" through whom "something of the Infinite Love" has shone, and these souls have embodied the common core of the faith, transcending sectarian division and confusion. Similarly, the books of such souls from various periods and traditions have created a shared Catholic and Protestant heritage. These works sometimes contain matters of doctrine to which our reason may not assent, but they are marked by a "Divine seal" and are "permeated with a certain sweetness and savor of life."[53] "The meditations of the devout monk of Kempen are the common heritage of Catholic and Protestant."[54] The tradition described in broad strokes by Whittier is that cited by Poiret and Upham—it includes not only Augustine and à Kempis but also Tauler, the author of the *Theologia Germanica*, Fénelon, and, of course, Woolman and Greenwell.

In sketching his view of devotional literature, Whittier also articulates a theory of reader response based on the standard of shared experience. "Such books know no limitations of time or place," he says. "They have the perpetual freshness and fitness of truth; they speak out of profound experience: heart answers to heart as we read them; the spirit that is in man, and the inspiration that giveth understanding, bear witness to them." Reading devotional literature is an encounter with the truth as experienced by another soul, and the Holy Spirit facilitates this recognition. Furthermore, the books in this tradition, both Catholic and Quaker, stress "self-renunciation" and "reconcilement to the Divine will," a life of suffering for the good of others, and the guidance of the "indwelling Spirit" that leads to truth that is "even in our hearts." These books avoid creeds, doctrine, and ritual, centering on "simple faith and holiness of life."[55]

After describing Greenwell's poetry and giving examples of several poems, Whittier turns to the issue of whether such devotional poetry leads to absorption in the self at the expense of one's duties to one's neighbors. He thus casts the issue of inner piety in the context of nineteenth-century reform as had, for example, Harriet Beecher Stowe in her articles for the *New-York Evangelist*. "But surely," says Whittier, "the benevolent unrest, the far-reaching sympathies and keen sensitiveness to the suffering of others, which so nobly distinguish our present age, can have nothing to fear from a plea for personal holiness, patience, hope, and resignation to the Divine will." Both Tauler and Woolman are cited as examples of "earnest teachers of the inward life" who were noted for "practical benevolence."[56] Whittier concludes that he hesitated to publish this volume, given the "troubled state of the country," but decided that the call to the "inward and spiritual" and Greenwell's message of hope would be an antidote to the civil strife.

The theoretical and hermeneutical principles suggested by the Metcalf and Whittier prefaces suggest how reprints promoted the criteria of experience and of guidance by the Holy Spirit in finding the truth within devotional literature. Further, the logocentric assumption was ever-present that the reader communed with the writer as though he or she were present. The circle of interpretation was all-embracing and universal, overcoming cultural and doctrinal barriers, because of the basis in shared experience.

Additional examples of reprints of Fénelon also illustrate the force of the tradition of the literature of the inner life and of the nature of its dissemination. In chapter 6, the analysis of editions and translations of Fénelon's devotional works in the earlier nineteenth century demonstrated how American readers were presented with selections of his meditations, letters, instructions and advice chosen from a variety of previous French editions and translations into English. Metcalf had been rather systematic in the way he chose his material for his anthology, but a specific example illustrates how the ensuing publication history of Quietist material over the next century and a half would become increasingly far from the original and homogenized into American culture. Fénelon's *Instructions et Avis sur divers points de la morale et de la perfection chrétienne* had previously been translated straightforwardly as *Instruction and Advice on Various Points of Morality and Christian Perfection*. For his anthology Metcalf entitled his translation (based on an 1810 edition entitled *Avis chrétiens, Christian Counsel*). In 1874, E. P. Dutton (New York) published a new edition, *Christian Counsels, selected from the devotional works of Fénelon, Archbishop of Cambrai*. This new abridged translation was by A. M. James and was based on the Didot French edition. The same publisher then produced another edition of Fénelon's *Spiritual Letters to Men* in 1877. Such editions of Fénelon usually contained around thirty extracts, as had the earlier editions of *Pious Reflections* for each day of the month. The topics are by now familiar: "On Pure Love," "On Prayer and the Principal Exercises of Piety," "On Humility," "On Self-abandonment," "On Fidelity in Small Matters," and "On the Presence of God."

By the twentieth century, Fénelon, as a canonic author, was still in the mainstream. In 1947, Harper and Row brought out a new edition of the *Instructions et Avis*, which had been chosen as the Lenten Book by the Episcopal Presiding Bishop. The English title was *Christian Perfection*.[57] This was a reliable edition by Charles F. Whiston of the Church Divinity School of the Pacific. The reputable translation by Mildren Whitney Stillman was based on an 1858 Paris edition that Whitson also compared with an 1823 edition. Stillman had previously published this spiritual counsel under the title of *Spiritual Letters*. The forty-one translated pieces, written mostly for devout members of the court, were all included in the French edition; the translator and editor did some reordering for thematic unity. French subtitles were given to each chapter. Only one section from the chapter on pure love was excised.

The topics of *Christian Perfection* range from "The Use of Time" to "Fidelity in Little Things," "Suffering Love," "Interior Peace," "Knowing God," and "Self-Renunciation." (The earliest translations and reprints into English, based on other editions, had, of course, printed many of these letters, often as tracts or in very small format.) An extract from the famous piece, "Fidelity in Little Things," is a good example of how this translation brought Fénelon's Quietist emphasis on disinterested love to twentieth-century American readers. The soul, says Fénelon, that neglects small things soon becomes accustomed to unfaithfulness.

> True love sees nothing as little. Everything which can please or displease God always seems great to it. It is not that true love throws the soul into fussing and scruples, but it does place no limits on its fidelity. It acts simply with God, and as it is quite untroubled by the things which God does not ask of it, it also never wants to hesitate a single instant in that which God does ask of it. Thus, it is not by fussiness that we become faithful and exact in the smallest things. It is by a feeling of love, which is free from the reflections and fears of the anxious and scrupulous. We are as though carried away by the love of God. We only want to do what we are doing, and we do not want to do anything at all which we are not doing.[58]

As in the preceding two examples (Metcalf and Whittier), the preface to this edition directed readers as to how to approach devotional literature. Whiston says that their minds cannot be "critical, analytical, argumentative and energetic." "In devotional reading our whole being (not only our intellects) must be quieted; and made open, receptive, expectant; and above all else, humble. It is not so much the work of the intellect as the attentive receptiveness of the whole man."[59] This reading will be done slowly, over time, with a spirit of waiting for the book to reveal itself to us much like a painting might reveal itself to us or the slow sprouting and growth to maturity of a seed. Behind the book also is the saint—Fénelon.

> We turn to and use this book not primarily to expose our minds and spirits to ideas and thoughts, but rather to seek to enter into companionship with this friend of God, that through it we may enter into a deeper and richer and truer fellowship with Fénelon's God.[60]

Whiston thus reiterates a hermeneutic that is both Quietist and logocentric, one in which the reader's openness allows him or her to encounter the spirit of the writer and enter into a friendship with that saint. In so doing, we learn how to enter into companionship with God.

The publishing fate of this translation of *Christian Perfection* also illustrates succinctly how popular evangelical Protestantism continued to make use of Catholic authors, adapting them to its own ends. In 1973, Banner Publishing reproduced a paraphrased version of the Stillman translation under the title *Let Go: Living by the Cross and by Faith* that would remain in print into the twenty-first century. In the introduction, the publisher says that the volume had previously appeared under the title *Spiritual Letters*, translated by Stillman. "After re-reading them, it was decided that a modern paraphrased version would help twentieth century Christians understand the message more clearly." (Letting go is the letting go of the bondage of self.) However, portions of this short preface are unacknowledged paraphrases of the introduction to the Harper and Row edition of *Christian Perfection* by Whiston. After noting that Fénelon wrote the letters to give spiritual direction to a "small number of earnest people" who were seeking "to live a life of true spirituality" in the midst of the corrupt court of Louis XIV, the writer broaches the issue of how to read the book. It is to be read "in a devotional mood" so that it can reveal the spiritual wisdom of "a truly great spiritual giant." "It must be read slowly," it says: "Consider turning to this book not primarily to expose your mind to ideas, but rather to seek to enter into companionship with this friend of God."[61] Forty letters made up this cheaply produced paperback edition under such headings as "The Advantages of Humility," "The Source of Peace Is in the Surrender of the Will," "The Discovery and Death of Self," "Our Knowledge Stands in the Way of Our Becoming Wise," "If You Have Love, You Have Everything," "Surrender is Not a Heroic Sacrifice, But a Simple Sinking Into the Will of God," and "Suffering Belongs to the Living. Not the Dead."

Ironically, Bethany House, another conservative evangelical publisher, reproduced intact the Harper and Row text, with a heading on the cover: "Devotional reflections on the Christian life by a seventeenth-century mystic."[62]

The narratives of transmission surrounding Fénelon that I have just traced are more than the details of a publishing history. They show a continuity of readership and a broad community of believers united by their interest in a higher, deeper, sanctified Christian life. The actual texts that were read, however, were increasingly distant from the originals so that a justifiable question remains. Whose experience were these readers confronting—that of the Quietists themselves or their very own?

Chapter 9

The Legacy of Madame Guyon from 1850 to 2000

From Romantic Sentimentalism to the Charismatic Movement

Phebe Lord Upham and Devotional Literature

Phebe Upham (1804-1882) began to contribute articles to the *Guide to Christian Perfection* in September of 1840; these early pieces were short "Sacred Meditations," usually based on a verse or phrase of Scripture.[1] There was a Quietist flavor to many of the devotionals; they were also permeated by the language of sentiment that touched the hymnody, poetry, and personal testimonies of those caught up in the revivalism of the deeper life or of personal holiness. (Phebe's husband Thomas, so analytic in his treatises on the psychology of the inner life, wrote devotional poetry of a sentimental vein, as we have seen, and he continued to contribute such poems to the *Guide* for many years.)[2] Of the Scripture's "How precious are thy thoughts unto me; how great is the sum of them," Phebe commented,

> The soul that reposes itself always in God, has an inward sense of his love, of his loving kindness and tender mercy, such as the heart wandering from God has no conception of. The sweet rest, the blissful repose of such a soul cannot be expressed; it rests on the bosom of infinite, unchangeable love.[3]

These meditations were gathered into a "neat little pocket volume," *Sacred Meditations*, according to the *Guide* in 1846. "It is one of the very best devotional books we ever saw, and we hope our readers will be ready to buy, read and distribute [it] at once."[4] Thus, Phebe Upham's little volume took its place in the long tradition of devotional manuals growing out of the *lectio divina* that entered the Protestant tradition from Catholicism. Such manuals, giving a method for meditating on either visual imagery or texts (Scripture or others), were probably best known to American Protestants via François de Sales.[5] They contributed to the development of a "religious self." Growing out of this long tradition, via Puritanism, as well, devotional literature came to include letters of spiritual direction, daily devotional readings, biographies and autobiographies, and poetry.[6] In mid-nineteenth-century America, the development of a mass market for readers coincided with the "feminization" of culture evident in the success of romances and domestic novels and also in intense devotional piety among both Catholics and Protestants.[7] Amanda Porterfield has called the general phenomenon "the domestication of theology," characterized by the "deification of femininity" and the "feminization of God." "In an era of soft religion," she writes, "many religious women found great personal strength and wielded authority accordingly, compelling the allegiance of nearly all sectors of their culture to the religious values they preserved in family life."[8] This domestication of theology carried over to the reading of devotional literature. By 1857, as pre-Civil War revivalism was intensifying, the editors of the *Guide to Holiness*, in a short book review, "[hailed] it as among the favorable omens of the present age, that works of a devotional character are in increasing demand."[9]

Thomas Upham's writings on the interior life and his contextualization of the American search for sanctification or holiness within Continental mysticism thus coincided with the spread of sentimental taste and also influenced it. Phebe Upham's devotional publications illustrate how holiness revivalism, spreading across denominations, was part of this phenomenon. Nor was she alone. We have already seen Harriet Beecher Stowe's link to the spirituality of the inner life. Two other examples illustrate this coalescence between popular piety and sentimental culture. Susan Warner (1819–1885), Stowe's contemporary and a Presbyterian, published the immensely popular *The Wide, Wide World* in 1850, a novel in part about the formation of the orphan Ellen's Christian character. Warner's many publications also included *Walks from Eden*, a series of narratives for young readers designed to illustrate Scripture. Her sister Anna, with whom she collaborated to a limited extent, was more heavily identified with Christian juvenile didactic literature and also wrote songs such as "Jesus Loves Me." Susan herself was touched by the search for a deeper inner life, had contacts with Methodists, and read Boardman's *The Higher Christian Life*.[10] Lucy Larcom (1824–1893), a Congregationalist who became an Episcopalian, was initially a mill worker in Lowell, Massachusetts, before going on to teach and to write. Best known for her poetry and for her autobiography, *A New England Girlhood*, Larcom became an adept compiler as well, producing a number of inspirational and devotional volumes. Such books grew out of the long tradition of commonplace books and devotional manuals. These compilations included *Beckonings for Every Day: A Calendar of Thought*, *Breathings of the Better Life*, and *The Cross and the Grail*. These particular anthologies contributed to the genre of "daily devotional readings" and also brought selections from great authors into one handy volume for the popular reader.

Phebe Upham adapted the writings of Madame Guyon to readers' taste for devotional literature, publishing samples of her own translations of Madame Guyon's correspondence in *The Guide to Holiness*, starting in 1846; the first two letters, from Madame Guyon to Fénelon, appeared in January and February of that year. From the translations of various Guyon letters, Phebe developed a set of maxims ("select thoughts") that appeared in the *Guide* in 1855; a devotional edition, *Madam Guyon's Letters*, followed in 1858. This handy book was in a small format and contained sixty-two abstracted letters, always less than two pages in length. The format suggested the intended use of the letters as devotional reading. Like other translators and editors, Upham justified her project by saying that Madame Guyon's style was "somewhat diffuse" and that the correspondence was voluminous so that the selection entailed condensing and rewriting the original texts. Upham, like the writer of the preface to the 1767 edition that she used, indicates that, next to the "Sacred Oracles," she has received the most spiritual benefit from these letters.[11]

Indirectly, Phebe's volume invited her readers to meditate on a set of devotional themes that were already apparent in Thomas Upham's interpretation of the life and religious experience of Madame Guyon. A sampling of entry titles makes this clear: "Turn away from Self to Christ," "Humility the effect of Love," "Joy in Persecutions," "Spiritual Oneness," "Simplicity and the Power of the Word," "Forgetfulness of Self," "Live in the Present," "Repose of the Soul in God," and "Concise View of the Interior Way." The uses to which the letters of spiritual counsel were put paralleled the ways in which Fénelon's spiritual direction had been been organized for Protestant readers. A few examples reinforce themes already encountered.

> When Jesus Christ is formed in the soul, he imparts not only a clear understanding of the word, but is himself the Word, reproduced in the soul. Those only in whom Christ dwells, fulfill the word, or have the word accomplished in them. Such only are able fully to interpret the word. It is not learning which best explains the truths of God, but the reproduction of these truths in the life—the experience of them.

The time is short; wherefore spend it in the compass and surroundings of self? The single eye sees only God. You act as a person who being called before a king, instead of regarding the king and his benefits, is occupied only with his own dress and appearance. God wishes to dis-arrange you—to destroy self; and you wish to preserve what he would destroy. Be more afraid of self than of the evil one. It is the spirit of Satan to exalt self above God, and this spirit is fostered by these con-tinual returns you make upon your own doings and misdoings, which leave no place in your mind for the occupation of God.

Having given up myself wholly to God, and loving Him far better than myself, how can I find any opposition to his good pleasure? How can I do otherwise than yield to one I love better than myself? How can a soul withdraw from the dominion of a Sovereign, that it loves with the whole heart? "What can separate us from the love of God, in Christ Jesus?" Although, while we remain in this life, there is a possibility of sinning, and of separation from God, and it is true, that the soul remains in oneness with Him, only by the continuance of his mercy, and that if he should leave it, it would immediately fall into sin, I cannot have the least fear, that my God will leave me, or that I shall ever separate myself in any degree from his love.[12]

Who read Upham's devotional edition of the spiritual letters of Madame Guyon? As in the case of Fénelon, the readership can be traced from the revivals following the Civil War and the ensuing holiness asso-ciations and denominations to the charismatic movement of the late twentieth century. The publishing house founded by Phoebe Palmer and her husband reprinted the Upham edition in 1870, and G. W. McCalla, of the National Association for the Promotion of Holiness, printed the book in 1895.[13] In the later twentieth century, Gene Edwards, of The Seed Sowers, an arm of Christian Books Publishing House, a charismatic press, reprinted the McCalla edition as *Guyon's Spiritual Letters* and then reissued it in 1989 as *Jeanne Guyon Speaks Again*. The title page indicated that this was an edition in "modern English"; in reality it was an updating of Phebe Upham's paraphrased translation, as printed by McCalla. For example, the last citation above, concerning "Complete Rest," was cast in the following breezy style in the Edwards text:

My desire is to give myself totally to God and to love Him far more than I love myself. Why would I oppose anything that pleases Him? How can I do anything but give myself completely to Him? Who could run from the reign of a king whom one loves wholeheartedly? "What can separate us from the love of God in Christ Jesus?"

I realize that while you are in this life there is room to sin and to be separated from God. It is also true that you remain in fellowship with God only through His continual mercy, and if He should leave you to yourself you would immediately fall into sin. Yet, I just cannot have the smallest fear that you will be separated from His love.[14]

All of Madame Guyon's writings came to be viewed as "devotional literature." This was the position of D. D. Lowery of the United Brethren, who published an anthology of her writings in 1904, defining devotional literature as "literature of a highly spiritual and deeply inspirational character." This transformation of Madame Guyon into a devotional author within Protestant traditions emerging from the tumultuous religious history of the nineteenth century meant that she became not only a spiritual authority, but also a role model and a source of emotional elevation.

Collections of daily devotional readings (a Scripture passage, followed by a commentary or excerpt and then a prayer) became a staple of popular piety in the nineteenth century and well into the twentieth century. Most striking was the ecumenical and eclectic flavor of the excerpts included in these devotional manuals. Mrs. Charles E. (Lettie) Cowman's *Streams in the Desert*, first published in 1923, went through innumerable printings and illustrates well the merging of the religious traditions of the interior way. Cowman (1870–1960) spent the years 1901–1917 with her husband Charles as a missionary in Japan and China. Although Lettie Cowman was first a Methodist, the Cowmans belonged to the International Holiness Union and Prayer League that would eventually become the Pilgrim Holiness Church in 1922. Charles Cowman's missionary partner was Ernest A. Kilbourne, and the missionary endeavor, a "faith" work, would become the Oriental Missionary Society.[15] In 1922, Mrs. Cowman began to write columns for *God's Revivalist and Bible Advocate*, published by God's Bible School, a nondenominational holiness institution in Cincinnati. (Male students from God's Bible School had assisted in the Cowman-Kilbourne missionary endeavor in Tokyo.) Charles Cowman died in 1924 after a long illness, and his wife emerged as a figure in her own right.[16]

The format of the daily devotionals in *Streams in the Desert* included a daily Scripture verse, excerpts from writers, including poetry, and commentary by Cowman; a short continuous text resulted, making attributions of the material sometimes difficult. These meditations are "a primary example of twentieth-century popular piety unmediated by minister or theologian."[17] In general, Mrs. Cowman's message is that spiritual depth is achieved through and in suffering, that rest in God's love and acceptance of God's providence lead to endurance and triumph, and that piety is a matter of the centered soul.

There is a limit to affliction. God sends it, and removes it. Do you sigh and say, "When will the end be?" Let us quietly wait and patiently endure the will of the Lord till He cometh. Our Father takes away the rod when His design in using it is fully served.

If the affliction is sent for testing us, that our graces may glorify God, it will end when the Lord has made us bear witness to His praise. [February 16]

In the present day there are those who live intermittent Christian lives because they have become occupied with the outward, and center in circumstances; in place of centering in God. God wants us more and more to see Him in everything, and to call nothing small if it bears us His message. [July 24]

Is there any note of music in all the chorus as mighty as the emphatic pause? Is there any word in all the Psalter more eloquent than that one word, Selah (Pause)? Is there anything more thrilling and awful than the hush that comes before the bursting of the tempest and the strange quiet that seems to fall upon all nature before some preternatural phenomenon or convulsion? Is there anything that can touch our hearts as the *power of stillness?*

There is for the heart that will cease from itself, "the peace of God that passeth all understanding," a "quietness and confidence" which is the source of all strength, a sweet peace "which nothing can offend," a deep rest which the world can neither give nor take away. There is in the deepest center of the soul a chamber of peace where God dwells, and where, if we will only enter in and hush every other sound, we can hear His still, small voice. [November 24][18]

Mrs. Cowman chose her excerpts to suit her Scripture verse and the theme she wished to develop for the day in question. Her sources ranged from Jonathan Edwards and John Wesley to the popular poets Henry Van Dyke and Annie Johnson Flint, from Emerson and Longfellow to *The Sunday School Times* and *The Canadian Ladies Home Journal.* She often cited A. B. Simpson of the Christian and Missionary Alliance. What is striking is that the excerpts, in all their eclectic scatteredness, represented much of the tradition of inner piety and holiness in which the writings of Madame Guyon played a part. Cowman's use of such extracts, however informal, echoed the practices of many other compilers before her but was closest to nineteenth-century periodical literature, such as *The Guide to Holiness* or *The Ladies' Repository.* In *Streams in the Desert,* we find the Catholic François de Sales quoted, but also Tauler, Zinzendorf, George Fox the Quaker, and Hannah Whitall Smith, the Quaker of holiness leanings who was part of the Keswick movement. And two quotes from Madame Guyon figure in the volume—both from the Phebe Upham collection of letters and two poems. An admonition not to give in to melancholy is included on June 1 for the verse from Isaiah 28:12, "This is the rest wherewith ye may cause the weary to rest; and this is the refreshing." Madame Guyon's concluding sentence is "God's designs regarding you, and His methods of bringing about these designs, are infinitely wise."[19] On October 12, when the imprisonment of Joseph in Genesis 39 occasions the theme of imprisonment because of serving God and the danger of self-pity, Mrs. Cowman quotes the poem "A little bird I am," and concludes with a striking quotation from Madame Guyon, "I have learnt to love the darkness of sorrow; there you see the brightness of His face."[20]

Versions of the Life of Madame Guyon

Thomas Upham's study of the life and religious experience of Madame Guyon spawned a range of editions of her autobiography, as well as retellings of her biography among those touched by holiness revivalism. The readership of the Upham book via its many editions was considerable, both in North America and in Great Britain. The off-shoots—other editions of the Guyon autobiography and short versions of her life for a popular audience—added to that readership. The genre of women's autobiographies was an important part of the Wesleyan holiness tradition where women were accepted as leaders and as ordained clergy as churches were formed. *Experience* (1793) and *Spiritual Letters* of Hester Ann Rogers (1756-1794), the well-known Methodist class leader, were read, along with Phoebe Palmer's *The Way of Holiness* and Madame Guyon's account of her life. Such experiential narratives were models for the autobiographies of women preachers within the American holiness tradition.[21] In fact, a number of these women, as identified by Susie Stanley, mentioned reading Madame Guyon; these included Hannah Whitall Smith and less well-known figures such as Lela McConnell, Sara Cooke, and Lizzie Miller.[22]

In chapter 1, I commented that by the beginning of the twentieth century, Madame Guyon was regularly included in collections of biographical sketches of individuals who illustrated the experience of sanctification. J. O. McClurkan's anthology *Chosen Vessels* placed her in the company of people like Whitefield, Frances Willard, and Charles G. Finney.[23] In 1911, J. Gilchrist Lawson, an evangelist, published a collection emphasizing a theology of the baptism of the Holy Spirit, *Deeper Experiences of Famous Christians*, that was printed by a Church of God press in the United States. Lawson's approach represented the appropriation of Madame Guyon and Fénelon by the Pentecostal branch of the holiness movement. Both Madame Guyon and Fénelon figured on a list that ranged from Savonarola to George Fox, Bunyan, Wesley, and Whitefield to Billy Bray, Jacob Knapp, George Mueller, D. L. Moody, and General Booth. Old Testament and New Testament characters were also included. In his introduction, Lawson explained that his collection could not begin to include all the examples of the "deeper experiences" of Christians from all periods of history. Those omitted included mystics such as St. Bernard, Hildegarde, Catherine of Siena, St. Frances de Sales, and many other Christians from various traditions around the world. For Lawson, the terminology used to describe "deeper" spiritual experiences might differ, but there is a "harmony" in the accounts: "It is the baptism, or filling, or gift of the Holy Spirit, and the experience resulting from being 'filled with the Spirit.'"[24] In presenting Madame Guyon, Lawson suggested that her teachings resembled those of modern Quakers and attributed a huge influence within France to her ministry in her lifetime.

> Her soul was all ablaze with the unction and power of the Holy Spirit, and everywhere she went she was besieged by multitudes of hungry, thirsty, souls, who flocked to her for the spiritual meat that they failed to get from their regular pastors. Revivals of religion began in almost every placed visited by her, and all over France earnest Christians began to seek the deeper experience taught by her.[25]

This genre of saints' lives illustrates the appeal of Madame Guyon to women readers within the broad holiness movement. Clara McLeister brought together short sketches of Men and Women of Deep Piety that appeared under the imprint of the Wesleyan Methodist Publishing Association in 1920. Her portraits were much briefer than those of Lawson, but it is apparent that a sensitivity to the need for women role models lay behind the work. In addition to the familiar figures ranging from Thomas à Kempis to Fénelon and William Wilberforce, Mrs. McLeister included Fanny Crosby, Anne Cutler, Mary Fletcher, Madam Guyon, Frances Havergal, Selina Shirley Huntingdon (Lady Huntingdon), Lizzie Johnson, Florence Nightingale, Mrs. Phoebe Palmer, Hester Ann Rogers, Minnie Shelhamer, Susanna Wesley, Frances Willard, and Mrs. E. M. Whittemore.

> To write brief sketches of pious women was the author's first design. This to her seemed an unassuming way of becoming a blessing to her sisters in the Lord who, having many cares and perplexities, hear much more frequently of holy men and their achievement than of pious, successful mothers and hand-maidens of the Lord. It was at the request of

the publisher that the writing of sketches of holy men was also undertaken and included in the volume.[26]

Madame Guyon, according to Mrs. McLeister, was not one of those individuals who were great becaused they embodied the age in which they lived; rather, she bucked the tide and the "gleams of [her] saintly and triumphant life" stood out "in a dark and forbidding age."[27]

This feminization of the legacy of Madame Guyon is also apparent in the versions of her autobiography that appeared in the wake of Upham's study. In 1880, a two-part edition of the *Autobiography of Madame Guyon* prepared by Edward Jones was published by the Bible House in New York City. This version would set the tradition for subsequent abridgments and paraphrases within the holiness and broader evangelical traditions. The Jones edition was quickly reprinted.[28] This particular edition was an abridgment but it reproduced, with some modernization, the anonymous James Gough text of the 1775 Dublin edition (often erroneously attributed to Digby Brooke) as it had passed into America via the 1804 Philadelphia edition printed by Crukshank. Thus, the popularized autobiography of Madame Guyon that circulated so widely among American holiness readers, whether in the Wesleyan or Pentecostal traditions, was a simplified and sanitized story, freed to a large degree of the details of its Catholicism—the mystic states and dogmatic controversy. Jeanne Guyon's yieldedness—her Quietist acceptance of persecution and suffering as a gift from God and her triumph over her ecclesiastical adversaries—became major themes. With some historic licence, Jones himself commented:

> Viewed from a human standpoint, it is a sublime spectacle, to see a solitary woman subvert all the machinations of kings and courtiers; laugh to scorn all the malignant enginery [sic] of the Papal inquisition, and silence, and confound the pretensions of the most learned divines. She not only saw more clearly the sublimest truths of out most holy Christianity, but she basked in the clearest and most beautiful sunlight while they groped in darkness. She grasped with ease the deepest and sublimest truths of holy Writ, while they were lost in the mazes of their profound ignorance.[29]

A series of women, whom we might label women of deep piety, published versions of either the autobiography or biography of Madame Guyon. Abbie C. Morrow (b. 1844) provides an interesting example from the end of the nineteenth century. Morrow was connected with the Pentecostal holiness tradition and was a deaconess and a superintendent of a home, and, like others in this period when holiness and sentimental piety often coalesced, she was a devotional writer. She authored *Joy and Rejoicing: Pentecostal Bible Readings, Bible Morning Glories, Bible B's,* and *Prayers for Public Worship, Private Devotions, and Personal Ministry.* In 1898 Morrow, following the Jones edition, abridged even further the Guyon autobiography, publishing it under the title *Sweet Smelling Myrrh: The Autobiography of Madame Guyon.*[30] By now, Madame Guyon's original text had been reduced to a straightforward narrative of 191 pages—easily assimilable by the common reader. When Madame Guyon had gone through her dark night of illness and depressive self-doubt in Savoy, she came to an inner assurance of her new apostolic vocation. American readers would absorb texts like the following in adding Jeanne Guyon to their mental storehouse of mythic pious women.

> Jesus was living in me; I lived no more. [. . .] He showed me all the world in a rage against me, without any one daring to appear for me, and assured me in the ineffable silence of His eternal Word, that he would give me vast numbers of children, which I should bring forth by the cross. I left it to Him to do with me whatever he pleased, esteeming my whole and sole interest to be placed entirely in His Divine Will.[31]

This tradition of abridging the Guyon autobiography and of modernizing its language would continue for a very long time and would include the broader evangelical world at the end of the twentieth century. Jan Johnson, whom we cited in chapter 2, published a short, paraphrased version of the autobiography in 1999 that was brought out by Bethany House, an affiliate at the time of the Bethany Fellowship Mission. She consulted an electronically produced version of the autobiography, a 1995 reprint originally brought out by the Moody Press in 1980. The Moody Press edition was based on an abridged version brought out by the Christian Witness Company in 1917. This entire publishing history demonstrates the continuity of the reading tradition surrounding the Guyon autobiography, as republished by Jones in 1880, but going back to James Gough's anonymous edited translation in the eighteenth century. Yes, Jeanne Guyon was always a Catholic, but she was, like Proteus, ever metamorphosing into a multifacted Protestant.[32]

Short biographies of Jeanne Guyon, usually written by women, also followed in the wake of nineteenth-century holiness revivalism. These were part of the educational effort to promote the cause of holiness by providing reading matter directed toward the general reader. Henrietta Matson's *Life of Madame Guyon* was published around the turn of the century.[33] Matson (1839–1905) was a Congregationalist who became active in the Pentecostal Alliance, a cross-denominational holiness group in Nashville, growing out of revivals in that city, of which J. O. McClurkan was the best-known figure.[34] A member of the 1862 class at Oberlin College, she had been a missionary in Mendi, West Africa, but had been forced to return home due to health problems. Matson was a member of the American Missionary Association that was actively involved in educational efforts in the South after the Civil War. In 1870 she arrived at Fisk University, serving as matron and as an instructor but also playing a key role in the revivals during the early years of the institution. Matson was also an author; she produced a novel, *Mississippi Schoolmaster*, in 1893,[35] and several biographies for the Pentecostal Mission Publishing Company, including *Life of George Mueller*, *Recollections of Chas. G. Finney*, and *Celebrated Missionaries*. These books and others on sanctification and the second coming by holiness leaders such as McClurkan and B. F. Haynes had often appeared in a short form in holiness-oriented newspapers.[36]

Henrietta Matson plays the role of the no-nonsense interpreter of the life of Madame Guyon in her little ninety-six-page biography. Her aim is to cut through the mysticism of Guyonian spirituality and to show that Jeanne Guyon had embarked on the way of holiness.

> For more than two hundred years devout souls have delighted in reading the memoirs of Madame Guyon. Her experiences are constantly quoted by the deeply spiritual, but are often misunderstood, especially by those who try to follow her, because God does not deal with any two human souls alike, for the same diversity is found in the spiritual world that we see in nature. The mystic and ascetic elements which prevail in Madame Guyon's writings have always been a fascination to some who read them. [. . .] But perhaps only few who read her life realize that she lived and loved and suffered as we do today, and that she found the King's highway of holiness in much the same way that we do in this twentieth century.[37]

Like Upham, whom she probably used as a reference, Henrietta Matson explains the religious experience of Madame Guyon in terms of conversion and sanctification, using the stock phraseology of experimental holiness as preached by Phoebe Palmer and others of holiness revivalism. God used the trials and suffering of Jeanne's years of marriage to bring her to conversion and "full surrender." "She had never heard of the 'Second work' of grace in her heart; the first work by which she had been 'born again' was entirely misunderstood by nearly all of those to whom she could go. Only one, here and there, in that day and age believed in, or experienced what we know as conversion."[38] Madame Guyon "laid herself and her all on the altar" and she had to learn that "His full and complete indwelling in her soul left no room for unholy desires."[39] Eventually, periods of inner desolation and crucifixion were followed by deep and complete peace and a sense of inner purity. "Every sanctified soul," says Matson, "knows what that means when living under the precious cleansing blood."[40]

After Madame Guyon's period of wandering and teaching, upon her arrival in Paris she continued her vocation, but now among the most distinguished people in France.

> The fire was burning in her soul, kindled by the Holy Ghost Himself, and following the divine leading, she cultivated this new field of labor with the same simplicity and holy fervor that characterized her work among the lowly. It was not long, however, before her teaching such new and unheard of doctrines as conversion and sanctification by faith alone, attracted very general attention.[41]

Jeanne Guyon and Father LaCombe would become "martyrs of the Holy Ghost" in the ensuing drama of religion and politics. Fénelon comes to know God as his "sanctifier" under the influence of Madame Guyon whose piety and "mental powers" had made her into a great religious reformer. She intercedes with God on his behalf. "Is it any wonder that God did so much for this remarkable man, whose influence has been felt by multitudes in the world who knew nothing of Madame Guyon?"[42] Matson goes on to depict clearly and succinctly the opposition of Louis XIV, Madame de Maintenon, and Bossuet to Madame Guyon, her imprisonments, Fénelon's exile, and then Jeanne's final exile to Blois. Jeanne Guyon may have been a martyr, but it was her conversion and sanctification that really drew the interest of Henrietta Matson.

Henrietta Matson's life of Madame Guyon was one of many short biographies, sometimes published as prefaces or as magazine articles, sometimes published as books, that figured among publications within the holiness movement and conservative evangelicalism. In 1946 Bessie Olson, a graduate of John Fletcher College and an instructor at Pilgrim Holiness, Nazarene, and Wesleyan institutions, brought out a forty-seven-page life of Madame Guyon as one of several portraits that included John Fletcher, Charles Spurgeon, William Carey, D. L. Moody, Adam Clarke, John Bunyon, and Henry Ward Beecher. Like Matson and others, Olson saw Madame Guyon as a reformer in France. "She was *in* the Catholic church, but not *with* it; in it in *form*, but not with it in *spirit*."[43] As late as 1984 the Christian Literature Crusade published another popular biography that also emphasized how Madame Guyon stood apart from the institutional church: "Like Martin Luther, who dared to point out in his *Ninety-Five Theses* certain errors and false practices of the Roman Catholic

Church, Madame Guyon taught that justification came by faith in Jesus Christ alone. And sanctification, too. In fact, it was her reliance upon personal faith in the crucified and resurrected Jesus as the foundation of the Christian life—simple, unembellished faith—that the Roman Catholic Church found to be the most objectionable."[44]

A Tradition of Devotional Reading

The legacy of Madame Guyon, like that of Fénelon, indicates the strikingly ecumenical taste among "holiness" readers of devotional literature, a taste that crossed denominational lines and included Catholic authors who were deemed to have the same experimental theology of purity of heart. By the end of the nineteenth century, the publisher G. W. McCalla in Philadelphia was advertising these "Works on the Interior Life":

Parable of a Pilgrim. Walter Hilton, 1433.
The Seven Overcomings. G. W. McCalla.
Practice of the Presence of God. Nicholas Herman [Brother Lawrence].
Life of Dr. John Tauler, with a summary of the doctrine.
Inward Divine Guidance. T. C. Upham.
Theologia Germanica.
The Living Flame of Love. John of the Cross.
The Prayer of Silence. John Falconi.
An Exhortation. Isaac Penington.
Spiritual Letters. Mrs. P. L. Upham.
The Journeyings of the Children of Israel. Thomas Bromely.
The Nature of Salvation by Christ. Job Scott.
Footprints of a Pilgrim. Mrs. A. E. Bennett.
Spiritual Letters. Fenelon.
Spiritual Letters. Madam Guyon.
Concise View of the Way to God, and of the State of Union. Madam Guyon.
The Crucified and Quickened Christian. William Dell.
Entire Conformity to the Divine Will.
Reminiscences of Port Royal. M. Angelique Arnauld.
Autobiography of Madam Guyon.
Christian Counsel. Fenelon.
The Spiritual Guide. Michael De Molinos.[45]

This broad canon of holiness devotional literature, featuring Madame Guyon and Fénelon, existed at the very moment that holiness associations that grew out of camp meetings were becoming institutionalized in the early twentieth century. The splintering of the holiness movement over issues of dispensationalism and the nature of the baptism of the Holy Spirit (particularly speaking in tongues) led to the creation of Pentecostal

and holiness denominations that were all part of broader Fundamentalism that emerged as a response to the threat to the biblical faith and to
personal salvation perceived to be posed by liberal theology in mainline
denominations. The preceding editions of devotional literature based on
Madame Guyon were early expressions of the diverging Wesleyan and
Pentecostal branches of the old holiness movement.[46]

A. W. Tozer's anthology, *The Christian Book of Mystical Verse*, published
in 1963, shows that this canon of devotional readings existed within the
broader camp of Fundamentalism well after the early holiness movements had subsided. Tozer (1897–1963) was a gifted, largely self-educated
preacher and writer who grew up on a farm in Pennsylvania; his family
eventually moved to Akron, Ohio, so that his father could find factory
work. After a conversion experience at the age of eighteen, Tozer initially
joined the Methodist Church. Beginning to preach not long after, he
became a member of the Christian and Missionary Alliance, where he
was given access to the pulpit. A. B. Simpson was a significant influence
on his thought, but the young Tozer also practiced an intense devotional
life of Bible study and prayer.[47] As did others in the holiness tradition
(whether Wesleyan or non-Wesleyan), he linked the high value of Scripture with the experiential reality of an interior life of inner piety. Tozer's
pastorates of Alliance churches began in 1919, with his most influential
service taking place on the south side of Chicago from 1928–1959, followed by a position as preaching minister at the Avenue Road Church in
Toronto. The power of Tozer's preaching was such that students from the
Moody Bible Institute and Wheaton College flocked to his Sunday evening services. The generation of Billy Graham and the new evangelicals
heard Tozer's preaching on the deeper Christian life, total commitment
to Christ, and the filling of the Holy Spirit for a life of service.[48] This
type of preaching was key to Tozer's ministry in Toronto where he again
attracted university students, particularly those aligned with the nondenominational InterVarsity Christian Fellowship, a parachurch student
group founded first in England. Tozer's brand of holiness placed him less
in the Wesleyan tradition than in that of the Keswick conventions, for
which he also preached.[49]

Tozer identified himself as an evangelical, but his emphasis on Scripture and on witnessing and the contrast he painted between himself and
"liberals" placed him within the camp of Fundamentalism. However, the
intensity of his own inner life of devotion and his interest in the interior
life as it spanned Catholic and Protestant theology situated him within
the tradition represented by Madame Guyon and Fénelon, setting him
apart from many other Fundamentalists. Tozer himself argued for "the

essential interiority of true religion. [. . .] That which is external must become internal; [. . .] the objective Reality which is God must cross the threshold of our personality and take residence within."[50]

Tozer was also a widely read author, first through his articles in *The Alliance Weekly*, later known as *The Alliance Witness*, of which he became editor in 1950. In his most influential books, *The Pursuit of God* (1948) and *The Knowledge of the Holy* (1961), he set forth a demanding form of inner piety characterized by complete commitment and a high view of God, as opposed to the increasingly acculturated views of the born-again experience in popular American evangelicalism. Although seeped in Scripture and in Pauline theology, Tozer freely recommended books on the interior life that included *The Imitation of Christ*, *The Confessions*, *Introduction to the Devout Life* (de Sales), *A Guide to True Peace* (Fénelon, Guyon, and Molinos), *The Practice of the Presence of God* (Brother Lawrence), *The Spiritual Guide* (Molinos), and the *Theologica Germanica*. But the list of authors was much longer and inclusive—Böhme, John of the Cross, Julian of Norwich, Nicholas of Cusa, Tersteegen, Suso, and others.[51]

Tozer had a long-standing interest in verse and hymnody, so *The Christian Book of Mystical Verse*, published at the time of his death, brought together many of the strands of his thinking about the experience of the interior life.[52] In his introduction, Tozer notes that very few of the authors he has included are classic mystics and that "gospel churches" have traditionally rejected mystics as "unstable," "visionary," and "unsound theologically." The poems of this volume are "God-oriented; they begin with God, embrace the worshipping soul and return to God again."[53] Tozer defines the mystic in a way that explains much of the tradition outlined in this book.

> I refer to the evangelical mystic who has been brought by the gospel into intimate fellowship with the Godhead. His theology is no less and no more than is taught in the Christian Scriptures. He walks the high road of truth where walked of old prophets and apostles, and where down the centuries walked martyrs, reformers, puritans, evangelists and missionaries of the cross. He differs from the ordinary orthodox Christian only because he experiences his faith down in the depths of his sentient being while others do not. He exists in a world of spiritual reality. He is quietly, deeply, and sometimes almost ecstatically aware of the Presence of God in his own nature and in the world around him. His religious experience is something elemental, as old as time and the creation. It is immediate acquaintance with God by union with the Eternal son. It is to know that which passes knowledge.[54]

The volume is geared toward worship and private devotion, not study, and an effort has been made to exclude the sentimental. Like the other editors of devotional literature whom we have encountered, Tozer invites his readers not to read as they would read other books but to "try rather to enter its mood, to capture and be captured by its spirit."

The organization of the anthology conveys Tozer's theology of devotion:

> Adoration of the Godhead
> [. . .] Meditation on the Cross of Christ
> Penitential Reflections on Our Sins
> Rejoicing in Forgiveness and Justification
> Yearning for Purity of Heart
> Aspirations after God
> Delighting in God's Presence
> The Raptures of Divine Love
> The Rest of Faith
> The Spiritual Warfare
> Victory Through Praise
> The Prayer of Quiet
> The Bliss of Communion
> Joyous Anticipation of Christ's Return
> Immortality and the World to Come.[55]

We find poets and hymnodists whom we would expect—Isaac Watts, Charles Wesley, and Christian Rossetti—as well as others who are unknown today, but also Catholics ranging from Bernard of Clairvaux and Peter Abelard to Madame Guyon and Frederick Faber (1814–1863). In fact, the two most represented poets/hymnodists are Faber and the radical Pietist Gerhard Tersteegen. A much-published hymnodist, Faber was an English Catholic parish priest and monk who was touched by the nineteenth-century search for a deeper life of holiness. He authored, as well, books such as *Growth in Holiness; or, The Progress of the Spiritual Life.*[56]

There are seven poems by Jeanne Guyon in Tozer's anthology; although the sources are not indicated, four of the poems are in Cowper's paraphrased translation. (Editions of her poetry, primarily as translated by Cowper, had continued to appear in the nineteenth century.)[57] Tozer chose Guyon poems for meditating on aspiring after God, the raptures of divine love, the rest of faith, suffering (spiritual warfare), and the bliss of communion. Perhaps the translation of "I Love My God," included by Tozer in his collection summarizes much of Jeanne Guyon's experience as it passes through cultures and translations to speak to the American heart:

I love my God, but with no love of mine,
For I have none to give;
I love thee, Lord; but all the love is Thine,
For by Thy life I live.
I am as nothing, and rejoice to be
Emptied, and lost, and swallowed up in Thee.

Thou, Lord, alone, art all Thy children need,
And there is none beside;
From Thee the streams of blessedness proceed
In Thee the blest abide,—
Fountain of life, and all-abounding grace,
Our source, our center, and our dwelling-place.[58]

Epilogue

In speaking of the readers of the works of Madame Guyon and of Fénelon, I have featured both individuals and the broad faith communities that set the boundaries of their interpretative practices. However, many of these individuals saw themselves as part of one vast community of readers through the centuries because all were part of a continuum through time of those who had embarked on the interior way and had come to experience union with God or perfect love. The striking quality of these persons of "eminent piety" was their dynamism—their lively faith, their sense of purpose and calling, their awareness of being a part of a religious movement. Whether they were the Quietists themselves in the later seventeenth century, eighteenth-century Pietists, Quakers, or Methodists, or nineteenth-century perfectionists, they organized themselves into small groups or associations in order to facilitate renewal, spread the news that a spirituality of the heart was available to all, reach out to one another, and educate one another.

The article "Points in Holiness Theology" (1903) cited in chapter 1 takes on a richness of texture if examined in retrospect from the viewpoint of an entire tradition of piety. For the author, "holiness theology" was certain because of the proof of experience: "We know because of testing over centuries every promise." The dynamism of a religious movement was evident in the organic imagery used by the writer. Holiness theology was "a growth that reach[ed] across centuries" and developed from "studies of the holiest men and women this world has ever seen." The

Baconian proof of experience was coupled with a high view of the authority of the Bible "as understood by plain people [. . .] filled and guided by the Holy Spirit, [. . .] the author of the book." And the tradition was "non-sectarian," including Bernard of Clairvaux, Thomas à Kempis, Madame Guyon, and Fénelon, as well as Wesley, Fletcher, and Asbury.[1]

Indeed, reading was a part of the road to piety, a means by which spirituality became accessible to the common people. Madame Guyon's claim in her *Short and Easy Method of Prayer* that all, yes, all were called to inner prayer was an attempt to open to the laity the way to contemplative prayer and interior spirituality. She was sensitive to those who could not read in giving her instructions for the short route to God, attainable apart from a religious vocation and outside a convent or monastery. Yet, her handbook on prayer was read and passed around in both manuscript and print form in the seventeenth century; in small Quietist circles, it was also transmitted orally, along with the teaching of others who were "democratizing" spirituality. In the movements promoting renewal and inner spirituality that followed, efforts to promote the reading of devotional literature went hand in hand with the reading of the Bible and of instructional works such as Plutarch's *Lives* and Fénelon's *Telemachus*. Protestants drew upon Catholic devotional methods and writers, adapting meditation and contemplation to their own needs, so that an informal canon of devotional literature emerged. Thomas à Kempis was the most prominent author in this shared devotional tradition, but Jeanne Guyon and François de Fénelon were the most dramatic examples of Protestant claims to Catholic authors because of their place within the politics of religious persecution under Louis XIV.

In the late twentieth century, American readers were still turning to the spiritual writings of Madame Guyon and Fénelon, but a look at how their works were disseminated says much about the devotional tradition. Protestant Evangelicalism of the post-World War II era was succeeded by the dynamism of the charismatic renewal movement that crossed traditional church boundaries.[2] Personal piety, new forms of community and of worship, and an emphasis on the laity were part of this renewal. Even as the older holiness and Pentecostal associations that emerged from nineteenth-century revivalism became institutionalized as churches, the spirituality practiced by various intentional ecumenical communities broadened the conception of the Christian spiritual tradition. "The very term 'spirituality' [came] to reflect both the earlier Roman Catholic focus on prayer and the interior life with God, and an emerging, more comprehensive sense of the whole of life lived in the concrete world in relation to God and neighbor."[3]

Thus, Seed Sowers, cited previously, produced modernized and simplified translations of many of the works of Madame Guyon that had appeared in the wake of Thomas Upham's study of her life and religious opinions. These edited reprints included not only *The Short and Easy Method of Prayer*, under a new title, and *The Torrents*, but the commentary of the *Song of Songs* published in Madame Guyon's lifetime, the commentaries on Genesis, Exodus, and Jeremiah from her work on the entire Bible, her treatise on union with God, and excerpts from her correspondence as well as from *Justifications*.[4]

Particularly interesting is what happened to the canon of devotional literature with the growth of interest both in the charismatic movement and in spiritual formation. The Seed Sowers produced a Library of Spiritual Classics that also included Madame Guyon, Fénelon, Brother Lawrence, and Molinos. The Paraclete Press, of the Community of Jesus, brought out an updated series of classics in a "Living Library Series" that reprinted Augustine, Thomas à Kempis, Bunyan, Jeremy Taylor, Brother Lawrence, Fénelon, Hannah More, and Henry Foster. Fénelon's letters of spiritual direction appeared in two volumes, *The Royal Way of the Cross* and *Talking with God*.[5] Reprints of classics of spirituality continued to appear, often in anthologies. Fénelon's *Spiritual Letters to Women* was reprinted as late as 1984 and he also appeared in an anthology called *Living Water: An Anthology of Letters of Direction*.[6] These popular editions were readily available for sale on the Internet by the twenty-first century.

The emergence of a more formal canonic tradition of devotional literature that amalgamated Catholic and Protestant works was illustrated best by *The Spiritual Formation Bible*.[7] This edition reproduced the New Revised Standard translation of the Bible with marginal glosses consisting of quotations from devotional commentaries on Scripture and from the works of the Church fathers and of mystics (including women like Julian of Norwich and Teresa of Avila). Writers from all the major strains of Protestant piety were included—from Calvin, Spener, and Wesley to John Woolman, Phoebe Palmer, and Philip Yancey (from modern Evangelicalism). The subtitle to the Bible, "Growing in Intimacy with God through Scripture," placed the project in the camp of personal piety, but the explanatory material made clear that spiritual formation would lead to involvement with the world surrounding the reader. "In a life increasingly given to the guidance of the Holy Spirit, our new humanity in Jesus Christ gradually becomes more visible and effective in the world. Far from removing us from the messiness of the world, spiritual formation plunges us into the middle of the world's rage and suffering."[8]

Because the goal of *The Spiritual Formation Bible* was to encourage spiritual growth through the application of Scripture, it drew on the method of *lectio divina* and the Ignatian practice of imaging or entering into the narrative. The editors contrasted the informative study of the Bible with the method of formational Scripture reading under the guidance of the Holy Spirit. Adapting traditional practices to the modern reader, the editors recommended reading slowly, reading in depth, using short passages, savoring them, letting the text "master" the reader, and responding to the text. Jeanne Guyon was featured in one of the calligraphic quotations on the reading and meaning of Scripture featured in the edition. The others highlighted in this way were Theonas of Alexandria, Gregory the Great, Abba Philimon, Guigo II, John Calvin, Joan Chittister, Richard Baxter, William Law, Philipp Jakob Spener, Thomas à Kempis, Martin Luther, Catherine of Siena, Peter of Damaskos, Teresa of Avila, John Cassian, John Wesley, and Dietrich Bonhoeffer.

Madame Guyon's featured quotation was "Come before the Lord and begin to read. Stop reading when you feel the Lord drawing you inwardly to himself. Now, simply remain in stillness. Stay there for a while." This was actually the adapted translation previously published by the Seed Sowers and the most readily available version of *The Short and Easy Method of Prayer*.[9] In the original handbook on prayer, Madame Guyon treated reading in two ways, first as meditative or "meditated" reading that opened the way to prayer, and second, as a brief means of focusing the mind in the prayer of the presence of God. It was in the second context that she stated: "The manner of reading in this degree is that as soon as one feels a small [degree] of contemplation (*recueillement*) one must stop and remain in repose, reading little and no longer continuing as soon as one feels drawn within."[10] The American paraphrase and the citation in *The Spiritual Formation Bible* homogenized the details of the text, transforming it to a generalized American context. The paraphrased and reordered Seed Sower version of the treatise on prayer aimed to make it comprehensible to Protestants, but it merely followed the two-hundred-year-old tradition of Digby Brooke and Thomas Upham in recreating the text for a general reader.

Fénelon was cited twice in the glosses in the margins of *The Spiritual Formation Bible* on the themes of abandonment of self-love and the need for detachment through the love of God and of the need for constant self reexamination: "Expect nothing of yourself, but all things of God. Knowledge of our own hopeless, incorrigible weakness, with unreserved confidence in God's power, are the true foundations of all spiritual life."[11]

The editors of the Bible included one other Quietist proper, Pierre de Caussade, an eighteenth-century Jesuit mystic and spiritual director who was best known for his little book *Abandonment to Divine Providence* (*L'Abandon à la providence divine*).[12] But the attention of the compilers of the marginal citations was directed to other Catholics, Augustine, Kempis, John of the Cross, Teresa of Avila, and de Sales.

If *The Spiritual Formation Bible*, like Wesley's *Christian Library*, illustrated the living tradition of an inclusive western tradition of spirituality that still embraced Madame Guyon and Fénelon, we can infer as well that the fervor of readers was gradually receding. Perhaps, as in the case of my visit to Hollow Rock, the holiness camp meeting, I had encountered among the marginal glosses the evidence of the long, slow death of Jeanne Guyon and of Fénelon as spiritual authorities. I had indeed observed all the textual practices of their publishing history—the practices of paraphrase and of rewrites that caused their historical reality to fade farther into the past and that had recreated an American experience by means of the experimental theology of these two seventeenth-century Quietists.

Yet, at the very moment that some evangelicals were speaking of the need for a new, distinctive "spirituality" and for a vital intellectual and creative witness, here was evidence that the figures of Jeanne Guyon and François de Fénelon still endured, although their power had dimmed.[13] The historical reality of their writings and their personalities would be ever more elusive: Guyon, a forceful and single-minded teacher who synthesized a long spiritual tradition for a newly empowered laity; and Fénelon, the epitome of an intellectual as a cleric, writer, and member of the French Academy, who discovered that his intellect could be brought to life through the experience of divine love.

Notes

Preface

1   See W. R. Ward, *The Protestant Evangelical Awakening* (Cambridge: Cambridge University Press, 1992), 1–53.

2   Charles E. Hambrick-Stowe, *The Practice of Piety: Puritan Devotional Disciplines in Seventeenth-Century New England* (Chapel Hill: University of North Carolina Press, 1982), 25–39 and passim.

3   Sue Lane McCully and Dorothy Z. Baker, eds., *The Silent and Soft Communion: The Spiritual Narratives of Sarah Pierpont Edwards and Sarah Prince Gill* (Knoxville: The University of Tennessee Press, 2005), 50. The information on Sarah Prince Gill is from the "Introduction" by Dorothy Z. Baker, xxi–xxiv. This volume is hereafter cited as *The Silent and Soft Communion.*

4   W. R. Ward, *Early Evangelicalism: A Global Intellectual History, 1670–1789* (Cambridge: Cambridge University Press, 2006), 61–69, hereafter cited as *Early Evangelicalism.*

5   Melvin E. Dieter has noted the influence of Thomas Cogswell Upham and other revivalists in spreading interest in certain Catholic mystics. "Madame Guyon, Molinos, St. Catherine, Fénelon, Catharine Adorna, and others in the Christian mystical tradition remain on the active list of holiness 'saints.'" Dieter does not explain the affinity in detail. See his *The Holiness Revival of the Nineteenth Century,* 2nd ed. (Lanham, Md.: The Scarecrow Press, 1996), 48, hereafter cited as *The Holiness Revival of the Nineteenth Century.*

6   See, for example, Diogenes Allen, *Spiritual Theology* (Boston: Cowley Publications, 1997), 152–61.

7   The text of Surin's preface is reproduced by Michel de Certeau in *La Fable*

mystique, vol. 1, XVIe–XVIIe siècle (Paris: Gallimard, 1982), 246–47, hereafter cited as *La Fable mystique*. Surin achieved considerable attention in the seventeenth century by his participation as an exorcist in a famous incident at a community of Ursuline nuns in Loudun, which was supposedly placed under a spell. Surin himself fell ill afterwards. Nevertheless, he was an authority cited by Fénelon during the Quietist debates.

8   E. Brooks Holifield, *Theology in America: Christian Thought from the Age of the Puritans to the Civil War* (New Haven: Yale University Press, 2003), 157–394, hereafter cited as Holifield.

9   George M. Marsden, *Fundamentalism and American Culture*, 2nd ed. (New York: Oxford University Press, 2006), 73, hereafter cited as *Fundamentalism and American Culture*. Marsden gives a good summary of the "complex web of interactions connecting Methodist holiness and Reformed holiness doctrine" from Wesley through Fundamentalism, 73–101.

10   See, for example, Henri Joachim Delacroix, *Les Grands Mystiques chrétiens*, new ed. (1908, repr., Paris: Alcan, 1938) and Louis Cognet, *Crépuscule des mystiques: Bossuet, Fénelon*, new ed. updated by J. R. Armagathe (1958, repr., Paris: Desclée, 1991), hereafter cited as Cognet, *Crépuscule*.

11   Elizabeth Rapley gives a history and analysis of these issues of the cloistered life, lay communities, and the ways in which women, despite their subordinate status, sought to forge a religious identity in *The Dévotes: Women and Church in Seventeenth-Century France* (Montreal: McGill-Queen's University Press, 1990), hereafter cited as Rapley.

12   Timothy L. Smith, *Revivalism and Social Reform in Mid-Nineteenth-Century America* (Nashville: Abingdon, 1957), hereafter cited as *Revivalism and Social Reform*.

Chapter 1

1   In this chapter I give an overview of major examples of issues of the diffusion of the writings of Madame Guyon (to whom Fénelon was often linked) as illustrative of the following chapters of the book. I have placed these examples in an autobiographical context to clarify my point of view as the authorial voice of the narratives of transmission that follow.

2   Information on Johann Baer or Bär, the printer of the 1828 edition, is from a letter to the author from Frederick S. Weiser of The Pennsylvania German Society, dated September 6, 1977.

     Tersteegen's nineteenth-century edition is *Die heilige liebe Gottes und die unheilige Naturliebe nach ihren untershiedenen Wirkungen, in XLIV anmuthigen Sinnbildern und erbaulichen Versen vorgestellet . . . .* (Lancaster, Pa.: J. Schweitzer, gedruckt von Johann Bär, 1828).

     A detailed discussion of Madame Guyon's poetry to accompany emblems and of Tersteegen's translation is given in chap. 4.

3   Information on the Bradfords is from John Tebbel, *A History of Book Publishing in the United States*, vol. 1, *The Creation of an Industry, 1630–1865* (New York and London: R.L. Bowker, 1972), 39–41. On the Quakers and

on early translations of Madame Guyon and of Fénelon into English, see chap. 5.

4   This is a reference to an edition of Fénelon's letters as a spiritual director, *Christian Perfection*, ed. Charles F. Whiston, trans. Margaret Whitney (New York and London: Harper and Row, 1947; repr. Minneapolis, Minn.: Bethany House, 1975), hereafter cited as *Christian Perfection*.

5   On editions of Madame Guyon by American publishers linked to the charismatic movement, see chaps. 2, 8, and 9.

6   Henry E. Brockett, "She Paid the Price" (source unknown), 19.

7   In the foregoing comments about the rise of holiness camp meetings after the Civil War, I am relying on Charles Edwin Jones, *Perfectionist Persuasion: The Holiness Movement and American Methodism, 1867–1936*, ATLA Monograph Series, no. 5 (Metuchen, N.J.: 1974), 16–46; and Dieter, *The Holiness Revival of the Nineteenth Century*, 91–116. Jones is hereafter cited as *Perfectionist Persuasion*. Ellen Weiss treats the design and architecture of a great Methodist camp meeting and its relation to the entire tradition in *City in the Woods: The Life and Design of an American Camp Meeting on Martha's Vineyard* (Oxford: Oxford University Press, 1987).

8   Janice R. Kiaski, "Holiness at Hollow Rock," reprinted at http://www.hollowrock.org, 2006.

9   See Jones, *Perfectionist Persuasion*, 23, for information on the publishing activities of the National Camp Meeting Association.

10   On the *Christian Library* and Wesley's use of Continental writings on spirituality, see Jean Orcibal, "Les Spirituels français et espagnols chez John Wesley et ses contemporains," *Revue de l'histoire des religions* 139 (1951): 50–109, especially 63 for Heylin and 69–72 for Madame Guyon, hereafter cited as "Les Spirituels français et espagnols chez John Wesley."

11   John Wesley, "Preface," *An Extract of the Life of Madam Guion* (London: R. Hawes, 1776), iv–v.

12   I consulted an English edition of *A Christian Library* (London: T. Cardeaux, 1819–1827). The "Devotional Tracts" are to be found in volume 23.

     For bibliographic references to American editions of Madame Guyon, see my essay, "Madame Guyon in America: An Annotated Bibliography," *Bulletin of Bibliography* 52 (June 1995): 107–11. The reference there to Wesley's *Library* (107) should be corrected in that Wesley published a devotional extract by Madame Guyon, not her autobiography, and included instead an extract of the life of Antoinette Bourignon.

     For additional information on Wesley's changing attitude toward Madame Guyon as a Mystic and on Wesley and mysticism, see Martin Schmidt, *John Wesley: A Theological Biography*, trans. Denis Inman (London: Epworth Press, 1973), II, ii, 150, 247–48; and Henry D. Rack, *Reasonable Enthusiast: John Wesley and the Rise of Methodism*, 3rd ed. (London: Epworth Press, 2002), 101–2. The two works are subsequently identified as *John Wesley: A Theological Biography* and *Reasonable Enthusiast*.

     Wesley is treated in more detail in chap. 5.

13   *Principles of the Interior or Hidden Life* (Boston: Waite, Peirce and Co., 1843); *Life of Madame Catharine Adorna* (New York: Harper and Brothers, 1845); *The Life of Faith*, in three parts (Boston: Waite, Peirce and Co., 1845); and *Life and Religious Opinions and Experience of Madame de la Mothe Guyon*, 2 vols. (New York: Harper and Brothers, 1846). This last work will be referred to as *Life and Religious Opinions* throughout this book. Upham is treated in detail in chap. 7.

14   *Life and Religious Opinions*, 2:373 (emphasis in original).

15   On McClurkan, his theological contexts, his activities, and his publications, see Mildred Bangs Wynkoop, *The Trevecca Story* (Nashville, Tenn.: Trevecca Press, 1976), 27–85. Timothy L. Smith reviews in detail the Pentecostal Mission, McClurkan's role, and the final union with the Church of the Nazarene in *Called Unto Holiness: The Story of the Nazarenes; The Formative Years* (Kansas City, Mo.: Nazarene Publishing House, 1962), 180–99, hereafter cited as *Called Unto Holiness*. A biography of Madame Guyon that was published by the Pentecostal Mission is treated in chap. 9.

16   Amicus, "Points in Holiness Theology," *Living Water* (May 12, 1903), 3.

17   J. O. McClurkan, *Chosen Vessels* (Nashville, Tenn.: Pentecostal Mission Publishing Co., 1901). I am grateful to Charles Edwin Jones for this reference.

18   Donna Geer (assistant manager, The Seed Sowers, Auburn, Maine), letter to author, April 24, 1992.

19   "The Still Small Voice," *The Old Testament*, vol. 1, *The Holy Spirit or Power From on High* (Harrisurg, Pa.: Christian Publications, n.d.), 162.

20   *Inward Divine Guidance*, preface by Hannah Whitall Smith (Salem, Ohio: Schmul Publishing, 1989), 97. This is a reprint.

Chapter 2

1   Wesley, "Preface," *An Extract of the Life of Madam Guion*, ii. See also iv–vi.

2   Wesley, "Preface," viii.

3   This is Marie-Florine Bruneau's translation in her *Women Mystics Confront the Modern World: Marie de l'Incarnation (1599–1672) and Madame Guyon (1648–1717)* (Albany: State University of New York Press, 1998), 188–89, hereafter cited as *Women Mystics*.

4   Montesquieu, *Lettres Persanes*, préface de Jean Starobinski, coll. Folio (Paris: Gallimard, 1973), 299. This is the edition of 1754.

5   Again, this is Bruneau's translation in *Women Mystics*, 192. She describes the historiographical tradition surrounding Madame Guyon in terms of competing views of mysticism, modernity, and masculinity-femininity.

6   Diderot, "Sur les femmes," in *Qu'est-ce qu'une femme*, ed. Elisabeth Badinter (Paris: P. O. L., 1989), 171–72.

7   Reverend Pierre Pourrat, S.S., *Christian Spirituality IV: Later Developments, Part II; From Jansenism to Modern Times*, trans. Donald Attwater, IV (1927; repr. Westminster, Md.: The Newman Press, 1955), 182–85, 188. This multivolume work will hereafter be cited as *Christian Spirituality*.

8   Evelyn Underhill, *Mysticism* (1911 repr. New York: Doubleday, 1990), 472, hereafter cited as *Mysticism*.

9   R. A. Knox, *Enthusiasm: A Chapter in the History of Religion*, corrected ed. (Oxford: Clarendon Press, 1959), 333, 339, hereafter cited as *Enthusiasm*.

10   Françoise Mallet-Joris, *Jeanne Guyon* (Paris: Flammarion, 1978); and Marie-Louise Gondal, *Madame Guyon (1648–1717): Un nouveau visage* (Paris: Beauchesne, 1989). A colloquium held in 1996 in France presented a variety of approaches to the life and writings of Madame Guyon. See Joseph Beaude, et al., *Madame Guyon: Rencontres autour de la vie et l'oeuvre* (Grenoble: J. Millon, 1997), subsequently referred to as *Madame Guyon: Rencontres*.

11   For instance, Marie-Florine Bruneau wrote a dissertation, *Mysticisme et Psychose: l'autobiographie de Jeanne Guyon* (University of California, Berkeley), that was heavily Freudian. See *Dissertation Abstracts international* 42 (1981): 237A–38A. In "Un pur silence: la perfection de Jeanne Guyon," Julia Kristeva has treated issues of repression, narcissism, displacement of desire, silence or aphasia, and language and love in the life and work of Jeanne Guyon. See *Histoires d'amour* (Paris: Denoël, 1983), 277–95.

12   Jan Johnson, "Seeing God in the Valley," *Weavings* 16 (July/August 2001): 37–43, hereafter cited as Johnson. The Upper Room is an arm of the General Board of Discipleship of the United Methodist Church that is independent financially. It promotes spiritual formation.

13   Jan Johnson's abridged version of the autobiography is *Madame Guyon* (Minneapolis, Minn.: Bethany House, 1999). Bethany House is affiliated with the Bethany Fellowship Mission. As a basis for her version of the Guyon life, Johnson used an electronically produced version of the autobiography that was already an abridgment. I have consulted *Experiencing the Depths of Jesus Christ* (Auburn, Maine: Seed Sowers, ca. 1975). This is a version of the *Short and Easy Method of Prayer* and seems to have been edited by Gene Edwards. The quotation is from his epilogue (160).

14   Johnson, "Seeing God in the Valley," 37, 40–41, 43.

15   Cognet, *Crépuscule des mystiques: Bossuet-Fénelon*, passim.

16   Pourrat, *Christian Spirituality*, 4:161.

17   Rapley, 35–41, 79–93.

18   Certeau, *La fable mystique*, 1:25–26.

19   The material on Madame Guyon and Fénelon in this chapter and on Fénelon and Bossuet in the following chapter is based heavily on two articles by Louis Cognet: "Fénelon," in the *Dictionnaire de spiritualité* (Paris: Beauchesne, 1962), 5:152–70; and "Guyon," in the *Dictionnaire* (1967), 6:1306–36. Citations from Madame Guyon's autobiography are from *La Vie de Madame Guyon écrite par elle-même*, ed. Benjamin Sahler (Paris: Dervy-Livres, 1983). This edition is that of the original edition of 1720 by Pierre Poiret, with some modernization of spelling and punctuation. This work will be referred to as *Vie* in subsequent footnotes. A critical edition of major importance is *La Vie par elle-même et autres écrits biographiques*, ed.

Dominique Tronc (Paris: Éditions Champion, 2001). Tronc's introduction comprises pp. 7–102 and is hereafter cited as Tronc, but the literary study included in the introduction (pp. 56–77) is by Andrée Villard; this particular section will be referred to as Villard.

20   Rapley, 48–60.

21   Guyon, *Vie*, 33.

22   Pourrat, *Christian Spirituality*, vol. 3, *Later Developments: Part I; From the Renaissance to Jansenism* (1953), 272–321; the quotation is from p. 289.

23   Cognet, "Guyon," 1309.

24   Guyon, *Vie*, 73.

25   Guyon, *Vie*, 75.

26   Tronc emphasizes the importance of the spiritual direction of Geneviève Granger and Jacques Bertot (both of whom were Franciscan) in the "Introduction," 20–43, including a table of the traditions within which Jeanne Guyon was formed: the Carmelite (Laurent de la Résurrection), the Capucin, the Franciscan, and Quietist (via Father La Combe), 25.

27   Guyon, *Vie*, 151.

28   Guyon, *Vie*, 209.

29   Guyon, *Vie*, 213–14.

30   Guyon, *Vie*, 213–14.

31   Guyon, *Vie*, 241–42.

32   Marie-Louise Gondal, "La transformation spirituelle de Madame Guyon à Thonon," in Beaude, *Madame Guyon: Rencontres*, 15–33. See especially 32.

33   Madame Guyon, *Les Torrents et commentaire au Cantique des cantiques de Salomon*, ed. Claude Morali (Grenoble: Jérôme Millon, 1992), 156, hereafter cited as *The Torrents*.

34   See Villard, "Introduction," 58–63 and Certeau, *La fable mystique*, 1:225–42.

35   Guyon, *Vie*, 346.

36   Madame Guyon, *Le Moyen Court et autres écrits spirituels*, ed. Marie-Louise Gondal (Grenoble: J. Millon, 1995), 62, hereafter cited as the *Short and Easy Method*. Emphasis in original. Pourrat discusses the popularity of the "prayer of simple regard" in his discussion of "Pre-Quietists." Quietists, for Pourrat, of course, took this prayer too far. See *Christian Spirituality*, 4:124–32.

37   Pourrat, *Christian Spirituality*, 4:138–39.

38   A history and general discussion of Quietism can be found in Jean-Robert Armogathe, *Le Quiétisme* (Paris: Presses Universitaires de la France, 1973), subsequently referred to as *Le Quiétisme*. I have also extracted details from Pourrat's hostile account in *Christian Spirituality*, 4:148–49, 163–65.

39   Rapley, 96–100.

40   Cognet, "Guyon," 1318.

41   These are portions of a letter from January 1690, numbered 220 in Madame Guyon, *Correspondance*, vol. 1, *Directions spirituelles*, ed. Dominique Tronc

(Paris: Honoré Champion Éditeur, 2003), 460–61, hereafter cited as *Correspondance*.

42   The edition of *Correspondance* reproduces these poems, with the Fénelon poem, subtitled "Parodie" (578–79), preceding the Guyon poem (579–80).

43   Jacques Le Brun, *La Spiritualité de Bossuet* (Paris: Klincksieck, 1972), 441–695. The quote is on pp. 473–74. This volume is subsequently referred to as *La Spiritualité*.

44   Guyon, *Vie*, 572–73.

45   *Les Justifications de Madame J.M.B. de la Mothe Guyon* (Cologne [Amsterdam]: Jean de la Pierre, 1720), 1:v.

46   Le Brun, *La Spiritualité*, 523, 537.

47   Madame Guyon, *Récits de captivité*, ed. Marie-Louise Gondal (Grenoble: Jérôme Millon, 1992), 155–56.

Chapter 3

1   "Avertissement," *Explication des Maximes des saints*, in Fénelon, *Oeuvres*, ed. Jacques Le Brun (Paris: Gallimard, 1983), 1:1004–5, hereafter cited as *Oeuvres*, I.

2   Brother Lawrence would be read along with Kempis, Guyon, and Fenelon in the ensuing tradition of devotional reading. I cite Surin in my preface.

3   Quoted by Cognac in "Guyon," 1324.

4   Here I have reinterpreted Pourrat, *Christian Spirituality*, 4:219.

5   Fénelon, *The Adventures of Telemachus, the son of Ulysses, In five parts*, 2nd and corrected ed. (London, A. and J. Churchil, 1700), n.p.

6   "Dedication," *Instructions for the education of a daughter, by the author of Telemachus . . . Done into English and revised by Dr. George Hickes* (London: J. Bowyer, 1707), A2–A3 (emphasis in original).

7   Rapley, 118.

8   Tronc gives a summary of the lines of transmission, 47–51.

9   On Poiret, see Marjolaine Chevallier, *Pierre Poiret (1646–1719): Du protestantisme à la mystique* (Geneva: Labor et Fides, 1994) and her "Madame Guyon et Pierre Poiret," 35–49, in *Madame Guyon: Rencontres*; as well as Ward, *Early Evangelicalism*, 50–53, 54–57.

10   Ward, *Early Evangelicalism*, 55.

11   Guyon, *Correspondance*, vol. 2, *Années de combat* (Paris: Honoré Champion Éditeur, 2004), 686, 687.

12   On early translations of Fénelon in England and on Ramsay, see Jean Orcibal, "L'Influence spirituelle de Fénelon dans les pays anglo-saxons au XVIIIe siècle," *XVIIe siècle*, nos. 12–14 (1951): 276–282, hereafter cited as "L'Influence spirituelle." This essay by Orcibal and two others by him that are cited elsewhere have been reprinted in *Etudes d'histoire et de littérature religieuses XVIe–XVIIIe siècles*, ed. Jacques Le Brun and Jean Lesaulnier (Paris: Klincksieck, 1997).

      The main source of information regarding Fénelon's influence in the eighteenth century is Albert Cherel, *Fénelon au XVIIIe siècle en*

France (1715–1820): Son prestige–son influence (1917; repr. Geneva: Slatkine Reprints, 1970). My discussion of Ramsay relies heavily on 31–151.

    A recent essay adds further information on the originality and significance of Ramsay himself. See Bruno Neveu, "La 'science divine' du chevalier Ramsay," 177–96 in *Fénelon: Philosophie et spiritualité . . . .* , ed. Denise Leduc-Fayette (Geneva: Droz, 1996).

13   Donald F. Durnbaugh has written a useful introduction to Jane Leade. See "Jane Ward Leade (1624–1704)," in *The Pietist Theologians: An Introduction to Theology in the Seventeenth and Eighteenth Centuries*, ed. Carter Lindberg, 128–46 (Oxford: Blackwell, 2005), hereafter cited as *The Pietist Theologians*.

14   Andrew Michael Ramsay, *The Life of François de Salignac De la Motte Fenelon, Archbishop and Duke of Cambray* (London: Paul Vaillant and James Woodman, 1723), 27, hereafter cited as *Life*.

15   Ramsay, *Life*, 38–39.

16   Ramsay, *Life*, 79.

17   Ramsay, *Life*, 78–79.

18   Ramsay, *Life*, 163.

19   Here I am referring to the notions of community and interpretation in the thought of Stanley Fish (*Is There a Text in This Class? The Authority of Interpretive Communities* [Cambridge: Harvard University Press, 1980]) and of narrative, community, and character formation in Stanley Hauerwas (*Character and the Christian Life: A Study in Theological Ethics* [San Antonio: Trinity University Press, 1975]; and *A Community of Character: Toward a Constructive Christian Social Ethic* [Notre Dame, Ind.: University of Notre Dame Press, 1981]).

20   The reference is cited by Owen C. Watkins, *The Puritan Experience: Studies in Spiritual Autobiography* (New York: Schocken Books, 1972), 1. Of course, Baxter's advice explains why Plutarch's *Lives* were a staple, along with the Bible, of reading from the Renaissance to the late eighteenth century. The Pietist and Wesleyan traditions would push the notion of the power of the influence of reading exemplary lives into a confirmation of the same experimental truth. Watkins gives a useful overview of the autobiographical thrust of Puritan spiritual writing and reading.

    F. Ernest Stoeffler has taken the position that Puritanism and continental Pietism were all part of a broad pattern of Calvinistic piety, of which the characteristics were "experientialism, perfectionism, Biblicism, and protest." See *The Rise of Evangelical Pietism* (Leiden, Neth.: E. J. Brill, 1965), 29.

21   Argomathe summarizes much of this tradition in *Le Quiétisme*, 9–25, and my discussion is indebted to him.

22   Guyon, *The Torrents*, 152.

23   Cited by Argomathe, *Le Quiétisme*, 18.

24   Fénelon, *Oeuvres*, 1:1120–21.

25   Guyon, *The Torrents*, 118.

26   Guyon, *Correspondance*, 2:429–30.

27   Ted A. Carpenter, *The Religion of the Heart: A Study of European Religious Life in the Seventeenth and Eighteenth Centuries* (Columbia: University of South Carolina Press, 1991), 14–17. R. W. Ward has preferred to identify these European movements as supplying the intellectual roots of Evangelicalism, broadly defined (*Early Evangelicalism*, passim). A historical approach that takes into account both experimental or experiential strands, as well as intellectual strands, seems to give a more adequate account of the roots of Evangelicalism.

28   Guyon, *La Passion de croire*, ed. Marie-Louise Gondal (Paris: Nouvelle Cité, 1990), 210–11.

29   Leszek Kolakowski, *Chrétiens sans Eglise: La conscience religieuse et le lien confessionel au XVIIe siècle*, trans. Anna Posner (Paris: Gallimard, 1965), 532 and 544–45. Emphasis in original.

30   Guyon, *Short and Easy Method*, 81–82.

31   Guyon, *Short and Easy Method*, 61.

Chapter 4

1   Georges Gusdorf, *Dieu, la nature, l'homme au siècle des lumières* (Paris: Payot, 1972), 70. The citation is from a Pietist periodical of 1744, *Die Geistliche Fama*. Gusdorf contextualizes the new religious consciousness represented by Madame Guyon and others, leading to Rousseau's "Profession of Faith of the Savoyard Vicar" in *Emile* (39–57). Gusdorf's useful survey of European pietism, including Quietism, follows (58–85).

2   In this brief overview of elements within German Pietism that are relevant to the understanding of the transmission of Guyonian Quietism to America, I have relied on Hans-Jürgen Schrader, "Madame Guyon, le piétisme et la littérature de langue allemande," 83–129, in *Madame Guyon: Rencontres*, subsequently cited as Schrader. This essay also appeared in German. See *Jansenismus, Quietismus, Pietismus*, ed. Harmut Lehmann, Heinz Schilling, and Hans-Jürgen Schrader (Göttingen: Vandenhoeck and Ruprecht, 2002), 189–225. Very useful bibliographic notes giving an overview of German scholarship on the question of Madame Guyon's influence in Germany are included by Schrader. This volume is subsequently referred to as *Jansenimus, Quietismus, Pietismus*. I have also used Peter C. Erb's historical survey that serves as an introduction to his edited volume, *Pietists: Selected Writings* (New York: Ramsey; Toronto: Paulist Press, 1983), 1–27, hereafter cited as Erb; and Ward, *Early Evangelicalism*, 8–10, 20–50, 78–84, 99–118. Lindberg's volume, *The Pietist Theologians*, demonstrates how international Pietist movements were, if we think of them in the broad categories suggested by Gusdorf.

3   Ward, *Early Evangelicalism*, 9.

4   Klaus von Orde, "Der Quietismus Miguel de Molinos bei Philipp Jakob Spener," in *Jansenismus, Quietismus, Pietismus*, 106–18, especially 109 and passim.

5   See the article "Labadie," in *Dictionnaire de spiritualité* (Paris: Beauchesne, 1975), 8:1–7.

6   Hanspeter Marti, "Der Seelenfrieden der Stillen im Lande: Quietistische Mystik und Radikaler Pietismus—das Beispiel Gottfried Arnolds," in *Jansenismus, Quietismus, Pietismus*, 92-105.

7   Jacques Le Brun, "Madame Guyon et la Bible," in *Madame Guyon. Rencontres*, 63; the entire essay includes pages 63-82 and is hereafter cited as "Madame Guyon et la Bible."

8   Jacques Le Brun, "Présupposés théoriques de la lecture mystique de la Bible. L'exemple de *La Sainte Bible* de Mme Guyon," *Revue de théologie et de philosophie* 133 (2001): 287-89; the entire essay includes pages 287-302 and will hereafter be cited as "Présupposés."

9   Le Brun, "Madame Guyon et la Bible," 80.

10   Le Brun, "Madame Guyon et la Bible," 71-72.

11   Le Brun, "Présupposés," 290-91.

12   Le Brun, "Présupposés," 302.

13   Jeanne de la Mothe Guyon, *Le Nouveau Testament de Notre-Seigneur Jésus-Christ*, VIII (Cologne [Amsterdam]: J. de la Pierre, 1713), 9 and 12, hereafter cited as *Apocalypse*. Emphasis in original.

14   Guyon, *Apocalypse*, 99.

15   Guyon, *Apocalypse*, 109. Emphasis in original.

16   Guyon, *Apocalypse*, 319.

17   Guyon, *Apocalypse*, 346-47, 383, 393.

18   Guyon, *Apocalypse*, 409.

19   Guyon, *La Passion de croire*, 215.

20   Here I am relying on Jean-Marc Heuberger, "Les Commentaires bibliques de Madame Guyon dans *La Bible de Berleburg*," *Revue de théologie et de philosophie* 133 (2001): 303-23.

21   Quoted by E. Gordon Alderfer in his "Introduction" to Kelpius' *A Method of Prayer* (New York: Harper and Brothers, with Pendle Hill, 1951), 35-36, hereafter cited as the Pendle Hill edition. Much of my background information is based on Alderfer, including the reference to Seneca.

22   Cited by Julius Friedrich Sachse, *The German Pietists of Provincial Pennsylvania*, vol. 1, *1694-1708* (Philadelphia: Printed for the author, 1895), 102-3.

23   Johann Kelpius, *A Short, Easy and Comprehensive Method of Prayer: Translated from the German; And published for a farther Promotion Knowledge and Benefit of INWARD PRAYER* (Germantown, Pa.: Christopher Sower, 1741), 3, hereafter cited as Kelpius.

24   Kelpius, 8.

25   Kelpius, 11.

26   Kelpius, 29.

27   Quoted by Alderfer in the Pendle Hill edition, 33.

28   The material on Beissel and Ephrata is based on Donald F. Durnbaugh, ed., *The Brethren in Colonial America* (Elgin, Ill.: The Brethren Press, 1967),

67–68f., hereafter cited as Durnbaugh; Peter C. Erb, "Introduction" to his anthology and translations, *Johann Conrad Beissel and the Ephrata Community: Mystical and Historical Texts*, 3–54 (Lewiston, N.Y.: The Edward Mellen Press, 1985), hereafter cited as Erb, *Beissel*; and Walter C. Klein, *Johann Conrad Beissel, Mystic and Martinet: 1690–1768* (Philadelphia: University of Pennsylvania Press, 1942), hereafter cited as Klein.

29   See Jean Cadier, "Charles . . . de Marsay," in *Dictionnaire de spiritualité* (Paris: Beauchesne, 1977), 10:657. Cadier is partially superseded by Schrader, 108–9 and 121–26.

30   Quoted by Schrader, 108–9.

31   *L'Âme amante de son Dieu: Représentée dans les emblèmes de Hermannus Hugo sur ses pieux désirs et dans ceux d'Othon Vaenius sur l'amour divin*, ed. Pierre Poiret (Cologne [Amsterdam]: Jean de la Pierre, 1717), 18. This is the volume referred to in chapter 1 as *The Soul in Love with Its God*.

32   On Beissel and the Brethren, see Durnbaugh, 65–66, and for a general description of Ephrata and Beissel's thought, see Erb, *Beissel*, 21–22.

33   The material on Böhme is based in part on F. Ernest Stoeffler, *German Pietism During the Eighteenth Century* (Leiden, Neth.: E. J. Brill, 1973), 167–71, hereafter cited as Stoeffler; as well as Erb, *Beissel*, passim; and F. Braig, "Jacques Boehme," *Dictionnaire de spiritualité* (Paris: Beauchesne, 1927), 1:1745–51, subsequently cited as Braig.

34   See Braig, 1750.

35   Stoeffler, 169.

36   Erb's translations in *Beissel*, 73–74, 80, and 95.

37   Klein, 113.

38   Cited by Durnbaugh, 235.

39   The editions that I cite in what follows are based on the Early American Imprints series and on Lottie M. Bausman, *A Bibliography of Lancaster County, Pa., 1745–1912* (Philadelphia: Patterson and White, 1912).

40   Sauer's editions of *Der Kleine Kempis* are probably based on Tersteegen.

41   Useful summaries of Tersteegen's thought and life are to be found in Stoeffler, 191–202; Hansgünter Ludewig, "Gerhard Tersteegen," in *The Pietist Theologians*, ed. Carter Lindberg; and Bernd Jasper, "Tersteegen," in *Dictionnaire de spiritualité* (Paris: Beauchesne, 1991), 15:260–71. On Tersteegen and Madame Guyon, see Schrader, 99–100, 106–9, 118–21. My discussion is based in part on these sources.

42   The translation is by Stoeffler, 192–95; the reference to the Catholic tradition is from Jasper.

43   #46, "Gott und sein Wille, bringt Stille" and #141, "Wer Gott nur will, ist immer still," in *Geistliches Blumengärtlein inner Seelen . . . .* (Frankfurt: Peter Daniel Schmitz, 1793), 12, 33.

44   On emblems, see Karl-Ludwig Selig, "Emblèmes," in *Dictionnaire de spiritualité* (Paris: Beauchesne, 1966), 4:605–9. On the German transla-

tion of the 1717 Poiret edition of Madame Guyon's poetry to accompany the Hugo and Vaenius emblems, see Schrader 107–9. Schrader repeats the erroneous attribution to Tersteegen of a new German translation of this poetry, suggesting that the 1828 Lancaster, Pennsylvania reprint is the initial German translation (107, n. 67). This translation was entitled *Die Ihren Gott liebenden Seele vorgestellt in Sinnbildern des Herrn. Hugonis, über seine Pia Desideria; und des Ottonis Vaenii über die Liebe Gottes mit Neuen Kupffern und Versen welche zielen auf des innere Christenthum, aus dem Frantzösischem ins* Teutsche *übersetzt* (Regensburg: Heinr. Jonas Ostertag; Ausberg: Joh. Matthias Steidlin, 1719).

45   The series of poems translated by Tersteegen was *The Different Effects of Sacred and Profane Love* (*Les éfets diferens de l'Amour sacré & profane; représentés dans plusieurs Emblêmes, exposés en Vers Libres*), in Jeanne de la Mothe Guyon, *Poésies et cantiques spirituels sur divers sujets qui regardent la vie intérieure ou l'esprit du vrai christianisme*, 4:254–88 (Cologne [Amsterdam]: Jean de la Pierre, 1722). Subsequent references will be to *Sacred and Profane Love* in *Spiritual Poetry*.

46   The 1751 edition was printed in Solingen. I am referring to the 1787 edition (Muhlheim: J. C. Eyrich), *Die heilige Liebe Gottes, und die unheilige Naturliebe: nach ihren unterschiedenen Wirkungen, in XLIV. Anmuthigen Sinnbildern und erbaulichen Versen vorgestellet; aus dem Französischen der Madame J.M.B. de la Mothe Guion treulich verdeutschet, und mit ferneren Betrachtungen aus ihren sämtlichen biblischen Schriften erläutert*, von G.T.St. References to this edition will be to *Holy Godly Love and Unholy Natural Love*.

47   Tersteegen, *Holy Godly Love and Unholy Natural Love*, 449 and 463.

48   Tersteegen, *Sacred and Profane Love* in *Spiritual Poetry*, 4:168.

49   Tersteegen, *Holy Godly Love and Unholy Natural Love*, 172, 173.

50   Peter C. Erb, "Gerhard Tersteegen, Christopher Saur, and Pennsylvania Sectarians," *Brethren Life and Thought* 20 (1975): 153–57. The preceding citations are from Tersteegen's letter, reproduced on 154–55.

51   *Signposts to Eternal Life in Forty-two Contemplations and Edifying Verses* (*Wegweiser zum Ewigen Leben in Zweiundvierzig Betrachtungen und erbaulichen Versen*) (York, Pa.: J. L. Getz, 1834). The book is presented as a new printing, with a preface from Tersteegen's 1751 preface.

52   Franz Hildebrandt, ed. *Wesley Hymnbook* (repr., Kansas City, Mo.: Lillenas Publishing, 1963), no. 42.

53   Dominique Tronc has written an extensive note on Fleischbein and on Moritz in his edition of the autobiography of Madame Guyon. See Tronc, 1008.

54   Karl Philipp Moritz, *Anton Reiser: A Psychological Novel*, trans. John R. Russell (Columbia, S.C.: Camden House, 1996), 4, hereafter cited as *Anton Reiser*.

55   Moritz, *Anton Reiser*, 2.

56   Moritz, *Anton Reiser*, 12.

Chapter 5

1   John Hawkesworth's eighteenth-century translation of *Telemachus* was
     edited by O. W. Wight in volume 1 of the *Select Works of Fenelon* (New
     York: Hurd and Houghton, 1875); this volume included essays by Lamar-
     tine and Villemain on the life and works of Fénelon; it is a reprint of an
     earlier nineteenth-century edition. The 1875 printing is subsequently cited
     as Hawkesworth translation, 1875 American edition.
          Early American printings of the Hawkesworth translation were in
     New York: Printed by T. and J. Swords for David Longwork, 1797, with
     1815 editions published in both Philadelphia and New York.
          On eighteenth-century editions of *Télémaque*, see Richard Frautschi and
     Angus Martin, "French Prose Fiction Published between 1701 and 1750: A
     New Profile of Production," *Eighteenth-Century Fiction* 14 (2002): 745.

2   The preceding citations are from Paul Merrill Spurlin, *The French Enlighten-
     ment in America: Essays on the Times of the Founding Fathers* (Athens: Univer-
     sity of Georgia Press, 1984), 54–55.

3   See Howard Mumford Jones, *America and French Culture* (Chapel Hill: Uni-
     versity of North Carolina Press; London: Humphrey Milford, Oxford Uni-
     versity Press, 1927), 139–40, hereafter cited as Mumford Jones.

4   The Library Company of Philadelphia possesses the edition with Jackson's
     signature: *Les Aventures de Télémaque, Fils d'Ulysse . . . Nouvelle édition avec des
     Notes et des Remarques pour l'intelligence de la Mythologie & de ce Poëme* (Phila-
     delphia: Chez Boinod et Gaillard, 1784); a second title page shows that the
     book was simultaneously published in Leiden and that it was a reprint of
     a 1725 edition by J. de Wetstein in 1725. The text includes several engrav-
     ings. The wallpaper still exists in the restored Hermitage and was created
     in 1825 by Dufour and Leroy. It features scenes from the adventures of
     Telemachus on the island of Calypso: "Papier peint panoramique: Paysages
     de Télémaque dans l'île de Calypso."
          French editions of the book were published in Philadelphia in 1806–
     1807, 1812, 1824, 1830, 1832, and 1834. The popular two-volume bilingual
     edition by Joseph Nancrede was published simultaneously in Philadelphia
     and in New York in 1797.

5   Robert Darnton, "Readers Respond to Rousseau: The Fabrication of
     Romantic Sensibility," in *The Great Cat Massacre and Other Episodes in
     French Cultural History* (New York: Vintage, 1985), 231, 233, 232. Fénelon
     was a formative influence on Rousseau, but that relationship is outside the
     scope of this study.

6   This is Jacques Le Brun's reference to Fénelon's "Lettre à l'Académie" in
     the former's preface to his edition of *Les Aventures de Télémaque*, collection
     "Folio" (Paris: Gallimard, 1995), 8, hereafter cited as Le Brun, "Preface."

7   *The Adventures of Telemachus Son of Ulysses: From the French of Fenelon by the
     celebrated Jn. Hawkesworth L. L. D. Corrected and Revised by G. Gregory, D. D.*
     [. . .] (New York: Printed by T. and J. Swords for David Longworth, 1797),

I:8. The life of Fenelon is found in vol. 1, 7–39, and the English writer attributes to Fénelon considerable rational authority in his relationship to Madame Guyon: "Pity first made him her friend, and sympathy her proselyte and advocate. He gave some consistency to her rhapsodies, and held devout meetings, where that fair enthusiast met Madame de Maintenon and other ladies, the most eminent in rank and character at court. The refined sensibility of Platonism was cherished by this mystic circle, who persuaded themselves that their ardent love to God was uninfluenced by any selfish consideration" (22–23).

8   On the sacred and profane in *Telemachus*, see Le Brun, "Preface," 11–17.

9   For details of the publishing history and an introduction to Fénelon's treatise, see Jacques Le Brun's comments in *Oeuvres*, I, 1268–69 and 1259–68.

10   Citations are from the text of 1696 as presented by Jacques Le Brun in his edition of Fénelon's *Oeuvres*, I, subsequently cited as Fénelon, *Education*; this reference is to page 167.

11   Fénelon, *Education*, 95, 92–93.

12   Fénelon, *Education*, 159–60.

13   Quotes in paragraph are from Fénelon, *Education*, 110, 135.

14   For example, Christopher Sauer/Sower Jr. printed *A Pattern of Christian Education, agreable to the precepts and practice of our blessed Lord and Saviour Jesus Christ: Illustrated under the character of Paternus & Eusebius* in Germantown in 1756.

15   Litchfield, Conn: Repr. Collier & Buel; New Bedford, Mass.: J. Spooner; New York, N.Y.: Printed for Daniel Larence by Samuel Campbell. An additional printing was completed in New York in 1799.

16   Isabel Rivers, "Dissenting and Methodist Books of Practical Divinity," in *Books and Their Readers in Eighteenth-Century England*, ed. Isabel Rivers (Leicester: Leicester University Press; New York: St. Martin's, 1982), 127–28, hereafter cited as Rivers.

17   See *Oeuvres*, I, 1445, notes for pp. 656–57.

18   *Lettres chrétiennes et spirituelles sur divers sujets qui regardent la vie intérieure ou l'esprit du vrai christianisme*, 4 vols. (Cologne [Amsterdam]: Jean de la Pierre, 1717).

19   See Orcibal, "L'influence spirituelle," 278 and passim for Fénelon's significant impact in the British Isles.

20   "L'influence spirituelle," 278–79.

21   Mumford-Jones, 362–63.

22   See Rufus M. Jones, Isaac Sharpless, and Amelia Gummere, *The Quakers in the American Colonies* (1911; repr. New York: Russell & Russell, 1962), 417–18.

23   Francis Frost, "Quakers," in *Dictionnaire de spiritualité*, vol. 12, part 2 (Paris: Beauchesne, 1985), 2694. Compare Rufus Jones' discussion of the relationship between Quakerism and Quietism in the chapters "Quietism" and "Quietism in the Society of Friends" in *The Later Periods of Quakerism*, I (London: Macmillan, 1921), 32–56 and 57–103.

24 See Hugh Barbour and J. William Frost, *The Quakers* (New York: Green-wood Press, 1988), 98–101 and passim.

25 *Quakerism A-la-Mode: or, A History of Quietism, Particularly That of the Lord Arch-bishop of Cambray and Madam Guyone* [sic] (London: J. Harris, 1698).

26 Citations are from the 1750 edition of *The Archbishop of Cambray's Dissertation on Pure Love . . .* (Germantown: Christopher Sauer, 1750), xxiv, xxvii, xxx; hereafter referred to as "Dissertation."

27 Fénelon, "Dissertation," xlviii.

28 Fénelon, "Dissertation," liii–liv.

29 Fénelon, "Dissertation," 2, 14.

30 Fénelon, "Dissertation," 17–94.

31 Fénelon, "Dissertation," 41.

32 Fénelon, "Dissertation," 95–96.

33 Fénelon, "Dissertation," 107, 108.

34 John Woolman, *The Journal and Essays of John Woolman*, ed. Amelia Mott Gummere (Philadelphia: Friends' Book Store; London: Friends' Book-shop, 1922), 156, 157, hereafter cited as *Journal*.

35 Amelia Mott Gummere, ed., "Biographical Sketch," in *Journal*, 15.

36 *Memoir of John Woolman, chiefly extracted from a Journal of His Life and travels* (Philadelphia: Tracts Association of Friends, n.d., ca. 1810), 21, 23.

37 Rivers, 146, 155.

38 Rack summarizes the impact of such reading on the young Wesley in *Reasonable Enthusiast*, 96–105.

39 William McDonald, *Marquis de Renty: or, Holiness exemplified by a Roman Catholic, New and revised edition, To which is added an appendix containing some account of Madame Guyon and F.W. Faber* (Philadelphia: National Publishing Association for the Promotion of Holiness, 1881). (Faber will figure in the discussion of A.W. Tozer in chap. 9.) McDonald is cited by Charles Edwin Jones, *A Guide to the Study of the Holiness Movement*, rev. ed., vol. 1, *The Wesleyan Holiness Movement: A Comprehensive Guide* (Lanham, Md., Toronto, and Oxford: The Scarecrow Press and American Theological Library Association, 2005), 35, hereafter cited as *Guide to the Holiness Movement*.

40 See Schmidt, *John Wesley: A Theological Biography*, trans. Norman P. Goldhawk (Nashville: Abingdon, 1962), 1:140–47, 213–17. By using Schmidt's account, I am emphasizing Wesley's Pietist connections and the role of Poiret as an intermediary, but I do not wish to minimize his indebtedness to the English spiritual tradition. For example, Rivers develops a context for Wesley's works on practical divinity in the dissenting tradition (Rivers, 139–152).

41 The fifteenth-century Bohemian Moravians found refuge, renewal, and leadership under Count Nicholas Zinzendorf (1709–1760). Zinzendorf's theology was a Christocentric theology of the heart, with use of the vocabulary of marriage and childhood. Like others with Pietist roots, Zinzendorf was touched by Quietist values and was a reader of Madame Guyon. The

Moravians were missionaries and took on an ecclesiastical identity after Zinzendorf's death.

Rack points to Wesley's initial encounters with Pietists in Georgia and the two traditions he encountered there, emanating from Halle and from Zinzendorf. *Reasonable Enthusiast,* 120–23. Ward gives a very useful account of Zinzendorf's relationship with the Pietists of Halle, his relation to Madame Guyon (and Anna Nitchman's enthusiasm for Guyon), and his adoption of Bernard of Clairvaux's Jesus-centered spirituality in *Early Evangelicals,* 102–13.

42   See Schmidt, *John Wesley: A Theological Biography,* 1:150–51, 224–25.

43   Schmidt, *John Wesley: A Theological Biography,* 1:246–52.

44   On the conflict over Moravian stillness, see Rack, *Reasonable Enthusiast,* 202–7.

45   *The Journal of John Wesley,* ed. Nehemiah Curnock (1912, repr., London: Epworth, 1938), 3:18.

46   *The Journal of John Wesley,* 5:382–83. The citation from Lyttelton is from n. 1, 383.

47   *The Life of Lady Guion, Written by herself in French, Now Abridged, And translated into English* (by James Gough), 2 vols. (Bristol: S. Farley, 1772), hereafter cited as *The Life of Lady Guion.*

Wesley's comments are in a letter to Penelope Newman, October 23, 1772, *The Letters of John Wesley,* ed. John Telford (London: Epworth, 1931), 5:341.

48   Harold Lindström, Foreword to *Wesley and Sanctification: A Study in the Doctrine of Salvation,* by Timothy L. Smith (1946; repr. Grand Rapids: The Francis Asbury Press of Zondervan Publishing House, 1980), 129.

49   Rack, *Reasonable Enthusiast,* 401.

50   The original edition was published in Bristol by F. Farley. See the reference in chap. 1 to the American edition. The citations to follow will be from the English edition published simultaneously with the American printing, *A Christian Library,* vol. 23 (London: Kershaw, 1825), referred to as *Christian Library.*

51   Rivers discusses in some detail Wesley's editing principles, 152–57.

52   For an overview of the significance of Wesley's choices see Schmidt's chapter, "John Wesley as Theological Writer" in his *John Wesley: A Theological Biography,* 2, particularly 101–8. Jean Orcibal analyzes Continental influence on Wesley, emphasizing the *Library,* in "Les spirituels français et espagnols chez John Wesley," 50–109.

53   Orcibal, "Les spirituels français et espagnols chez John Wesley," 62–63.

54   *Christian Library,* 3, 3–4.

55   For example, the last quotation is an accurate version of the language of tenderness in the original: "Rien n'est si sec, si froid, si dur, si resserré, qu'un coeur qui s'aime seul en toutes choses. Rien n'est si tendre, si ouvert, si vif, si doux, si aimable, si aimant, qu'un coeur que l'amour divin possède et anime." Fénelon, *Oeuvres complètes,* ed. M. Gosselin

(1851–1852, repr. Geneva: Slatkine Reprints, 1971), 7:234. This edition will be subsequently referred to as the Gosselin edition. Gosselin does not distinguish among all the variants and editions in the tradition of Fénelon's manuscript and publication history, but he often provides access to the commonly known texts as they were disseminated without regard to complete accuracy.

56   Gosselin edition, 231–32.

57   *Christian Library*, 7, 8–9.

58   In the Gosselin edition, these reflections are found in VI: 28, 30–31, 32, 32–33, 33–34, 35, 35–36, 36, 36–37, 38, 40, 41–42, 47, 148–51. The passages in Gosselin seem to represent three publication histories.

59   *Christian Library*, 48.

60   Jeanne de la Mothe Guyon, "Instruction chrétienne d'une Mère à sa Fille," in *Discours chrétiens et spirituels sur divers Sujets qui regardent La Vie Intérieure, tirés la plupart de la Ste. Ecriture* (Cologne [Amsterdam]: Jean de la Pierre, 1716), 2:17–18, hereafter cited as *Discours*; and *Christian Library*, 56. Emphasis in original.

61   *Christian Library*, 61.

62   *Christian Library*, 65.

63   *Christian Library*, 69.

64   *Christian Library*, 78–79.

65   *Christian Library*, 101.

66   Charles Wesley, *Wesley Hymnbook*, #40.

67   *Memoirs of the Life, Religious Experiences, and Labours in the Gospel*, ed. John Gough (Dublin: Robert Jackson, 1781), 20–21.

68   *Memoirs*; Gough's version of Wesley's comments is on pp. 95 and 97.

69   Guyon, *The Life of Lady Guion*, 1:iii. The preface may refer to *Pilgrim's Progress*.

70   Guyon, *The Life of Lady Guion*, 1:199–228, 228–32, 237–39.

71   Guyon, *The Life of Lady Guion*, 2:309–24, 325–70.

72   Guyon, *The Life of Lady Guion*, 1:191–94.

73   Guyon, *The Life of Lady Guion*, 1:xvii.

74   This is my translation of the original as previously cited in chapter 2.

75   Guyon, *The Life of Lady Guion*, 1:63.

76   Guyon, *The Life of Lady Guion*, 1:127.

77   *The Exemplary Life of the pious Lady Guion, translated from her own account in the Original French, to which is added, a new translation of her "Short and Easy Method of Prayer,"* by Thomas Digby Brooke (Dublin: William Kidd, 1775). The treatise on prayer is found on pp. 447–509. (The sale list of the printer also includes Heylin's *Devotional Tracts concerning the Presence of God, and other Religious subjects* [p. 2].) This edition is subsequently cited as *Lady Guion*, 2nd ed.

78   *Lady Guion*, 2nd ed., xvii.

79   *Lady Guion*, 2nd ed., 489.

80   "Self is wholly a miser, it contracts what it possesses and at the same time attracts all that it does not possess. . . . Love, on the contrary, is a giving, not a craving; an expansion, not a contraction; it breaks in pieces the condensing circle of self, and goes forth in the delightfulness of its desire to bless" (2:160–61). "But when God is pleased to inform the will of the creature with any measure of his own benign and benevolent will, he steals it sweetly forth in affection to others; and a new and delightful dawning arises out of his spirit" (3:159). Henry Brooke, *The Fool of Quality; or, The History of Henry Earl of Moreland*, 3 vols. (Philadelphia: Printed for Robert Campbell, 1794).

81   *The Worship of God, in Spirit and Truth; or, A Short and Easy Method of Prayer . . . ; To which is added two letters, concerning a life truly Christian; and a discourse upon the universal love and goodness of God to mankind, in and through Jesus Christ; Extracted from two late authors* (Philadelphia: Francis Bailey, 1789).

Chapter 6

1   James Stillman Caskey, "Jonathan Edwards' 'Catalogue,'" B.D. thesis (Chicago Theological Seminary, 1931), 12–13, 17, 29. See also William Sparkes Morris, *The Young Jonathan Edwards: A Reconstruction* (Brooklyn, N.Y.: Carlson Publishing, 1991), 219–86. Austin Warren notes that Nathaniel Emmons, one of Edwards' disciples, copied passages from Fénelon in a commonplace book; Warren also suggests that Samuel Hopkins, another Edwardsian, was in the Quietist tradition because of his doctrine that a test of true Christianity was to be "'willing to be damned for the glory of God.'" See "Fénelon Among the Anglo-Saxons," in *New England Saints* (Ann Arbor: University of Michigan Press, 1956), 64, subsequently referred to as "Fénelon Among the Anglo-Saxons." Warren discusses in a general way, but without documentation, a number of the readers treated in this chapter.

2   I am indebted here to Stephen G. Post, "Disinterested Benevolence: An American Debate Over the Nature of Christian Love," *Journal of Christian Ethics* 14 (1986): 356–68 and *Christian Love and Self-Denial: An Historical and Normative Study of Jonathan Edwards, Samuel Hopkins, and American Theological Ethics* (Lanham, Md.: University Press of America, 1987), 21–55. The article is hereafter cited as "Disinterested Benevolence."

3   The translation here is from Whiston, *Christian Perfection*, 135.

4   *America and French Culture 1750–1848*, 411–48, particularly 439–40.

5   *Pious Reflections for Every Day in the Month*, trans. (*Manuel de piété*) J. Clowes (Boston: Loring, n.d). This is a miniature book. See also the following editions: Boston: Hall and Hiller, 1803; New Bedford, Mass.: A. Shearman, 1807; New York: Collins, 1811; and Newburyport: A.B. Allen, 1814.

       Apples of Gold, Gathered by Fénelon (Philadelphia: J. B. Lippincott, 1856) represents a late example of a hard-bound miniature, containing

"Pious Reflections," and other excerpted "apples" on topics such as humility, prayer, self-knowledge, charity, and death.

6   *The Archbishop of Cambray's Meditations and Soliloquies, on various religious subjects: With directions for a holy life, also a letter concerning religion* (New Bedford, Mass.: A. Shearman, 1802), n.p.

7   Fénelon, *Faithfulness in Little Things . . . Translated from the French into German, and thence into English* (Philadelphia: Kimber, Conrad, 1804). The title would be reprinted in 1815, also in Philadelphia, by Joseph Rakestraw.

8   John Kendall, Preface to *Extracts from the Writings of Francis Fenelon, Archbishop of Cambray . . . .* (Philadelphia: Kimber, Conrad, 1804), iv, vii. These citations are variations on the life of Fénelon presented both in the 1772 Bristol edition by James Gough of the life of Madame Guyon and in his *Select Lives of Foreigners, Eminent in Piety*, 2nd ed. (Bristol; repr. Dublin: James Gough, 1796), 113, 129–30.

9   On the Olney hymnbook, see James M. Gordon, *Evangelical Spirituality: From the Wesleys to John Stott* (London: SPCK, 1991), 70–92. D. Bruce Hindmarsh analyzes John Newton's hymnody at Olney in *John Newton and the English Evangelical Tradition, between the Conversions of Wesley and Wilberforce* (Oxford: Clarendon Press, 1996), 257–88, hereafter cited as *Newton and the English Evangelical Tradtion*. Cowper figures in this discussion, and the summary of the aesthetics of eighteenth-century hymnody is particularly helpful.

10   The Cowper translations have been examined in detail by Dorothy L. Gilbert and Russell Pope, "The Cowper Translation of Mme Guyon's Poems," *PMLA* 54 (1939): 1077–98 and by John D. Baird and Charles Ryskamp in their edition of *The Poems of William Cowper* (Oxford: Clarendon Press, 1995), 2:x–xi, xx–xxi, 322–37; the poems are given on 43–108. The essay will be referred to as Gilbert and Pope, the edition as Cowper.

11   For more details on American editions of the Cowper translations, see my "Madame Guyon in America: An Annotated Bibliography," 108–109. An example of Cowper's popularity is to be found in the extensive publication list of Benjamin and Thomas Kite of Philadelphia in 1807; they were selling Cowper's *Life* (3 vols.) and his *Poems* (3 vols.). See n. 26.

12   See, for example, the statistics on the growth between 1790 and 1860 in the number of Methodist churches given by Mark A. Noll, *America's God: From Jonathan Edwards to Abraham Lincoln* (Oxford: Oxford University Press, 2002), 166, hereafter cited as *America's God*; and his discussion of the hymns of early Methodism as a source of its theology, 332–33.

13   Guyon, *The Life of Lady Guion*, 440.

14   Guyon, *The Life of Lady Guion*, 441.

15   Guyon, *The Life of Lady Guion*, 447.

16   Guyon, *The Life of Lady Guion*, 444.

17   Guyon, *The Life of Lady Guion*, 449.

18   Cowper, 324.

19 For a detailed discussion of Cowper's changes in the original Guyon texts, see Gilbert and Pope, 1082–98.

20 These examples are cited in Gilbert and Pope, 1091 and 1092, although their interpretation is somewhat different from mine.

21 "L'ame amante trouve Dieu par-tout" ("The Soul that loves God finds him Everywhere"), stanza 3, cited by Gilbert and Pope, 1096.

22 Stanzas 1, 2, and 5, Cowper, 53, 54.

23 Stanzas 1, 2, and 15, Cowper, 106, 108.

24 "A Figurative Description of the Procedure of Divine Love Bringing a Soul to the Point of Self-Renunciation and Absolute Acquiescence," stanzas 1, 2, and 12 in Cowper, 47 and 49.

25 *The Exemplary Life of the pious Lady Guion, translated from her own account in the Original French: To which is added, a new translation of her "Short and Easy Method of Prayer,"* by Thomas Digby Brooke (Philadelphia: Joseph Crukshank, 1804); and *The Life of Lady Guion: now abridged, and translated into English, exhibiting her eminent piety, charity, meekness, resignation, fortitude and stability, her labours, travels, sufferings and services, for the conversion of souls to God, and her great success in some places, in that best of all employments on the earth: to which are added accounts of the lives of worthy persons, whose memories were dear to Lady Guion* (New Bedford, Mass.: Abraham Shearman, 1805).

26 *Select Lives of Foreigners, Eminent for Piety,* 3rd ed. (Philadelphia: Printed for Benjamin and Thomas Kite, 1807). See also n. 6. I will cite the second edition subsequently as *Select Lives,* as specified in n. 6.

27 *Select Lives,* n.p. The preface is identical in the American edition of the Kites.

28 See the editor's note, *Select Lives,* 99.

29 *Select Lives,* 146.

30 For details on these editions between 1820 and 1825, see my "Madame Guyon in America: An Annotated Bibliography."

31 *A Guide to True Peace, or, A Method of attaining to inward and spiritual prayer: Compiled chiefly from the writings of Fénelon, Archbishop of Cambray, Lady Guion, and Michael de Molinos* (Poughkeepsie, N.Y.: P. Potter; Philadelphia: S. Potter, 1818). See also *A Guide to True Peace; or, The Excellency of Inward and Spiritual Prayer . . . .* (New York: Harper and Brothers, published in association with Pendle Hill, 1946); this edition was reprinted in a pocket-size edition (Wallingford, Pa.: Pendle Hill, 1979). In his preface to the 1946 edition, Howard H. Brinton notes that the collection was published anonymously by two Quakers, William Backhouse and James Jonson, and went through twelve editions and reprintings between 1813 and 1877 (vii–xiii).

32 *Pious Reflections for Every Day of the Month. Translated from the French of FENELON. To which is prefixed, THE LIFE OF THE AUTHOR* (Boston: Lincoln and Edmonds, 1814), xii–xiii.

33 Another source for material on the life of Fénelon that was available in

America was by Charles Butler, an English Catholic. *The Life of Fénelon, Archbishop of Cambray* was published London in 1810, then quickly reprinted in Baltimore and Philadelphia in 1811, with other editions to follow. Howard Mumford Jones has pointed out that periodicals also began to treat Fénelon; for example, the *Christian Disciple* published "Sketches of the Life and Character of Fénelon," translated from the French, 4 (n.s.) (1822): 421–33.

34   Much of this biographical material is based on the entry in the *Dictionary of American Biography*, vol. 6, ed. Allen Johnson and Dumas Malone (New York: Scribner's, 1931), 491–92.

35   Henry Wadsworth Longfellow, *The Letters*, vol. 2, *1837–1843*, ed. Andrew Hilen (Cambridge, Mass.: Belknap Press of Harvard University Press, 1966), 480–81.

36   Mrs. Follen, ed. *Selections from the Writings of Fenelon, with a Memoir of His Life*, 5th ed. (Boston: Simpkins, 1844), vi, hereafter cited as *Selections*.

37   Follen, *Selections*, 22, 27.

38   Follen, *Selections*, 22.

39   Jacques Le Brun gives the history of the writing and publication of the two parts of this treatise, along with an excellent introduction, in Fénelon, *Oeuvres*, 2:1529–40.

40   *Demonstration of the Existence and Attributes of God followed by The Reflections of Father of Tournemine, a Jesuite, upon Atheism: Upon my Lord of Cambray's Demonstration, and upon Spinosa's System, which served for a preface to some of the former editions of the Demonstration by Mr Fenelon, The Late Famous Archbishop of Cambray, Author of Telemachus* (Harrisburg: William Gillmor, 1811). This text is based on a tradition derived from 1718, bringing parts 1 and 2 of Fénelon's anthology together, along with the Tournemine refutation.

41   See Holifield, 197–217.

42   *Catechism on the Foundations of the Christian Faith: For the use of both the young and old; followed by The celebrated Conversation of Mr. de Fenelon with Mr. de Ramsay; and by several extracts, on the existence of GOD, and on the Worship which is due to him, from the letters of the illustrious Archbishop of Cambray M. DE FENELON; Printed with the express approbation of Monseigneur Caroll Archbishop of Baltimore and New York* (New York: The Economical School, 1810).

43   Follen, *Selections*, 307.

44   William Ellery Channing, *On the Character and Writings of Fénelon* (Boston: n.p., 1829). I am quoting the second edition, *Remarks on the Character and Writings of Fenelon* (London: Edward, Rainford, 1830), 7, 8, 9, hereafter cited as Channing. Howard Mumford Jones has noted the original review in the *Christian Examiner* n.s. 6 (1829), 1–35, as an example of Fénelon's status as a favorite Catholic author in America; *America and French Culture*, 439. Joel Porte has emphasized Channing's rhetorical strategy of inviting readers to compare the career of Fénelon and that of the first Catholic

bishop of Boston, Jean-Louis Lefebre de Chenerus. See "Emerson's French Connection," in *Consciousness and Culture: Emerson and Thoreau Reviewed* (New Haven: Yale University Press, 2004), 98–100, hereafter cited as "Emerson's French Connection."

45   Channing, 16, 26.

46   Follen, *Selections*, x, xi, xiii.

47   Follen, *Selections*, xiii–xiv.

48   Ann Douglas, *The Feminization of American Culture* (1977, repr., New York: Avon Books, 1978), 185–86, 404–5, hereafter cited as *The Feminization of American Culture*. There will be further discussion of Douglas in chaps. 7 and 9.

49   The authoritative discussion of this early material and of Child's evolution within her culture is by Carolyn L. Karcher, *The First Woman in the Republic: A Cultural Biography of Lydia Maria Child* (Durham, N.C.: Duke University Press, 1994), 126–50; Karcher describes these biographies as moving toward more conventional portrayals of women, although they were built on wrenching personal dramas (147).

50   Lydia Maria Child, *The Biographies of Lady Russell and Madame Guyon*. The Ladies' Family Library, vol. 2. (Boston: Carter, Hendee, 1832), 251.

51   See Lydia Maria Child, *The Progress of Religious Ideas through Successive Ages*, 3 vols. (New York: C.S. Francis, 1855). For the discussion of Child within Unitarianism, see Holifield, 208.

52   Thomas C. Upham, "The Peculiar Dangers Attending a State of Holiness," *The Guide to Christian Perfection* 2 (1841): 56. It is interesting that Upham's initial reference to Madame Guyon is not entirely positive—he accuses her in this piece of the error of "discerning spirits."

      A journalistic biography was published in the "Little Journeys" series, vol. 3, for 1897: Elbert Hubbard, "Madame Guyon," in *Little Journeys to the Homes of Famous Women*, 43–78 (New York and London: G.P. Putnam's son, 1897). An art edition of this biography was produced by the Roycrofters as Elbert Hubbard, *Three Great Women: Being Little Journeys; Madame Guyon, Elizabeth Barrett Browning* (East Aurora, N.Y.: The Roycrofters, 1908).

53   *New England Saints*, 67.

54   Porte, "Emerson's French Connection," 103. Robert D. Richard Jr. ascribes Emerson's religious bent to his mother, who read authors who treated the practical day-to-day religious life and whose favorite author was Fénelon. *Emerson: The Mind on Fire* (Berkeley, Calif.: University of California Press, 1995), 21–22, 89, hereafter cited as *Emerson: The Mind on Fire*.

55   Richard Jr., *Emerson: The Mind on Fire*, 89–90.

56   Here I am relying on Holifield, 441–42.

57   Ralph Waldo Emerson, *The Early Lectures of Ralph Waldo Emerson*, vol. 1, *1833–1836*, ed. Robert E. Spiller and Wallace E. Williams (Cambridge, Mass.: Belknap Press of Harvard University Press, 1959).

58   Ralph Waldo Emerson, *The Journals and Miscellaneous Notebooks*, vol. 3, *1826–*

1832, ed. William H. Gilman and Alfred R. Ferguson (Cambridge, Mass.: Belknap Press of Harvard University Press, 1963), 172, 174; henceforth cited as *Journals*, with separate dates and editors for the volume in question.

59   Emerson, *Journals*, vol. 4, *1832–1834*, ed. Alfred R. Ferguson (1964), 83, 84.

60   Emerson, *Journals*, vol. 5, *1835–1838*, ed. Merton M. Sealts Jr. (1965), 5.

61   I have consulted the catalogue as reproduced in the appendix of *Bronson Alcott's Fruitlands with Transcendental Wild Oats by Louisa M. Alcott*, ed. Clara Endicott Sears (Boston: Houghton Mifflin, 1915), 175–85, hereafter cited as *Fruitlands*.

      Interest in mystical writers remained strong in Boston, and A. E. Ford, a Swedenborgian, translated *The Torrents*, adding parallel passages from Swedenborg at the bottom of the page as a kind of gloss. This was a complete, literal translation of the Guyon text. In the preface, Ford maintained that the "writings of Madame Guyon can be best appreciated by those who have accepted the heavenly doctrines of the New Jerusalem" (iii). This work was published after Thomas Upham's two-volume work on Madame Guyon had appeared (see chap. 7), but the translator indicates that readers of Madame Guyon may be surprised by the coincidence between her and the teachings of the New Church, on the deepest subjects of the interior life" (vi). Guyon, *Spiritual Torrents, with parallel passages from the writings of Emanuel Swedenborg* (Boston: Otis Clapp, 1853).

62   "Sketch of Childhood," cited in Louisa May Alcott, *Her Life, Letters, and Journals*, ed. Ednah D. Cheney (Boston: Roberts Brothers, 1889), 30–31, hereafter cited as *Life, Letters, and Journals*.

63   Cheney, *Life, Letters, and Journals*, 68.

Chapter 7

1   In his early study of the perfectionist and holiness movements, Benjamin Warfield was consistently critical because of his position as a Calvinist on the nature of sin. An abridged edition, *Perfectionism*, edited by Samuel G. Craig, was published in 1958 (Grand Rapids: Baker Book House). The most complete discussion of the holiness movement is Melvin Dieter's *The Holiness Revival of the Nineteenth Century*. Material on *The Guide to Holiness* is found on 1–3; on the Oberlin brand of perfectionism, see 18–20. Dieter's study was preceded by Timothy L. Smith's *Revivalism and Social Reform in Mid-Nineteenth Century America* in which he sought to demonstrate that holiness revivalism was not centered on inner piety alone but also led to social reform. A notable example was the abolitionist movement to which Oberlin College was linked. See also Dieter, 20–22. George M. Marsden presents a theological analysis of Finney as a synthesizer of holiness traditions and of the justifications for the social expression of holiness in the nineteenth century in *Fundamentalism and American Culture*, 73–74, 80–81.

2   Biographical data on Merritt is given in *The Encyclopedia of World Methodism*,

general ed. Nolan B. Harmon (Nashville, Tenn.: United Methodist Publishing House, 1974), 2:1552–53.

3   See S. B., "Experimental Holiness," *Guide to Holiness* 26 (1854): 114–15 and "The Close of the Year and Volume," *Guide to Holiness* 44 (1863): 185. Dieter treats the importance of the *Guide* in *The Holiness Revival of the Nineteenth Century*, 42. The Palmer publishing house took over the *Guide* in 1864.

4   "To the English Reader," *A Short and Easie Method of Prayer Which every one may learn and practise with great Facility, and thereby arrive, in a little time, to high degrees of Christian Perfection: Singularly useful to all Persons who seek God in Sincerity by Madam Guion* (London: Printed for R. Sympson at the Harp in St. Paul's-Church-Yard and J. Nutt near Stationers-Hall, 1704), A 2(1)–A 3, hereafter cited as "To the English Reader."

5   "To the English Reader," A 4(1)–A 5.

6   "To the English Reader," A 5(1)–A 6.

7   "To the English Reader," A 7.

8   "To the English Reader," A 9.

9   Gough, *The Life of Lady Guion*, xvii.

10   *Select Lives*, 11.

11   See Sandei, *Pro Theologia Mystica Clavis elucidarium onomasticon vocabulorum et loqutionum obscurum* (1640; repr., Heverles-Louvain: Editions de la Bibliothèque S.J., 1963), 204–5.

12   François de Sales, *Lettres*, vol. 9, bk. 2 of *Oeuvres complètes* (Paris: J.J. Blaise, 1821), 35.

13   Marie de l'Incarnation, *L'expérience de Dieu avec Marie de l'Incarnation*, ed. Guy-M. Oury (Saint-Laurent, Quebec: Fides, 1999), 57, 68, 86. See also Bremond, *Histoire littéraire du sentiment religieux en France*, 6:38–47.

14   This is a summary of Jacques Le Brun, "Expérience religieuse et expérience littéraire," in *La Pensée religieuse dans la littérature et la civilisation du XVIIe siècle en France: Actes du Colloque de Bamberg, 1983*, ed. Manfred Tietz and Volker Kapp, published as a volume of *Biblio 17: Papers on French Seventeenth Century Literature* 13 (1984): 123–46.

15   See Le Brun, *La Spiritualité de Bossuet*, 470–74. The Quietist controversy is discussed in detail on 441–695.

16   Bossuet, *Correspondance*, ed. Ch. [Charles] Urbain and E. [Eugène] Levesque, new ed. (Paris: Hachette, 1912), letter 921, 6:8, hereafter cited as Bossuet.

17   Bossuet, letter 933, 6:26–27.

18   Bossuet, letter to Madame d'Albert, letter 939, 6:57.

19   "Ce goût expérimental de la présence de Dieu," is the phrase to describe the experience preparatory to the second degree of prayer. *Moyen court*, 70.

20   *Justifications de la doctrine de Madame de la Mothe-Guyon* (Paris: Librairies Associés, 1790), 1:249. Additional references to the certainty of experiential knowledge and to the nature of the subject within the system of Madame Guyon's mysticism are to be found in J.-F. Marquet, "L'Expérience

religieuse de Jeanne Guyon," in *Fénelon: Philosophie et spiritualité*, ed. Denise Seduc-Fayette (Geneva: Droz, 1996), 155–76.

21 Johannes Wallmann gives this publication history in his chapter on Arndt in Lindberg, *The Pietist Theologians*, 21–22.

22 *Guide to Christian Perfection* 8 (1845): 49–51. Thomas Upham contributed the comments (49) and the abstracts: "Of the Transforming Power of Faith" and "Of the Purification of the Heart by Union with Christ." Upham seems to have been working with Wesley's *Christian Library*. Short maxims "Rules to Aid in Leading a Holy Life," drawn from Arndt were included in 8 (1845): 73.

23 The foregoing quotations are from an eighteenth-century printing of an English translation of Johann Arndt, *Of True Christianity . . . Wherein is contained the whole œconomy of God Towards Men; and the Whole Duty of man Towards God* (London: Printed for D. Brown and J. Downing, 1712), I: xliii, xliv, 42. John Weborg discusses the experiential and experimental aspects of Pietism in "Pietism: 'The Fire of God Which Flames in the Heart of Germany'" in *Protestant Spiritual Traditions*, ed. Frank C. Senn (New York: Paulist Press, 1986), 197–210; however, he assigns a more modern meaning to the term "experimental," discussing the practices of Pietism under that heading; this volume is hereafter cited as *Protestant Spiritual Tradtions*.

24 For a useful summary of Puritan spirituality, see E. Glenn Hinson, "Puritan Spirituality" in *Protestant Spiritual Traditions*, 165–82.

25 John Bunyan, *The Pilgrim's Progress*, Special tercentenary edition (New York: American Tract Society, 1934), 257, 259, 264, hereafter cited as *Pilgrim's Progress*.

26 Bunyan, *Pilgrim's Progress*, 264, 266.

27 Bunyan, *Pilgrim's Progress*, 267, 268.

28 Bunyan, *Pilgrim's Progress*, 367.

29 Holifield introduces his survey of Edwards' theology with this distinction, quoting the phrase from Edwards I have cited; Holifield also summarize's Edward's intellectual background. See *Theology in America*, 102, 102–4.

30 See Hambrick-Stowe, *The Practice of Piety*, 49 and 54–55.

31 I am referring here to the schematic representation in Lewis Bayly, *The Practice of Piety, directing a Christian how to walk, that he may please God*, amplifed by the author (London: Printed for Edward Brewster, 1702), 2.

32 The phrase is cited by Holifield, 102, who develops the distinction between the speculative and the practical.

33 Cited by Iain H. Murray in *Jonathan Edwards: A New Biography* (Edinburgh, Pa.: The Banner of Truth Trust, 1987), 35, hereafter cited as Murray.

34 Jonathan Edwards, *Sermons and Discourses 1723–1719*, ed. Kenneth P. Minkema (New Haven, Conn.: Yale University Press, 1997), 72, 74, 78, 79, 80, hereafter cited as *Sermons and Discourses*.

35 Edwards, *Sermons and Discourses*, 81.

36 Edwards, *Sermons and Discourses*, 253.

37 I am borrowing the phrase "Baconian style" from Holifield in *Theology in*

America, part 2, where it is used to describe a style of "empirical, inductive, and nonspeculative" thinking (159) in nineteenth-century American theology.

38   McCully, *The Silent and Soft Communion*, 13.

39   Jonathan Edwards, *Some Thoughts Concerning the Present Revival of Religion in New England*, in *The Great Awakening*, ed. C. C. Goen, *The Work*, vol. 4, ed. John E. Smith (New Haven, Conn.: Yale University Press, 1972), 341–42.

      Sarah Edwards became a model of religious piety for ensuing generations via the memoir of Samuel Hopkins (to be mentioned in chap. 8). For a useful commentary in the context of the tradition of Puritan marriage, see Amanda Porterfield, *Feminine Spirituality in America: From Sarah Edward to Martha Graham* (Philadelphia: Temple University Press, 1980), 19–50, hereafter cited as *Feminine Spirituality in America*.

40   Jonathan Edwards, *A Treatise Concerning Religious Affections*, ed. John E. Smith, *The Works*, vol. 2, ed. Perry Miller (New Haven, Conn.: Yale University Press, 1959), 410, 411. The page references refer to the first extended citation as well as the body of the paragraph. Murray gives a useful summary of Edwards' thinking on revivals, the emotions, and experience in chaps. 12 and 13 of his biography: "The Defence of Experimental Religion" and "The Religious Affections."

41   An excellent survey of the impact of Baconian thought in England is given by Richard Foster Jones in *Ancients and Moderns: A Study of the Rise of the Scientific Movement in Seventeenth Century England*, 2nd ed. (St. Louis, Mo.: Washington University Studies, 1961).

42   Cited by Hindmmarsh in *John Newton and the English Evangelical Tradition*, 49. Newton's reading included the texts of both English and Continental spirituality (79–80), and he led an intense devotional life (221–47).

43   See Noll, *America's God*, 233–34; Holifield, 159–60; and Marsden, *Fundamentalism and American Culture*, 55–56.

44   On Wesley and Locke, see for example Clifford J. Hindley, "The Philosophy of Enthusiasm: A Study in the Origins of 'Experimental Theology,'" *London Quarterly and Holborn Review* 182 (1957): 99–109 and (1957): 199–210; Frederick Dreyer, "Faith and Experience in the thought of John Wesley," *American Historical Review* 88 (1983): 12–30; and Donald A.D. Thorson, "Experimental Method in the Practical Theology of John Wesley," *Wesleyal Theological Journal* 24 (1989): 117–41. Wesley drew on the Anglican tradition but was particularly influenced by Peter Browne, Bishop of Cork, an interpreter of Locke and opponent of Deism.

45   David Watson gives a useful summary of the history of the holiness movement or, more accurately, of holiness movements in nineteenth-century America, with an emphasis on the ways in which this strain of revivalism was related to Methodist spirituality, in "Methodist Spirituality," in *Protestant Spiritual Traditions*, 217–73, particularly 254–63, hereafter cited as Watson. Timothy L. Smith gives an excellent overview of "The Resurgence of Revivalism 1840–1857" in *Revivalism and Social Reform in Mid-Nineteenth Century America*, 45–62.

46   Watson, "Methodist Spirituality," 255.

47   See Ann Taves, *Fits, Trances, and Visions: Experiencing Religion and Explaining Experience from Wesley to James* (Princeton, N.J.: Princeton University Press, 1999) for a history of experience as enthusiasm in America, particularly "Shouting Methodists" (76–117) and "Methodist Camp and Tabernacle Meetings" (232–40). Taves also summarizes naturalistic explanations of experience in the eighteenth century (20–46). This volume is subsequently referred to as Taves.

48   *On Experimental Religion* (Boston: Bowles and Dearborn, 1827), hereafter cited as *Experimental Religion*. Holifield refers to this tract in the context of his discussion of conservative Unitarianism in his *Theology in America*, 533, n. 33. He notes as well Samuel Barrett, *Doctrine of Religious Experience, Explained and Enforced* (Boston: Leonard C. Bowles, 1829); Barrett may well be the author of the 1827 tract. The reference to "losing religion" in my citation suggests a Methodist-Arminian, rather than Calvinist, theological context.

49   *Experimental Religion*, 5.

50   *Experimental Religion*, 11.

51   *Experimental Religion*, 12, 14.

52   *Experimental Religion*, 15.

53   See Holifield, 270; he discusses Methodist theology of perfection under the general heading of "Baconian Style," 268–72. David Watson gives a useful summary of "The Way of Holiness" in his essay, 257–61.

54   Here I am following the account of Holifield, 361–67.

55   Charles G. Finney, *The Memoirs of Charles G. Finney: The Complete Restored Text*, ed. Garth M. Rosell and Richard A.G. Depuis (Grand Rapids: Zondervan [Academic Books], 1989), 409.

56   For an overview of Palmer, her theology, and her ministry, see Dieter, *The Holiness Revival*, 22–42.

57   Quoted by Mark Noll in *America's God*, 361. In his discussion of Palmer, Noll concludes that she was not "building a theology from the resources of Methodist Christian experience." "Palmer in effect continued to insist that Wesleyanism had no formal theology" (361). See 359–62.

58   Phoebe Palmer, *The Way of Holiness, with Notes by the Way* . . . . 2nd ed. (New York: G. Lane and C.B. Tippett, 1848), 215, 230, and 234, hereafter cited as *The Way of Holiness*.

59   Palmer, *The Way of Holiness*, 31.

60   Palmer, *The Way of Holiness*, 42–43.

61   My reference here is to hymn no. 361 of the 1889 edition of the *Methodist Hymnal* for which the text is reproduced at http://wesley.nnu.edu/charles_wesley/hymns/300-399.htm (October 3, 2006).

62   Palmer, *The Way of Holiness*, 95.

63   Palmer, *The Way of Holiness*, 107.

64   Richard Wheatley, *The Life and Letters of Mrs. Phoebe Palmer* (New York:

Palmer and Hughes, 1884), 522; here Palmer is voicing her reservations about Upham's view of spiritual union. This volume is hereafter cited as *Life and Letters*.

65   Palmer, *The Way of Holiness*, 157.

66   Palmer, *The Way of Holiness*, 139.

67   Carl F. Price, *More Hymn Stories* (New York: Abingdon, 1929), 59.

68   The lines are quoted from *The United Methodist Hymnal* (Nashville, Tenn.: United Methodist Publishing House, ca. 1976), 369.

69   Information on Upham's life is based in part on Alpheus S. Packard, *Address on the Life and Character of Thomas C. Upham, D.D. . . . .* (Brunswick, Maine: Joseph Griffin, 1873), 9 and passim.

70   Wheatley, *Life and Letters*, 240, 241. The story of the Uphams' involvement in the Tuesday meeting is given on 238–42, and the details reveal the mentoring relationship Palmer had with them in 1840. Palmer notes that the Uphams established their own meeting in their house similar to the "Tuesday meeting." See also 577.

71   Wheatley, *Life and Letters*, 251.

72   Thomas C. Upham, "Testimony," in *Pioneer Experiences: Or the Gift of Power Received by Faith, Illustrated and Confirmed by the Testimonies of Eighty Lives; Witnesses of Various Denominations*, ed. Phoebe Palmer (New York: W. C. Palmer, Jr., 1868), 90, 91, hereafter cited as *Pioneer Experiences*.

73   Upham, *Pioneer Experiences*, 91, 92.

74   Upham, *Pioneer Experiences*, 92–94, 96, 97.

75   Upham, *Pioneer Experiences*, 98.

76   Thomas C. Upham, *Elements of Intellectual Philosophy*, 2nd ed. (Portland, Maine: Shirley and Hyde, 1828), 456. On the editions of Upham's major works, see Darius L. Salter, *Spirit and Intellect: Thomas Upham's Holiness Theology* (Metuchen, N.J.: The Scarecrow Press, 1986), 12, hereafter cited as Salter. Salter indicates that Upham's works of the 1840s on the interior life and on Madame Guyon went through eighteen and fifty-seven editions, respectively.

77   See Holifield, 179–196, and Salter, 183–212.

78   Thomas C. Upham, *A Philosophical and Practical Treatise on the Will* (Portland, Maine: William Hyde, 1834), 73, hereafter cited as *The Will*.

79   Upham, *The Will*, 218.

80   Upham, *The Will*, 233.

81   Thomas C. Upham, *American Cottage Life: A Series of Poems illustrative of American scenery, and of the Associations, feelings, and employments of the American cottager and farmer*, 2nd ed. (Brunswick, Maine: Joseph Griffin, 1836); see 124 for the quotation from the Guyon poem and for "The True Rest."

82   Thomas C. Upham, *The Manual of Peace*, embracing I. Evils and Remedies of War, II. Suggestions on the Law of Nations, III. Consideration of a Congress of Nations (New York: Leavitt, Lord; Brunswick, Maine: Joseph Griffin, 1836); for the reference to the temperance movement, see 193.

83 Thomas C. Upham, *Principles of the Interior or Hidden Life: Designed particularly for the consideration of those who are seeking assurance of faith and perfect love* (Boston: Waite, Pierce, 1843). The volume went through eight editions by 1873, and also appeared in abridged versions, for example, as late as 1950 in a series called Abridged Holiness Classics, published by the Beacon Hill Press, a publishing arm of the Church of the Nazarene.

84 Smith and her husband were Quakers and proponents of the deeper life of holiness as espoused by the international Keswick movement; this movement is discussed briefly in chap. 8 in the context of W. E. Boardman. On McCalla, see chap. 1. The Wesleyan Methodist Publishing Association also published an edition of *Inward Divine Guidance* with the Whitall Smith preface in 1905; a reprint by the Christian Witness Publishing Company appeared in 1907. The reprint that I cited in chap. 1, n. 15, was published by the Schmul Publishing Company as part of a Wesleyan Book Club and is referred to here as *Inward Divine Guidance*. For the citation from the Whitall Smith preface, see 6.

85 *Inward Divine Guidance*, 65.

86 *Inward Divine Guidance*, 104.

87 *Inward Divine Guidance*, 108–9.

88 *Inward Divine Guidance*, 119.

89 Thomas C. Upham, *Life of Madame Catharine Adorna, Including Some Leading Facts and Traits in Her Religious Experience: Together with Explanations and Remarks, tending to illustrate the doctrine of holiness*, 3rd ed. (New York: Harper and Brothers, 1858), 3–4; hereafter referred to as *Adorna*.

90 Upham, *Adorna*, 85–97.

91 Upham, *Adorna*, 114.

92 Upham, *Adorna*, 33. See 23–32.

93 Upham, *Adorna*, 82–83.

94 Upham, *Adorna*, 143.

95 Upham, *Adorna*, 236–37.

96 Upham, *Adorna*, 138–39.

97 I emphasize the influence of Poiret's *Théologie de l'amour, ou La Vie et les oeuvres de Sainte Catherine de Gênes* (Cologne [Amsterdam]: Jean de la Pierre, 1691) and of Upham's book on Adorna on *The Life and Religious Opinions and Experience of Madame de la Mothe Guyon* in "Madame Guyon and Experiential Theology in America," *Church History* 67 (1998): 492–94. Upham refers to the Poiret work in *Adorna*, 107.

98 *Life and Religious Opinions*, 1:v. Upham gives a "catalogue" of the major works he consulted, 1:xvii–xviii.

99 The quote from Upham about the nature of Madame Guyon's poetry is in the *Life and Religious Opinions*, 1:227. The poem from Cowper follows on 227–28; see my discussion of the stanza in question in chap. 6.

100 "Preface" to *Autobiography of Madame Guyon*, trans. Thomas Taylor Allen (London: Kegan Paul, Trench, Trübner; St. Louis, Mo.: B. Herder, 1897),

1:v, xxii. The Allen translation was later edited and abridged for the Shepherd Illustrated Classics series, with an introduction by Ruth Bell Graham, who said, "This is a strange autobiography, deeply inspiring, at times disturbing, always intensely personal." *The Autobiography of Madame Guyon*, trans. Thomas Taylor Allen, ed. Warner A. Hutchinson, introd. Ruth Bell Graham (New Canaan, Conn.: Keats, 1980), n.p.

101 *Enthusiasm*, 235–36.
102 *Life and Religious Opinions*, 1:65–66.
103 *Life and Religious Opinions*, 1:109; see also 137–41.
104 *Life and Religious Opinions*, 1:192.
105 *Life and Religious Opinions*, 1:193, 194.
106 *Life and Religious Opinions*, 1:238.
107 *Life and Religious Opinions*, 1:339.
108 *Life and Religious Opinions*, 1:398.
109 *Life and Religious Opinions*, 1:380–99.
110 *Life and Religious Opinions*, 1:60.
111 *Life and Religious Opinions*, 2:7–9.
112 *Life and Religious Opinions*, 2:77–78.
113 *Life and Religious Opinions*, 2:114–18; the citations are found on 115 and 118.
114 *Life and Religious Opinions*, 2:169.
115 *Life and Religious Opinions*, 2:207.
116 *Life and Religious Opinions*, 2:373; the preceding allusions are to 372.
117 Taves, 149–52.
118 See Dieter, *The Holiness Revival of the Nineteenth Century*, 46–49, on Upham, his impact, and the assimilation of the Quietists into the holiness movement. He notes that Upham's writings were also published in England and "prepared the way for the English holiness evangelism of the Palmers during the war; their influence moved on into the seventies opening doors for the holiness revival of the Smiths, Mahan, and Boardman. They continue on the active reading lists today. Through them Madame Guyon, Molinos, St. Catherine, Fénelon, Catharine Adorna and others in the Christian mystical tradition remain on the active list of holiness 'saints' as well" (48).

Chapter 8

1 See chap. 1 for illustrations of the influence of Upham and of the Quietists on adherents to "holiness."
2 Biographical information on Boardman is drawn from Timothy L. Smith, *Revivalism and Social Reform*, 106–7.
3 On Boardman's influence and on the theological significance of the Keswick Conventions, see Timothy L. Smith's *Called Unto Holiness*, 11, 21–25. Boardman's piece, "The Higher Christian Life," appeared in *The Guide to Holiness* 36 (1859): 109–11.

4   The citations are from the preface to *The Higher Christian Life* (Boston: Henry Hoyt; New York: D. Appleton, ca. 1858, dated 1859), v, vii. The text is subsequently referred to as Boardman.

5   Boardman, 35, 50.

6   Boardman, 59.

7   Boardman refers to a woman reader of Upham's *Interior Way* [sic] who wrote a contract of consecration. Boardman, 129.

8   On Hannah Whitall Smith and Upham, see chap. 7, n. 82.

9   Detailed discussions of Boardman, of the Keswick movement, and of holiness revivalism in Europe can be found in Smith, *Called Unto Holiness*, 23–24; and Dieter, *The Holiness Revival of the Nineteenth Century*, 49–52, 129–69. George Marsden examines the Keswick movement, including its American element, in *Fundamentalism and American Culture*, 75–80, 95–101. It should be noted, as well, that the Salvation Army, which was Wesleyan in its view of the life of holiness, grew out of the revivals in England. Madame Guyon was read among Salvationists, also.

10 Joel A. Carpenter makes this point in his foreword to vol. 2 of Jones, *Guide to the Study of the Holiness Movement, The Keswick Movement: A Comprehensive Guide* (2007), xi–xii.

11 Chap. 7, n. 100.

12 Elisabeth Elliot, "Introduction" to *Spiritual Letters to Women*, Shepherd Illustrated Classic edition, by Fénelon (New Canaan, Conn.: Keats Publishing, 1980), n.p.

13 Harriet Beecher Stowe, *Three Novels: Uncle Tom's Cabin, The Minister's Wooing, Oldtown Folks* (New York: Library of America, 1982), 12, hereafter cited as *Three Novels*.

14 See Joan D. Hedrick, *Harriet Beecher Stowe: A Life* (Oxford: Oxford University Press, 1994), 209–14, hereafter cited as Hedrick.

15 Stowe, *Three Novels*, 213. I give a fuller discussion of Stowe, Fénelon, and the novel in "Fénelon Among the New England Abolitionists," 86–92. Thomas Gossett has discussed Tom and Fénelon in *Uncle Tom's Cabin and American Culture* (Dallas, Tex.: Southern Methodist University Press, 1985), 105. Lawrence Buell emphasizes Stowe's revolutionary intentions in *New England Literary Culture: From Revolution through Renaissance* (Cambridge: Cambridge University Press, 1986), 189.

16 "Religious Character and Experience of Phebe Ann Jacobs,—Written by her Friend, P. L. U.," *Guide to Holiness* (1850), 18:3, 5, 7.

17 Hedrick, 156.

18 All citations are from Harriet Beecher Stowe, "De Rance and Fenelon—A Contrast," *New-York Evangelist* 13 (1842): 105.

19 I have discussed in detail this novel and the spirituality of women as depicted by Stowe and Phoebe Palmer in a paper, "Harriet Beecher Stowe and Phoebe Palmer on Women's Spirituality," presented at a symposium

at Fuller Seminary honoring Charles Edwin Jones (February 2006). See also Lawrence Buell, "Calvin Romanticized: Harriet Beecher Stowe, Samuel Hopkins, and *The Minister's Wooing*," in *Critical Essays on Harriet Beecher Stowe*, ed. Elizabeth Ammons, 259–75 (Boston: D. K. Hall, 1980).

20   Samuel Hopkins, "Appendix," in *The Life and Character of the Late Reverence, Learned, and Pious Mr. Jonathan Edwards*, 2nd ed. (Glasgow, 1785), 113. Consulted at http://galenet.galegroup.com/servlet/ECCO.

21   Joseph A. Conforti, *Jonathan Edwards, Religious Tradition, and American Culture* (Chapel Hill: University of North Carolina Press, 1995), 137–46.

22   Edwards A. Park, "Memoir," in vol. 1, *The Works of Samuel Hopkins* (Boston: Doctrinal Tract and Book Society, 1852), 211.

23   See Hedrick, 276–77; Smith, *Revivalism and Social Reform*, 160–61; and Post, "Disinterested Benevolence," passim. William James, citing Upham, would compare Sarah Edwards and Madame Guyon in his discussion of saintliness. *The Varieties of Religious Experience*, Centenary edition (London: Routledge, 2002), 216, 224.

24   Folder 70, no. 6, of the Beecher-Stowe Collection, Arthur E. and Eliza Schlesinger Library of the History of Women in America, Radcliffe College, Harvard University, hereafter cited as Beecher-Stowe Collection. I am grateful to the Schlesinger Library for permission to quote from this unpublished letter.

25   "The Interior or Hidden Life," *New-York Evangelist*, 16 (April 17, 1845) pagination unavailable; all quotations in the following paragraph are from this article.

26   Harriet Beecher Stowe, "The Interior Life, or Primitive Christian Experience," *New-York Evangelist*, 16 (1845): 97; subsequent citations are from this essay. The *Guide to Christian Perfection* reprinted this article in July (1845), 8:13–18. The term "primitive Christian experience" was also used by Lyman Beecher, as reported in the *Guide*, in an article, "Dr. Lyman Beecher on Sanctification," in which Beecher calls sanctification the "primitive standard of Christian attainment" (1845), 8:139.

27   The letter by Catharine Beecher to Phoebe Palmer was dated September 30, 1845. Charles Edward White cites only short phrases in *The Beauty of Holiness: Phoebe Palmer as Theologican, Revivalist, Feminist, and Humanitarian* (Grand Rapids: Zondervan Publishing House, Francis Asbury Press, 1986), 61:271, n. 158.

28   A letter of May 29, 1850, cited by Charles Edward Stowe, *The Life of Harriet Beecher Stowe* (Boston: Houghton Mifflin, 1889), 133.

29   Beecher-Stowe Collection, folder 70, fragment; reprinted by permission of the Schlesinger Library.

30   Harriet Beecher Stowe, *Religious Studies, Sketches, and Poems* (Boston: Houghton Mifflin, 1896), 120.

31   Holifield, 452. See 452–66 for a useful overview and analysis of Bushnell's thought.

32   *The Feminization of American Culture*, 154.

33   The account of Bushnell's wife is presented at length in his daughter's account of his life. See Mary A. Cheney, *Life and Letters of Horace Bushnell* (New York: Charles Scribner's Sons, 1903), 191–92, hereafter cited as Cheney. Timothy L. Smith summarizes the Cheney account in *Revivalism and Social Reform*, 106, placing Bushnell in the camp of the theology of Finney and Wesley as it was being preached at the time.

34   Cheney, 192, 193.

35   Cheney, 192.

36   Horace Bushnell, *God in Christ* (Hartford, Conn.: Brown and Parsons, 1849), 55, hereafter cited as *God in Christ*.

37   Bushnell, *God in Christ*, 67.

38   Bushnell, *God in Christ*, 71.

39   Bushnell, *God in Christ*, 81, 95.

40   Bushnell, *God in Christ*, 346–47.

41   Bushnell, *God in Christ*, 264.

42   Bushnell, *God in Christ*, 308, 309.

43   Bushnell, *God in Christ*, 335, 343–44.

44   Bushnell, *God in Christ*, 328.

45   Bushnell's advocacy of a new age of spirituality is echoed in Henry Theodore Cheever's *Correspondences of Faith and View of Madame Guyon: A Comparative Study of the Unitive Power and Place of Faith in the Theology and Church of the Future* (New York: Anson D. F. Randolph, ca. 1885).

46   Bushnell, *God in Christ*, 346, 347.

47   The issues of a piety of heart versus a theology of the intellect in Stowe and Bushnell were also apparent in the discourse in 1850, referred to earlier in this chapter, of Edwards A. Park on "The Theology of the Intellect and the Theology of Feelings" (discussed in *The Feminization of American Culture*, 174–81). *The Guide to Holiness* reported on the Park address in which he called for the integration of feeling and intellect in his conclusion. Parks was quoted: "We do hope and believe, that the intellect will yet be enlarged so as to gather up all the discordant representations of the heart, and employ them as the complements, or embellishments, or emphasis of the whole truth; that the heart will be so expanded and refined as to sympathize with the most subtle abstractions of the intellect; that many various forms of faith will yet be blended into a consistent knowledge, like the colors in a single ray; and thus will be ushered in the reign of the Prince of peace, when the lion shall lie down with the lamb." *Guide to Holiness* (1850), 18:67.

48   "The Immediate Knowledge of God," in Horace Bushnell, *Sermons on Living Subjects* (New York: Charles Scribner's Sons, 1892), 115, hereafter cited as *Sermons*.

49   Bushnell, *Sermons*, 117, 118, 119, 120.

50   Bushnell, *Sermons*, 127.

51   James W. Metcalf, ed. *Spiritual Progress; or, Instructions in the Divine Life of*

the Soul: From the French of Fénelon and Madame Guyon (New York: M. W. Dodd, 1853), n.p. The Fénelon material was based on the 1810 edition of his works, volume 4; and the Guyon material, on the 1704 edition of her *Opuscules*, as well as 1790 editions of her works and those of Lacombe.

G. W. McCalla reprinted Metcalf's anthology as *Christian Counsel on Divers Matters Pertaining to the Inner Life* (Philadelphia: G. W. McCalla, 1899). Charles Blanchard's annotated copy of this particular edition is located in the Blanchard Collection of the Buswell Library of Wheaton College. The advertisements for "Works on the Interior Life" (that also included Fénelon's *Spiritual Letters*) occur at the end of this edition. (See chap. 1, p. 8.)

Charles Blanchard's story of his spiritual life, *President Blanchard's Autobiography: The Dealings of God with Charles Albert Blanchard* (Boone, Iowa: The Western Alliance Publishing Company, 1915), makes clear his inner piety, as well as his activities on behalf of such organizations as the National Christian Association (active against secret societies) and the distribution of tracts. His book on prayer, *Getting Things from God: A study of the Prayer Life* (Chicago: The Bible Institute Colportage Association, 1915), relies heavily on Andrew Murray and E. M. Bounds. Murray was connected with the Keswick movement, and his theology is represented in such books as *The Deeper Christian Life* (New York: H. H. Revell, 1896) and *The Two Covenants and the Second Blessing* (New York: H. H. Revell, 1898). Bounds was active first in southern holiness circles.

The Metcalf volume was reproduced on the Internet as part of the Christian Classics Ethereal Library, a site maintained at Calvin College. Available online at http://www.ccel.org/ccel/fenelon/progress, verified in August of 2007.

On the translation of Madame Guyon's *The Torrents* (also in 1853), with parallel passages from Swedenborg, see chap. 6, n. 54.

52   "The Three Silences of Molinos," in Henry Wadsworth Longfellow, *The Poetical Works of Longfellow*, with a new introduction by George Monteiro, reprint of the Cambridge edition (Boston: Houghton Mifflin, 1975), 320.

[. . .]
These Silences, commingling each with each,
Made up the perfect Silence that he [Molinos] sought
And prayed for, and wherein at times he caught
Mysterious sounds from realms beyond our reach.
[. . .]
Hermit of Amesbury! Thou too hast heard
Voices and melodies from beyond the gates,
And speakest only when thy soul is stirred!

53   John Greenleaf Whittier, "Dora Greenwell," in *The Prose Works* (Boston: Houghton Mifflin; Cambridge, Mass.: Riverside, 1892), 3:284, hereafter cited as "Dora Greenwell."

54 Whittier, "Dora Greenwell," 284.

55 Whittier, "Dora Greenwell," 285; this reference is to the entire preceding paragraph.

56 Whittier, "Dora Greenwell," 301–2.

57 See chap. 1, n. 3.

58 Whiston, *Christian Perfection*, 35.

59 Whiston, "Preface," *Christian Perfection*, ix.

60 Whiston, "Preface," *Christian Perfection*, x.

61 Robert E. Whitaker, "Introduction," *Let Go: Living by the Cross and by Faith* (Monroeville, Pa.: Banner Publishing, 1973), n.p. Later editions appeared with Whitaker House as the publisher in New Kensington, Pa. under the title *Let Go*.

62 This was a paperback edition. Bethany House Publishers was a division of Bethany Fellowship in Minneapolis, Minnesota. See chap. 1, n. 4.

Chapter 9

1 Phebe Upham also contributed to the *Guide* "The Song of Songs; or, The Soul Wedded to Christ," a commentary which appeared in several parts in volumes 20 (1851) and 26 (1854). She viewed the Old Testament book as prophetic, "referring to that period of the church when Christ will become all in all to her; and perhaps the time is near, when the marriage of the Lamb is to take place, and the bride is to make herself ready" (26:109). This stance suggests how participants in the holiness renewal saw themselves in the context of nineteenth-century millennialism. Phebe Upham's interest in *The Song of Songs* may have been spurred by her reading of Madame Guyon.

2 Here is one of Thomas Upham's poems, "Entire Consecration": "If men of earth, for earth's renown, / Are willing long to wait or toil, / Nor shrink to lay existence down / Upon the war-field's bloody soil;– // If there is nought they'll not endure, / If there is nought they will not dare, / To make their hopes, their purpose sure, / Their wealth to gain, their wreath to wear,– // Oh, say, shall we, who bear a name / That intimates our heavenly birth, / Behold our efforts put to shame, When placed beside the zeal of earth? / 'Tis Jesus calls. For his dear sake, / If they their all for earth have given, / Oh, let us haste his cross to take, / And give our hearts, our all for heaven." *Guide* 15 (1849): 91.

3 *Guide* 2 (1840): 83.

4 *Guide* 9 (1846): 71.

5 For example, an excerpt from de Sales on peace and humility of the soul appeared in the *Guide* 4 (1843): 175–76.

6 Margaret R. Miles gives a useful synthesis and critique of this tradition in *The Image and Practice of Holiness* (1988; repr. London: SCM, 1989), 126–44.

7 Here I am referring to Douglas, *The Feminization of American Culture*, particularly 275–409, and to Ann Taves, *The Household of Faith: Roman Catholic*

Devotions in Mid-Nineteenth-Century America (Notre Dame, Ind.: Notre Dame University Press, 1986), 4–19. Taves analyzes the emergence of a mass market for books, the publication of Catholic prayer books and devotional guides, and the distribution of these works via parish missions.

8   Porterfield, *Feminine Spirituality in America*, 78 and 51–81.

9   *Guide* 31 (1857): 64.

10   Susan wrote under the name of Elizabeth Wetherell and Anna used the pseudonym Amy Lothrop. Sharon Y. Kim indicates Susan's roots in the spirituality of Jonathan Edwards in "Behind the Men in Black: Jonathan Edwards and Nineteenth-Century Woman's Fiction," in *Jonathan Edwards at Home and Abroad: Historical Memories, Cultural Movement, Global Horizens,* ed. David W. Kling and Douglas A. Sweeney, 137–53 (Columbia: University of South Carolina Press, 2003). I am grateful to Sharon Kim for discussing Susan Warner's religious orientation with me. Warner wrote in her journal of 1860 that she had spent the morning reading "The Higher Christian Life" and then went on to say in her entry for December 31: "Thank the Lord for this year—how good it has been! And the problem at which I have worked for twenty years is, I believe, solved at last. I have been taught the secret, and I am wholly the Lord's. The Lord keep me. And he will. And his name shall be praised." Anna Bartlett Warner, *Susan Warner* (New York: G. P. Putnam's, 1909), 425, 427. Edward Halsey Foster gives an overview of the sisters in *Susan and Anna Warner,* Twayne Authors Series (Boston: G. K. Hall, 1978).

     The information on Larcom as a devotional writer is based, in part, on Cheryl Forbes, *Women of Devotion through the Centuries* (Grand Rapids: Baker Books, 2001), 138–40, hereafter cited as *Women of Devotion through the Centuries.* Basic biographical information on Lucy Larcom and Susan Warner is given in Douglas, *The Feminization of American Culture,* 404–7.

11   *Letters of Madam Guyon,* trans. P[hebe]. L[ord]. Upham (Boston: Henry Hoyt, 1858), iii–iv, hereafter cited as Guyon, *Letters,* trans. P. Upham. Upham also includes a biographical note in which she calls Madame Guyon a reformer "in advance of the common standard of poetry" (1) and also indicates other recent translations, as well as the two volumes on Guyon by her husband. Cowper's translations of "A Little Bird I Am" and "God Everywhere, to the Soul That Loves Him" form an epilogue to this edition.

12   The extracts, in order, are from letter 29, "Simplicity and Power of the Word," letter 30, "Forgetfulness of Self," and letter 59, "Repose of the Soul in God," in Guyon, *Letters,* trans. P. Upham, 80, 82, and 142.

13   W. C. Palmer Jr. published the letters in New York in 1870; McCalla reprinted them as *Spiritual Letters* in Philadelphia in 1895.

14   Jeanne Guyon, *Jeanne Guyon Speaks Again* (Auburn, Maine: Christian Books Publishing House, 1989), 121. This edition includes an introduction by Gene Edwards in which he speaks of retracing the life of Madame Guyon during a trip to France. "Personally, I read Guyon because I am stirred and challenged. Her eccentricities I ignore, the categorization of her teachings I leave to scholars (who fare no better than the rest of us in

coming to any kind of consensus on the place of her life and teachings in church history)" (xv). Fourteen letters between Madame Guyon and Fénelon are also included in the volume. On Edwards' editions of the writings of Madame Guyon see chap. 2, n. 9.

15 Information on the Cowmans and on the Oriental Missionary Society is based on Jones, *Guide to the Study of Holiness*, 1:731, 750; 2:1037. The missionary effort stressed the creation of indigenous churches and began with the massive distribution of Bibles to individual homes. The Pilgrim Holiness Church merged with the Wesleyan Methodist Church in 1968.

16 Cheryl Forbes discusses Mrs. Cowman in the context of "daily devotionals" as a genre of women's writing in *Women of Devotion through the Centuries*, 19–56, and some details of my discussion are based on Forbes.

17 Forbes, *Women of Devotion through the Centuries*, 37.

18 Mrs. Chas. E. Cowman, compiler, *Streams in the Desert* (Los Angeles: The Oriental Missionary Society, 1945), 52 (this appears to be attributed to C. H. Spurgeon), 218–19 (attributed to C. H. P.), 337 (selected). This copy, which belonged to my mother, was the 24th printing of *Streams*.

19 *Streams in the Desert*, 165; Guyon, *Letters*, trans. P. Upham (slightly edited by Cowman), 27.

20 *Streams in the Desert*, 296.

21 See Susie C. Stanley, *Holy Boldness: Women Preachers' Autobiographies and the Sanctified Self* (Knoxville: University of Tennessee Press, 2002), passim, hereafter cited as *Holy Boldness*. Useful documents regarding the role of women in Wesleyan and broader revival traditions are to be found in *Women and Religion in America*, ed. Rosemary Radford Ruether and Rosemary Skinner Keller (San Francisco: Harper and Row, 1981), 1:12–45, and (1983) 2:351–65.

22 Stanley, *Holy Boldness*, 31–32. Stanley notes that George Scott Railton of the Salvation Army had published a pamphlet on Madame Guyon that was reprinted in the United States in 1885 and that B. T. Roberts of the Wesleyan Methodist Church mentioned Madame Guyon as an example of leadership by women in the church in *Ordaining Women* (30).

23 See chap. 1, n. 12. The 1901 edition of McClurkan was also reprinted; for example, *Chosen Vessels* (Salem, Ohio: The Allegheny Wesleyan Methodist Connection, 1978).

24 J. Gilchrist Lawson, *Deeper Experiences of Famous Christians, Gleaned from Their Biographies, Autobiographies and Writings* (Anderson, Ind.: The Warner Press, ca. 1911), viii, hereafter cited as *Deeper Experiences*. David Bundy has given examples of "orthodox" spirituality within American Pentecostalism and has noted the citation of Upham's version of the life of Madame Guyon in international holiness periodicals that became aligned with Pentecostalism. See "Visions of Sanctification: Themes of Orthodoxy in the Methodist, Holiness, and Pentecostal Traditions," *Wesleyan Theological Journal* 39 (2004): 127–35.

25 Lawson, *Deeper Experiences*, 103. The chapter of "Madam Guyon" includes

pp. 87–104. Fénelon's portrait follows (pp. 107–18). "Not only in France but throughout the world, his name is today a household synonym for piety" (107).

26   Mrs. Clara McLeister, *Men and Women of Deep Piety*, ed. E. E. Shelhamer (Syracuse, NY: Wesleyan Methodist Publishing Association, 1920), 5, hereafter cited as *Men and Women of Deep Piety*. "Madam Guyon" is treated on pp. 209–15.

27   McLeister, *Men and Women of Deep Piety*, 209.

28   *Autobiography of Madame Guyon*, complete in two parts (New York: ed. Jones, 1880), hereafter cited as *Autobiography*, ed. Edward Jones. Jones somewhat modernized the language and reduced parts two and three of the original translation he consulted, creating a continuous narrative, emphasizing Madame Guyon's spiritual experiences and ministry before going to Paris, and giving minimal details of events after her stay in the Visitation Convent in 1688. Other printings by holiness publishers followed in 1880 and 1886; G. W. McCalla's editions went through several printings until 1905. For details, see my "Madame Guyon in America: An Annotated Bibliography," 108.

29   Jones, ed. *Autobiography*, iv.

30   For biographical details see Jones, *The Wesleyan Holiness Movement*, 2:1399. Morrow's edition was brought out by the God's Revivalist Office; Lettie Cowman's publisher brought out an edition slightly later. Abbie C. Morrow, ed., *Sweet Smelling Myrrh: The Autobiography of Madame Guyon* (Cincinnati, Ohio: God's Revivalist Office, 1898), hereafter cited as *Sweet Smelling Myrrh*. Morrow published some other books with this publisher.

31   Morrow, *Sweet Smelling Myrrh*, 140–41.

32   See chap. 2, p. 4 and n. 8. Jan Johnson, *Madame Guyon* (Minneapolis, Minn.: Bethany House, 1999). In her preface, Johnson points to some of the cultural differences between the society of seventeenth-century France and that of modern America. The electronic text that Johnson consulted for her short paraphrased version was the Web site of Christian Classics–Ethereal Library, for which the 2003 Web site was www.ccel.org. The text on the Web site was *Madame Guyon: An Autobiography* (Chicago: Moody Press, 1995), reprint from about 1980. The Moody book was based on the *Autobiography of Madame Guyon* (Chicago: Christian Witness Company, 1917). This particular publishing history is more related to the ministry of Dwight L. Moody and the non-Wesleyan interest in the deeper Christian life or a life of consecration to service.

A slightly earlier abridged version, also emanating from Chicago, was Anna C. Reiff's *Madam Guyon: An Autobiography* (Chicago: Evangel Publishing House, 1911), which also included headings and summaries of chapters, two poems, "Love Constitutes My Crime" and "Prisons Do Not Exclude God," and a chapter called "Spiritual Nuggets: Culled from Madam Guyon's Writings." Reiff noted: "We make no apology for putting another edition before the public. The Christian world is just beginning to appreciate the depths in God this martyr spirit reached" (2).

33 Henriette Matson, *Life of Madame Guyon* (Nashville, Tenn.: Pentecostal Mission Publishing Company, n.d.), hereafter cited as Matson.

34 See chap. 1, p. 9 and notes 10, 11, 12. Timothy L. Smith summarizes the history of the holiness movement among Methodists, Cumberland Presbyterians, and others in Tennessee that led J. O. McClurkan to organize the Pentecostal Alliance or Pentecostal Mission in Nashville in 1898. This group initially had close ties to the Christian and Missionary Alliance but eventually became a part of the Church of the Nazarene. See *Called Unto Holiness*, 180–99.

35 The novel was based on Matson's experiences in Memphis before she went to Fisk, as well as on the experiences of some Fisk students. It was published, with an introduction by Rev. M. E. Striehy, in Boston by the Congregational Sunday-school and Publishing Society. It was reprinted in the Black Heritage Collection, Freeport, N.Y.: Books for Libraries Press, 1972.

36 For details on Henrietta Matson see the *General Catalogue of Oberlin College, 1833–1908* (Oberlin, Ohio: 1909); her brother Henry Matson was the librarian at Oberlin from 1874–1877. On her role at Fisk University, see Joe M. Richardson, *A History of Fisk University, 1865–1946* (Tuscaloosa: University of Alabama Press, 1980), 10–11, 178; and Andrew Ward, *Dark Midnight When I Rise: The Story of the Jubilee Singers Who Introduced the World to the Music of Black America* (New York: Farrar, Strauss and Giroux, 2000), passim. Ward calls Henrietta Matson "perhaps the most fervid [sic] evangelical in the history of Fisk" (97). I am grateful to Charles Edwin Jones for bringing Henrietta Matson's biography of Madame Guyon to my attention as well as the discussions of her in Richardson and Ward.

37 Matson, 5–6.

38 Matson, 21–22.

39 Matson, 26, 27.

40 Matson, 42.

41 Matson, 54.

42 Matson, 75.

43 Bessie G. Olson, *Madame Guyon: A Great Heroine* (Des Moines, Iowa: The Boone Publishing Company, 1946), 2. Olson's biographical sketches were part of "The Hall-of-Fame Series" of this press. All the biographies were between 46 and 48 pages in length. Guyon was the only woman listed as part of this series.

44 Dorthy Gawne Coslet, *Madame Jeanne Guyon: Child of Another World* (Fort Washington, Pa.: Christian Literature Crusade, 1984), 115–16. Coslet claims that Madame Guyon rejected the worship of Mary and the other saints.

45 This list is found in the 1899 edition of *Christian Counsel* at the end of the text by Fénelon.

46 Timothy L. Smith surveys the various regional expressions of the nineteenth-century holiness movement as they gave birth to the Church of the Nazarene in *Called Unto Holiness*, 27–90. George M. Marsden discusses the relationship between the holiness movement and Fundamentalism, the

ensuing conflicts, and the American Keswick movement in *Fundamentalism and American Culture*, 93–101.

47 The preceding biographical information is drawn from E. Lynn Harris, *The Mystic Spirituality of A.W. Tozer, A Twentieth-Century American Protestant* (San Francisco: Mellen Research University Press, 1992), 17–30, hereafter cited as Harris.

48 For Tozer's mature career, I consulted Lyle W. Dorset, *A Passion for God: The Spiritual Journey of A.W. Tozer*, chaps. 5, 6, 7 (Chicago: Moody Publications, 2008), in manuscript form.

49 The Moody Bible Institute continues to make available Tozer's sermons at http://www.MoodyAudio.com. For example, one can buy sermon series such as "Four Stages on the Path Toward Spiritual Perfection" (1957). I listened to a rebroadcast of "Forward with Christ in Total Commitment" dating from January 13, 1957. In this sermon, Tozer addressed himself to "evangelicals," not "liberals," and said that true Christian faith is attachment to Christ. This attachment is intellectual (theological knowledge), volitional (a choice of the will), exclusive (setting aside all that is contrary to Christ), inclusive (accepting of all the people of God, not denominational), and irrevocable (a final commitment). Tozer cited the Nicene creed on the nature of Christ and "the old writers" on the dark night of the soul, while claiming he was not a mystic in that he had never had "wild dreams."

50 Cited by Harris, 79, from the preface to *The Divine Conquest*.

51 Harris gives a list of Tozer's recommended books on mysticism on p. 139. Tozer is supposed to have handed out copies of Brother Lawrence's *The Practice of the Presence of God*, and it is possible that Tozer's enthusiasm for Brother Lawrence contributed to the popularity of this work among the evangelicals of the latter half of the twentieth century. See, for example, the modern paraphrase, Brother Lawrence, *The Practice of the Presence of God* (New Kensington, Pa.: Whitaker House, 1982), continuously in print.

52 A[iden] W[ilson] Tozer, ed., *The Christian Book of Mystical Verse* (Harrisburg, Pa.: Christian Publishers, 1963), hereafter cited as *Mystical Verse*. Tozer's introduction comprises v–viii.

53 Tozer, *Mystical Verse*, v, vi–vii.

54 Tozer, *Mystical Verse*, vi.

55 Tozer, *Mystical Verse*, ix–xiv.

56 Charles Edwin Jones includes Faber in *Guide to the Study of Holiness, The Keswick Movement*, 19. Faber's works were often printed in the United States. For example, *Growth in Holiness; or, The Progress of the Spiritual Life* appeared in 1855 (Baltimore: John Murphy; Pittsburgh: George Quigley). *Hymns, selected from Faber*, ed. R. Pearsall Smith, was printed in 1874 in Boston by the Willard Tract Repository. Taves notes that Faber was influenced by de Sales and that his was an "affective" form of devotion. See *The Household of Faith*, 71, 79.

57 For example, *The Poems of Madame de La Mothe Guyon*, edited and arranged with a Short Life by the Rev. A. Saunders Dyer (New York: A. C. Armstrong

and Son, 1890); this volume was essentially an edition of Cowper's translations and was originally printed in Glasgow.

58   This is the text as reproduced in *Mystical Verse*, 65. Tozer also included "The Fervor of Holy Desire" (53–54), "The Acquiescence of Pure Love" (64–65), "Resignation" (74–75; this is the Cowper translation of "A Little Bird I Am," usually published under that title), "The Benefits of Suffering" (81), "Sorrow and Love" (81–82), and "Aspirations of the Soul After Christ" (101–2; this is the Cowper translation, usually titled "Aspirations of the Soul After God.")

Epilogue

1   See chap. 1, n. 15.

2   Here I am referring to the emphasis on the baptism of the Holy Spirit and the speaking in tongues in groups outside of traditional Pentecostalism; these groups were to be found within established denominations and in independent churches and organizations. See Vinson Synan, *The Holiness-Pentecostal Tradition: Charismatic Movements in the Twentieth Century*, 3rd ed. (Grand Rapids: William B. Eerdmans Publishing Company, 1997), 220–78; and Vinson Synan, et al., *The Century of the Holy Spirit: 100 Years of Pentecostal and Charismatic Renewal, 1901–2001* (Nashville, Tenn.: Thomas Nelson Publishers, 2001), particularly 149–232.

3   Don E. Saliers, "Christian Spirituality in an Ecumenical Age," in *Christian Spirituality: Post-Reformation and Modern*, ed. Louis Dupré and Don E. Saliers, vol. 18, *World Spirituality: An Encyclopedic History of the Religious Quest* (New York: Crossroad, 1989), 521.

4   Seed Sowers was an imprint of Christian Books Publishing House (Auburn, Maine). The reprint of *Justifications* is of interest because, according to the publishers, it was a reproduction of an abridgment published privately by George W. McCall in 1915. (This is probably the publisher G. W. McCalla of the National Holiness Association who worked out of Philadelphia and those editions went through many reprints.) *Justifications* was a collection of excerpts removed from the context of the argument over particular theological issues, which Madame Guyon was accused of and which were really part of a long church tradition. She cited extensively from a wide range of authoritative writings to justify the point in question. American readers, on the other hand, were given a series of topical excerpts (e.g. "What is the Most Courageous of All Abandonments," "God Cannot be Found Outside of Himself," and "The Consummation of the Interior Life") and short "nuggets" from *Justifications*, followed by several short excerpts from the commentary on the Bible.

    The editor's preface to the Seed Sowers reprint includes the comment: "*Justifications* has been largely overlooked and/or neglected through the centuries. A modern rewrite of these available excerpts seems to indicate that *Justifications* might be among [Madame Guyon's] best works. Or did the translator simply glean the best out of 1200 pages, giving the cream to us in this 10 percent?" *Final Steps in Christian Maturity*, new ed. (Auburn, Maine: Christian Books Publishing House, 1985), xi.

5   I consulted Fénelon, *Talking with God*, Modern English version by Hal M.
        Helms (Brewster, Mass.: Paraclete Press, 1997).

6   *Spiritual Letters to Women* was reprinted by Zondervan Publishing House.
        Living Water, edited by Robin-Baird Smith, was published by W. B. Eerd-
        mans Publishing Company in Grand Rapids, Michigan, in 1987. Although
        Zondervan is linked to the broad evangelical movement, its roots are in the
        reformed theological tradition, as are those of Eerdmans. These references
        are from *The Spiritual Formation Bible*, 1667, 1672.

7   *The Spiritual Formation Bible: Growing in Intimacy With God Through Scrip-
        ture* (Grand Rapids: Zondervan Publishing House, 1999), hereafter cited
        as *The Spiritual Formation Bible*. This was a joint project of Zondervan and
        of The Upper Room, so that it linked reformed and Wesleyan traditions,
        although The Upper Room is ecumenical in its mission to promote spiri-
        tual formation.

8   *Spiritual Formation Bible*, xiii.

9   The citation is featured between pp. 926–27 of *The Spiritual Formation Bible*
        and is found in *Experiencing the Depths of Jesus Christ*, 79.

10   *The Short and Easy Method*, 92–93.

11   *The Spiritual Formation Bible*, 1245. See also p. 404.

12   Caussade's work was not published until 1861; he also wrote a treatise on
        the prayer of the heart and spiritual instructions. See Frank Paul Bowman,
        "Pierre de Caussade, an Eighteenth-Century Mystic," *Holy Cross Magazine*
        76, no. 8 (1965): 9–13; and Michel Olphe-Galliard, *La Théologie mystique en
        France au XVIIIe siècle: Le Père de Caussade* (Paris: Beauchesne, 1984).

13   Here I am thinking of Alister McGrath's call for the articulation of an
        evangelical spirituality to counteract "feel good spiritualities" or else risk
        losing evangelicals to the Catholic tradition ("Borrowed Spiritualities,"
        Christianity Today [November 8, 1993], 20–21). Robert Wuthnow noted
        the need for the development of spiritual practices in his *After Heaven:
        Spirituality in America Since the 1950s* (Berkeley: University of California
        Press, 1998), 197. Mark A. Noll decried the intellectual sterility of Ameri-
        can Fundamentalism in *The Scandal of the Evangelical Mind* (Grand Rapids:
        W. B. Eerdmans Publishing Company; Leicester, England: Inter-Varsity
        Press, 1994).

        "The specific tenets of dispensational, Holiness, and Pentecostal the-
        ologies are not the exact point at issue for a more general consideration
        of the intellect. It is, rather, the patterns of thinking encouraged by these
        theologies. Whatever the contemporary fate of individual parts of those
        theologies, their habits of mind still loom large among evangelicals as the
        twentieth century draws to a close" (142).

Bibliography

Primary Sources
Editions in French

Bossuet, Jacques Bénigne. *Correspondance*. Vol. 6. Edited by Ch[arles] Urbain and E[ugène] Levesque. New edition. Paris: Hachette, 1912.

Fénelon, François de Salignac de la Mothe-. *Les Aventures de Télémaque, Fils d'Ulysse* . . . . New edition. Reprint of 1715 edition by J. de Wetstein. Philadelphia: Boinod and Gaillard, 1784.

———. *Les Aventures de Télémaque*. Preface by Jacques Le Brun. Collection folio. Paris: Gallimard, 1995.

———. *Oeuvres*. Edited by Jacques Le Brun. 2 vols. Bibliothèque de la Pléiade. Paris: Gallimard, 1983, 1997.

———. *Oeuvres complètes*. Vols. 6 and 7. Edited by M. [Jean Edme Auguste] Gosselin. First published 1851–1852. Geneva: Slatkine Reprints, 1971.

Guyon, Jeanne de la Mothe. *L'Âme amante de son Dieu: Représentée dans les emblèmes de Hermannus Hugo sur ses pieux désirs et dans ceux d'Othon Vaenius sur l'amour divin*. Edited by Pierre Poiret. Cologne (Amsterdam): Jean de la Pierre, 1717.

———. *Correspondance*. Edited by Dominique Tronc. 3 vols. Paris: Éditions Honoré Champion, 2003–2005.

———. *Discours chrétiens et spirituels sur divers Sujets qui regardent La Vie Intérieure, tirés la plupart de la Ste. Écriture*. Vol. 2. Edited by Pierre Poiret. Cologne (Amsterdam): Jean de la Pierre, 1716.

———. *Les Justifications*. Edited by Pierre Poiret. 3 vols. Cologne (Amsterdam): Jean de la Pierre, 1720.

——. *Justifications de la doctrine de Madame de la Mothe-Guyon.* Vol. 1. Paris: Librairies Associés, 1790.

——. *Le Moyen Court et autres écrits spirituels.* Edited by Marie-Louise Gondal. Grenoble: Jérôme Millon, 1995.

——. *Le Nouveau Testament . . . avec des explications & réflexions qui concernent la vie intérieure.* Vol. 8. Edited by Pierre Poiret. Cologne (Amsterdam): Jean de la Pierre, 1713.

——. *Les Opuscules spirituels.* 1720. A facsimile of the first edition with foreword by Jean Orcibal. Hildesheim: G. Olms, 1978.

——. *La Passion de croire.* An anthology edited by Marie-Louise Gondal. Paris: Nouvelle Cité, 1990.

——. *Poésies et cantiques spirituels sur divers sujets qui regardent la vie intérieure ou l'esprit du vrai christianisme.* Cologne (Amsterdam): Jean de la Pierre, 1722.

——. *Récits de captivité.* Edited by Marie-Louise Gondal. Grenoble: Jérôme Millon, 1992.

——. *Les Torrents et commentaire au Cantique des cantiques de Salomon.* Edited by Claude Morali. Grenoble: Jérôme Millon, 1992.

——. *La Vie de Madame Guyon écrite par elle-même.* Edited by Benjamin Sahler. Text of Pierre Poiret with modernizations. Paris: Dervy-Livres, 1983.

——. *La Vie par elle-même et autres écrits biographiques.* Critical edition with "Introduction" by Dominique Tronc. Literary study by Andrée Villard. Paris: Éditions Champion, 2001.

Translations, Abridgments, Anthologies

Fénelon, François de Salignac de la Mothe-

The Adventures of Telemachus, Son of Ulysses. Translated by John Hawkesworth. Corrected and revised by G. Gregory. 2 vols. New York: David Longworth, 1797.

The Adventures of Telemachus, the son of Ulysses, In five parts. 2nd ed. corrected. London: A. and J. Churchil, 1700.

Apples of Gold, Gathered by Fénelon. Anthology in miniature format. Philadelphia: J. B. Lippincott, 1856.

The Archbishop of Cambray's Dissertation on Pure Love, with an account of the life and writings of the lady, for whose sake the archbishop was banish'd from Court. Translated by Josiah Martin. Philadelphia: Andrew Bradford, 1738. First published 1735 by Luke Hinde (London). Philadelphia: Andrew Bradford, 1738. Reprinted as *The Archbishop of Cambray's Dissertation on Pure Love . . . .* (Germantown, Pa.: Christopher Sauer, 1750).

The Archbishop of Cambray's Meditations and Soliloquies, on various religious subjects: With directions for a holy life, also a letter concerning religion. New Bedford, Mass.: A. Shearman, 1802.

Catechism on the Foundations of the Christian Faith . . . followed by The celebrated Conversation of Mr. de Fenelon with Mr. de Ramsay; and by several extracts, on the existence of GOD, and on the Worship which is due to him, from the letters of the illustrious Archbishop of Cambray M. DE FENELON. New York: The Economical School, 1810.

Christian Perfection. Edited by Charles F. Whiston. Translated by Margaret Whitney. New York: Harper and Row, 1947. Reprint, Minneapolis, Minn.: Bethany House, 1975.

Demonstration of the Existence and Attributes of God followed by The Reflections of Father Tournemine, a Jesuite [sic], upon Atheism . . . . Harrisburg, Pa.: William Gilmor, 1811.

Extracts. Preface by John Kendall. Philadelphia: Kimber, Conrad, 1804.

Faithfulness in Little Things: Translated from the French into German, and thence into English. Philadelphia: Kimber, Conrad, 1804.

Instructions for the education of a daughter, by the author of "Telemachus" . . . . Translated into English and revised by Dr. George Hickes. London: J. Bowyer, 1707.

Let Go: Living by the Cross and by Faith. Abridgment of *Spiritual Letters*, an earlier version of Christian *Perfection*. Introduction by Robert E. Whitaker. Monroeville, Pa.: Banner Publishing, 1973. Reprinted as *Let Go*. New Kensington, Pa.: Whitaker House.

Pious Reflections for Every Day of the Month. (*Manuel de piété.*) Translated by J. Clowes. Miniature edition. Boston: Loring, n.d.

Pious Reflections for Every Day of the Month . . . To which is prefixed, THE LIFE OF THE AUTHOR. Boston: Lincoln and Edmonds, 1814.

Selections from the Writings of Fenelon, with a Memoir of His Life. Edited by Mrs. [Eliza Cabot] Follen. 5th ed. Boston: Simpkins, 1844.

Some Advice to Governesses and Teachers: Written by the author of The Evidence of the Existence of God . . . . New York: printed for Daniel Lawrence by Samuel Campbell, 1795. Reprinted in Litchfield, Conn.: Collier & Buel; New Bedford, Mass.: J. Spooner, 1795.

Spiritual Letters of Archbishop Fénelon. Vol. 1, *Letters to Men.* Vol. 2, *Letters to Women.* New York: E. P. Dutton, 1877, 1878. Reprinted as *Spiritual Letters to Women.* Introduction by Elisabeth Elliot. Shepherd Illustrated Classics. New Canaan, Conn.: Keats Publishing, 1980.

Talking with God. Modern English edition by Hal M. Holms. Brewster, Mass.: Paraclete Press, 1997.

Telemachus. Translated by John Hawksworth. Vol. 1, *The Select Works of Fenelon.* Edited by O. W. Wight. New York: Hurd and Houghton, 1875.

Guyon, Jeanne de la Mothe

Autobiography of Madame Guyon. Complete in two parts. New York: ed. Jones, 1880. Abridgment of 1880 edition, *Sweet Smelling Myrrh: The Autobiography of Madame Guyon.* Edited by Abbie C. Morrow. Cincinnati, Ohio:

God's Revivalist Office, 1898. Abridgment of 1880 edition, *Autobiography of Madame Guyon*. Chicago: Christian Witness Company, 1917. Reprint, Chicago: Moody Press, 1980. Reproduced at http://www.ccel.org. Paraphrased abridgment based on this electronic text, edited by Jan Johnson. *Madame Guyon*. Minneapolis, Minn.: Bethany House, 1999. Abridgment of 1880 edition, *Madam Guyon: An Autobiography*. Edited by Anna C. Reiff. Chicago: Evangel Publishing House, 1911.

Autobiography of Madame Guyon. Translated by Thomas Taylor Allen. 2 vols. London: Kegan Paul, Trench, Trübner. St. Louis, Mo.: B. Herder, 1897. Reprinted with an introduction by Ruth Bell Graham. Shepherd Illustrated Classics. New Canaan, Conn.: Keats, 1980.

The Exemplary Life of the pious Lady Guion, translated from her own account in the Original French: To which is added, a new translation of her "Short and Easy Method of Prayer," by Thomas Digby Brooke. Dublin: William Kidd, 1775. Reprint, Philadelphia: Joseph Crukshank, 1804.

Experiencing the Depths of Jesus Christ. (The Short and Easy Method of Prayer.) Auburn, Maine: Christian Books Publishing House, 1975.

Final Steps in Christian Maturity. (Justifications.) New edition. Auburn, Maine: Christian Books Publishing House, 1985.

Die heilige Liebe Gottes and die unheilige Naturliebe nach ihren untershiedenen Wirkungen, in XLIV anmuthigen Sinnbildern und erbaulichen Versen vorgestellet . . . . (Les éfets diferens de l'Amour sacré & profane . . . .) Compiled and translated by Gerhard Tersteegen. First published in Solingen, Ger., 1751 and Muhlheim, Ger.: J. C. Eyrich, 1787. Lancaster, Penn.: J. Schweitzer, gedruckt von Johann Bär, 1828.

Die Ihren Gott liebenden Seele vorgestellet in Sinnbildern des Herrn. Hugonis, über seine Pia Desideria . . . ins Deutsche ubersetzt. (L'Âme amante de son Dieu.) Regensburg, Ger.: Heinr. Jonas Ostertag; Augsburg, Ger.: Joh. Matthias Steidlin, 1719.

Jeanne Guyon Speaks Again. (Spiritual Letters.) Auburn, Maine: Christian Books Publishing House, 1989.

Letters. Translated by Phebe Lord Upham. Boston: Henry Hoyt, 1858. Reprint, New York: W. C. Palmer Jr., 1870. Reprinted as *Spiritual Letters*. Philadelphia: W. G. McCalla, 1895.

The Life of Lady Guion Written by herself in French, Now Abridged, And translated into English (by James Gough). 2 vols. Bristol: S. Farley, 1772. Reprint, New Bedford, Mass.: Abraham Shearman, 1805.

Poems: Translated from the French of Madame De La Mothe Guion, by the late William Cowper. Philadelphia: Kimber, Conrad, 1804.

Poems. "Introduction" and "Life of Madame Guyon." Edited by Rev. A. Saunders Dyer. First published in Glasgow; New York: A. C. Armstrong & Son, 1890.

Selections from the Devotional Writings of Madame de la Mothe-Guyon. Preface by D. D. Lowery. The Devotional Series. Dayton, Ohio: United Brethren Publishing House, 1904.

A Short and Easie Method of Prayer. Preface, "To the English Reader." London: Printed for R. Sympson at the Harp in St. Paul's-Church-Yard and J. Nutt near Stationers-Hall, 1704.

Spiritual Torrents. With parallel passages from the writings of Emanuel Swedenborg. Translated and edited by A. E. Ford. Boston: Otis Clapp, 1853.

Spiritual Torrents. Auburn, Maine: Christian Books Publishing House, 1990.

Union With God. Auburn, Maine: Christian Books Publishing House, 1981.

Wegweiser zum Ewigen Leben in Zweiundvierzig Betrachtungen und erbaulichen Versen. Preface by Gerhard Tersteegen from the 1751 edition of his translation of *Les éfets diferens de l'Amour sacré & profane.* York, Pa.: J. L. Getz, 1834.

The Worship of God, in Spirit and Truth: or, A Short and Easy Method of Prayer . . . . Extracted from two late authors. Philadelphia: Francis Bailey, 1789.

Anthologies

A Guide to True Peace; or, A Method of attaining to inward and spiritual prayer: Compiled chiefly from the writings of Fénelon . . . , *Lady Guion, and Michael de Molinos.* Poughkeepsie, N.Y.: P. Potter; Philadelphia: S. Potter, 1818.

A Guide to True Peace; or, The Excellency of Inward and Spiritual Prayer. New York: Harper and Brothers, 1946. Published in association with Pendle Hill. Reprint, Wallingford, Pa.: Pendle Hill, 1979.

Metcalf, James W., ed. *Spiritual Progress; or, Instructions in the Divine Life of the Soul.* From the French of Fénelon and Madame Guyon. New York: M. W. Dodd, 1853. Reprinted as *Christian Counsel on Divers Matters Pertaining to the Inner Life.* Philadelphia: G. W. McCalla, 1899. Reprinted at Christian Classics Ethereal Library and available online at http://www.ccel.org/ccel/fenelon/progress.

Tozer, A[iden] W[ilson], ed. *The Christian Book of Mystical Verse.* Harrisburg, Pa.: Christian Publishers, 1963.

Other Primary Sources

Alcott, Louisa May. "Sketch of Childhood." In *Her Life, Letters, and Journals.* Edited by Ednah D. Cheney. Boston: Roberts Brothers, 1889.

Arndt, Johann. *Of True Christianity* . . . *Wherein is contained the whole œconomy of God Towards Men; and the whole Duty of man Towards God.* Vol. 1. London: Printed for D. Brown and J. Downing, 1712.

Barrett, Samuel. *Doctrine of Religious Experience, Explained and Enforced.* Boston: Leonard C. Bowles, 1829.

Bayly, Lewis. *The Practice of Piety, directing a Christian how to walk, that he may please God.* Amplified by the author. London: Printed for Edward Brewster, 1702.

Boardman, W. E. *The Higher Christian Life.* Boston: Henry Hoyt; New York: D. Appleton, 1859.

Brooke, Henry. *The Fool of Quality; or, The History of Henry Earl of Moreland.* 3 vols. Philadelphia: Printed for Robert Campbell, 1794.

Bunyan, John. *The Pilgrim's Progress.* Special tercentenary edition. New York: American Tract Society, 1934.

Bushnell, Horace. *God in Christ.* Hartford, Conn.: Brown and Parsons, 1849.

——. *Sermons on Living Subjects.* New York: Charles Scribner's Sons, 1892.

Butler, Charles. *The Life of Fénelon, Archbishop of Cambray.* First published in London, 1810. Philadelphia: A. Finley, 1811.

Channing, William Ellery. *On the Character and Writings of Fénelon.* Boston: n.p., 1829.

Cheever, Henry Theodore. *Correspondences of Faith and View of Madame Guyon: A Comparative Study of the Unitive Power and Place of Faith in the Theology and Church of the Future.* New York: Anson D. F. Randolph and Company, ca. 1885.

Child, Mrs. [Lydia Maria]. *The Ladies' Home Library.* Vol. 2, *The Biographies of Lady Russell and Madame Guyon.* Boston: Carter, Hendee, 1832.

Coslet, Dorothy Gawne. *Madame Jeanne Guyon: Child of Another World.* Fort Washington, Pa.: Christian Literature Crusade, 1984.

Cowman, Mrs. Charles E. *Streams in the Desert.* 24th printing. Los Angeles: The Oriental Missionary Society, 1945.

Diderot, Denis. "Sur les femmes." In *Qu'est-ce qu'une femme?* Edited by Elisabeth Badinter, 163–85. Paris: P. O. L., 1989.

Edwards, Jonathan. *The Works of Jonathan Edwards.* Vol. 2, *A Treatise Concerning Religious Affections.* Edited by John E. Smith. Vol. 4, *The Great Awakening.* Edited by C. C. Goen. Vol. 14, *Sermons and Discourses: 1723–1729.* Edited by Kenneth P. Minkema. New Haven: Yale University Press, 1959, 1972, 1997.

Emerson, Ralph Waldo. *The Journals and Miscellaneous Notebooks.* Vol. 3, *1826–1832.* Edited by William H. Gilman and Alfred R. Ferguson. Vol. 4, *1832–1834.* Edited by Alfred R. Ferguson. Vol. 5, *1835–1838.* Edited by Merton M. Sealts Jr. Cambridge, Mass.: Belknap Press of Harvard University Press, 1963, 1964, 1965.

Finney, Charles Grandison. *The Memoirs: The Complete Restored Text.* Edited by Garth M. Rosell and Richard A. G. Depuis. Grand Rapids: Zondervan Academic Books, 1989.

Gough, James. *Memoirs of the Life, Religious Experiences, and Labours in the Gospel.* Edited by John Gough. Dublin: Robert Jackson, 1781.

———. *Select Lives of Foreigners, Eminent for Piety*. 3rd ed. Philadelphia: Printed for Benjamin and Thomas Kite, 1807.

The Guide to Christian Perfection. Edited by Timothy Merritt et al. Volumes 1–8. Boston: T. Merritt and other publishers, 1839–1845.

The Guide to Holiness. Edited by D. S. King et al. Volumes 9–44. Boston: George C. Rand and other publishers, 1846–1863.

Hedrick, Joan D. *Harriet Beecher Stowe: A Life*. Oxford: Oxford University Press, 1994.

Hopkins, Samuel. *The Life and Character of the Late Reverend, Learned and Pious Mr. Jonathan Edwards* . . . . 2nd ed. Glasgow: Printed by David Niven Brown for James Duncan, jun; sold by him and John Brown, 1785. Eighteenth Century Collections Online. Gale Group. http://galenet.galegroup.com/servlet/ECCO. 2004.

Hubbard, Elbert. "Madame Guyon." In *Little Journeys to the Homes of Famous Women*. New York: G. P. Putnam's Son, 1897.

Kelpius, Johann. *A Short, Easy and Comprehensive Method of Prayer: Translated from the German; And published for a farther Promotion Knowledge and Benefit of INWARD PRAYER*. Germantown, Pa.: Christopher Sower, 1741.

Lawson, J. Gilchrist. *Deeper Experiences of Famous Christians*. Anderson, Ind.: The Warner Press, ca. 1911.

Longfellow, Henry Wadsworth. Vol. 2, *The Letters, 1837–1843*. Edited by Andrew Hilen. Cambridge, Mass.: Belknap Press of Harvard University Press, 1966.

———. *The Poetical Works*. New introduction by George Monteiro. Reprint of the Cambridge edition. Boston: Houghton Mifflin, 1975.

Marie de l'Incarnation. *L'Expérience de Dieu avec Marie de l'Incarnation*. Edited by Guy-M. Oury. Saint-Laurent, Quebec: Fides, 1999.

McClurkan, J. O. *Chosen Vessels*. Nashville, Tenn.: Pentecostal Mission Publishing Company.

McLeister, Mrs. Clara. *Men and Women of Deep Piety*. Edited by E. E. Shelhamer. Syracuse, N.Y.: Wesleyan Methodist Publishing Association, 1920.

Methodist Hymnal. 1889 edition. http://wesley.nnu.edu/charles_wesley/hymns/index.htm#methodist. HTML conversion by Paul Leler and George Lyons. © 2001 Wesley Center for Applied Theology. Northwest Nazarene University.

Molinos, Michael de. *The Spiritual Guide which Disentangles the soul; and brings it by the inward way to the getting of perfect Contemplation and the Rich Treasure of Internal Peace*. Translated from the Italian version. London: n.p., 1699.

———. Miguel de. *Golden Thoughts from The Spiritual Guide*. Preface by J. Henry Shorthouse. New York: Charles Scribner's Sons, 1883.

Montesquieu. *Lettres persanes*. Preface by Jean Starobinski. Collection folio. Paris: Gallimard, 1973.

Moritz, Karl Philipp. *Anton Reiser: A Psychological Novel.* Translated by John R. Russell. Columbia, S.C.: Camden House, 1996.

Matson, Henrietta. *Life of Madame Guyon.* Nashville, Tenn.: Pentecostal Mission Publishing Company, n.d.

McCully, Sue Lane, and Dorothy Z. Baker, eds. *The Silent and Soft Communion: The Spiritual Narratives of Sarah Pierpont Edwards and Sarah Prince Gill.* Knoxville, Tenn.: University of Tennessee Press, 2005.

Olson, Bessie G. *Madame Guyon: A Great Heroine.* The Hall-of-Fame series. Des Moines, Iowa: The Boone Publishing Company, 1946.

On Experimental Religion. Boston: Bowles and Dearborn, 1827.

Palmer, Phoebe. *The Way of Holiness, with Notes by the Way . . . .* 2nd ed. New York: G. Lane and C. B. Tippett, 1848.

A Pattern of Christian Education, agreeable to the precepts and practice of our blessed Lord and Saviour Jesus Christ: Illustrated under the character of Paternus & Eusebius. Germantown, Pa.: Christopher Sauer Jr., 1756.

Poiret, Pierre. *Théologie de l'amour, ou La Vie et les oeuvres de Sainte Catherine de Gênes.* Cologne (Amsterdam): Jean de la Pierre, 1691.

Quakerism A-la-Mode; or, A History of Quietism, Particularly That of the Lord Archbishop of Cambray and Madam Guyone [sic]. London: J. Harris, 1698.

Ramsay, Andrew Michael. *The Life of François de Salignac De la Motte Fenelon, Archbishop and Duke of Cambray.* London: Paul Vaillant and James Woodman, 1723.

Sales, François de. *Oeuvres complètes.* Vol. 9, bk 2. Paris: J. J. Blaise, 1821.

Sandei. *Pro Theologia Mystica Clavis elucidarium onomasticon vocabulorum et loqutionum obscurum.* Herverlée-Louvain: Editions de la Bibliothèque S. J., 1963. First published 1640.

Simpson, A. B. *The Holy Spirit or Power From on High.* Vol. 1, *The Old Testament.* Harrisburg, Pa.: Christian Publications, n.d.

The Spiritual Formation Bible. Growing in Intimacy with God Through Scripture. Grand Rapids: Zondervan Publishing House, 1999.

Stowe, Harriet Beecher. Folder 70. Correspondence. The Beecher-Stowe Collection. Arthur E. and Eliza Schlesinger Library on the History of Women in America. Radcliffe Institute, Harvard University.

———. "De Rance and Fenelon—A Contrast." *New York Evangelist* 13 (1842): 105.

———. "The Interior or Hidden Life." *New-York Evangelist* 16 (1845): n.p.

———. "The Interior Life, or Primitive Christian Experience." *New-York Evangelist* 16 (1845): 97.

———. *Three Novels: "Uncle Tom's Cabin," "The Minister's Wooing," "Oldtown Folks."* New York: Library of America, 1982.

Tersteegen, Gerhard. *Geistliches Blumengärtlein inner Seelen . . . .* Frankfurt: Peter Daniel Schmitz, 1793.

Theologia Germanica: Which setteth forth many fair Lineaments of divine Truth, and faith very lofty and lovely things touching a perfect Life. Translated by Susanna

Winkworth. Introduction by Calvin E. Stowe. Andover, Mass.: W. F. Draper; Boston: John P. Jewett, 1856.

Tozer, A[iden] W[ilson]. "Forward with Christ in Total Commitment." Sermon. January 13, 1957. http://www.MoodyAudio.com.

Upham, Thomas C. *American Cottage Life*. 2nd ed. Brunswick, Maine: Joseph Griffin, 1836.

———. *Elements of Intellectual Philosophy*. 2nd ed. Portland, Maine: Shirley and Hyde, 1828.

———. *Inward Divine Guidance*. Preface by Hannah Whitall Smith. Reprint, Salem, Ohio: Schmul Publishing Company, 1989.

———. *Life and Religious Opinions and Experience of Madame de la Mothe Guyon*. 2 vols. New York: Harper and Brothers, 1846.

———. *The Life of Faith*. Boston: Waite, Peirce, 1845.

———. *Life of Madame Catharine Adorna*. 3rd ed. New York: Harper and Brothers, 1858.

———. *The Manual of Peace*. New York: Leavitt, Lord; Brunswick, Maine: Joseph Griffin, 1836.

———. *A Philosophical and Practical Treatise on the Will*. Portland, Maine: William Hyde, 1834.

———. *Principles of the Interior or Hidden Life*. Boston: Waite, Peirce, 1843.

———. "Testimony." In *Pioneer Experiences*. Edited by Phoebe Palmer. New York: W. C. Palmer Jr., 1868.

Wesley Hymnbook. Edited by Franz Hildebrandt. Reprint, Kansas City, Mo.: Lillenas Publishing Company, 1963.

Wesley, John, ed. *A Christian Library*. Vol. 23. London: Kershaw, 1825.

———. *The Journal*. Vols. 3 and 5. Edited by Nehemiah Curnock. London: Epworth, 1938. First published 1912.

———. *The Letters*. Vol. 5. Edited by John Telford. London: Epworth, 1931.

———. "Preface." In *An Extract of the Life of Madam Guion*. London: R. Hawes, 1776.

Whittier, John Greenleaf. "Dora Greenwell." In vol. 3 of *The Prose Works*. Boston: Houghton; Cambridge, Mass.: Riverside, 1892.

Woolman, John. *The Journals and Essays*. Edited by Amelia Mott Gummere. Philadelphia: Friends' Book Store; London: Friends' Bookshop, 1922.

———. *Memoir of John Woolman, chiefly extracted from a Journal of His Life and travels*. Philadelphia: Tracts Association of Friends, n.d., ca. 1810.

Secondary Sources

Alderfer, E. Gordon. "Introduction." In *A Method of Prayer* by Johann Kelpius, 7–72. New York: Harper and Brothers, 1951.

Allen, Diogenes. *Spiritual Theology*. Boston: Cowley Publications, 1997.

Amicus. "Points in Holiness Theology." *Living Water* (May 12, 1903), 3.

Argomathe, Jean-Robert. *Le Quiétisme*. Paris: Presses Universitaires de France, 1973.

Barbour, Hugh and J. William Frost. *The Quakers*. New York: Greenwood Press, 1988.

Bausman, Lottie M. *A Bibliography of Lancaster County, Pa. 1745–1912*. Philadelphia: Patterson and White, 1912.

Beaude, Joseph, et al. *Madame Guyon: rencontres autour de la vie et l'oeuvre*. Grenoble: Jérôme Millon, 1997.

Bowman, Frank Paul. "Pierre de Caussade, An Eighteenth-Century Mystic." *Holy Cross Magazine* 76, no. 8 (1965): 9–13.

Braig, F. "Jacques Boehme." In *Dictionnaire de spiritualité*. Vol. 1, 1745–51. Paris: Beauchesne, 1927.

Bremond, Henri. *Histoire littéraire du sentiment religieux en France depuis la fin des guerres de religion jusqu'à nos jours*. Vol. 6, *La conquête mystique*. Paris: Bloud et Gay, 1926.

Brockett, Henry E. "She Paid the Price." Source unknown.

Bruneau, Marie-Florine. *Mysticisme et psychose: l'autobiographie de Jeanne Guyon*. University of California, Berkeley. *Dissertation Abstracts International* 42 (1981): 237A–38A.

——. *Women Mystics Confront the Modern World: Marie de l'Incarnation (1599–1672) and Madame Guyon (1648–1717)*. Albany: State University of New York Press, 1998.

Buell, Lawrence. "Calvin Romanticized: Harriet Beecher Stowe, Samuel Hopkins, and *The Minister's Wooing*." In *Critical Essays on Harriet Beecher Stowe*. Edited by Elizabeth Ammons. Boston: D. K. Hall, 1980.

Bundy, David. "Visions of Sanctification: Themes of Orthodoxy in the Methodist, Holiness, and Pentecostal Traditions." *Wesleyan Theological Journal* 39 (2004): 127–35.

Cadier, Jean. "Charles . . . de Marsay." In *Dictionnaire de spiritualité*. Vol. 10, 657. Paris: Beauchesne, 1977.

Carpenter, Ted A. *The Religion of the Heart: A Study of European Religious Life in the Seventeenth and Eighteenth Centuries*. Columbia: University of South Carolina Press.

Caskey, James Stillman. "Jonathan Edwards' Catalogue." B.D. thesis. Chicago: Chicago Theological Seminary, 1931.

Certeau, Michel de. *La Fable mystique*. Vol. 1, *XVIe-XVIIe siècles*. Paris: Gallimard, 1982.

——. "Labadie." (Adapted from Certeau). In *Dictionnaire de spiritualité*. Vol. 8, 1–7. Paris: Beauchesne, 1975.

Cheney, Mary A. *Life and Letters of Horace Bushnell*. New York: Charles Scribner's Sons, 1903.

Cherel, Albert. *Fénelon au XVIIIe siècle en France (1715–1820): son prestige–son influence*. First published 1917. Paris: Slatkine Reprints, 1970.

Chevallier, Marjolaine. *Pierre Poiret (1646–1719): Du protestantisme à la mystique.* Geneva: Labor et Fides, 1994.

Child, Lydia Maria. *The Progress of Religious Ideas through Successive Ages.* 3 vols. New York: C. S. Francis, 1855.

Cognet, Louis. *Crépuscule des mystiques: Bossuet, Fénelon.* New edition updated by J. R. Armagathe. Paris: Desclée, 1991.

——. "Fénelon." In *Dictionnaire de spiritualité.* Vol. 5, 152–70. Paris: Beauchesne, 1962.

——. "Guyon." In *Dictionnaire de spiritualité.* Vol. 6, 1306–36. Paris: Beauchesne, 1967.

Conforti, Joseph A. *Jonathan Edwards, Religious Tradition, and American Culture.* Chapel Hill: University of North Carolina Press, 1995.

Darnton, Robert. "Readers Respond to Rousseau." In *The Great Cat Massacre and Other Episodes in French Cultural History.* New York: Vintage, 1985.

Delacroix, Henri Joachim. *Les Grands Mystiques chrétiens.* New edition. Paris: Alcan, 1938.

Dictionary of American Biography. Edited by Allen Johnson and Dumas Malone. Vol. 6. New York: Scribner's, 1931.

Dieter, Melvin E. *The Holiness Revival of the Nineteenth Century.* 2nd ed. Lanham, Md.: The Scarecrow Press, 1996.

Dorset, Lyle W. *A Passion for God: The Spiritual Journey of A. W. Tozer.* Chicago: Moody Publications, 2008.

Douglas, Ann. *The Feminization of American Culture.* First published 1977. New York: Avon Books, 1978.

Dreyer, Frederick. "Faith and Experience in the Thought of John Wesley." *American Historical Review* 88 (1983): 12–30.

Durnbaugh, Donald F., ed. *The Brethren in Colonial America.* Elgin, Ill.: The Brethren Press, 1967.

Erb, Peter C. "Gerhard Tersteegen, Christopher Saur, and Pennsylvania Sectarians." *Brethren Life and Thought* 20 (1975): 153–55.

——, ed. "Introduction." In *Johann Conrad Beissel and the Ephrata Community: Mystical and Historical Texts,* 3–54. Lewistown, N.Y.: Edward Mellon Press, 1985.

——. "Introduction." In *Pietists: Selected Writings,* 1–27. New York: Ramsey; Toronto: Paulist Press, 1983.

Forbes, Cheryl. *Women of Devotion through the Centuries.* Grand Rapids: Baker Books, 2001.

Foster, Edward Halsey. *Susan and Anna Warner.* Twayne Authors Series. Boston: G. K. Hall, 1978.

Frautschi, Richard and Angus Martin. "French Prose Fiction Published Between 1701 and 1750: A New Profile of Production." *Eighteenth-Century Fiction* 14 (2002): 745.

Frost, Francis. "Quakers." In *Dictionnaire de spiritualité*. Vol. 12, part 2, 2694. Paris: Beauchesne, 1985.

Gilbert, Dorothy L. and Russell Pope. "The Cowper Translation of Mme Guyon's Poems." *PMLA* 54 (1939): 1077-98.

Gondal, Marie-Louise. *Madame Guyon 1648-1171: Un nouveau visage.* Paris: Beauchesne, 1989.

Gordon, James M. *Evangelical Spirituality: From the Wesleys to John Stott.* London: SPCK, 1991.

Gusdorf, Georges. *Dieu, la nature, l'homme au siècle des lumières.* Paris: Payot, 1972.

Hambrick-Stowe, Charles E. *The Practice of Piety: Puritan Devotional Disciplines in Seventeenth-Century New England.* Chapel Hill: University of North Carolina Press, 1982.

Harmon, Nolan B., ed. *Encyclopedia of World Methodism.* Vol. 2. Nashville, Tenn.: United Methodist Publishing House, 1974.

Harris, E. Lynn. *The Mystic Spirituality of A. W. Tozer: A Twentieth-Century American Protestant.* San Francisco: Mellon Research University Press, 1992.

Heuberger, Jean-Marc. "Les Commentaires bibliques de Madame Guyon dans *La Bible de Berleburg*." *Revue de théologie et de philosophie* 133 (2001): 303-23.

Hindley, Clifford J. "The Philosophy of Enthusiasm: A Study of the Origins of 'Experimental Theology'." *London Quarterly and Holborn Review* 182 (1957): 99-109, 199-210.

Hindmarsh, Bruce. *John Newton and the English Evangelical Tradition, between the Conversions of Wesley and Wilberforce.* Oxford: Clarendon Press, 1996.

Holifield, E. Brooks. *Theology in America: Christian Thought from the Age of the Puritans to the Civil War.* New Haven: Yale University Press, 2003.

James, Henry. *The Varieties of Religious Experience.* Centenary edition. London: Routledge, 2002.

Jasper, Bernd. "Tersteegen." In *Dictionnaire de spiritualité*. Vol. 15, 260-71. Paris: Beauchesne, 1991.

Johnson, Jan. "Seeing God in the Valley." *Weavings* 16 (2001): 37-43.

Jones, Charles Edwin. *A Guide to the Study of the Holiness Movement.* Vol. 1, *The Wesleyan Holiness Movement: A Comprehensive Guide.* Vol. 2, *The Keswick Movement: A Comprehensive Guide.* Revised edition. Lanham, Md.: The Scarecrow Press and American Theological Library Association, 2005, 2007.

———. *Perfectionist Persuasion: The Holiness Movement and American Methodism, 1867-1936.* Metuchen, N.J.: The Scarecrow Press, 1974.

Jones, Howard Mumford. *America and French Culture.* Chapel Hill: University of North Carolina Press; London: Oxford University Press, Humphrey Milford, 1927.

Jones, Richard Foster. *Ancients and Moderns: A Study of the Rise of the Scientific*

Movement in Seventeenth Century England. 2nd edition. St. Louis, Mo.: Washington University Studies, 1961.

Jones, Rufus M. *Later Periods of Quakerism.* Vol. 1. London: Macmillan, 1921.

Jones, Rufus M., Isaac Sharpless, and Amelia Gummere. *The Quakers in the American Colonies.* First published 1911. New York: Russell & Russell, 1962.

Karcher, Carolyn L. *The First Woman in the Republic: A Cultural Biography of Lydia Maria Child.* Durham, N.C.: Duke University Press, 1994.

Kiaski, Janice R. "Holiness at Hollow Rock." Reprint. http://www.hollowrock.org. 2006.

Kim, Sharon. "Behind the Men in Black: Jonathan Edwards and Nineteenth-Century Women's Fiction." In *Jonathan Edwards at Home and Abroad: Historical Memories, Cultural Movement, Global Horizons.* Edited by David W. Kling and Douglas A. Sweeney. Columbia: University of South Carolina Press, 2003.

Klein, Walter C. *Johann Conrad Beissel, Myatic and Martinet: 1690–1768.* Philadelphia: University of Pennsylvania Press, 1942.

Knox, Ronald A. *Enthusiasm: A Chapter in the History of Religion.* Corrected edition. Oxford: Clarendon Press, 1959.

Kolakowski, Leszek. *Chrétiens sans église: La conscience religieuse et le lien confessional au XVIIe siècle.* Translated by Anna Posner. Revised edition. Paris: Gallimard, 1965.

Kristeva, Julia. "Un pur silence: la perfection de Jeanne Guyon." In *Histoires d'amour,* 277–95. Paris: Denoël, 1983.

Le Brun, Jacques. "Expérience religieuse et expérience littéraire." In *La Pensée religieuse dans la littérature et la civilisation du XVIIe siècle en France: Actes du Colloque de Bamberg, 1983.* Edited by Manfred Tietz and Volker Kapp. *Biblio 17: Papers on French Seventeenth Century Literature* 13 (1984): 123–46.

——. "Présupposés théoriques de la lecture mystique de la Bible: L'exemple de *La Sainte Bible* de Madame Guyon." *Revue de théologie et de philosophie* 133 (2001): 287–302.

——. *La Spiritualité de Bossuet.* Paris: Klincksieck, 1972.

Lehmann, Hartmut, Hans-Jürgen Schrader, and Heinz Schilling, eds. *Jansenismus, Quietismus, Pietismus: Im Auftrag der Historischen Kommission zur Erforschung des Pietismus.* Göttingen, Ger.: Vandeenhoeck & Ruprecht, 2002.

Lindberg, Carter, ed. *The Pietist Theologians: An Introduction to Theology in the Seventeenth and Eighteenth Centuries.* Oxford: Blackwell, 2005.

Lindström, Harold. *Wesley and Sanctification: A Study in the Doctrine of Salvation.* Foreword by Timothy L. Smith. First published 1946. Grand Rapids: The Francis Asbury Press of Zondervan Publishing House, 1980.

Mallet-Joris, Françoise. *Jeanne Guyon.* Paris: Flammarion, 1978.

Marquet, J. -F. "L'Expérience religieuse de Jeanne Guyon." In *Fénelon: Philoso-*

phie et spiritualité . . . . Edited by Denise Leduc-Fayette, 155–76. Geneva: Droz, 1996.

Marsden, George M. *Fundamentalism and American Culture*. 2nd ed. New York: Oxford University Press, 2006.

———. *Jonathan Edwards: A Life*. New Haven: Yale University Press, 2003.

McGrath, Alister E. "Borrowed Spiritualities." *Christianity Today* (November 8, 1993): 20–21.

Miles, Margaret R. *The Image and Practice of Holiness*. First published 1988. London: SCM, 1989.

Morris, William Sparkes. *The Young Jonathan Edwards*. Brooklyn, N.Y.: Carlson Publishing, 1991.

Murray, Iain H. *Jonathan Edwards: A New Biography*. Edinburgh, Pa.: The Banner of Truth Trust, 1987.

Neveu, Bruno. "La 'science divine' du chevalier Ramsay." In *Fénelon: Philosophie et spiritualité* . . . . Edited by Denise Leduc-Fayette, 177–96. Geneva: Droz, 1996.

Noll, Mark A. *America's God: From Jonathan Edwards to Abraham Lincoln*. Oxford: Oxford University Press, 2002.

———. *The Scandal of the Evangelical Mind*. Grand Rapids: William B. Eerdmans Publishing Company; Leicester, England: Inter-Varsity Press, 1994.

Olphe-Galliard, Michel, S.J. *La Théologie mystique en France au XVIIIe siècle. Le Père de Caussade*. Paris: Beauchesne, 1984.

Orcibal, Jean. *Études d'histoire et de littérature religieuses XVIe-XVIIIe siècles*. Edited by Jacques Le Brun and Jean Lesalnier. Paris: Klincksieck, 1997.

———. "L'Influence spirituelle de Fénelon dans les pays anglo-saxons au XVIIe siècle." *XVIIe siècle* nos. 12–14 (1951): 276–82.

———. "Les Spirituels français et espagnols chez John Wesley et ses contemporains." *Revue de l'histoire des religions* 139 (1951): 50–109.

Packard, Alpheus S. *Address on the Life and Character of Thomas C. Upham, D.D.* Brunswick, Maine: Joseph Griffin, 1873.

Park, Edwards A. "Memoir." In *The Works of Samuel Hopkins*. Vol. 1, 9–266. Boston: Doctrinal Tract and Book Society, 1852.

Porte, Joel. "Emerson's French Connection." *Consciousness and Culture: Emerson and Thoreau Reviewed*. New Haven: Yale University Press, 2004.

Porterfield, Amanda. *Feminine Spirituality in America*. Philadelphia: Temple University Press, 1980.

Post, Stephen G. *Christian Love and Self-Denial: An Historical and Normative Study of Jonathan Edwards, Samuel Hopkins, and American Theological Ethics*. Lanham, Md.: University Press of America, 1987.

———. "Disinterested Benevolence: An American Debate Over the Nature of Christian Love." *Journal of Religious Ethics* 14 (1986): 356–68.

Pourrat, Pierre, S. S. *Christian Spirituality*. Vol. 3, *Later Developments: Part I. From the Renaissance to Jansenism*. Vol. 4, *Later Developments: Part II. From Jansenism to Modern Times*. Translated by Donald Attwater, IV. First published 1927. Westminster, Md.: The Newman Press, 1953, 1955.

Price, Carl F. *More Hymn Stories*. New York: Abingdon, 1929.

Rack, Henry D. *Reasonable Enthusiast: John Wesley and the Rise of Methodism*. 3rd ed. London: Epworth Press, 2002.

Rapley, Elizabeth. *The Dévotes: Women and Church in Seventeenth-Century France*. Montreal: McGill-Queen's University Press, 1990.

Richard, Robert D., Jr. *Emerson: The Mind on Fire*. Berkeley: University of California Press, 1995.

Richardson, Joe M. *A History of Fisk University, 1865-1946*. Tuscaloosa: University of Alabama Press, 1980.

Rivers, Isabel. "Dissenting and Methodist Books of Practical Divinity." In *Books and Their Readers in Eighteenth-Century England*. Leicester: Leicester University Press; New York: St. Martin's, 1982.

Ruether, Rosemary Radford and Rosemary Skinner Keller. *Women and Religion in America*. Vols. 1 and 2. San Francisco: Harper and Row, 1981, 1983.

Sachse, Julius Friedrich. *The German Sectarians of Pennsylvania: A Critical and Legendary History of the Ephrata Cloister and the Dunkers*. Vol. 1, *1708-1742*. Philadelphia: Printed for the author, 1899.

Saliers, Don E. "Christian Spirituality in an Ecumenical Age." In *World Spirituality: An Encyclopedic History of the Religious Quest*. Vol. 18, *Christian Spirituality: Post-Reformation and Modern*, edited by Louis Dupré and Don E. Saliers, 520-44. New York: Crossroad, 1989.

Salter, Darius L. *Spirit and Intellect: Thomas Upham's Holiness Theology*. Metuchen, N.J.: The Scarecrow Press, 1986.

Schmidt, Martin. *John Wesley: A Theological Biography*. Vol. 1. Translated by Norman P. Goldhawk. Nashville, Tenn.: Abingdon Press, 1962.

——. *John Wesley: A Theological Biography*. Vol. 2. Translated by Denis Inman. London: Epworth Press, 1973.

Sears, Clara Endicott, ed. *Bronson Alcott's Fruitlands with Transcendental Oats by Louisa M. Alcott*. Boston: Houghton Mifflin, 1915.

Senn, Frank C., ed. *Protestant Spiritual Traditions*. New York: Paulist Press, 1986.

Smith, Timothy L. *Called Unto Holiness. The Story of the Nazarenes: The Formative Years*. Kansas City, Mo.: Nazarene Publishing House, 1962.

——. *Revivalism and Social Reform in Mid-Nineteenth-Century America*. Nashville: Abingdon Press, 1957.

Spurlin, Paul Merrill. *The French Enlightenment in America: Essays on the Times of the Founding Fathers*. Athens: University of Georgia Press, 1984.

Stanley, Susie C. *Holy Boldness: Women Preachers' Autobiographies and the Sanctified Self.* Knoxville: University of Tennessee Press, 2002.

Stoeffler, F. Ernest. *German Pietism During the Eighteenth Century.* Leiden, Neth.: E. J. Brill, 1973.

——. *The Rise of Evangelical Pietism.* Leiden, Neth.: E. J. Brill, 1965.

Synan, Vinson. *The Century of the Holy Spirit: 100 Years of Pentecostal and Charismatic Renewal, 1901–2001.* Nashville, Tenn.: Thomas Nelson Publishers, 2001.

——. *The Holiness-Pentecostal Tradition: Charismatic Movements in the Twentieth Century.* Grand Rapids: William B. Eerdmans Publishing Company, 1997.

Taves, Ann. *Fits, Trances, and Visions: Experiencing Religion and Explaining Experience from Wesley to James.* Princeton, N.J.: Princeton University Press, 1999.

——. *The Household of Faith: Roman Catholic Devotions in Mid-Nineteenth-Century America.* Notre Dame, Ind.: Notre Dame University Press, 1986.

Tebbel, John. *A History of Book Publishing in the United States.* Vol. 1, *The Creation of an Industry, 1630–1865.* New York: R. L. Bowker, 1973.

Thorson, Donald A. D. "Experimental Method in the Practical Theology of John Wesley." *Wesley Theological Journal* 24, no. 1 (1989): 117–41.

Underhill, Evelyn. *Mysticism.* First published 1911. New York: Doubleday, 1990.

United Methodist Hymnal. Nashville, Tenn.: United Methodist Publishing House, 1976.

Ward, Andrew. *Dark Midnight When I Rise: The Story of the Jubilee Singers Who Introduced the World to the Music of Black America.* New York: Farrar, Strauss and Giroux, 2000.

Ward, Patricia A. "Fénelon Among the New England Abolitionists." *Christianity and Literature* 50, no. 1 (2000): 79–93.

——. "Madame Guyon and Experiential Theology in America." *Church History* 67 (1998): 484–98.

——. "Madame Guyon in America: An Annotated Bibliography." *Bulletin of Bibliography* 52 (1995): 107–11.

Ward, W. R. *Early Evangelicalism: A Global Intellectual History, 1670–1789.* Cambridge: Cambridge University Press, 2006.

——. *The Protestant Evangelical Awakening.* Cambridge: Cambridge University Press, 1992.

Warfield, Benjamin Breckinridge. *Perfectionism.* Edited and abridged by Samuel G. Craig. Grand Rapids: Baker Book House, 1958.

Warner, Anna Bartlett. *Susan Warner.* New York: G. P. Putnam's, 1909.

Warren, Austin. "Fénelon Among the Anglo-Saxons." In *New England Saints.* Ann Arbor: University of Michigan Press, 1956.

Watkins, Owen C. *The Puritan Experience: Studies in Spiritual Autobiography.* New York: Schocken Books, 1972.

Weiss, Ellen. *City in the Woods: The Life and Design of an American Camp Meeting on Martha's Vineyard*. Oxford: Oxford University Press, 1987.

Wheatley, Richard. *The Life and Letters of Mrs. Phoebe Palmer*. New York: Palmer and Hughes, 1884.

Wuthnow, Robert. *After Heaven: Spirituality in America Since the 1950s*. Berkeley, Calif.: University of California Press, 1998.

Wynkoop, Mildred Bangs. *The Trevecca Story*. Nashville, Tenn.: Trevecca Press, 1976.

Index

Lopez, Gregory, 94, 166
love (pure or disinterested), 7, 42,
   98–99, 107-8, 114, 187, 205
Lowery, D. D., 193

Mahan, Asa, 145, 147, 170
Maintenon, Madame de, 16, 33–39,
   41
Malaval, François, 28, 48
Mallet-Joris, Françoise, 14
Marie of the Incarnation, 17, 24,
   132–33
Marsay, Charles de, 67–68, 81
Marsden, George, xii, 214n9
Martin, Josiah, 89, 103; *see also*
   Quakers
Matson, Henrietta, 198–200
McCalla, G. W., 8, 155, 192, 201
McClurkan, J. O., 8-9, 195, 199
McLeister, Clara, 197–98
Mennonites, 2, 71
Merritt, Timothy, 129, 145
Metcalf, James W., 183–84, 187
Methodism: and the American
   holiness movement, 3-4, 6, 129,
   142–43, 145–47, 150, 152, 166,
   169, 190; *see also* holiness
millennialism, 176
Miramion, Madame de, 30
Molinos, Miguel, 6, 7, 13, 30, 42, 60,
   61, 71, 95, 116, 156, 166, 246n52;
   Spiritual Guide, ix, 30, 61–62, 101
Montesquieu (Charles de Secondat,
   baron de), 12–13
Moody, Dwight L., 171, 200
Moody Bible Institute, 202
Moody Press, 198
Moravians, 71, 95–96, 97; *see also*
   Zinzendorf
Moritz, Karl Philipp, 80; *Anton Reiser*,
   80–82
Morrow, Abbie C., 197–98
Mueller (Müller), George, 184, 196,
   198
mystical theology, 53–54, 63–64,
   157, 203; twilight of mysticism, 17;
   union of unity, 23

National Camp-Meeting Association
   for the Promotion of Holiness, 5;
   National Association for the Pro-
   motion of Holiness, 192; National
   Holiness Association, 8, 184; *see
   also* camp meetings
Nazarene, Church of, xiv, 5, 8
New Catholics, 24, 34
Newton, John, 110, 141
Noailles, Louis Antoine de, 36, 39, 43
Noll, Mark, 141–42, 254n13

Oberlin College, 129, 145, 199
Oberlin Evangelist, 129, 147
Oberlin revivalism, 145–46, 173, 176
Olson, Bessie, 200-1
Oriental Missionary Society, 193

Palmer, Phoebe, 146-50, 155, 166,
   169, 171, 177; Biblicism, 148, 151;
   language, 149–50; opposition to
   mysticism, 149, 151, 159; *Pioneer
   Experiences*, 151; theology of sanctification, 146; Tuesday Meeting for
   the Promotion of Holiness, 146,
   150; *Way of Holiness*, 147–50, 177,
   195; Uphams, relationship to, 146,
   149, 150–52
Paraclete Press, 209
Park, Edwards A., 107, 175, 245n47
Pascal, Blaise, 6, 46
Penn, William, 2, 60–61
Pentecostal Alliance, 8, 198–99
Pentecostal Mission Publishing Company, 199
Pentecostalism, 196
perfection (Christian), 97, 129,
   144–46
Philadelphians, 49, 67
Pietism, 47, 55, 167, 182, 208-9,
   221n27; German: 47, 60–62; Quietism and, 60, 61, 65; in Pennsylvania, 65–67, 68–71, 71–72
Pilgrim Holiness Church, 193
Poiret, Pierre, 46–48, 116, 132,
   158–59, 167, 184, 241n97; editions
   of Madame Guyon, 46, 48, 62, 64,